Columbus, Georgia, 1865

Columbus, Georgia, 1865

The Last True Battle
of the Civil War

Charles A. Misulia

THE UNIVERSITY OF ALABAMA PRESS
Tuscaloosa

The University of Alabama Press
Tuscaloosa, Alabama 35487-0380
uapress.ua.edu

Hardcover edition published 2010.
Paperback edition published 2019.
eBook edition published 2019.

Inquiries about reproducing material from this work should be addressed to
the University of Alabama Press.

Typeface: Bembo

Cover image: *Top*, unidentified Confederate flag (captured at Columbus),
"WD 461," Museum of the Confederacy, Richmond, Virginia; *bottom*, "City
of Columbus," *Harpers Weekly: A Journal of Civilization*, September 19, 1868,
New York
Cover design: Erin Bradley Dangar / Dangar Design

Paperback ISBN: 978-0-8173-5976-8
eBook ISBN: 978-0-8173-9290-1

A previous edition of this book has been catalogued by the Library of
Congress as follows:
Library of Congress Cataloging-in-Publication Data
Misulia, Charles A., 1980–
Columbus, Georgia, 1865 : the last true battle of the Civil War / Charles A.
Misulia.
p. cm.
Includes bibliographical references and index.
ISBN 978-0-8173-1676-1 (cloth : alk. paper) 1. Columbus, Battle of,
Columbus, Ga., 1865. I. Title.
E477.96.M57   2010
973.7'38—dc22
                                                            2009018500

To
Dr. & Mrs. Andrew G. Misulia
my parents
for all of their love

Our whole army, . . . like a besom of destruction, had swept through one of the fairest cities of the South, and left but little of it, and nothing in it.

    —Columbus as remembered by one of Wilson's Raiders

Contents

Illustrations

MAPS

Preface

It was fought by professional soldiers and by untrained civilians. It was fought for possession of one of the South's most important military-industrial centers. It was fought on Easter Sunday over a mile-and-a-half-long series of forts and earthworks. It was decided at a bridge one thousand feet in length. It determined the fate of a city. Today, it is almost completely forgotten. It was arguably the last battle of the Civil War—and it was fought at Columbus, Georgia.

The story of the Battle for Columbus has significance for several reasons. The battle and the two days of Union occupation and destruction that followed are of considerable importance to the history of Columbus, Georgia; Phenix City, Alabama; and the Chattahoochee valley. Determined in blood and consumed by fire, Columbus's fortunes, which had become linked to those of the Confederacy, were dealt a notable setback. Additionally, and despite the extent to which its memory has been erased by the passing of time, the battle and its aftermath remain the most exciting and perilous days in the city's history.

Furthermore, although it had no effect on the ultimate outcome of the hostilities, the engagement that took place on the day and night of April 16, 1865, marks what might be reasonably argued was the last real *battle* of the Civil War (see appendix 1). Just as Fort Sumter marks the "first shot," Antietam the "bloodiest day," Gettysburg the "high tide," and the skirmish at Palmetto Ranch the "last blood drawn in anger on American soil during the war," so, too, the Battle for Columbus deserves recognition for its place in the annals of Civil War history.

Although I am a longtime Civil War enthusiast and resident of the state of Georgia, it was not until 2001 that my good friend Mike Rankin first took me to see the remains of the Confederate defenses over which the struggle for possession of the city of Columbus once raged. Map in hand, we explored the hills and valleys of Phenix City and stood beside what little survives of the earthen forts and gun emplacements. My curiosity sufficiently aroused, I began to investigate the particulars of the action. To my surprise, I discovered there existed no detailed secondary account.

Noting my enthusiasm for the subject and after reviewing some preliminary research, family and friends encouraged me to consider expanding my research in order to compile a comprehensive study of the engagement and its aftermath. With that goal in mind, I embarked on what turned into a six-year endeavor to tell the whole story of the Battle for Columbus.

To recount how I discovered each diary, memoir, photograph, and map over the past six years would take a book in itself. Suffice it to say that I met many wonderful people, and some not so wonderful, visited many new and interesting places, got lost, ate some good food, and some bad, and felt at times as if I should be on a first-name basis with the staff at Motel 6. In the end, however, after I had tracked down hundreds of leads, burned up thousands of dollars' worth of gasoline, collected enough material to stuff my file cabinets well beyond capacity, and spent sufficient hours sitting at my computer for my friends to begin to question whether the project might never end, the work was finally completed.

Within the pages of this book, the reader will discover a comprehensive, hour-by-hour account of the events that took place in and around Columbus between April 15 and April 18, 1865. To provide context to the story, I outline the final phases of General James H. Wilson's Alabama-Georgia Raid, the situation affecting the Chattahoochee valley during close of the Civil War, and the effects of the battle on Columbus's early reconstruction. I have often included eyewitness testimony so the reader might gain a sense of who the participants were and how they interpreted the events that unfolded around them.

To make the excerpts easier to read, I have corrected many misspellings and grammatical errors and have converted many handwritten symbols to words where doing so enhances the clarity of the statements. In the process I have attempted to maintain the integrity of the material, and the reader will notice, at times, passages where phonetic spellings or incorrect words have been retained in order to preserve the flavor of the original turns of phrase. I have avoided the use of [*sic*] throughout.

It is my sincere hope that this volume will spark interest in the people and events involved in the Battle for Columbus and raise awareness about the role Columbus and the Chattahoochee valley played in the Civil War. Finally, I hope it will generate remembrance of the struggles and sacrifices made by those individuals on both sides who, in fighting for their convictions, lost their lives, their homes, or their fortunes.

Acknowledgments

Credit for the completion of this work is due to many people in addition to the one whose name appears as author. In particular, Dr. Andrew G. Misulia and Mrs. Carney L. Misulia, my parents, deserve generous thanks for all they have done to make this work possible. Throughout this undertaking they have worked to ensure that I was provided with all of the resources and tools that I needed, and it is only through their love, encouragement, and unfaltering devotion to me and to this venture that it was ever completed.

To my wife, Marilyn, I wish to extend special credit for her unflagging faith in me and in this project. Her patience and understanding have been of enormous comfort to me.

Thanks is extended to my friend Mike Rankin, who took me to visit the forts and earthworks in Girard for the first time and who sparked my interest in the battle. Dr. Mark Berger, for whom I wrote my first paper on the battle, motivated me to contemplate expanding my research, and gave me valuable instruction on how to organize and use historical materials.

Bob Holcombe and Jeff Seymour reviewed and edited preliminary (and much longer) versions of this work. I appreciate their having spent time and energy to make this history more accurate and more enjoyable for the reader. They are fine historians and friends.

Special thanks also to the following institutions and their staff:

Abraham Lincoln Presidential Library, Springfield, Illinois
Alabama Department of Archives and History, Montgomery
Andersonville National Historic Site, Andersonville, Georgia
Auburn University, Auburn, Alabama
Bartholomew County Public Library, Columbus, Indiana
Bowling Green State University, Bowling Green, Ohio

City of Columbus Clerk of Counsel's Office, Columbus, Georgia
Clapp Factory Cemetery Preservation Group, Columbus, Georgia
The Columbus Museum, Columbus, Georgia
Columbus Public Library, Columbus, Georgia
Columbus State University, Columbus, Georgia
Emory University, Atlanta, Georgia
Georgia Archives, Morrow
Georgia Historical Society Library and Archives, Savannah
Historical Society Library of Delaware, Wilmington
Historic Chattahoochee Commission, Eufaula, Alabama
Historic Columbus Foundation, Columbus, Georgia
Historic Linwood Cemetery Foundation, Columbus, Georgia
Idaho Military History Society, Boise
Illinois State Historical Society Library, Springfield
Indiana Historical Society, Indianapolis
Iowa Gold Star Military Museum, Johnston
Kenan Research Center, Atlanta History Center, Atlanta, Georgia
The Kentucky Historical Society Library, Frankfort
Library of Congress Department of Archives and History, Washington, D.C.
Missouri History Museum Library and Research Center, St. Louis
Missouri State Department of Natural Resources, Jefferson City
Missouri State Museum, Jefferson City
Museum of the Confederacy, Richmond, Virginia
National Archives and Records Administration, Washington, D.C.
National Civil War Naval Museum at Port Columbus, Columbus, Georgia
Newberry Library, Chicago, Illinois
Ohio Historical Society State Archives, Columbus
Old Dominion University, Norfolk, Virginia
Phenix City Public Library, Phenix City, Alabama
Pittsburg State University, Pittsburg, Kansas
Pomona Public Library, Pomona, California
Regent University, Virginia Beach, Virginia
Rutherford B. Hayes Presidential Library, Spiegel Grove, Fremont, Ohio
State Historical Society Library of Iowa, Des Moines
State Historical Society Library of Iowa, Iowa City
State Historical Society Library of Missouri, Columbia
U.S. Army Military History Institute, Carlisle, Pennsylvania (U.S. Army
Heritage and Education Center)
United States Naval Observatory, Washington, D.C.
University of Georgia, Athens
University of Iowa, Iowa City

University of Michigan, Ann Arbor
University of Mississippi, Oxford
University of Missouri, Columbia
University of North Carolina, Chapel Hill
Valdosta State University, Valdosta, Georgia
Virginia Wesleyan College, Norfolk
Wallace State College, Hanceville, Alabama
Wisconsin State Historical Society, Madison

In addition to those mentioned above, literally dozens of individuals have contributed to this effort. I dare not attempt to list all who have lent their resources, time, and energy to this project for fear that I might inadvertently overlook one. Nevertheless, I extend to each my sincerest appreciation, and express my hope that this work will be a credit to them. Any success will be largely attributable to their contributions, and any shortcomings I claim as my own. Thank you all.

1
Wilson's Raid

Six miles east of Tuskegee, Alabama, on the evening of April 15, 1865, as the twilight sky streaked with lightning, twenty-seven-year-old Brevet Major General James H. Wilson stepped out of the torrential rains and up onto the porch of a large plantation home that was to be his headquarters for the night. Tearing off his heavy raincoat and saturated kepi, the Union general peered through the storm at the seemingly endless columns of cavalry that trudged toward the east through the driving rain.

Thanks to Wilson, the veteran troopers who slogged along the muddy roadway were a part of no mere cavalry raid, but instead were a part of a "great campaign with an army of mounted men." They were highly trained, well mounted and equipped, and superbly armed. Their morale was high, their fighting prowess unparalleled. They were confident in their commanders and sure of themselves, to the point that, according to staff member Private Ebenezer N. Gilpin, "it would require awful carnage to convince them they were not invincible." They were Wilson's masterpiece, a magnificent assembly of veteran cavalrymen marching "in compact, well-balanced columns, men and horses in perfect form, disciplined, well officered, and sure of themselves." They were the pride of the army and their young commander. But it had not always been so. It had been an interesting set of circumstances, and a heroic effort on the part of Wilson, that had produced the grand cavalry corps and brought it successfully into southeastern Alabama that night.[1]

From the very beginning of the Civil War, the Union cavalry branch in the western theater had been poorly led, disorganized, and thoroughly ineffective in the field. By late summer of 1864 the Federal cavalry in the West was in critical need of restructuring and leadership in order to make it of any significant use to the army. General William T. Sherman was frustrated with the cavalry's inability to aid his army's operations in any substantial manner, and he desperately needed a new commander to fix the problems. After consultations with General Ulysses S. Grant, Sherman was supplied with an officer ready to take charge as the Military Division of the Mississippi's chief of cavalry. The man who was chosen was General James H. Wilson.[2]

Wilson was born to Harrison and Katherine Wilson at Shawneetown, Illinois, on September 2, 1837. When he was fourteen his father died, leaving James the head of the household and the family's sole breadwinner. Immediately he set to work, taking over the responsibilities of the farm and trying his hand at several other endeavors, proving himself successful in all. Managing seemed to come naturally to him, and while he provided for his family he polished skills that would prove handy later in life. His early elevation into the world of adulthood and success also led him to develop a keen sense of independence and self-worth, characteristics that would prove both motivator and stumbling block in his future.

After attending McKendree College in Illinois for a year, Wilson was accepted to the Military Academy at West Point, where he graduated in 1860, sixth in his class. After graduation he was sent west as a topographical engineer, where he watched as the country's regional differences escalated. Once the first guns of the war sounded, he was determined not to be left out. Through maneuvering with political contacts and by untiring ambition, promotions came fast, although for one so clamorous for advancement, not always fast enough. From 1861 through 1863, Wilson was promoted from second lieutenant of topographical engineers to aide on General George McClellan's staff, to inspector general of the Army of the Tennessee during the Vicksburg campaign, and eventually to chief engineer and brigadier general. Recognized for his organizational skills, familiarity with cavalry tactics, and superior horsemanship, in early 1864 he was made chief of the Cavalry Bureau in Washington, D.C.

The Cavalry Bureau had been created in order to streamline the purchase of horses to mount Union volunteers and also to secure for them sufficient arms and equipments specific to that service. However, in the months since its creation, the bureau's performance had proved markedly unsatisfactory. Realizing that what was needed was an "intelligent and swift-moving administrator," Grant agreed to part with Wilson for sixty days. Wilson, eager for a field command, agreed to take the prestigious "desk job" with the understanding that he would rejoin active operations when the spring brought renewed activity.

At the bureau, Wilson was in his element. Immediately, he used his developed organizational skills to weed out corruption and streamline the management of affairs. He overhauled the government's system for purchasing horses for the army and cut out many of the underhanded dealings that were siphoning money from the government into the pockets of crooked contractors. He also kept a close eye on where the government's resources were being spent, and tried to limit those expenditures that he saw as not yielding rewards great enough to justify the outlay. In the process, he angered many politicians and government workers who either were benefiting from the profiteering or who desired government funding for pet projects that would benefit them politically. Among the latter was the provisional governor of Tennessee, Andrew Johnson, whom Wilson denied authority to raise or provision loyal Tennessee cavalry regiments, which he felt were of little value to the army.[3]

Of all that Wilson accomplished at the bureau, however, probably his greatest contribution was to promote the Spencer repeating rifle as a cavalry weapon and to order its increased production. Wilson had been quick to see the advantages that repeating arms brought to his branch of service, and after reviewing positive reports about the Spencer, including a conspicuous endorsement by President Abraham Lincoln, Wilson became convinced that it was the rifle his troopers needed.

The Spencer's magazine held seven self-contained metallic rimfire cartridges that were fed through the action by the manipulation of a lever underneath the rifle. The weapon could be "loaded with seven charges more quickly than a muzzle-loading gun . . . [could] be loaded with its single charge." The speed of the loading process was enhanced by the fact that percussion caps were not needed to fire the weapon, "for the cartridge contains the fulminate." The absence of a "ramrod or detached parts, the loss of which makes loading impossible," was a further advantage.

The greatest quality of the Spencer rifle lay not in its loading, however, but in its capacity to deliver rates of fire almost unequaled during the war. It could "be fired seven times in twelve seconds, and with ease twenty times per minute." This rate eclipsed that of the average conventionally armed soldier and gave its user a firepower advantage of nearly 700 percent. "In the hands of scouts or sharpshooters, or regular troops," claimed Warren Fisher Jr., treasurer of the Spencer Repeating Arms Company, "the Spencer Rifle is so effective as to render one man with it fully equal to half a dozen men armed with single-loading muskets."

The claim was more than mere boasting. Unlike so many other weapons tested during the Civil War, the Spencer quickly proved itself in combat. Nearly as soon as the new weapons began to make their way into the hands of Federal troops and onto the battlefield, their reliability, ruggedness, and nearly unparalleled performance became well known. Wilson later remembered the Spencer to be "by all odds the most effective firearm of the day." Though he had no way of knowing it at the time, his endorsement of the

Spencer would soon prove a great asset in his career and greatly increase the effectiveness of his soldiers at the Battle for Columbus. By the end of the war, the weapon itself would be solidly associated with Wilson's name.[4]

In the spring of 1864, Wilson was transferred to command of the 3rd Cavalry Division of the Army of the Potomac. As commander of this division he gained much-needed field command experience, and although he made several serious blunders, he learned quickly from his mistakes and gained a sense of what cavalry was capable of accomplishing. He also discovered how effective cavalry could be when deployed en masse as mounted infantry. Wilson quickly developed the idea of using the cavalry as a highly mobile, self-supporting strike force. On the proper composition of the cavalry branch of the army, Wilson summed up his theory by stating that "the best cavalry is the best infantry, mounted."[5]

In September 1864, Sherman asked Grant to send him someone capable of turning the fortunes of his western horsemen around. Wilson was the man selected. Though only twenty-seven years of age, Wilson received a glowing endorsement from Grant, was promoted to brevet major general, and was ordered to take command of Sherman's cavalry.

Immediately, Wilson sought Sherman's permission to consolidate, re-equip, and deploy the cavalry in force. Wilson believed that if his troopers could be molded into a tight-knit, stand-alone corps they could be deployed against the enemy with telling effect. Sherman, already doubtful of the cavalry's ability to accomplish anything of major import, and busy readying his army for his campaign toward Savannah, consented, saying: "Do the best you can with it, and if you make any reputation out of it I shall not undertake to divide it with you." With free rein over the organization and restructuring of the cavalry, Wilson began building what he soon designated the Cavalry Corps, Military Division of the Mississippi.[6]

Using many of the same organizational skills he had employed at the Cavalry Bureau, Wilson quickly began a major overhaul of the divisions under his command. Officers were replaced, troopers were rounded up from detached duties that had spread them to points all over the western theater, and Wilson's headquarters became the head of all of the army's cavalry operations. Throughout the fall of 1864, Wilson's efforts slowly began to transform the corps.

Although his task was formidable, with inexhaustible ambition Wilson endeavored to consolidate, refit, remount, and properly arm his command, which consisted of seventy-two regiments—"by far a greater number than any other general of comparable rank, Federal or Confederate, had ever commanded." In the winter of 1864, though the reorganization was incom-

Fig. 1. General James H. Wilson. Courtesy Massachusetts Commandery, Military Order of the Loyal Legion (MOLLUS), and the U.S. Army Military History Institute.

plete, Wilson was forced to put his partially restructured Cavalry Corps in the field. To Wilson's credit, his troopers successfully aided General George Thomas's Military Division of the Mississippi in repulsing Confederate general John B. Hood's campaign into Tennessee.[7]

After Hood's retreat, Wilson put his campaign-weary troopers into winter quarters near Gravelly Springs, Alabama. January and February 1865 were spent refitting his command and obtaining horses and weapons. Wilson was consumed by the effort. Thousands of horses were rounded up and put into service, though their numbers fell short of meeting all of the corps' needs. Thousands more Spencers were also ordered in hopes of outfitting the entire corps with the rapid-fire weapon. Wilson also instituted a daily regimen of rigorous drill and instruction. His by-the-book personality and adherence to strict codes of discipline stood in marked contrast to the devil-may-care attitudes prevalent in many western theater regiments. "We have to drill now, have dress parade, guard mount, & etc.," remembered veteran trooper Sergeant Samuel Bereman of the 4th Iowa Cavalry, who added, "we are getting stylish in our old days [and] General Wilson is the cause of it all."[8]

While Wilson oversaw this work, plans were set in motion for a campaign against Mobile, to be led by General Edward Canby. Much to Wilson's dismay, divisions of his Cavalry Corps were ordered to be detached to support that operation and also to fight Confederate irregulars in Tennessee. Wilson was further frustrated when he got word that the plans for the capture of Mobile included sending another part of his Cavalry Corps on a purely diversionary raid into Alabama to take pressure off of Canby's forces. Though Grant suggested Wilson might direct his raid toward Tuscaloosa or Selma and even "attack as much of the enemy's force as possible," it was Grant's impression that neither would be "so important as the mere fact of penetrating deep into Alabama." The plan did not sit well with Wilson, and ran counter to his ideas on the proper employment of cavalry.[9]

In late February, Wilson and Thomas conferred at Wilson's headquarters about plans for the proposed raid. Wilson was unwilling to accept any plan that would further reduce or divide his command or which would require him to lead his corps on a pointless diversionary mission. He was sure that, given proper authority, his large, well-equipped cavalry force could easily undertake an independent campaign. Eager to convince Thomas, Wilson staged a parade. "In passing seventeen thousand troopers in review before Thomas," remembered Wilson, "I convinced him that . . . if permitted to go with my whole available force into Central Alabama, I would not only defeat Forrest and such other troops as I might encounter, but would capture Tuscaloosa, Selma, Montgomery, and Columbus, and destroy the Confederacy's last depots of manufacture and supply and break up its last interior line of railway communications."

Wilson finally got what he had been working for; the opportunity to employ his Cavalry Corps in a major independent campaign in which he was left with broad command discretion. The launch date for the campaign was set for March 5. Wilson's objectives would be to destroy General Nathan B. Forrest's Confederate forces in Alabama, to relieve the pressure on Canby in Mobile, to destroy the industrial and supply centers of lower Alabama and south Georgia, and, if possible, to ride east to link up with Grant in either Virginia or the Carolinas for an anticipated final campaign to destroy the Confederate army under General Robert E. Lee. Riding fast, Wilson's men would sweep down into Alabama and across Georgia, taking only the essentials in order to keep the supply trains short and moving quickly. Once in central Alabama, the corps would live off the land

and follow whatever course Wilson believed necessary to secure his objectives. Much as Sherman had in his "March to the Sea," Wilson also would "go down a hole," cutting all communication with the rest of the armies. It was a bold plan.[10]

After sending away several divisions to aid in Sherman's march, Canby's Mobile campaign, and the operations in Tennessee, Wilson was left with only four divisions under his control. Of these, one was mostly without mounts. Realizing he had no time to spare in requisitioning additional horses or weapons, Wilson decided to strip that division of its remaining horses and Spencers and to use those to outfit the rest of his force. The dismounted division would be issued infantry equipment and left behind with Thomas's army.[11]

In all, the corps Wilson assembled to make the campaign into Alabama and Georgia was composed of three divisions; the 1st Division, under Brigadier General Edward M. McCook; the 2nd Division, under Brigadier General Eli Long; and the 4th Division, under Brevet Major General Emory Upton. The force was well trained, marvelously equipped, and battle-tested. In total they numbered just over thirteen thousand troopers, of which all but a few hundred were equipped with Spencers. It seemed an impressive force, particularly when after some trial and calculation, "it was estimated that the whole expedition . . . could fire over eighty thousand balls in a minute" (see appendix 2).[12]

Attached to each of the three divisions and adding their firepower to that of the troopers were three batteries of horse artillery that had been specially outfitted with teams of eight or ten horses each, as opposed to the normal six, to lessen the fatigue of the animals and to help the batteries keep pace with the swift-moving cavalry. The 18th Indiana Light Artillery and the Chicago Board of Trade Battery were assigned to the 1st and 2nd divisions, respectively. Attached to the 4th Division was Lieutenant George B. Rodney's Battery I, 4th U.S. Artillery, which was composed of four 12-pounder Napoleon light field guns.[13]

Each trooper of Wilson's Cavalry Corps would begin the campaign with five days' rations. According to Adjutant William F. Scott of the 4th Iowa Cavalry, "The small allowance of bread and grain was intended to provide only for the march through the northern part of Alabama, a region very poor at best, and now wasted by two years of war within its borders." Beyond this, there were pack animals, a 250-wagon supply train that carried "forty-five days' coffee rations, twenty of sugar, fifteen of salt, and [each soldier's additional] eighty rounds of ammunition." It was anticipated that the needs of Wilson's men would be met after reaching central Alabama by foraging and "living on the country." Additionally, Wilson took along fifty-eight wagons loaded with thirty canvas pontoon boats and lumber enough to span some of the rivers he would encounter along the campaign.[14]

Besides seeing to it that his troops were excellently equipped, Wilson ensured that they would be equally well led. At Wilson's request, General Upton, commander of the 4th Division, was made second in command of the expedition. Upton had been one year Wilson's junior at West Point, where they met and became friends. Like Wilson, Upton was extremely ambitious and had made it clear even at the academy that he intended to pursue a general's rank and make a name for himself in the army. The opening shots of the war had already been fired when Upton graduated in 1861, and he had immediately thrown himself into the struggle for the preservation of the Union.

Initially commissioned as an artillery officer, Upton rapidly gained recognition for bravery on the battlefield and for coolness under fire. Wilson and Upton deepened their friendship when they served together for a time in the Shenandoah Valley, in 1864. At the Battle of Opequan, Upton was severely wounded by a piece of shell that tore away a chunk of flesh on the inside of his right thigh. In a characteristic display of fearlessness, Upton, determined not to give up his command, disobeyed an order by General Philip Sheridan to leave the field and ordered a tourniquet applied to his leg. He then had himself borne around the battlefield on a stretcher until the engagement was concluded. He had only recently recovered enough from his wound to again take the field when he was assigned to command the 4th Division.

Because of their relative youth (Wilson was twenty-seven, Upton twenty-five) and their similar backgrounds, attitudes, ideals, and struggles, the two generals further cemented their bonds of friendship when Upton was assigned to Wilson's command. As one of the other commanders of the corps noted, Upton became "omnipresent in the mind of Wilson and . . . constantly associated with him, where duty permitted or otherwise."[15]

Upton's division was composed of six regiments and one battery, divided into two brigades containing three regiments each. Wilson had approved this structure for his corps because he believed that the previous system of organization, which placed three brigades in each division, was unnecessary. He felt that by placing only two brigades in each division he could eliminate the tendency to leave one whole brigade (usually composed of three or four regiments) in reserve and better employ all the troops at his disposal in the field.[16]

For command of the 2nd Brigade of Upton's division, Wilson called on another of his associates from back east, Brevet Brigadier General Andrew

J. Alexander. Alexander had been Wilson's adjutant-general at the Cavalry Bureau, and Wilson found him to be a man of skill and integrity. Their closeness grew during Wilson's short time in Washington, and when Wilson was transferred to command of Sherman's cavalry he made Alexander his adjutant-general and chief of staff. Four years Wilson's senior, Alexander was striking in appearance. "He was a pure Saxon in coloring," Wilson recalled after the war, "with hair and beard that glistened like gold in the sunshine, and a complexion that bid defiance to the sun and wind. Standing over six feet in height, he was as trim and commanding a figure as it was ever my privilege to behold." Wilson was also keenly aware of Alexander's abilities as an aggressive commander: "He was a hard and rapid hitter; methodical, careful and prudent, looking out for his men and his horses with just as much care as he did for his papers, . . . but never failing to go for the enemy with all his might. . . . He never believed in or adopted half measures . . . and scarcely ever failed to do what was expected of him."[17]

The three cavalry regiments composing Alexander's brigade were the 1st Ohio, 7th Ohio, and 5th Iowa. The 1st Ohio was led by Colonel Beroth B. Eggleston, a forty-six-year-old former Ohio farmer. Before settling on farming Eggleston had tried several occupations, including dry goods, postmaster, and law, but had found each unsatisfactory. He enlisted in 1861, and by 1863 he had been promoted to colonel of the 1st Ohio.[18]

Supporting the 1st Ohio was the 7th Ohio, under the command of Colonel Israel Garrard. This regiment had seen a lot of active service in the western theater, and though assigned to Alexander's brigade for the campaign, many of the men still lacked mounts. Captain R. C. Rankin of the unit was placed in charge of the dismounted men of the division, numbering about five hundred, and was informed that he and his troopers would follow along until horses could be acquired.[19]

Last in the brigade was the 5th Iowa, under the command of Colonel John Morris Young. Young had a petite build and fiery red hair that matched his enthusiastic personality. One of his soldiers remembered him as "a brave little cuss" who "led us gallantly."[20]

Command of the 1st Brigade of Upton's division fell to Brevet Brigadier General Edward F. Winslow. Born and raised in Maine, Winslow moved in 1856 to Mount Pleasant, Iowa, where he established a mercantile business and worked as a bank clerk. Shortly before the outbreak of war he became involved in the construction of railroads, a career for which he seemed to have a passion. When the war began he joined the 4th Iowa Cavalry, where he was named captain of Company F. By 1863 he had risen to the rank of colonel and was serving as chief of cavalry to the 15th Corps. From 1863 until the assignment of Upton to the 4th Division, though he held only a colonel's rank, Winslow assumed the responsibilities of both brigade and division command.

Despite his field experience, Winslow possessed no formal military training and was passed over for command of the 4th Division when Upton was assigned. Even so, initially Upton and Winslow's relationship was cordial. But while Winslow appears to have had respect for Upton as a commander, Winslow's lack of promotion, their very similar personalities, and Upton's close friendship with Wilson seem to have quickly placed Winslow and Upton somewhat at odds.

Both Winslow and Upton were self-assured, consumed by a desire for recognition and promotion, and driven by a yearning to be respected by their peers. One of Winslow's contemporaries described him as possessing "an intelligent and pleasing countenance, and a feminine voice. . . . He is a man of great energy, great ambition and unlimited self-confidence. . . . His worst fault, if it can be termed a fault, is his self-conceit, which sometimes discovers itself immodestly."

In the contest for approbation that followed, Winslow undoubtedly came out the loser. Not only did Wilson (a West Pointer and eastern theater commander) overlook Winslow's experience, but Upton (another eastern theater associate of Wilson's and a professional soldier) was appointed as Winslow's commander. When Alexander (who had served as an assistant to Wilson at the Cavalry Bureau) was put in command of the 4th Division's 2nd Brigade, Winslow was unmistakably the odd man out. While Wilson, Upton, and Alexander renewed and deepened their friendships, Winslow, as the newcomer to the leadership, was never able to penetrate the group. All the clout Winslow had managed to amass in the western cavalry service was instantly made worthless when Wilson's new leadership took the reins.[21]

Three regiments were under Winslow's command. First was his own, the 4th Iowa Cavalry, of which he was still officially the colonel. Composed of 872 troopers, it was led in his absence by Lieutenant Colonel John Peters. The regiment had a poor, almost mutinous reputation early in the war, but by 1865 it was considered an excellent unit.[22]

Next was the 3rd Iowa Cavalry, made up of 948 troopers and led by Colonel John W. Noble, a thirty-four-year-old Yale-educated lawyer from Keokuk, Iowa. Noble had enlisted in 1861, and by 1864 he had been promoted to colonel of his regiment. He was said to be "a small, black-haired, black-eyed man, with good education, good ability, and of remarkable energy and courage."[23]

Last was the 10th Missouri Cavalry, composed of 551 men and led by Lieutenant Colonel Frederick W. Benteen. Born in Petersburg, Virginia,

Fig. 2. General Edward F. Winslow. Courtesy Massachusetts Commandery, MOLLUS, and the U.S. Army Military History Institute.

Benteen moved as a young man to St. Louis, Missouri. While his father was a secessionist, Benteen harbored strong Union sentiments that were supported by his sweetheart and later bride. When war broke out he joined the Federal army, much to the dismay of his father, who proclaimed upon hearing the news, "I hope the first god damned bullet gets you." By 1862, Benteen had been promoted from lieutenant to second major. Shortly thereafter he was promoted to lieutenant colonel following an officers' fistfight and shootout, which left the colonel dead, the lieutenant colonel convicted of murder, and the senior major relieved of his command. Benteen was described as being "tall (5′ 10″) and broad-shouldered. He had a large torso, long muscular arms, and huge hands." He was very quiet and was known to use sarcasm to avoid confrontation most of the time, but was prone to explosive rage when pushed too far.[24]

Once his corps was finally readied for the field, Wilson felt confident that they would "do good service" against the enemy in Alabama and Georgia. He had faith in both his subordinate commanders and his troops. His soldiers were veterans. They knew the stresses of campaigning and were accustomed to the smoke and confusion of battle. They were well armed, well drilled, and for the most part, well mounted. There was little doubt in Wilson's mind that his troopers would "turn out a heavier fighting force than ever before started on a similar expedition in this country." By March 5, the campaign's launch date, all that was uncertain to Wilson was whether the weather would cooperate. Unfortunately, it did not.[25]

2

The Road to Columbus

The spring of 1865 in north Alabama was an unusually wet one. Heavy rains swelled the Tennessee River and made crossing impossible, forcing Wilson and his corps to remain in camp until the water receded. After crossing the river there was another series of postponements, ending with a wait for rations that were late in being delivered. Finally, on March 22, seventeen days after the campaign was slated to begin, the army headed south toward its first objective, Selma, and the untouched heart of the Confederacy.

Wilson's Raiders, three divisions strong, headed south via slightly divergent routes to help conceal their force's true number. The maneuver also made them vulnerable to attack by General Forrest's Confederate cavalry. Fortunately for Wilson, Forrest's command was spread out and it would take time to consolidate it. On March 29, having met no real resistance, Wilson detached General John Croxton's brigade (part of the 1st Division) for a mission to capture Tuscaloosa and to screen the corps from possible attempts by the Confederates to harass his rear. Croxton's brigade was to carry out its orders and reunite with the main body, which in the meantime would push on toward Selma.[1]

Wilson's Raiders continued their march unopposed for nine days until they ran into waiting Confederate forces at Montevallo. At first the engagement went against them, and the Confederate cavalry seemed to be getting the upper hand. Realizing that the 4th Division was near, however, Wilson politely prompted, "Upton I think you've let them come far enough; move out!" Upton immediately sent in his whole division, broke the Confederate lines, and by nightfall they had driven the enemy nearly eighteen miles.

Morale was high after the corps' first major victory. It would continue to rise after the capture of a Confederate messenger who was carrying a copy of Forrest's plans for the defense of the state, which disclosed the lo-

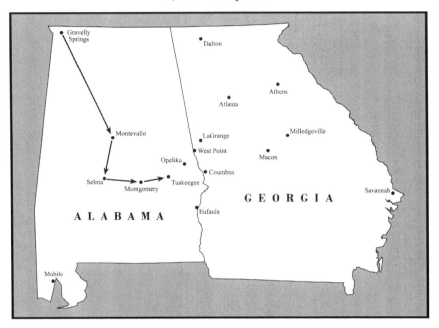

Map 1. Route of Wilson's Raid across Alabama, March 22–April 15, 1865. March 22: Gravelly Springs. April 2: Selma. April 12: Montogmery. April 15: Tuskeegee.

cations of all Confederate forces in Alabama. It was a turn of events that put Wilson at a distinct advantage. The captured dispatches told of Forrest's plans to intercept the Union advance while a smaller party circled around behind the Federals to fall upon their rear. Seizing the opportunity provided by the intelligence, Wilson detached the remainder of the 1st Division, under McCook, to burn a strategic bridge and to recall Croxton's brigade. Beating the Confederates to the span, McCook succeeded in the first of his goals, but he failed to find Croxton and was forced to return without him. In the meantime, Wilson pushed the remainder of the corps more rapidly toward Selma.[2]

On April 1, Wilson's men again encountered Confederate forces twenty miles north of Selma at Ebenezer Church. The fight was hot. The 2nd Division was the first of Wilson's Raiders engaged. They were eventually joined by Alexander's 2nd Brigade of the 4th Division. The numbers and overwhelming firepower of the Federal troopers broke the Rebel defense and sent them flying back toward Selma and its heavy fortifications.

Fortune was with Wilson and his corps. At Montevallo a "nameless heroine" had provided the Federals with "some late Montgomery papers and a written note to Gen. Wilson, giving a detailed account of the number and disposition of the Rebel forces . . . at Selma and Montgomery." Soon after continuing their march toward Selma on April 2, Wilson's men overtook an English engineer who admitted that he had helped design the defenses at Selma and who, at Wilson's insistence, "took a stick and drew a diagram of the forts and rifle pits there in the sandy soil at his feet, also giving the location and number of troops defending the town."[3]

Now with detailed plans for both the enemy's defenses and strategy, Wilson confidently inspected the ground over which his troopers would assault Selma and organized an attack to be carried out at dusk on April 2. Upton would lead the 4th Division on an assault through a swamp along the main road into the city. Meanwhile, Long and his 2nd Division would attack via another road farther to the Union right. The signal for the attack was to be the discharge of a battery of Federal artillery.[4]

All went according to plan until late in the afternoon, when some of Forrest's cavalry fell upon the rear of Long's division as they tried to cut their way through to aid their comrades within the fortifications of Selma. Long, finding his rear harassed, decided to go ahead and initiate the main assault. Under a withering fire of small arms and artillery, the troopers of the 2nd Division blasted their way over the outer defenses of the city. Though somewhat confused by the premature start to the battle, Upton realized that the attack had begun and threw his troopers into the fight. Wilson himself rode into the fray, accompanied by the nearly 350 men of the 4th U.S. Cavalry who acted as his personal escorts and bodyguards. What at first was a stern defense by the Confederates soon turned into a rout as Federal troopers poured into the city, capturing thousands of prisoners and causing the rest to take to their heels. As darkness fell on April 2, the last of Selma's defenders either fled into the gathering darkness or surrendered to the Union cavalrymen.[5]

Following the battle, some of the Union soldiers got carried away in the excitement over their triumph and began merrymaking in the streets of the city. The looting of houses and businesses followed, and fires were started that burned a portion of the town before they could be brought under control. Eventually, however, with the assistance of Federal provosts, the pillage was mostly halted, the exuberant soldiers were bedded down, and order was established.[6]

Wilson's Raiders remained at Selma for a week, destroying government stores and military industry that Wilson knew the Confederates could ill afford to lose. The Federals also supplied their dismounted men with captured Confederate horses. Indeed, horseflesh was seized in such abundance at Selma that even after remounting the fifteen hundred soldiers who had begun the campaign afoot or whose horses had been worn out or wounded, there yet remained over five hundred animals, which the commanding general ordered corralled, driven into the Alabama River, and shot.[7]

While others busied themselves with the destruction of Selma's military infrastructure, the men of the 12th Missouri began assembling supplies to lay a pontoon bridge across the overflowing Alabama. The construction would prove no easy undertaking. The thirty canvas pontoon boats brought along were insufficient to span the seven hundred feet from bank to bank. Sixteen additional wooden pontoons were discovered, but even they were not enough. Eventually, two large barges filled the remaining gap, but as it turned out, assembling the supplies proved only half the battle. Several times during the laying, the bridge was broken apart by the swift current, the sinking of leaky boats, or drifting debris.[8]

In the meantime, Wilson met with Forrest under the pretext of a prisoner exchange, but in actuality with an eye to discovering the whereabouts of his detached brigade under Croxton, which had failed to arrive at Selma as expected. During the generals' meeting, held at a mansion in Cahawba, Forrest inadvertently revealed that the missing brigade was moving without serious opposition through west-central Alabama. Wilson had the information he needed. He now knew that the detached brigade was in no serious danger. After concluding the meeting with Forrest, Wilson set his sights eastward toward the symbolically important city of Montgomery, the Confederacy's first capital, and on Columbus, Georgia, the Confederacy's second-largest producer of war material.[9]

On April 8 and 9, Wilson's Raiders carefully crossed the fragile pontoon bridge spanning the Alabama. Several times during the transit, the bridge was split apart by the fast-moving current or from the impact of driftwood and had to be repaired. On the night of April 9, while the last of the corps was crossing the bridge, General Alexander, while reaching for a rope in an attempt to keep a floating tree from smashing the bridge, overturned his skiff, and he along with two soldiers were thrown overboard. "He was pitched out and disappeared under the surface of the swiftly flowing stream," recalled Wilson. "Being a strong swimmer, however, he soon came to the top, and by a few vigorous strokes brought himself to the bow of one of the pontoons, which he seized with both hands, but just as he began to lift himself from the water the upper part of his body was caught by the butt of the drifting log and crushed against the bow of the boat till his ribs cracked audibly." Fortunately for Alexander, several men on the bridge and in the pontoons came to his aid (including one who jumped into the water and held onto the general until others could retrieve him)

Fig. 3. General Andrew J.
Alexander. Courtesy
Massachusetts Com-
mandery, MOLLUS, and
the U.S. Army Military
History Institute.

and saved him from drowning. For the next several days he would command his brigade from an ambulance.[10]

On April 10, Wilson and his raiders set out eastward toward Montgomery. Realizing that Forrest's forces were virtually destroyed, Wilson "determined to move by the way of Montgomery into Georgia, and after breaking up railroads and destroying stores and army supplies in that state, to
march thence as rapidly as possible to the theater of operations in North
Carolina and Virginia." Because no agreements had been reached between
the two armies regarding the exchange of prisoners, and because Wilson
realized the impossibility of dragging along several thousand Rebel captives, he was forced to come up with a solution. He "adopted the plan of
marching those captured at Selma through the country, and as they gave
out to parole and allow them to straggle back to Selma or to their homes
as best they could. . . . [I]t gave every white man who fell into our hands
a severe lesson as to what might happen to men captured in arms against
their country," remembered Wilson, adding, "the plan worked well." The

practice also freed Wilson from the irksome responsibilities of feeding and guarding a large number of slow-moving prisoners, the provisions for whom would have to be scoured from the surrounding population.[11]

Wilson also devised ways of dealing, at least partially, with the thousands of runaway slaves who flocked to his army. He organized some of the able-bodied male blacks into three regiments, which would later be uniformed and armed with captured Confederate supplies. These regiments, composed at Selma of about five hundred soldiers each (eventually to be designated the 136th, 137th, and 138th United States Colored Troops), then followed along in the rear of the corps both on foot and upon surplus horses and mules procured along the route. As for the thousands of other black followers who flocked to the army, Wilson could do little more than try to get rid of them by burning bridges across streams and creeks in his rear. The tactic proved to be of little success.[12]

April 11 found Wilson and his corps struggling eastward over poor roads and skirmishing with a Confederate cavalry brigade under the command of Brigadier General Abraham Buford. At a particularly poor stretch, the Union troopers were obliged to "carry rails from the adjoining farms and make a corduroy road." Wilson's diary reads, "Crossing of Big Swamp very bad—stream naturally difficult and now swollen. Command very much delayed." The day's developments were not all bad, however. News from captured Confederate newspapers printed in Montgomery revealed that General Canby had forced the evacuation of Mobile, which meant success there was certain. It also meant that Wilson could now consider himself free from any obligation to support Canby. Of further interest to Wilson was the news that the defenses of Petersburg had been broken, that Richmond had been captured, and that President Jefferson Davis and the Confederate government had fled.[13]

The next day, April 12, the advance of Wilson's Cavalry Corps moved cautiously toward Montgomery, expecting to fight for its possession. Confederate cavalry west of the city threw up barricades and obstructions and kept up a running skirmish, but as the head of the column approached the outskirts the resistance evaporated and the Northern soldiers were surprised to see smoke rising from the city. When they reached the place they were met by the mayor and a group of councilmen, who, to their surprise, surrendered the capital unconditionally. The smoke was from eighty-five thousand bales of cotton that the fleeing Confederates had set on fire to prevent its falling into Union hands.[14]

Hurrying ahead of the rest of the corps, Captain Edward C. Dale procured two United States flags from a citizen and with one climbed atop the capitol building and hoisted it aloft the dome. The flag had belonged to a renowned Alabama militia unit that had originally been formed in 1836 to fight the Creek Indians, but Dale probably chose it because of the ironic yet fitting words emblazoned upon its folds—"Montgomery True Blues." On the hills outside town, the approaching troopers received the signal with elation. "We ascended a hill overlooking the city of Montgomery," remembered Private Gilpin of Upton's staff. "General Wilson came up, and . . . there before us was . . . the first capital of the Confederate States; now from the dome floated the 'old flag!' In a moment, every hat and cap flew off, and three cheers loud and long, were given!"[15]

Wilson quickly dispatched the 4th U.S. Cavalry, his escort, to secure the city and then had his corps prepare to enter with as much panache as possible. "Division and brigade flags unfurled, guidons flying, sabers and spurs jingling, bands playing patriotic airs," remembered Wilson, "the war-begrimed Union troopers, batteries, ambulances, and wagons passed proudly through the city." As they did, a large number of those citizens who remained in Montgomery turned out to get a glimpse of the boys in blue. A particularly amused Union sergeant recalled passing "a little boy . . . [who] with wide eyes and mouth exclaimed, 'Lawd! I didn't know there was so many Yankees in the world!'"[16] The spectacle, while grand, caused only little delay in the Federals' march. Soon, the advance elements of the Union column again engaged Confederate cavalry under General Buford east of the city and drove them back on the road toward Columbus for twelve miles. The rest of the corps burned the government and military supplies found in the city, then bivouacked on its eastern outskirts.

Once in Montgomery, Wilson tried to secure the latest information about developments in other theaters of operation. "The air was full of rumors," and although he was able to determine that Richmond had fallen, Wilson still had no idea of the recent surrender of the Army of Northern Virginia to Union forces at Appomattox Courthouse on April 9. "No one would admit that he knew positively what had taken place in Virginia," remembered Wilson, "and not a word reached me indicating that Lee had surrendered."

Despite the lack of official confirmation, the news of Richmond's fall was encouraging to the war-weary Union troopers, and many believed that "at an early day the Confederate bubble would burst." Wilson felt convinced that "my command was operating in exactly the right line to produce the greatest effect in the final windup of the great drama. The situation as I still saw it made it my duty to continue 'breaking things' along the main line of Confederate communications through central Alabama, Georgia, and the Carolinas."[17]

Wilson's Raiders spent April 13 destroying Confederate property and resting themselves and their mounts. During their stay about three thousand prisoners were paroled and the corps' growing number of sick and wounded were transported to St. Mary's Hospital, where they were left along with "sufficient quantities of commissary stores and medicines." Messages were dispatched to Canby and to Thomas outlining the successes of the campaign thus far and announcing that the "fall of Richmond and defeat of Lee [at Petersburg] have deprived the rebels in this section of their last hope." According to Wilson, "If I can now destroy arsenals and supplies at Columbus and divide their army in the Southwest, [they] must disintegrate for lack of munitions."

Not all the activity in the city was directed toward official business. Amusements and sightseeing were the order of the day for many of Wilson's Raiders, who appear to have been well treated by the remaining residents of Montgomery. Many of Montgomery's ladies gave bouquets of flowers to the boys in blue. The statehouse and the first capitol of the Confederacy were sites frequented by many of the soldiers. One Federal officer even drank a toast with a paroled Confederate "to the Union forever."[18]

While some of the officers of the Cavalry Corps spent the afternoon amusing themselves in Montgomery, Wilson and Upton planned the army's next move. It was Wilson's impression that the 2nd Division "had borne the brunt of the attack at Selma, and it was naturally Upton's turn to have the post of honor at Columbus." Wilson believed that he had already accomplished enough with his corps to win him national renown. He also knew how clamorous Upton was to have a major victory to his credit. "No knight of old was ever more absorbed in dreams of military glory, nor more grimly determined to win it," remembered Wilson. "There was no enterprise too perilous for Upton, if only he might hope to gain credit or promotion thereby. No proper understanding can be had of Upton's character without giving full force and effect to this peculiarity."

Eager to accommodate his friend and colleague's ambitions, Wilson assigned to Upton the responsibility for capturing Columbus and securing passage over the Chattahoochee River into Georgia. To bolster Upton's force, Wilson placed Colonel Oscar LaGrange's 2nd Brigade of the 1st Division under Upton's command. After their meeting, Wilson issued orders informing the corps that they would move toward Columbus the next morning and that Upton would take the lead.

Before dawn on April 14, Upton and his division began their march toward Columbus. Upton feared, however, that the bridges spanning the Chattahoochee at Columbus might be destroyed before his arrival in order to prevent the city's capture. To ensure a crossing of the river elsewhere, Upton informed LaGrange that his brigade would soon be dispatched to seize the crossing at West Point until it could be seen whether or not the bridge at Columbus could be secured intact. The possession of a bridge over which the corps could pass into Georgia was extremely important. Even if the pontoons that the corps used to cross the Alabama River had not been mostly destroyed, the steep banks of the Chattahoochee and the river's breadth would have rendered the employment of the pontoon bridge inadequate.[19]

Despite being placed under Upton's authority, not all of LaGrange's brigade moved at the head of the army with orders to march to West Point. One regiment, the 4th Kentucky Cavalry, which had been on a mission to destroy several steamboats, and a detachment of the 1st Wisconsin Cavalry, which was acting as provost in Montgomery, were absent from the brigade. Both took up their line of march that day at the rear of the corps' main column, and would follow it to Columbus rather than to West Point.

Even so, with the majority of LaGrange's brigade leading the way, the Cavalry Corps resumed its eastward trek. Though Upton had assumed control of LaGrange's brigade, which added significantly to his command, he also was forced to leave some of his own division behind in Montgomery. Six companies (E, F, G, H, L, and M) of the twelve composing Noble's 3rd Iowa were placed under the command of Major George Curkendall and detailed to act as provost guards in the city until the rear of the huge Cavalry Corps departed. After leaving the city late in the afternoon, Major Curkendall's battalion began a rapid march to try to overtake the rest of their regiment, which was hurrying eastward toward Tuskegee, but only managed "16 miles and went into camp."[20]

As soon as the Union columns began to march, they encountered Confederate resistance. "On every crook and corner of the road the enemy would fortify and barricade with rails, give us a volley, and fall back," remembered Captain Charles Hinrichs of the 10th Missouri Cavalry. "At every plantation we were sure to receive their welcome, our boys, however, cared but little for their barricades, but as soon as the enemy fired charged right on them." Though the fights that day were usually brief and often ended with the Confederates disappearing into the forests and swamps, in a few cases some of the enemy were captured. In one instance, several soldiers from the 72nd Indiana Mounted Infantry took a bunch of skirmishers "on their own hook." When the prisoners asked what would become of them, one of the Union soldiers "dismounted, took their guns and broke them around a tree, and told them to go home and stay there." "As the boys rode off the rebels hallooed after them, 'Good bye, boys; that's much better than we expected.'"

Skirmishers were not the only hindrance to the corps' movements that day. Bridges, swamps, and creeks aided the Confederate's delaying action, but they could not ultimately stop the Union columns. At Line Creek the Confederates tried to ignite the bridge but were swooped down upon so rapidly that they were sent "flying and bareheaded, throwing away their guns as they went." According to Captain Hinrichs, "We heard from a white lady that some of them cried when their captain tried to rally them for another stand."[21]

For some of the Union troopers, the swamps themselves were of greater concern than the skirmishing. Numerous, large, and often ominous in appearance, eastern Alabama's swamplands and the creatures that inhabited them made many of the Federal cavalrymen extremely uncomfortable. "We passed through . . . the biggest and most horrid and difficult swamp . . . so dense and gloomy that we could rarely see the sun," recalled Sergeant Josiah Conzett of the 5th Iowa's Company E. "Alligators of immense size we saw—in large numbers, sleeping on logs, and snakes of all kinds and size, and other kinds of reptiles we never saw before were all around us. It gave us the Horrors. . . . We were all glad when we finally got across that fearful swamp for had our horses made a misstep and thrown us over, it would surly have been the last of us. It gives me the creeps even now to think of it."[22]

In addition to the fighting and the poor roads that served to slow the Union advance, the vast numbers of runaways that each mile attached themselves to the army were another major problem that had to be remedied. Otherwise, as Sergeant Benjamin F. McGee of the 72nd Indiana Mounted Infantry put it, "the negro element was likely to become an elephant on our hands." Orders were sent that day to the various commands instructing them to relieve their black, male noncombatants so that they could be mustered into the colored regiments and armed with captured Confederate weapons and equipment. This would also unencumber the Union troopers in case of battle, since "there were nearly as many negroes in each regiment as there were soldiers."

Apparently, however, the orders were not well received by Wilson's Raiders or by the contrabands. "This order caused considerable confusion and dissatisfaction in some of the companies," remembered McGee. "They had always led our pack mules for us and helped about the cooking, and very materially lightened our labors, and we determined not to give them up." The blacks themselves were also averse to the idea of being removed to the rear, as "their present position suited them much better than soldiering." "It was amusing to see the stratagems resorted to by us and them to keep from being taken away from us," recalled McGee.[23]

The next morning, April 15, the head of the column resumed its march on Columbus by way of Tuskegee. The day started bright and clear. The terrain over which much of the corps passed in those early hours appeared more hospitable than had the swamps of the previous afternoon. "The country through which we passed today is the finest we have ever seen," remarked Sergeant Thomas Giles of Company L, 4th U.S. Cavalry. "The fields as far as the eye can reach are level, slightly rolling, and filled with seed of various kinds."

Skirmishing resumed along with the advance as Wilson's Cavalry Corps drove on toward the east. Six miles outside Tuskegee, members of the 3rd Ohio Cavalry encountered, engaged, and overwhelmed a portion of the 12th Mississippi Cavalry, capturing the regiment's flag and its commander. Suddenly, however, at midmorning, as the head of the Union column began to approach Tuskegee, the Confederate resistance evaporated. The approaches to the town grew peaceful and quiet.[24]

Tuskegee in 1865 was a town of between three and four thousand citizens. "It was the seat of education and refinement for an extensive region," remembered Wilson, "and contained several private schools and seminaries for both girls and boys, which contributed much to its importance." Just days before the arrival of Union troops, Confederate military authorities were using the town to help coordinate efforts to consolidate a force to defend Columbus and also to orchestrate efforts to slow the Federal cavalry.

On the morning of April 15 the Confederates abandoned the town, probably in hopes that it might be spared from destruction. As hoped, the surrender of the town was its best protection. "Here, as at Montgomery, the mayor and leading citizens met our advance guard and surrendered at discretion, begging only protection for person and property," remembered Wilson. "I promptly granted their request and told off the trusty Fourth [U.S.] Cavalry again to guard the town and maintain order . . . and all the usual precautions were taken, not only to prevent straggling and marauding, but to impress the people with the good behavior and discipline of the Northern cavalrymen."

Wilson also indulged his flair for the dramatic that morning and afternoon. "As was now the rule," he recalled, "corps, division, and brigade flags, regimental colors, and company guidons were unfurled, the bands played patriotic airs to the accompaniment of clanking saber and jingling spur as brigade after brigade . . . passed on to the eastward." As the troopers of the 4th Division entered the town they encountered a particularly fine mansion estate. When one of Upton's staff inquired at the home, he discovered that it was owned by a former schoolmate who, after making a brief reacquaintance, was provided a guard to see that nothing was disturbed while the Union army passed.[25]

As the Federal cavalry entered Tuskegee, the soldiers were struck by the town's elegant layout, fine homes, and splendid gardens. "It is one of the finest towns I have ever met with in the South," remembered Major Steven Von Shipman of the 1st Wisconsin Cavalry. Having been an architect by trade before the war, Shipman noted that "the architecture of the public and private residences was quite as good if not better than at Montgomery." He went on to comment that "The most exquisite taste is manifested in the ornamentation of the ample grounds around each dwelling. There is the greatest variety of evergreens and the magnolia in great abundance. We saw ripe strawberries and green peas. The evergreen arches through the hedges were finer than I ever saw before." Wrapped in its spring foliage and showered by the morning sunlight, according to Private Alva C. Griest of the 72nd Indiana, Tuskegee appeared to be "a town like a flower garden, a paradise on a small scale the gardens are so tastefully arranged."[26]

While the foliage and gardens might have been enough to impress many of the troopers, for some there were other things of interest in the town— the girls' schools located there made sure of that. Lieutenant Charles D. Mitchell, an adjutant on Upton's staff, explained that Tuskegee had "fine homes, beautiful lawns, and pretty girls. That's a good combination." Another veteran scrawled in his journal as he passed through the town: "Amazing, the most beautiful town I ever saw . . . it has beautiful gardens and girls, and an abundance of them too." Some of the Union cavaliers apparently wallowed in the attention they received. "The citizens, with their good ladies and daughters, came thronging out to see us and seemed quite friendly," remembered Private Gilpin, adding: "We convinced them that we were quite a gentlemanly set of soldiers."[27]

At Tuskegee, LaGrange's brigade turned north toward West Point. Under orders from Upton, LaGrange was to march via Opelika to that city, seize the bridge across the Chattahoochee, and then communicate with Upton at Columbus. From that point on, his mission became separate from that of the rest of the army.

Under Upton's watchful guidance, the 4th Division continued directly east toward Columbus, to be followed by the remainder of the corps. The Confederate skirmishers who had disappeared just prior to arrival in Tuskegee immediately resumed the contest just outside town. "Rebs in our advance burning bridges and piling rails as usual," an aggravated officer in the lead reported.[28]

While Upton dealt with the details of the corps' movements, Wilson made his headquarters at a hotel and met with the civilians of the town to address their concerns. "One of the first callers was a dignified and serious woman," Wilson recalled, "who said that a detachment of men under the direction of an officer were threatening to destroy her printing press and type because, as the officer alleged, they were used in the publication of a rebel newspaper." This woman, the owner of the *Tuskegee Press,* was ultimately allowed to keep her printing equipment but was forced to sign a five-thousand-dollar bond, drawn up by Colonel Noble of the 3rd Iowa, a former lawyer, agreeing " 'so long as water runs and grass grows,' to publish nothing against the Government or the Constitution of the United States, but to confine her printing establishment to the publication of Bibles and schoolbooks."[29]

Elsewhere in the city, soldiers were making their way through the town, gathering supplies, resting, and feeding their horses. Of the soldiers engaged in the latter activity, many found that the partially completed Methodist Church of Tuskegee provided an excellent place to stable their horses and for the troopers to get a view of the village from its mostly completed tower.

Either resting or passing through, the troopers of the Cavalry Corps from seemingly every rank took the opportunity to try to find out the latest word on the progress of the war. Many of the Union soldiers had not previously heard that Richmond had been captured. "I rode up to a man standing by the fence in his yard and asked him what news there was, and how things were going in the armies," remembered Sergeant Conzett. "He put his finger on his nose and grinning told me that was the way folks were feeling in Richmond—that our folks were in full possession of the city and that the war was about over." Strange though the reply, Conzett attested to the enthusiasm of its reception: "You should have heard the hurrahs of our boys when the news passed along our line."

Others heard the good news about the developments in the armies, too. Unfortunately, however, as Lieutenant James O. Vanorsdol of the 4th Iowa explained, there was no official word, and no way to tell if what was being relayed was true. "Rumors of peace and that Grant had whipped Lee were rife throughout the day, but nothing definite was known by us—only rumors by the Rebels and citizens which afterwards proved to be true."[30]

By about 5 P.M., Wilson began to notice the rear elements of his corps entering town and decided to press on to the east. Upton was ahead, seeing to the advance of his division and planning their further movements toward Columbus. Before Wilson could leave, however, he was required to entertain one more group of citizens. "I was about to take leave," he later recalled, when "the ladies connected with the seminaries . . . called to pay their respects, after which they decked my horse with garlands and prepared a letter thanking and commending me and my command for our

forbearance and good behavior." Wilson soon found "the situation was becoming embarrassing" and was "anxious to put an end to it." Fortunately
for the general, "a violent rainstorm broke upon the scene," driving in-
doors the assembled crowd and allowing Wilson to expedite his departure
through a "pelting rain to a rich and favorably located plantation six miles
beyond."[31]

Though Wilson settled in for the evening early at the plantation, his veteran troopers trudged forward their heads bent against the stinging rain.
"We got a thorough soaking as we had to face a real southern thunderstorm," remembered one soldier, "and I . . . lost my hat." The gathering
darkness and the raging storm set the scene for a strange sight at the village of Society Hill, fourteen miles east of Tuskegee. There, according to
Captain Hinrichs, the soldiers met "white ladies standing in the rain waving handkerchiefs and *hurraying for Lincoln*." It was the first such "show of
Union sentiment among the people . . . met on the expedition," remembered another soldier. Responding promptly, according to Hinrichs, "the
boys cheered them as we passed."

If it caused the Union troopers discomfort, at least the storm had one
positive effect—it drove off the harassing parties of Confederate skirmishers. After the rain began, "the rebels were seen only in small, vanishing parties of mounted men," remembered Adjutant Scott of the 4th Iowa, and
"after passing Society Hill in a drenching rain, the whole force went into
bivouac," Upton establishing his headquarters at a plantation known as Buchanan's House. The head of Upton's division halted and encamped just a
few miles west of Crawford, and only twelve to fifteen miles west of Columbus by the most direct route. Upton knew that the next day's march
would bring them to the city.[32]

All the information Upton had gathered during the afternoon told him
that the Confederates were preparing to defend Columbus, but with what
force, he had no idea. He also had no reliable intelligence about the bridges
at Columbus. What information Upton possessed told him that there were
at least two bridges spanning the Chattahoochee between the small town
of Girard, Alabama, and Columbus, Georgia—one, a footbridge at the south
of the city, the other, a railroad bridge farther north. Only time would tell
how accurate his information was and what condition the bridges would
be in when he arrived.

What Upton was sure of, however, was that there was one potentially
major obstacle standing between his division and the town of Girard, opposite Columbus. Uchee Creek was a rain-swollen, sluggish stream that
ran across his line of march east of the small village of Crawford. It was

Fig. 4. General Emory Upton. Courtesy National Archives Collection, U.S. Army Military History Institute.

spanned by a bridge that Upton hoped had not yet been destroyed, and which, if it could be captured at least mostly intact, would enable his forces to cross without having to halt while another was built.

Lastly, Upton realized that half of Noble's 3rd Iowa (Curkendall's battalion, detached as provosts in Montgomery) still had not caught up to his division and were likely encamped somewhere near Tuskegee for the night. Knowing that he might need all the troops at his disposal to bolster his numbers in a fight for Columbus, Upton ordered that only two companies from the division be detailed to guard the baggage train, "to be relieved by the six companies . . . that have not yet come up, if they should arrive."

Confident that all else was satisfactory, Upton drew up his order of march for the next day. The march to Columbus would begin at 5 A.M. Alexander's brigade would lead the division, detailing six companies "to push forward as rapidly as possible and secure the bridge over the Uchee, beyond Crawford." Following closely behind would be Rodney's Battery I, 4th U.S. Artillery, and the pioneers, who could "repair the bridge if necessary." Winslow's brigade would follow behind the battery and try to keep closed up on the road as much as possible. Finally, the division and brigade headquarters wagons were ordered to "move immediately in rear of the troops and the pack trains in rear of the entire command."[33]

With his dispositions made, Upton could do little else but wait for morning. His moment had arrived. This was the opportunity he had waited for—the chance to prove his abilities as a cavalry commander in the eyes of his superiors and his friend, General Wilson. More importantly, this was his chance to win the fame that he desired. That night, while the torrential rains pooled and swirled in turbulent puddles outside his headquarters, Upton reviewed his meticulous calculations in preparation for the Battle for Columbus.

3
Gathering Darkness on the Chattahoochee

By the beginning of April 1865, the outlook for Columbus, Georgia, and the Confederacy was bleak. The tide of fortune had turned and was on the verge of overwhelming the Confederacy. In nearly every quarter, things were going badly for the armies. Lee's Army of Northern Virginia, after nearly nine months of siege, was still hemmed in at Petersburg, while its commander tried to devise a way to save his ragged, war-weary, and disillusioned force from an agonizing death in the trenches.

The Army of Tennessee was in even poorer condition. The suicidal Tennessee campaign undertaken by General Hood in the winter of 1864 had wasted the army on monumentally ill-conceived assaults that broke the spirit of its soldiers. The reinstatement of General Johnston to command of the army in late February helped momentarily to stem the tide of desertions and defeatism, but major defeats in March at Averasboro, North Carolina, and then again at Bentonville undid the army's last hope.[1]

On April 2, Richmond, the capital of the Confederacy, was abandoned and the Confederate government fled south. On April 9, Lee surrendered his army to Grant at Appomattox Courthouse. By April 12, word of the surrender reached Union and Confederate forces opposing one another in North Carolina. The news sparked a wave of desertions from the Army of Tennessee that its disillusioned commanders were powerless to prevent. "My small force is melting away like snow before the sun," Johnston complained, "and I am hopeless of recruiting it."

After consulting with President Jefferson Davis, Johnston drafted a letter and sent it to General Sherman. Its object was "to make a temporary suspension of active operations, and . . . to permit the civil authorities to enter into the needful arrangements to terminate the existing war." On the evening of April 14, Sherman agreed to the request and hostilities in the Carolinas ceased. Though orders were at once dispatched by both armies directing the immediate postponement of destructive operations, the disruption of the lines of communication during the recent fighting in Georgia meant that word of the developments would not reach central and south Georgia or Alabama for nearly a week. For both Wilson's Raiders and the soldiers and civilians of the Chattahoochee valley, there was still time to plan, to fight, . . . and to die.[2]

In Columbus in April 1865, times were hard. The collapse of the Confederate economy and transportation systems had crippled the once powerful city. The lack of adequate numbers of soldiers to garrison its defenses was also worrisome. It was a much different atmosphere than had prevailed in Columbus for much of the war.

Situated on the east bank of the Chattahoochee River in Muscogee County, Columbus was a city of major importance to the Confederacy. Founded in 1828 as a trading town, in subsequent years it had grown into a major industrial and trade center. Columbus's position at the head of navigation on the river meant that cotton could be easily loaded aboard steamers bound for Apalachicola, Florida, where it was shipped on to markets, foreign and domestic. The river's falling waters on the north end of the city also provided power to run productive textile mills. An ironworks, a paper mill, and a steam engine manufactory also added to Columbus's production capacity, while railroad connections facilitated the movement of goods into and out of the city.[3]

By 1860, Columbus's population was estimated at about ten thousand. The number increased as the beginning of hostilities drove the need for increased production, and nearly two thousand additional workers relocated to the city. By the height of the war, the influx of factory women, mechanics, and other laborers expanded the combined permanent and temporary population to an estimated seventeen thousand.[4]

From 1861 to 1865, Columbus played a major role in providing the Confederacy with supplies. In fact, the city was recognized as one of the South's leading producers of war material, "furnish[ing] more manufactured articles of every kind to the Confederate Quartermaster department than any place in the Confederacy except Richmond, which had all the protection and fostering care of the government. This superiority was not relative, according to population, but absolute, producing more clothing, shoes, hats, cooking utensils, axes, spades, harness, etc."

Columbus's clothiers produced a tremendous number of uniforms for Confederate forces. The government depot acquired "a large number of sewing machines" early in the war and in June 1862 delivered to Richmond its monthly production of "240 wooden boxes of uniforms, which filled fourteen railroad cars." Among the most productive of Columbus's private uniform manufactories were the shops at Empire Mills. This establishment alone supplied approximately three thousand completed suits per month to the Confederate quartermaster department, and though records are fragmentary, surviving documents show that this operation managed to turn out at least 32,016 uniforms between June 1863 and June 1864. In fact, the Columbus Depot uniform was one of the most common uniforms worn by Confederate troops in the western theater. It may even have been one of the most widely produced in the Confederacy, behind the Richmond Depot uniforms.[5]

Uniform production in Columbus was facilitated by the extraordinary manufacturing capabilities of its textile mills. Georgia jeans, cassimeres, and kerseys were manufactured in amazing quantities. The Columbus Factory, also known as Clapp's Factory, made war materials of all kinds, but in 1861 it reported annual production of "300,000 yards of cotton cloth and 75,000 yards of woolen goods, plus 40,000 pounds of yarn and thread." Eagle Mills, Columbus's largest, had a daily production rate during the war of "2,000 yards of tweed for uniforms . . . 1,500 yards of cotton duck for tents . . . [and] $1,500 worth of cotton 'stripes' for army shirts, osnaburgs, sheeting and yarn. The plant's production in 1862 also included up to 1,000 yards a week of 'India rubber cloth' and 1,800 pounds a week of rope." Though production varied greatly from month to month, this factory managed in June 1864 to turn over a staggering 103,184 yards of cotton goods to the Confederate quartermaster department in the city.

Other products of use to the army were produced in Columbus in huge quantities. Two factories produced both conventional brogans and shoes with wooden soles. When leather became scarce, the uppers of the wooden shoes were made with canvas from the mills in town. What the wooden-soled shoes may have lacked in comfort, they made up for in thrift. Whereas leather shoes commanded premium prices by mid-war, often in excess of seventy-five dollars per pair, the government could purchase wooden-soled shoes with cloth or canvas uppers for as little as ten dollars.

Beyond uniforms and shoes, Columbus supplied the armies of the South with buttons, oil cloth, ammunition, rifles, carbines, revolvers, swords, bayonets, and musical instruments. The Navy Yard and its capacity to aid the Confederate naval service, and even to build a torpedo boat and ironclad, added weight to Columbus's standing as a major manufacturing center for the Confederate government. Columbus was also responsible for helping to feed the armies, producing "two hundred and fifty barrels [of flour] a day for transportation to Confederates in Virginia."[6]

In addition to the small arms produced in Columbus, including the famous J. P. Murray rifle and the Columbus Firearms Company revolver, Columbus was responsible for sending nearly one hundred pieces of artillery to the field. The Columbus Iron Works began production of artillery in the summer of 1861, and by June 1862 the production capabilities had increased to the point that "the firm announced that they were prepared to cast six and furnish four cannon per week." Among the guns known to have been produced there was a 12-pounder field howitzer made of donated brass named "The Ladies Defender," as well as an experimental breech-loading gun fashioned from the wheel shaft of the river steamer *John C. Calhoun.* In September 1862 the facility was leased to the Confederate government and placed under the control of Chief Engineer James H. Warner of the Confederate navy. From that point on, the Confederate Naval Iron Works engaged in the production of ship machinery.

The Columbus Arsenal, which began to produce artillery in 1863, was Columbus's major cannon manufacturer. The equipment used by the facility was that of the old Baton Rouge Arsenal, which had been forced to relocate after the capture of New Orleans. The focus of the arsenal was to produce 12-pounder Napoleon light field guns, and estimates of total Napoleon production range between sixty and seventy. The Columbus Arsenal also may have produced as many as twenty 9-pounder field guns.[7]

After the fall of Atlanta, the strain on Columbus industries to keep up with demand increased. As depot after depot in the South fell into Union hands, the machinery from those facilities was packed up and sent to Columbus. The threat of Sherman marching his army on Columbus was considered real in 1864, but it passed when he decided to move instead toward Savannah.

While the ability to produce items needed by the troops was still excellent in early 1865, getting the goods into the hands of those who needed them was becoming increasingly difficult. Goods from Columbus piled up with no means to move them. By April 1865 the railroad ties between the armies and Columbus had been mostly destroyed. Those that remained were incomplete, and because the railroads were constantly harassed by Federal cavalry, the materiel carried on them was increasingly at risk. Further inhibiting was the Union blockading fleet off Apalachicola, which had long since cut off any chance of moving goods south via the river for transport by sea.[8]

With such a substantial portion of the Confederacy's goods coming from Columbus, it had been decided early in the war that defenses should be constructed to protect it from an enemy raid. The city's geography, however, made preparing a defense problematic. Columbus lay in a flat valley surrounded by hills on the east and bordered by the Chattahoochee on the west. Across the river in Alabama lay a small suburb of Columbus called Girard, which also lay in a bare, flat valley compassed about by steep ridges. Several small creeks cut through both towns. With the twin cities thus situated in a giant bowl, it would be impossible to construct defenses immediately around them that would not be vulnerable to bombardment by enemy artillery occupying the surrounding hills. The only alternative, therefore, was to build fortifications farther out on the high ground that encircled the Chattahoochee valley.[9]

Work on defenses for the city was begun in 1862. Attack from the west was considered the most likely, so a series of forts and earthworks was begun with the intention of protecting Columbus's industry and the bridges that connected Columbus with Girard. Progress was slow at first, but when General Lovell Rousseau led a Federal cavalry raid in 1864 that passed just north of Columbus, the work was renewed and new defenses were planned. Forts were begun as far out as two miles from the town of Girard on high hills that would provide excellent points of observation and interlocking fields of fire. The forts were strategically placed on prominent hills overlooking the main roads into Girard from Crawford, Opelika, Summerville, and Eufaula.[10]

Of prime importance to the constructors of the defenses was the protection of the three bridges that connected Girard to Columbus. Of Columbus's three bridges that spanned the Chattahoochee, the oldest connected Bridge Street in Girard with Dillingham Street in Columbus and was known as the City Bridge. Originally built in 1833–34, this bridge was destroyed by a flood and rebuilt in 1841. It was of a covered design with only small windows in the sides for the admittance of light. The bridge's length has generally been estimated at about three hundred yards.[11]

The most important bridge in Columbus was constructed to connect Girard's Brodnax Street with Columbus's Franklin Street. Called the Franklin Street Bridge, it was slightly longer than the City Bridge, at just over one thousand feet in length. It, too, was of covered design with small windows, but it was large enough for the passage of two carriages and was operated as a toll bridge.[12]

The third bridge that spanned the Chattahoochee at Columbus was the bridge of the Columbus and Western Railroad. It lay just north of the Franklin Street Bridge. Another bridge connected Alabama with Georgia three miles north of the city at Clapp's Factory, but it lay outside of the city's defenses and was mainly used by factory workers.[13]

Although the forts were excellent in design and well constructed, there was one major problem with the city's defenses: they were too extensive. According to General Jeremy F. Gilmer, an engineer who oversaw part of the construction, "The country around Columbus is of such a character that it is difficult to locate a line of defensive works without giving a development too great for any garrison that we can hope to place there." Despite Gilmer's doubts about the lack of manpower to utilize the city's defenses, construction continued through 1863 and until late 1864.[14]

When in late 1864 it was feared that Union forces under Sherman might march south from Atlanta to capture Columbus, work on the western side of the river came to an abrupt halt. Construction efforts were redirected to the eastern side of Columbus, where earthworks were hastily thrown up in a ring around the city. This shift of focus may have cost the loss of precious time and resources that could have been used to finish and equip the forts west of Columbus, which were neglected until it was proved that Union forces intended to move toward Savannah rather than Columbus.[15]

When the focus finally returned to the western side of the line in April 1865, there was too little time and too few resources, human and materiel, to get many of the forts prepared. Nearly all the forts occupying the outer defensive ring were complete but had yet to be furnished with artillery and, therefore, were useless. What would be of use to the defenders were the forts constructed on the northern edge of the original line, and a newer, inner line of works that was quickly being finished even as the Federals approached.[16]

Two men who understood the problems associated with the defenses of Columbus well were Major General Howell Cobb and Colonel Leon Von Zinken. Cobb was born in Cherry Hill, Georgia, on September 7, 1815. After attending college in Georgia, he was admitted to the bar in 1836. In 1842 he was elected to the U.S. Congress as a representative from Georgia, a position that he held for three consecutive terms until 1849, when he was made Speaker of the House. In 1852 Cobb left the Democratic Party and was elected governor of Georgia on the Union ticket, a platform opposed to national dissolution. Shortly after his election, Cobb switched his party affiliations back to the Democratic Party, but he had sufficiently perturbed his peers enough to prevent his election to a U.S. Senate seat after his term as governor. After his first major political defeat, Cobb returned to the practice of law.

In 1856 Cobb became an ardent supporter of James Buchanan's bid for election in his successful presidential race, and was named shortly thereafter secretary of the treasury. While he had at one time been a strong Unionist, Secretary Cobb saw what he believed to be Northern radicalism tearing the nation apart. Though for union, he was not for union at any price, and when Abraham Lincoln was elected Cobb resigned his post and returned home.

The early months of the Confederacy were an exciting time for Cobb, who was unanimously chosen to be the president of the Provisional Con-

Fig. 5. General Howell Cobb. Courtesy Hargrett Rare Book and Manuscript Library, University of Georgia Libraries.

federate Congress and administered the oath of office to President Davis at the capital in Montgomery on February 18, 1861. After a regular congress was established for the fledgling government, Cobb set out to become a military man. He was given authority to raise a regiment, and eventually became the colonel of the 16th Georgia Infantry and was sent to Virginia. Cobb remained with his unit until 1863, when he was transferred south and was made the commandant of middle Florida, a position that gave him the responsibility of protecting western Florida and southwest Georgia. By March 1865 Cobb held the rank of major general and was in command of the Department of Tennessee and Georgia, as well as Georgia's Reserve Force.[17]

The Georgia Reserve Force was a unusual organization. Established in April 1864, it replaced Georgia's previous militia organizations whereby citizens were called into service for the protection of the state and to provide for local defense. It was instituted under Confederate authority and was composed of able-bodied males between seventeen and eighteen as well as those between forty-five and fifty years of age. Its ranks were also bolstered by volunteers of all ages from seventeen to fifty who were not already in Confederate service and by men who were on detail from the provisional army. It was designed to be called into the field only in the case of emergency and to be limited mainly to service within Georgia's borders. Clothing, equipment, arms, and other necessary materiel were often purchased for the units by their officers or through contributions from

the communities where the various units were raised. As commander of
the Georgia Reserve Force, Cobb was in charge of organizing these units
under Confederate authority and readying them for duty, should they be
needed. They were needed almost immediately, when Sherman launched
his Atlanta campaign in May 1864.[18]

Even so, Cobb was largely inhibited in his efforts to raise the reserves
through the maneuvering of Georgia's governor, Joseph Brown. Besides
having an intense dislike for Cobb, Brown detested what he saw as the
Confederate government's encroachment upon the sovereignty of his state.
Early in the war, Brown was handled roughly by Confederate authorities
and by another personal enemy, President Davis. A series of controversies,
and most recently Brown's diminished authority over the mustering and
employment of the state's militia, made Brown unwilling to cooperate
with Cobb's efforts. Though Brown had at his disposal nearly three thousand militia officers within Georgia who were capable of helping assemble
troops to serve in the reserves, his obstinacy ensured that Cobb's Reserve
Force would marshal only about six thousand soldiers. Cobb's further efforts to convince Brown to allow him to draft detailed men or those acting as part of the state's civil administration caused heated disagreement,
but ultimately the governor won.[19]

Though the reserves were supposed to remain in the field only so long as
the emergency lasted, the prolonged sojourn of Sherman's army in Georgia
kept them on duty for much longer than anyone had initially expected. It
was only following the Union army's March to the Sea and its subsequent
movement into the Carolinas that, much to the pleasure of its members and
their families, most of the reserves were allowed to return home. A substantial portion, however, were never released, but were retained on duty
to garrison cities, guard prisoners, and perform other essential tasks. A significant contingent was engaged in transporting a large body of Union
prisoners of war from Andersonville to Jacksonville, Florida, to be exchanged.[20]

This latter operation had begun earlier in 1865 when Generals Cobb,
D. H. Maury, and Gideon Pillow took it upon themselves to relieve the
strained resources of Georgia of the burden of Federal prisoners. Cobb
and the others realized that Union forces had long since ceased entering
into arrangements for prisoner exchanges. Yet, it was the belief of Cobb
and Maury that Union officials would not be opposed to the Confederates
simply paroling and giving over custody of Union prisoners to Federal authorities without exchange. Under this assumption, Cobb arranged an initial trial in which fifteen hundred Union prisoners were released from An-

dersonville, transported by rail to Jackson, Mississippi, and then successfully turned over to Union army authorities.

Although this trial was successful, General Richard Taylor refused to allow another such release in Mississippi, fearing that the Union prisoners might pick up information about Confederate dispositions along the route that could be used against his forces. Undeterred, in March 1865 Cobb and others looked for another opportunity. After careful study, it was agreed that should Union forces accept, the prisoners would be moved via rail to Columbus, from thence down the Chattahoochee River to (near) Quincy, and on from there by rail to Jacksonville, from which point it would only be a short march to Union-held St. Augustine. To oversee the arrangements, Cobb appointed his aide Colonel Charles A. L. Lamar.

Lamar was a prominent and infamous citizen of Savannah who, as the son of a wealthy and influential Georgia industrialist, won notoriety before the war for his fiery temper, competitive nature, seamanship, and activities as an illegal slave trader. At the onset of war he volunteered with and then promptly resigned his commissions from at least three different units, preferring instead to use his knowledge of seafaring and smuggling to engage in the more exciting and lucrative business of blockade running. Lamar partnered with his father to establish and operate "a state subsidized blockade running line" for Georgia. At this, Lamar was very successful. Traveling to Europe several times, he helped to procure at least five fast steamships that succeeded in delivering greatly desired goods to the state. According to historian Tom Wells, "One of them, the *Little Hattie,* is supposed to have made sixty round trips." Lamar's exploits even won him an endorsement for the position of Georgia state agent for the export of cotton.[21]

Upon his final return from Europe, Lamar, who was a cousin of Cobb's wife, was made an aide on Cobb's staff. He was also recommended by Cobb to Governor Brown to take up the state's blockade running where Lamar's father had been forced to leave off after the fall of Savannah to Sherman's army. Indeed, when Savannah fell, Lamar's father, in an effort to save what he could of his large fortune, attempted to convince the Union occupiers that, despite his active participation in blockade running, he was in truth a Unionist. His attempts were partly fruitful, and in keeping with his newfound loyalty, the elder Lamar attempted to convince his son to give up the smuggling enterprise, sell the ships, and invest the money abroad where it could not be confiscated by the U.S. government. All of this the devoted secessionist and eager entrepreneur, Charles Lamar, could not do.[22]

Instead of selling the ships, Lamar defied his father and offered their continued services to Governor Brown under new and potentially more profitable terms. Then, in February 1865 Lamar proposed another, more controversial venture. Apparently, several Southern-sympathizing Northern businessmen were willing to partner with Lamar and financially back a mission to run in needed supplies in exchange for payment in cotton. Eager to obtain approval for the mission and to reap the handsome monetary rewards for such an effort, Lamar promoted the scheme and earned the support of Cobb and Brown. This was not hard to do considering that, despite public regulations prohibiting such activity, at least in Georgia the trading of cotton for needed supplies with Northern agents had been in practice for some time by the spring of 1865.[23]

The colonel promised that he could supply "the country between the Savannah River on the Atlantic & the Apalachicola River on the Gulf" with desperately needed war materiel. "I have two of the fastest ships in the world, all ready to go immediately into the business," claimed Lamar. "I want no advances from the government," he further announced, but "will demand cotton upon delivery of the goods."[24]

Cobb enthusiastically accepted the application and forwarded it to President Davis, announcing, "I am clearly and decidedly of opinions that we should obtain all the supplies which our cotton will get for us." "I have for months urged this policy on our government," opined the general, "and have the gratification of knowing that our brave soldiers in the field have been indebted to it for many of the necessities and comforts with which they have been furnished." He even went so far as to pronounce that "If Lincoln himself would exchange arms, ammunition, clothing, shoes, meat, salt, medicines, and many other articles too tedious to mention, for the cotton of our government and people, I avow, without hesitation, I would make the exchange with them." In hopes of prompting action, Cobb urged that the government "should not hesitate to make such a contract with Mr. Lamar whom I know, and whose ability to carry out his proposition I have no doubt about." But hesitate the government did.[25]

For more than a month, Cobb's endorsement was lost amid the bureaucratic shuffle in Richmond. Unwilling to delay longer, in March 1865 Cobb ordered Lamar and a group of associates to travel to Savannah under a flag of truce with the official mission of arranging the prisoner turnover at St. Augustine, but also with the ulterior intention of making arrangements necessary to facilitate the blockade-running attempt. For the trip, Lamar secured passage to Savannah down the Ocmulgee River aboard the steamer *Comet*. Before the ship could depart, however, suspicions were raised about its intended purpose and destination. Apparently, Lamar's associates onboard were "well known as speculators and blockade runners," the ship was loaded with a large amount (two hundred bales) of cotton, and word got out that the vessel was destined to rendezvous with a Federal transport. Much to the frustration of Lamar and the rest of his entourage, as well as to Cobb, a group of concerned citizens at Hawkinsville, headed by Confederate captain Norman McDuffie, boarded the ship, seized and removed the cotton, and arrested the boat's captain and part of Lamar's band. Indeed, Lamar and two of his associates were only able to avoid being detained themselves by disclosing the written orders of their official business issued by Cobb.[26]

Though Lamar was ultimately allowed to continue on to Savannah overland and was able to begin the prisoner exchange negotiations, the episode sparked a flurry of contentious public correspondence between McDuffie and both Cobb and Lamar. McDuffie claimed that Cobb had overstepped his authority by granting permission to the group to sell cotton to the Federals and that the whole affair had the "coloring of a slightly whitewashed effort to trade with the enemy for private advantage." Cobb defended his position by claiming that he had granted permission to take the cotton along as an afterthought and that it was only to be used to defer expenses associated with the trip. This public denial was necessary not only for Cobb's personal protection but also in order to protect the secret nature of the arrangements.[27]

Despite the controversy, the Confederate envoy to Savannah received encouragement from the Federal authorities that the proposed prisoner turnover would be accepted. Under the guard of three regiments of the Georgia Reserve Force, more than six thousand prisoners were shipped off in hopes of restored freedom.[28] Shortly thereafter, Cobb ordered Lamar to Jacksonville to take charge of the negotiations. This was an especially convenient assignment, as it placed Lamar near the St. Mary's River where in early April the CSS *Owl,* carrying a cargo of lead, niter, saltpeter, Enfield rifles, bacon, flour, coffee, and other goods, managed to slip past the Union blockaders and up the river. The ship's cargo had been secured through an agent in New York, and was sent (it was claimed) with the permission of Federal authorities. The run was only partly successful, however. "The *Owl* only discharged about one third of her cargo before she had to put off, with the blockaders after her."[29]

The other man whose life would become intertwined with the fate of Columbus was Colonel Leon Von Zinken. "Son of a Prussian general and himself once a Prussian officer," noted one biographer, "he entered the war as a major of the German Battalion of the Twentieth Louisiana." At the Battle of Shiloh, Tennessee, Von Zinken was recognized by his commanding general as having "performed well his part, having three horses

Fig. 6. Colonel Leon Von Zinken. Collection of the author.

shot under him during the conflict." The Battle of Shiloh also appears to be the first of several instances where he would be wounded. According to the colonel of the 20th Louisiana, "Maj. Leon Von Zinken bravely led several attacks with the colors in his hand, but was disabled early on the second day by the fall of his horse, which was killed under him."[30]

Von Zinken became lieutenant colonel of his regiment in June 1862 and also served as inspector general on General John C. Breckinridge's staff until September 1863. During that time he further distinguished himself as a competent staff officer and commander and had at least two more horses shot from under him in combat. In September 1863 "he was relieved from duty as Inspector of the Division at his own request . . . in order to take command of the 13th & 20th Louisiana Regiment" and was made its colonel. While Von Zinken may have intended to command his regiment in the field, only one month after he was named colonel he was ordered to be detached for duty as the commandant of the post of Marietta, Georgia.[31]

Von Zinken remained at his post until the approach of Sherman's army in the summer of 1864 forced him back into the field. Unfortunately for Von Zinken, this time he earned no praise for his efforts. After the Battle of Ezra Church on July 28, 1864, General Randall Gibson, his brigade commander, in his report of the battle, accused Von Zinken of acting without authority and placing the brigade in jeopardy. Von Zinken paid for his blunder. During the engagement he was seriously wounded by a bursting shell that crippled his hand and forearm, thereby ending again his field command. On September 4, after recuperating from his wounds, Von Zinken was sent orders that read: "You are to assume command of [the] post at Columbus."[32]

Upon arrival in Columbus, Von Zinken inspected the city and its defenses. It soon became obvious to him that serious work had to be undertaken to put things in readiness to meet the enemy should they move that way. He had the cooperation of city officials and the confidence of most of his superiors, a fact reflected in an inspection report from Columbus in October: "Leon Von Zinken . . . appears to be an excellent officer and well suited for this position, with an accurate knowledge of his duties, zealous and energetic in their performance."

The fact that Von Zinken was "zealous and energetic" may also have made him easy for some in Columbus to dislike. In February 1865, only five months after his assignment to the post, Von Zinken became the target of potential violence when one of the city provosts stopped a Confederate soldier and prominent Columbus resident named John Lindsay, who was wounded and home on furlough. Lindsay was "creating a disturbance," and when confronted by the provost he insolently refused to show his pass. The provost guard immediately reported the infraction. Determined to take hold of the situation, Von Zinken ordered "the guard to bring him to his headquarters 'dead or alive.'" The next day Lindsay again refused to show his pass or heed the instructions of the guard, and as Lindsay mounted his horse the provost "shot a ball through his head, killing him instantly."[33]

The shooting sparked a wave of resentment toward Von Zinken. A mob soon gathered at the colonel's headquarters. Soldiers passing through the city joined the throng, and "a large body of Wheeler's Cavalry was . . . shouting, 'Hang him! Hang him!'" Lindsey's brother and a group of citizens "rushed into Von Zinken's office, seized him, and sent for a rope." It was only through the efforts of the slain soldier's father that more bloodshed was averted.

Though Von Zinken escaped with his life that day, a court-martial was ordered and he was charged with murder. Fortunately for him, however, within the last several months Von Zinken had earned the respect and confidence of his commander, the very successful and influential Howell

Cobb. Cobb defended Von Zinken in his trial and won an acquittal. Shortly thereafter, Cobb received command of the Department of Tennessee and Georgia. When he did, he assigned Von Zinken to command of the sub-district that encompassed his post.[34]

Among the many responsibilities thrust upon Von Zinken by his new position was the rounding up of Confederate deserters within his sub-district who were forming bands and camps in the countryside. It was his job to ensure the safety of the community from these gangs by breaking them up and returning the men to their commands. In this, Von Zinken had a good deal of trouble.

First, the pursuit of these bandits required absence from his post at Columbus, and Von Zinken was anxious to have some other individual placed in charge of it so that he might not be so divided in his efforts. Second, there was a jurisdictional dispute between Von Zinken and General William Wofford (whose command was supposed to be limited to north Georgia) over the latter's interference in operations within Von Zinken's subdistrict. Apparently, Von Zinken found Wofford's cavalry constantly and, at least according to Von Zinken, illegally recruiting among the deserters he was attempting to roust out. (This is somewhat ironic as one of Wofford's missions was to round up deserters who were causing disturbances in the northern part of the state.)

In a telegram to Cobb, Von Zinken explained: "First, I would respectfully ask whether General Wofford has any authority to recruit amongst deserters in my district? Second, if he has such authority, there is no chance to return men to their commands as they are organizing companies which are a terror to the country." Von Zinken's concern with deserter bands was short-lived, however. The growing possibility of a Federal raid on Columbus necessitated a refocusing of efforts toward putting the defenses of Columbus in order.[35]

As the Confederacy edged toward collapse during the early spring of 1865, Cobb and Von Zinken both realized that Columbus was in danger. With the Army of Tennessee pinned down in North Carolina, there was no force available except the Georgia Reserve Force and Forrest's command, most of which was spread thin all over Alabama, to stop a raid against the city either from Thomas's Union army in Tennessee or from the south or west. As early as late February, both Cobb and Von Zinken were trying to devise ways to garrison the city. Cobb even sought permission from Confederate authorities "to stop at Columbus men and officers returning to the army." The worsening situation in Virginia and the Carolinas held center stage, however, and their efforts went largely ignored outside Georgia.[36]

Von Zinken could plainly see that he faced a serious challenge in trying to prepare a defense for Columbus. The fortifications were too extensive, and he had too few troops at his disposal to complete them or to man them. He also knew that there were no troops to spare. Every man the army had was needed in the field or was already doing service elsewhere. Working under the assumption that he would never be able to defend Columbus using the fortifications already in place, Von Zinken began a new, smaller line of entrenchments that would form a *tête-de-pont,* the military term used to describe defenses constructed on the enemy side of a bridge or causeway to protect the structure and allow its use as a route of communication or reinforcement.[37]

The bridges Von Zinken chose to enclose within his new semicircle of entrenchments in Girard were the Franklin Street Bridge and the Columbus and Western Railroad Bridge. To expedite the construction, he incorporated three already nearly completed and excellently situated forts into his defensive plan. At the west end of the Franklin Street Bridge, in Girard, there stood a conspicuous knoll known as Red Hill, atop which was a small square fort capable of sheltering a couple hundred soldiers and four cannons. This fort, designated Fort 1 by Confederate engineers, was situated so as to present a view of the City Bridge, the town of Girard, and the approaches to the south and west. It would anchor the south end of Von Zinken's defenses.[38]

Running northward from the Alabama end of the Franklin Street Bridge for about a mile and a half, paralleling the Chattahoochee River to the east and the Summerville Road to the west, was a very large, and in places steep, ridge known as Ingersoll Hill. At the northernmost terminus of this hill occurred a steep slope that facilitated an excellent view of the northern approaches to the city and the Summerville Road. Here a massive, two-hundred-yard-long, crescent-shaped, four-gun fort, designated Fort 2, along with an attached one-gun redoubt, anchored the north end of Von Zinken's *tête-de-pont.*

With Forts 1 and 2 anchoring either end of his main line, Von Zinken began the construction of a series of trenches and rifle pits running north to south that would connect them. "These breastworks consisted of trenches eight feet wide and six feet deep . . . [with] a single opening about ten feet wide being left untouched to allow for ingress and egress. The earth of the trenches was banked on the outer edge." Additionally, near the north end of the entrenchments he initiated construction of a two-gun lunette (crescent-shaped redoubt) whose guns could rake the Summerville Road with enfilading fire.[39]

As an added measure of protection from any threat that might present itself along the Summerville Road, Von Zinken incorporated into his de-

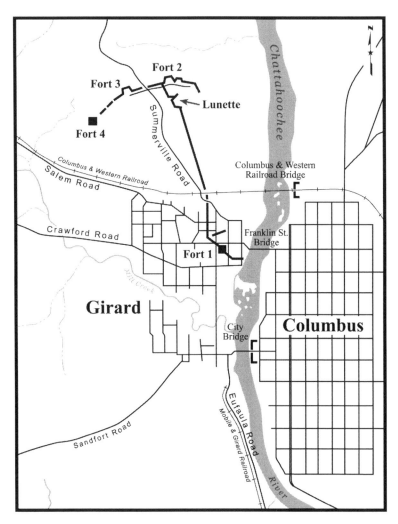

Map 2. Columbus, Girard, and Confederate defenses, April 1865. Charged with protecting Columbus, Von Zinken quickly realized the futility of trying to man all of the city's defenses. Abandoning the outer works, Von Zinken began construction of a *tête-de-pont* around the Columbus and Western Railroad Bridge and the Franklin Street Bridge. Incorporated into his line would be Forts 1–4.

fenses another large, crescent-shaped, three-gun fort on the western side of the Summerville Road on a hill opposite Fort 2. This fort, designated Fort 3, would be connected by a set of entrenchments to Fort 2, crossing the Summerville Road, forming a curtain to the main line. Additionally, extending from Fort 3's western flank was a series of rifle pits that ran in the direction of another nearby fort that had yet to be completed. When ready, Von Zinken's defenses would resemble an upside-down and backward "L" with Fort 1 at the base, Fort 2 at the top center, and Fort 3 at the top left (see map 2).[40]

Von Zinken's defensive positions were strong. In addition to the forts and earthworks that his less-than-adequate work details were trying to complete, the ground itself offered obstacles to any force that might attempt to assail the line. Between the Summerville Road and the main line of the *tête-de-pont* ran a small creek in a depression that, at its deepest, descended almost forty feet before rising again to the entrenchments. This depression was also cut through by several steep ravines that would prove imposing obstacles.[41]

Work on the fortifications continued at a slow pace through March 1865. With only a skeleton garrison of Confederate soldiers and a small body of government-contracted slave labor available to work, the improvements were necessarily delayed. Meanwhile, Cobb tried unsuccessfully to convince Georgia's governor to let him have the thousands of able-bodied men on detached service, or part of the civil government, to help prepare to defend the state, should an emergency arise. Both tasks proceeded slowly until April 3 and 4, when word of the fall of Selma and the rout of Forrest's army spread through southwest Georgia.[42]

4
Conflict on the Horizon

Week One

On the evening of Monday, April 3, 1865, news of the fall of Selma reached Columbus, setting off the first week of what would be a two-week explosion of activity that would culminate in the Battle for Columbus. Preparations to defend the city immediately took on a new level of urgency. Von Zinken met with Columbus's mayor, Francis G. Wilkins, to discuss what could be done to prepare the city to meet the enemy. Among Von Zinken's first concerns was that he had very few soldiers to man the trenches being built across the river. It was a situation he had been working to remedy for weeks.[1]

Von Zinken saw Columbus's large black population as a perfect source for building a garrison. "Many negroes offered daily to volunteer [and I] could raise a brigade in a short time," he had pleaded with Secretary of War John C. Breckinridge in hopes of gaining consent to arm Columbus's blacks. Firing off a fresh request on April 3, Von Zinken politely urged action, asking: "Have telegraphed twice on the subject. Please answer." Wilkins was easier to convince. Von Zinken was quickly able to persuade the mayor that without additional manpower, of whatever sort, there was little hope of defending the city. Unwilling to wait, Von Zinken asked Wilkins to write Cobb asking for whatever assistance the general could provide from Georgia's Reserve Force, and also for permission to initiate the raising of a colored brigade.[2]

At his headquarters in Macon, on April 4, Cobb received the news of Selma's capture with complete surprise. He had no idea up to that point that any Federal force was even moving through Alabama. Cobb quickly realized that the Union army had cut him off from communication with his commander, Lieutenant General Richard Taylor, in Meridian, Mississippi. Beyond the reports that were starting to trickle in, Cobb knew nothing of the strength or movements of the Union cavalry, nor anything about the dispositions of either Taylor's or Forrest's command. Desperate to receive some communication, Cobb ordered a special messenger to ride through the country to Taylor and then to return with his reply. Cobb needed to know what he was up against. Also, as he explained, "I am particularly anxious to know what assistance you could give us and what your operations are likely to be so far as they bear upon the defense of this section of the country." Cobb knew that even if his message made it through to Taylor, a response would be a long time coming. There was no time to waste.[3]

Though Cobb had no information about the enemy except the reports that were beginning to arrive over the telegraph, he realized that the proximity of the Union force put his state in danger, particularly southwest Georgia. It seemed only reasonable that an enemy at Selma would turn its army toward the Confederacy's last remaining major manufacturing and supply centers at Columbus and Macon. With this in mind, Cobb plunged headlong into the task of recruiting Georgia's forces to repel an invasion he felt was imminent. It would not be an easy task.

When Sherman's Union army marched into North Carolina in March 1865, Georgia's state of emergency was considered to have passed, and most of the Reserve Force was granted leave to go home and tend their fields. Those who remained on duty were spread out in all corners of the state and were occupied with various tasks. The significant contingent engaged in transporting the Union prisoners of war from Andersonville to Jacksonville were meeting with constant impediment. Cobb, now desperate to have the mission completed and the reserves returned, ordered the overseeing officer to use his soldiers to impress all transportation necessary to complete the mission. "The prisoners must be forwarded without delay," Cobb instructed.[4]

Elsewhere around the state, other units were equally occupied. At several cities, soldiers were detailed to guard supplies and watch for enemy movements. One outfit was assisting in the delivery of a wagon train bound for Milledgeville. A couple others were guarding prisoners at Andersonville. Still others were dealing with problems caused by civil insurrectionists, who, disillusioned with the war, were causing disturbances in several towns, but chiefly in Augusta.[5]

Cobb realized that without more specific reliable information about the enemy's forces and their intentions toward Georgia, he could not call to duty the remainder of Georgia's reserves, who had only recently been released to go home after almost ten months of service. He also realized that the few troops he had on hand would be inadequate to meet any serious threat. Even so, for the next several days Cobb attempted to get whatever forces he could muster moving toward southwest Georgia. "The fall of

Selma and the movement of the enemy . . . makes it necessary that I should gather all the forces I can for the defense of the state in that direction," he telegraphed General Brickett Fry in Augusta. "Regarding the necessity as imperative," Cobb asked Fry to send the reserves stationed in Augusta by rail via Atlanta to Macon, a circuitous route that involved the "least amount of marching." Cobb also authorized Fry to grant short furloughs to "any man among his reserves who could promise to return with another able bodied recruit." Cobb then sent out messages asking the commanders of various other reserve organizations to promptly report their strengths and to stand by to be called into action if the situation warranted.[6]

Cobb also sought support from forces outside his control. Almost immediately, he petitioned Confederate authorities to have the men of General Wofford's Department of North Georgia placed under his command. He also appealed directly to Davis for assistance, saying, "The movements in Alabama put in immediate danger arsenals and public stores at Columbus . . . as well as the resources of Southwestern Georgia. . . . These important resources," explained Cobb, "require more means of defense than I have with militia."[7]

While Cobb was still reeling from the news of Selma's fall, and trying to establish what, if any, of Georgia's reserve forces could be mustered to meet the threat, his headquarters began to be bombarded with telegraphs and letters from concerned civil and military authorities from all over south Georgia. There was no shortage from either Von Zinken or Wilkins. On April 4, Wilkins sent a lengthy message asking what forces Cobb could send to garrison Columbus. Cobb, unsure about his ability to gather enough soldiers to defend the state, and for the most part uninformed about the strength and intentions of the enemy, answered honestly: "You will appreciate . . . the difficulties in the way of saying at this time, what can or will be done for the defense of Columbus." He added: "Much depends upon the force that I may be able to bring into the field—much also depends on the movements of the enemy."

Despite his uneasiness over the lack of soldiers at his immediate disposal, and the apparent approval of Columbus's mayor, Cobb had no intention of granting Von Zinken's request to garrison Columbus with black soldiers. "In reference to the arming of the negroes I must say to you, that I am utterly opposed to it and can only give it my sanction, where ordered to do so, by higher authority," announced Cobb. "Instead," he suggested, "let us prepare by any means for our defense and if our citizens will do their duty, we will not be driven to the necessity of making our negroes win our liberty for us."

Ironically, Von Zinken's request was later approved by Davis, who en-

dorsed the measure and instructed Secretary Breckinridge to "confer authority . . . to raise companies . . . officers to be appointed hereafter." Unfortunately for Von Zinken, the flight of the Confederate government and
the poor state of communications between south Georgia and the rest of
the Confederacy ensured that the president's directive never arrived. There
would be no arming of Columbus's blacks. Cobb's reply seems to have
settled the question.[8]

Questions were in abundance, however, and Von Zinken had many more.
In the days following the news of Selma's fall, Cobb's office was inundated
by messages from Columbus's post commandant asking permission to take
various actions. "Three hundred effective arms retained at West Point by
your order are much needed here, can I send for them?" asked one telegram. "Artillery [in Columbus] ought to be provided with horses, do you
sanction impressments?" asked another. When Von Zinken inquired as to
whether, because of his dual responsibilities as post and subdistrict commandant, another post commander should be appointed, Cobb replied,
"when it becomes necessary at times for you to visit the district you can
temporarily put on duty any officer reporting to you, . . . but . . . your duties of commandant of post and subdistrict are not incompatible."[9]

Initially, Cobb obliged Von Zinken's constant querying, until he learned
that Von Zinken had attempted go over his head by petitioning the state
inspector general directly about the need for troops in Columbus. Shortly
thereafter, when Von Zinken began to send Cobb messages suggesting
courses of action—for example, one that read, "I suggest that the Georgia
State Line be sent here, [and] also that Gen. Woffords Cavalry be ordered
to West Point to watch movements of enemy"—Cobb put a stop to it. He
informed Von Zinken that all of his suggestions had already been considered and that Wofford's command was outside his authority. After explaining that the disposition of Georgia's forces would be dictated by the
movements of the enemy, Cobb asked: "In the meantime, I wish to ascer-
tain what force you will be able to command at Columbus . . . advise me
fully upon the points using every effort in your power."[10]

Von Zinken got the message. The number of telegrams decreased, and
he turned to focusing on his own efforts within the city. Although he had
little infantry or cavalry with which to protect Columbus, Von Zinken
did have a substantial artillery force under the command of Major James F.
Waddell. Waddell was born in 1826, in Hillsboro, North Carolina. During
the Mexican War he served with the 12th U.S. Infantry and was promoted
to second lieutenant. After the war he served for a time as consul to Mata-
moras. In 1857 Waddell moved to Russell County, Alabama, where he lived
until the outbreak of hostilities in 1861. In that year he joined and was ap-

Fig. 7. Major James F.
Waddell. Courtesy State
of Alabama Department
of Archives and History.

pointed a captain in the 6th Alabama Infantry. After one year of service
he organized a battery of artillery after he was granted permission to take
twenty men from each company of the 6th Alabama.[11]

Waddell and his battery were captured at Vicksburg in July 1863 but
were exchanged that September and immediately began the task of reorganization. The unit was increased to battalion strength and designated
the 20th Battalion Alabama Light Artillery. It was divided into three companies, or batteries—Emery's battery, Bellamy's battery, and the Arkansas
Helena Battery. The last battery was detached and did not serve with the
battalion, but was replaced by the 2nd Battalion Alabama Light Artillery,
Company D, known as Sengstak's battery, under the command of Captain
Henry Sengstak. Waddell was promoted to major, and the battalion joined
the Army of Tennessee during the Atlanta campaign. By April 1865 Waddell's command was stationed at Columbus and had grown to include Barrett's 10th Missouri Battery.[12]

Companies A and B of the battalion, known as Emery's battery and Bellamy's battery, respectively, were mostly outfitted with Parrott and other rifled guns. The 10th Missouri appears to have been outfitted with four 12-pounder howitzers. Together, these batteries were placed in the forts and behind the redoubts of the *tête-de-pont* as well as in positions across the river in Columbus where they could support the infantry manning the trenches, if any were ever sent. In addition to Waddell's battalion, Captain Nathaniel Clanton's Alabama Battery was also stationed in the city, and was likely armed with two 12-pounder howitzers and two 10-pounder Parrotts.[13]

Though the battalion had a sufficiency of weapons and ammunition, reinforced by a seemingly endless supply from the stockpiled arsenals, armories, and depots of Columbus, they desperately needed horses. Von Zinken made repeated attempts to impress enough horseflesh to remount the batteries, but met with only limited success. In Columbus, as in many other parts of the South by this late time in the war, the people's willingness to give up their valuable livestock had long since waned. With little expectation of success, Von Zinken began contemplating how best he could distribute and utilize his semi-static artillery.[14]

He also turned his attention toward the completion of the *tête-de-pont,* behind the walls of which his artillery would be stationed. Shortly before the word of Selma's fall reached Columbus, a large contingent of black prisoners of war were sent to the city to aid in the construction of the city's defenses. These laborers were put to work digging entrenchments and rifle pits to connect Forts 1, 2, and 3. They also began felling trees outward from the works to create a field of fire. By sharpening the ends of the branches and laying them in interlaced rows, they created an impressive obstructive slashing that was, in many places, one hundred yards in depth. The line was further reinforced by a series of abatis (sharply pointed stakes planted in the ground with the points toward the enemy at a forty-five-degree angle) that ran the length of Von Zinken's main line.[15]

Supervising the black prisoners were men from the 26th Battalion Georgia Infantry, who made up Columbus's small infantry garrison. Unfortunately for Von Zinken, however, the 26th Battalion was "badly disciplined and almost in a state of disorganization." This greatly hindered the work. In a letter to Cobb, Von Zinken noted that "the morning report of the 26th Georgia Battalion [has been] invariably showing a number of men absent without leave." Despite Von Zinken's requests that convalescents, who "could do the duty equally as well," be sent to Columbus, and that the 26th Battalion be put "in the field" where their discipline and future usefulness could be improved, the serious lack of manpower available in the state meant that the 26th Battalion would stay on in the city as guards.[16]

Critically in need of reliable soldiers but unwilling to risk perturbing

Cobb further by suggesting courses of action, Von Zinken again met with Mayor Wilkins. This time Von Zinken asked the mayor to contact Cobb and encourage him to speak with Governor Brown about calling out the reserves. Wilkins, eager to see an increase in the number of soldiers in Columbus, willingly complied, and this time his requests were welcomed at Cobb's headquarters. Cobb knew that if he pressed the issue of mustering the militia with Brown independently he would likely meet with failure, due to Brown's contention that the already weak economy of the state would be dealt a hard blow by its male workforce again being put into military service. However, armed with the request of Wilkins, a concerned and influential mayor of one of Georgia's most important cities, the inquiry might fall on more receptive ears. Cobb immediately forwarded the request.

Within a short time, Cobb had his answer, as did Wilkins and Von Zinken. Brown responded that while he was willing "to call out the militia for the defense of the state, as soon as the emergency requires it . . . he [was] anxious not to call them from their homes, sooner than necessity compels it." To Brown, the news that a large Union force had captured a major city only 180 miles from Georgia's western border was not alarming enough to warrant immediate action. With little else he could do, Cobb instructed Wilkins to "make all the preparation you can for the defense of your city—arouse your people to a sense of their duty, and you shall have from the military authorities, all the co-operation and assistance that can be rendered." It was little consolation.[17]

While news of Selma's capture elicited mixed degrees of concern in Georgia, in Montgomery, only forty-five miles from Selma, the response from the civil authorities and the public was universal—panic. Valuables were hidden; citizens loaded wagons and carts and drove them out of town. At the railroad depot there was a rush for passes to any destination east of the city, and masses of humanity, their possessions in tow, soon began to cram the platforms. Governor Thomas H. Watts called on the state's reserves and all able-bodied male citizens to assemble at the capital: "The stern resolve of men determined to remain free will nerve your arms . . . and hearts for the perils of the contest." He also called for assistance from Brigadier General Buford and his small brigade of cavalry.[18]

Though initially unwilling to take sides in the conflict, Buford, who had graduated from West Point in 1841 and served during the Mexican War, cast his lot with the Confederacy in 1862 and was quickly promoted to brigadier general. He was known as a "man of enormous proportions." At an engagement in 1864, a Union major attempting to force his capitulation in a running fight struck Buford repeatedly on the head with his saber, all the while shouting, "Surrender you damn big Rebel." Though Buford managed to kill his assailant, his wounds placed him temporarily out of action. By the spring of 1865, however, he had recovered sufficiently to retake the field. Placed under the command of Brigadier General Daniel Adams, he took charge of the small brigade of cavalry composed of the consolidated ranks of the 7th and 4th (Russell's) Alabama Cavalries. Dispatched to aid in the defense of Selma, Buford's brigade arrived too late to take part in the fight and fell back to Montgomery.[19]

Shortly after Buford's arrival in the city, Brigadier General Adams, the commander of all of Alabama's forces north of the District of the Gulf, also arrived. At the insistence of Adams and Watts, Buford took over command of the city's garrison. To all three men—Watts, Buford, and Adams—it seemed almost certain, considering how swiftly Wilson's Raiders had moved through Alabama to capture Selma, that Union forces would soon attack Montgomery. A quick survey of the troops present in the city revealed a serious need for reinforcements and equipment.[20]

General Taylor sent out calls for reserve soldiers in Mobile to be rushed up via rail to join the citizen soldiers forming companies in the streets. Buford and Adams even sent a telegram to Von Zinken, asking him to forward to the city whatever troops he had at his disposal. Of course, Von Zinken transmitted the message directly to Cobb in Macon, but with the annotation that of troops "I have none but merchants, which I do not deem advisable to send." Another inspection by Buford of the city's garrison soon revealed that although able-bodied men were heeding the call to arms, they lacked weapons. To address the problem, Watts issued a proclamation calling for residents of the surrounding countryside to rush to Montgomery and "to bring all the arms and ammunition you have or can get." Adams telegraphed Cobb: "Please send five hundred stand [of] arms and any force to assist in defense of this place."[21]

The message fell on deaf ears. Cobb had no forces to send to Alabama to aid in the defense of Montgomery. He, as yet, had hardly any to defend Georgia. Additionally, from what he was learning from reports of the enemy's movements, the Union army, which Cobb by now knew was Wilson's Raiders, would likely capture Montgomery before the requested weapons could get there. He could not help.

Back in Montgomery, for the next several days preparations continued while the Union forces remained at Selma with no indication of any intention to move. This interlude gave Buford and his small force an opportunity to fortify the city and expand the garrison. It also gave the city's military authorities time to begin loading the valuable commissary and quartermaster stores, machinery, and other government property onto cars bound for Columbus. In the meantime, Watts telegraphed Davis asking that he direct Cobb to come to his aid: "With troops spared from Georgia, [we] can probably save Montgomery, retake Selma, and save Mobile," his wildly optimistic message reported. Davis, unsure of the possibilities, wired Cobb, instructing him to act in the matter as "discretion indicates," but added, "of the practicality, I cannot judge here."[22]

Watts was not alone in his appeals for help. On April 7, Buford informed Secretary Breckinridge that the enemy was still at Selma and that he believed they would move with their main body toward western Alabama in pursuit of routed Confederate forces under Taylor and Forrest. But, explained Buford, if the enemy should move instead against Montgomery, "[I] will make the best fight possible." The next day, in a bid to coerce Cobb into sending what soldiers he had to Montgomery immediately, Adams telegraphed Davis, assuring him that "if speedily re-enforced" with troops from Georgia, there might be a chance to save the city.[23]

The cries for help from Montgomery were too numerous to be ignored. Davis again contacted Cobb, asking him to consider using those forces he could control to assist in the protection of Alabama's capital. Davis did not fully understand the situation. Cobb had very few troops at his command. Moreover, Brown opposed the immediate calling up of additional soldiers until he was convinced it would be absolutely necessary to defend Georgia's interests. Furthermore, the majority of Cobb's forces were reserves who were averse to serving outside Georgia's borders. Taking them out of the state would require surmounting significant resistance from both Brown and the reserves themselves. In reality, there was no significant help to be had.[24]

Of more serious consequence, however, was that while Montgomery was symbolically significant to the Confederacy, the resources of Columbus and Macon were much more important to maintaining the war effort. If any spot in the South was still worth defending, to Cobb, it was southwest Georgia. Cobb explained to Davis that Wilson's Raiders put in danger all of the vital resources surrounding Columbus and Macon and that he believed it was "their policy to devastate that section. . . . The only arsenals that will be left on this side of the Mississippi must fall if the enemy is permitted to overrun the state," Cobb explained.[25]

It was time for boldness. Cobb needed reinforcements from the Army of Tennessee, and he needed them quickly. Without soldiers, all the correspondence and strategy in the world would be for naught. Cobb explained to Davis that while at first it appeared as if the Union forces would march directly on Montgomery and then Columbus, for some reason they were delaying. Therein lay the opportunity needed to get the required troops in position to protect the Confederacy's last depots and supply centers. It was an opportunity Cobb felt should not be squandered. "I submit that it is a matter of your consideration to see what force can be placed in position to protect these interests, not merely important, but as far as I can see, essential to our success," he asserted.[26]

Cobb could not have been more displeased with the replies he received on April 8. They demonstrated just how badly disconnected Davis and the on-the-run administration were from the realities that existed within what was left of the Confederacy. Though Cobb was given authority to direct the operations of Wofford's command, and even to remove them from the state if he thought it prudent, he received no other assurances of any aid from Confederate troops. In a tremendously unhelpful message, Breckinridge counseled Cobb that he should "call on the governor of Georgia for all assistance practicable." The answer was clear. Cobb was on his own. He would have to defend the state as best he could, with whatever force he alone could assemble.[27]

The next day proved a frustrating one for Cobb. In the morning he was handed a message stating that the Union commanding general in Jacksonville was delaying the prisoner exchange deal, citing the necessity of gaining permission from Grant in Virginia, and it appeared that he might renege altogether. Also, the rations taken along to feed the prisoners were nearly exhausted. Cobb needed all the troops he could gather to garrison Columbus, especially the three regiments of that part of Georgia's Reserve Force that were engaged in guarding the prisoners. He had only one option. Cobb terminated the negotiations and ordered the three regiments to return the prisoners to Andersonville.[28]

A few hours later the situation intensified. Apparently, Watt's cries for help rang louder in Davis's ears than did Cobb's, and the president instructed Cobb to help defend Montgomery. To Cobb it was now obvious that Davis and the government had no clue how best to direct the situation. Even so, Cobb had no choice. He ordered the railroad superintendent to put in readiness a special train to deliver him to Montgomery so that he could "form a satisfactory judgment in reference to the policy of sending . . . troops . . . out of the state." The train would leave that evening.[29]

In preparation for departure, Cobb sent a message to Wofford in Atlanta directing him to "telegraph to Montgomery what number of infantry . . . [he] could forward to that place and what number of cavalry . . . [he] could move in that direction." Cobb knew that Wofford's soldiers would resist any attempt to send them out of the state, so he coached Wofford's explanation. "You can say to your men that they will only be ordered there in the event it is found necessary for the defense of Georgia," explained Cobb, adding, "a prompt response on their part to this call would greatly strengthen their claims to the favorable consideration of the government in reference to their future service." In closing, Cobb instructed Wofford to stop at Atlanta the 3rd Georgia Reserves who were en route from Augusta until it could be seen whether they should be forwarded to Montgomery or Columbus.[30]

Before he left, Cobb also contacted Brown explaining his situation. Cobb made it clear that he had been directed by Davis to help defend Montgomery if at all possible, but that he felt uncertain about sending Georgia's reserves out of the state "without first informing . . . [himself] of the position of the enemy, and the condition of affairs on our side." He tried to make clear to the governor that he was doing everything possible to best protect Georgia: "If I should be satisfied upon looking over the whole ground, that it is the best policy to send forward such troops as I can command to Montgomery, I shall do so and . . . endeavor by the most energetic action at that point to save Georgia from the invasion of the enemy." Additionally, Cobb petitioned Brown to allow him, if the situation warranted, to take the 1st and 2nd regiments of the Georgia State Line across the border into Alabama.[31]

The two regiments of the Georgia State Line had been formed as part of what Brown considered his personal army, which, though commanded in the field by others, was created by and subject only to his authority. Cobb knew that in the past Brown had sternly opposed the movement of his regiments out of the state, but he hoped that the governor might reconsider in the light of the present circumstances. With no time to waste, Cobb asked: "I request that you answer me by telegraph in Montgomery as I must act promptly if I do anything."[32]

On the evening of April 9, the already bleak prospects of success at either Montgomery or Columbus turned black. In the moments before Cobb was to board the train bound for Alabama, his ability to coordinate a concerted effort to defend Georgia was dealt another blow. In the depot, Cobb read—at first with disbelief, then with almost uncontrollable frustration—a message outlining the details of a general order to be published the next day. The order decreed that, in an effort to fill the rapidly dwindling ranks of the Confederate armies, "all men between eighteen and forty-five in the reserves, whether officers or privates, [were] to be sent to conscript camp for assignment [to some other preexisting Confederate unit]."

"Where is the necessity for it?" Cobb fumed. He had ardently petitioned against the order, which had been speculated upon for some time, and had tried to explain to its supporters that the soldiers in the reserves were not seeking to shirk their duties, but were "willing to be transferred *with their organizations* to the army in the field. . . . It breaks up and destroys the reserve organizations in this state, and will produce more disaffection and distrust than [anyone] . . . can imagine," he had argued. "Besides," he pointed out, "in Georgia you need them all and will have active work for them all." The order, which the reserves would have abhorred under any circumstances, could not have come at a worse time.

As the train waited, Cobb dictated an unofficial letter to Breckinridge. In it, his anger and frustration with the policies of the Confederate government could not be concealed. In no uncertain terms, he presented his case against the order and called upon the secretary to use his powers to rescind it before it was too late. "General—let me say to you that the policy of the government in forcing everybody into conscript camp is crushing out the spirit of our people and this order takes another turn of the screws which will be felt as more unjust and degrading than anything that has gone before it. . . . The spirit of our young men revolt at the idea. . . . For God sake, for the sake of the cause and the country, and for the sake of the noble young men of the country, do not put this last strain on the country's back. I feel that I plead the cause of the country, and though I write hurriedly, I write earnestly."[33]

There was no way Cobb would have even considered dividing his meager forces in the face of the enemy to send a part to conscript camp. He would keep them together until the emergency passed. Even so, he could do little to shield his men from learning of the order. He knew how the officers and men from the reserves would feel about the government's policy. He knew that the men of the regiments under his authority would not stand for it. He could only hope that word of the order would not reach his soldiers until the coming actions were decided.

That evening, as his train steamed toward Alabama, the matter must have weighed heavily on Cobb's mind. The policies of the Confederacy were now undermining the ability and desire of its soldiers to protect it. Furthermore, the civil leadership was detached from reality and could provide no support, yet they intended to direct the armies' efforts in distant areas where communication was inhibited and they did not know the situation. As the train jostled and swayed along the tracks leading westward toward Montgomery, the general contemplated the confused state of the government and military, and likely wondered how much longer the Confederacy could hold on.

The Enemy Approaches

Week Two

As the train steamed up to the depot in Montgomery on the morning of April 10, 1865, the scene that confronted Cobb must have seemed terribly different from when he had administered the oath of office to Davis a little over four years earlier. The city was in an uproar. Extending from its outskirts was a long, snakelike procession of refugees moving out along the roads leading into the countryside. Within the city, carriages and wagons jammed the streets. Piles of military stores were being loaded aboard railcars to be run out of town, and at the depot citizens crowded the trains, eagerly awaiting their first opportunity to get out of the path of the armies. Soldiers gathered under the command of Buford and Adams were digging in for a fight, and news of the approach of the Federal cavalry alarmed the population. Soon, Cobb learned that the cavalry had crossed the Alabama River at Selma, broken the lines of the 7th and 4th Alabama cavalries, and was marching rapidly on a direct route for the capital.[1]

Cobb also learned that just that morning Adams had clashed with Montgomery's mayor, Walter Coleman, over whether the city should be surrendered. Coleman feared for the safety of the capital and proposed, in order to spare the residents the calamity visited on Selma, to form a surrender delegation. Adams refused to endorse the idea or to disclose any part of his strategy or intentions to Coleman. Negotiations were further embittered when Coleman confronted Adams about rumors that all the cotton in the city was to be burned to prevent its capture and discovered the general's firm resolve on that point. In disgust, Coleman left the meeting vowing to form the delegation in spite of whatever actions Adams took.[2]

Cobb hurried to the capitol, where he met with Watts and Adams about the prospects of saving the city. There he learned that for the past week, Buford, with the aid of Watts, had been trying to assemble troops, with limited success. What forces had been sent were mainly small units rushed up from Mobile. They included "two regiments State Reserves, Third and

Fourth Alabama, 700 men; Seventh Alabama Cavalry, 300 men, and two battalions light artillery, with guns but no horses . . . [and] one gun and one caisson of Winston's battery [that] came with Third Alabama Reserves." The situation looked hopeless.[3]

As requested, Brown telegraphed Cobb in Montgomery to tell him that he wanted the Georgia State Line regiments to be halted at Columbus un-til the situation showed more clearly that their removal from Georgia was necessary. In plain terms, it meant "permission denied." Wofford's telegram was equally disappointing. Furthermore, Cobb learned that the Union cav-alry force under Wilson was massive, well equipped, and armed with re-peating rifles. He heard how in less than two weeks they had marched from north Alabama, turning back every force sent against them, and then routed Forrest at Selma.[4]

It did not take Cobb long to assess the situation. The Federals would arrive at the capital within two or three days, too soon for Cobb to even hope of assembling some force from his command. With the few troops already in the city and the fewer that might be assembled from Georgia after wrangling with Brown, Cobb decided that attempting to do battle at Montgomery would be to invite disaster.

Whatever Watts and Adams thought of Cobb's refusal to commit Geor-gia's resources to a fight for the capital, it soon was a matter beyond ne-gotiation. While the meeting was still under way, Cobb's efforts to con-tact Taylor six days earlier paid off when a dispatch rider arrived bearing orders from Taylor instructing Adams to "send all the infantry assembled in Montgomery to Columbus by rail, and to fall back slowly with the cavalry."[5] The orders from Taylor were clear, and they worked to shift the focus of operations decisively to Columbus as the point at which a stand would be taken. Hurriedly, Watts, Adams, Buford, and Cobb formulated a plan whereby Montgomery would surrender in hopes of receiving merci-ful terms, while Adams and Buford would use their cavalry to harass the enemy as it advanced on Columbus. Their combined efforts would, it was hoped, slow the Federal forces enough to buy time for Cobb to get Geor-gia's troops assembled and in position. Combined with the forces that had already been assembled under Buford in Montgomery and that could be rapidly redeployed eastward, there arose a hope of consolidating a formi-dable defensive force. Additionally, Taylor offered to have part of Mobile's garrison, which had been forced to abandon their defenses on April 9, "fitted up" for transportation to Columbus. The latter proposal was never acted upon, as the breakup of communications between Taylor and south Georgia inhibited the deployment. Even so, with renewed confidence that there yet remained some prospect of turning back the enemy and saving

Columbus and south Georgia, Cobb boarded the train and rode the rails back to Macon.[6]

For four days after Cobb's return to Macon on April 10, his headquarters swirled with activity as preparations to defend Columbus reached fever pitch. Cobb ordered what troops he had at his immediate disposal to "rush forward at once to Columbus" and to report there to Von Zinken for further orders. Many of Cobb's reserve officers commanded detachments of only a company or two. Numerous other units were not prepared to move yet at all, but were ordered to rendezvous their men, report their strength, and proceed to the city as soon as their commands were in readiness.[7]

For those troops farther away from the city, wherever possible, Cobb arranged for transportation via rail to speed their movement. The 1st and 2nd regiments of the Georgia State Line, which had been acting as part of the capital's garrison at Milledgeville but had recently established an encampment south of Macon, received orders to "move to Columbus, Ga. at once on arrival of the train which . . . [would] be sent as soon as possible." Not all of Cobb's efforts were fruitful, however. Several of the units ordered to hurry to Columbus were occupied with important duties and could not be immediately relieved. Some were out of direct communication, and it would take time for them to receive Cobb's instructions.[8]

Watts and Adams in Alabama joined the effort. Those troops who had assembled in Montgomery but who were not attached to Buford's brigade boarded trains bound for Columbus. Additional soldiers who had escaped Mobile's defenses by rail before its capture were also arriving in the city and were rerouted eastward. Also, Watts called on the militias of eastern Alabama to assemble and place themselves at the disposal of Columbus's military authorities.[9]

In Columbus, too, preparations intensified. One of the first to get word of Cobb's decision to make a stand at Columbus was Von Zinken, who instantly began recruiting forces on both sides of the Chattahoochee. Realizing that time was growing short, he sent messengers out through the countryside to put the local reserves on standby and deliver the call to arms. "Ten Cavalrymen sent to Union Springs [and I] have called on county militia commandants in Alabama to turn out—Governor Watts is assisting," Von Zinken reported.[10]

At the small schoolhouse near Silver Run, Alabama, "just after school had begun for the day, a courier on horseback was seen approaching the building at a rapid gait." After reading and answering the message borne by the rider, the headmaster, Colonel John M. Brannon, "walked back and forth over the school house floor two or more times, then addressing his pupils, said, 'Children, gather up your books and slates and go quietly to your homes. It is rumored that a Yankee raid is coming in this direction . . . and I am ordered to get the reserves ready to meet it.'" As soon as school was dismissed, Brannon commenced readying his unit, the Russell County Reserves, which "was composed of several companies of old men, over 45, and boys under 16 years of age." Soon afterward, one of the students, Charles Martin, "found the citizens of the village all in a hustle of excitement, packing knapsacks with clothing and filling haversacks with rations for the members of the families who were expecting to be ordered to the front at any minute."[11]

Assisting Von Zinken in Columbus was Mayor Wilkins, who called on the citizens of Columbus, Girard, and the surrounding area to prepare themselves to fight for their city and state. In one proclamation, Wilkins declared:

> *Citizens of Columbus:* The time has arrived when it is necessary for every man who is determined to protect his family and home, to arouse themselves to the necessity of organizing into companies to repel the invading foe, with which we are now threatened. The Commandant of the Post is ready and anxious to arm and equip as many of the citizens as will organize. I therefore call upon and request the citizens of Columbus and county, to delay no longer, but meet together and organize, we have men sufficient with the force our Government can furnish, to drive the enemy back, so never let it be said that Columbus fell without a struggle. Organize and protect your homes.[12]

While the mayor tried to motivate and organize the citizens of Columbus, Von Zinken oversaw the completion of the earthworks and the disposition and refitting of those troops on hand. Among the many items he still desperately needed were horses to outfit the batteries. One message printed in the newspaper entreated: "Patriots to the Rescue. . . . One hundred and fifty horses are needed for equipping batteries, necessary for the defense of our city. Come forward and nobly *offer* your *horses. Do not wait for Impressment.*"[13]

Unfortunately for Von Zinken, however, the patriotism of Columbus's citizens proved insufficient to meet the army's needs. Despite a notice stating that volunteered "horses may be needed only temporarily," the pitiful results prompted the colonel to authorize Captain J. G. McKee, the sub-district's inspector of field transportation, to begin collecting animals. Indeed, so active was this endeavor that all military entities passing through Columbus to the armies with horses were ordered to register them at the commandant's post in order to receive a written exemption from impressment.[14]

Also making their way into the city during this time were the shattered remnants of units that were either mostly captured or routed at Selma. Among them was a small group of artillerymen from Ward's Alabama Battery (also known as Cruse's battery) who, upon reporting to Von Zinken at Columbus, were assigned to duty with Waddell's artillery. Additionally, Von Zinken took command of troops arriving from Montgomery and ordered them to work finishing the entrenchments and forts in Girard. By this time, Von Zinken could see that with the small number of soldiers he might hope to have at his disposal, the completion of the earthworks would be essential to a successful defense of the city.[15]

Von Zinken also established a system that would allow him to rapidly assemble his forces in case of emergency. Reprinted each day in Columbus's newspapers was a message that had originally appeared on April 4 in which Von Zinken stated: "In case of alarm, six guns will be fired by the artillery on Broad street, in front of Post Headquarters, at which signal, all military organizations at this Post will immediately assemble at their respective rendezvous, fully armed and equipped, with twenty-four hours rations, ready to take the field, and await orders from these Headquarters."[16] It was also at about this time that a group of visiting officers questioned the colonel about what he intended to do with the cannons out in the street in front of his office. Von Zinken is reported to have responded in his distinctive Prussian accent, "Vell, if tem dam Yankees come here, I make vun 'ell of a tam fuss!"[17]

While Von Zinken prepared to put up a fight in Columbus, just over seventy-five miles to the west, Buford's brigade, with ranks swelled by conscripts and volunteers to about fifteen hundred men, was preparing to abandon Montgomery. As darkness fell over the capital on the evening of April 11, the last train, carrying Alabama's reserves, steamed out for Georgia. The exodus of civilians hoping to escape the invaders continued, and the roads leading east were jammed with refugees. In a final act of defiance, Adams ordered the destruction of eighty-five thousand bales of cotton to prevent it falling into Union hands. Once they were ablaze, Buford led his troopers out of the defenseless city on the road leading eastward toward Tuskegee and Columbus.[18]

The next morning, Montgomery, the first capital of the Confederacy, fell without a fight. The Federals marched triumphantly through the city, bands

Fig. 8. General Abraham Buford. Courtesy Massachusetts Commandery, MOLLUS, and the U.S. Army Military History Institute.

playing, under the stars and stripes of a United States flag that was hurriedly hoisted above the capitol's dome. The revelry was short-lived, however. The Confederate cavalry had taken up position just outside Montgomery to the east, and "on the morning of the 12th the enemy's advance struck the little line of battle of the Seventh and Fourth [Alabama Cavalry] Regiments." Fighting continued throughout the day until by evening the Confederates had been pushed back to within twenty miles of Tuskegee.[19]

Frustrated by the day's reverses, and lacking intelligence concerning Forrest's whereabouts and whether or not he could expect any help from "the wizard" in delaying the Union advance, Buford confided in one of his scouts: "I have sent . . . [Forrest] two couriers and neither of them have reported. I don't know what became of them, whether they have been captured, killed, or run away." The scout, a French-born immigrant named Isaac Hermann, realizing the desperate nature of the situation, replied, "I think I can carry a dispatch that will land. . . . I can change my clothes for some civilian clothes." "Hermann, you are an angel," the general responded enthusiastically. Within a short time, under the cover of darkness, the scout set off.[20]

All did not go as planned, however. When still within a short distance from the Confederate camp, Hermann and two comrades surprised and captured a group of three Federals who had broken into a slave cabin and were warming by the fire. With these prisoners, Hermann returned and at daybreak reported back to Buford's headquarters. "I thought you were on your way to Selma," said Buford when roused from his sleep. "I met with an accident," replied the scout, adding, "I accidentally captured three Federals and got me a horse."[21]

Fortunately for Buford, the next day, April 13, the Union army rested, giving the Confederate cavalry time to regroup. It also gave Buford time to interrogate the prisoners, who, as it turned out, "were very reticent and evaded many of his questions." "General Buford was very anxious to find out the strength of his adversary . . . and their destination," but their lips were shut. "I suggested that I change my clothing for the uniform of one of the prisoners who was my size and ride in their line," remembered Hermann. "That is a very dangerous business," responded Buford; "if you are trapped they will hang you." "I am in for the war," replied the scout. "I'll take the chances."[22]

After midnight, Hermann, dressed as a Federal trooper, rode through the lines and, after convincing the picket that he was a returning forager, slipped into the Union camp. There he lounged by a fire with several soldiers, learning what he could of the army's disposition, their strength, and their intention to smash into and across Georgia. Hermann had not been in camp long, however, when suddenly "the bugle blast 'Call to Horse' and everything was active." "What's the matter?" asked Hermann of his new companions. A trooper replied, "Did you not get three day's rations?" "Yes," replied the imposter. "Well, we are going to advance," came the reply. It was time to escape.

> I ran to my horse and mounted. I felt that I had to advise General Buford of this move. . . . I took [off] down the railroad track . . . but to my surprise there was a vidette post there of two sentinels. They halted me, saying, "You can't pass." . . . There being a nice spring of water in sight, just to the left of the road, [I said] I wanted to fill my canteen. . . . I suggested that I would fill theirs if they wished me to. . . . So they handed me their canteens and I put the spurs to my horse . . . and at full gallop rode into our camp. . . . I at once rode up to the general's quarters, was admitted by the sentinel, and made my report. He [Buford] was still in bed, but he got up and ordered two

companies . . . to the front and deployed in a skirmish line. In less than an hour we heard the firing.[23]

Meanwhile, back in Columbus, as Buford was pumping his prisoners for information on the afternoon of April 13, the last trains from Montgomery crossed the Chattahoochee and hissed into the station. With them came news, sometimes accurate, at other times wildly speculative, about the current disposition of the advancing Federal army in Alabama and also about operations in other theaters. At his home known as The Cedars, John Banks, age sixty-seven, wrote in his diary of the latest developments as he knew them: "We have been compelled to evacuate Richmond and the seat of the Confederate government; not determined yet where it will be. Macon and Columbus are both spoken of. The Yankees have taken Selma, Alabama, and now threatening Montgomery. Much excitement and fears of their approach to Columbus. Our prospects very gloomy. . . . Some efforts have been made for a treaty of peace but nothing short of subjugation will do the enemy. Hence we have renewed the war, preferring to fight to the bitter end rather than accept subjugation."[24]

What Banks did not realize was that the situation was gloomier than even he or others in Columbus knew, and that "the bitter end" had already come for most of the armies. By April 13, not only had Richmond been evacuated, but Lee had already surrendered to Grant at Appomattox Courthouse. All major hostilities in the Carolinas had ceased, and arrangements for the surrender of the Army of Tennessee had been initiated. The Union forces that overran the last of the Mobile's defenses at Fort Blakely were now occupying that city. Montgomery was already in its second day of occupation after surrendering without a fight. All major fighting outside east Alabama and west Georgia was suspended. The war was over. The Confederacy had lost. These developments were unknown to the people of Columbus on April 13, however. Nor were they known by Wilson's Raiders. In the Chattahoochee valley there was still time for men on both sides of the conflict to pursue a "bitter end."

While accurate and timely intelligence about the armies in Virginia and the Carolinas was unavailable due to broken communications, there was in Columbus's newspapers a conspicuous attempt by the editors to diminish the danger posed to the city by the approaching Union cavalry, whose proximity alone should have encouraged more substantive warning. The misinformation must have seemed strangely at odds with the news being brought into Columbus by the refugees from Montgomery, including Governor Watts. On receipt of the news of the skirmish at Mount Meigs, east of Montgomery, between Buford's brigade and the advance of Wilson's

Raiders, for example, the *Columbus Daily Sun* advised readers: "This [news] we are inclined to believe is incorrect. . . . But it is thought the scouts must have been deceived, and mistook a Yankee picket or scouting party for an advance of the enemy."[25]

Fortunately, many of Columbus's citizens were not so naive and began preparing for the worst. Many women of Columbus "concealed jewelry and valuables, and buried their silver." "My father and mother hired or borrowed a horse and buggy and had brought a wooden box about eighteen inches square containing silver plate, gold and silver watches, finger rings and other jewelry, which they wanted me to hide in some secret place in the woods," remembered a young boy, Charles Martin, who had been sent to his father's plantation in Alabama for safety. "My father and I carried the box to the edge of a new ground about 400 yards from the quarters and hid it in an old hollow chestnut log and covered the end of the log with dead leaves," he recalled.[26]

Columbus's civic leaders were taking no chances either. While soldiers across the river were trying to complete the last of the rifle pits and to drill the citizens of the city who had already volunteered, the city council called a special, secret meeting, the notes of which reveal that "His honor [the mayor] stated the discourse of the meeting to be to take into consideration the danger of the city from a raid by the enemy, and to adopt some measures necessary for the welfare and defense of the city."[27]

Though not everything discussed at the meeting is known, the council's notes reveal that several measures were adopted. In a effort to show solidarity, the city council voted to "approve of any measures which the mayor . . . [might] think proper to take in reference to the defense of the city." They also resolved "that the citizens of the city and adjacent country, be earnestly requested to organize themselves and report forthwith to the commandant of this post, and hold themselves subject to his order, at all times, until such time as the emergency shall cease." Additionally, they entrusted to the mayor the responsibility of restricting the consumption "of all spiritous liquors within the corporate limits of the city, even to cause its destruction, if in his judgment he think it advisable." In a final motion, probably in order to avoid a panic, it was resolved that "the proceedings of the board were to be considered secret, excepting that part requesting the organization of citizens."[28]

While the city council moved to get the mayor to be more vocal in calling on support from residents, it appears that some Columbus citizens were already doing just what was expected of them. Later that night, another meeting took place at the council chamber in which members of a local militia unit known as the Typo Guards met "for the purpose of organizing." They even announced that "citizens who are not connected with some other organization and who desire to unite . . . are invited to attend and participate."[29]

April 14 saw the continuation of Cobb's efforts in Macon to get his forces to Columbus and into position. The arrival in Columbus of the 1st and 2nd regiments of the Georgia State Line greatly added to the garrison's strength, and it appears that they were ordered over the bridge into Girard by Von Zinken without any further consultation with Brown. Also arriving in the city were volunteers from Muscogee, Russell, and surrounding counties. As these soldiers arrived they were assigned to a company and sent to one of several camps established on the eastern outskirts of Columbus. Joining them was the Georgia Reserve Force's chief of staff, former general and Confederate secretary of state Robert Toombs. The garrison was further strengthened by fifty-seven sick and wounded soldiers from the city's hospitals who were released and reported to Von Zinken for duty. Indeed, the convalescents who answered the call greatly strengthened Von Zinken's force. Between April 10 and April 14 at least 163 sick or disabled men volunteered for duty.[30]

Despite the resolve of the convalescents and the arrival of more militia, the confidence of some of Columbus's citizens seemed to decline. "Everything in Columbus is in commotion," remarked Rev. Charles Todd Quintard, the Second Episcopal Bishop of Tennessee, who was acting as temporary rector of Trinity Episcopal Church in Columbus. "Preparations are being made to defend the place, but it is absurd," he elaborated; "the force that can be gathered here is too insignificant."[31]

On the evening of April 14, unconfirmed reports that the Union army had struck out from Montgomery and was rapidly moving east reached Von Zinken in Columbus. Immediately, the word was relayed to Cobb in Macon. Despite the somewhat sketchy nature of the information that was being gathered, Cobb decided that the time had come for him to travel to Columbus to help coordinate the city's defense efforts and to get closer to the reports coming in from the west. That evening he again prepared to board a westbound train. This time, however, it appeared certain that before he returned to Macon he would either check the Federal invasion or be defeated at Columbus.[32]

6

Time Runs Out

"Rumors—They are as plentiful as blackberries in June," headlined one editorial from the *Columbus Daily Sun* on the morning of Saturday, April 15, 1865. As the day dawned bright over Columbus, despite what the commanders of the Confederate forces in the city knew about the approach of the Federal cavalry, the morning papers offered a combination of unrealistic optimism and urgent warning. Strangely, printed right next to impassioned pleas from the mayor, Von Zinken, and other officials and officers for assistance in repelling the impending attack of the Union army were articles claiming that the city was in no immediate danger.[1]

In one column, Mayor Wilkins implored "the citizens to organize, report to, and receive arms and equipments from the commandant of the post . . . without delay." He even made desperate appeals to the people's patriotism so that it would "never . . . be said that Georgians were too degraded to appreciate their liberties or too cowardly to defend them." Even so, printed prominently in the same paper were strange editorials, probably published in a futile effort to prevent panic, which stated: "From information in our possession we are satisfied that the enemy will not move in any considerable force from Montgomery for some days to come. It is even doubtful whether they contemplate any immediate movement in this direction, until after the river has been cleared between Montgomery and Mobile, and a base established at the former place."[2]

That the writer's analysis was fallacious was apparent to the citizens of Columbus. It was obvious from the desperate appeals of the city's commanders, the flood of refugees from Alabama (including Governor Watts), and the heightened military presence and activity that something important was about to unfold. Furthermore, firsthand reports coming from eastern Alabama that morning warned of imminent danger. Some credit is due the newspaper, however, in at least admitting that "this [news] . . . is merely an opinion of our own, and may prove erroneous."

If the flawed reporting of Columbus's newspapers was due only to poor information gathering or simply a lack of understanding about the unfolding situation, it might have been overlooked. However, what was printed next in that day's columns cast suspicion on the paper, its editor, and its employees. Just when it appeared that all the efforts of the military and civil authorities were being directed toward consolidating a force to oppose the approaching enemy, and when one might expect that calls would have been made to set aside differences in order to defeat a common foe, the paper began to print articles designed to undermine the authority and support of Columbus's leaders.[3]

In particular, the paper published statements seemingly designed to instill a lack of confidence on the part of some citizens in Von Zinken's abilities as a commander. This may have been partially due to some hard feelings in relation to the shooting incident two months earlier, or, as the paper hints, because of some recent improprieties on the colonel's part involving overindulgence in spirits. In any case, the paper called for another officer to be assigned to command the forces gathering in the city. "If Columbus should be threatened and the Confederate authorities deem this a point of sufficient importance to make at least one manly effort for its defense, our people demand it as their right that an officer of known ability and sobriety be at the head of affairs. They will be satisfied with none other," one article announced. "The presumption is that an officer of higher grade than any one here now, will be assigned to duty should the defense of the city be decided upon," the article stated. In an obvious jab at Von Zinken, the writer further elaborated: "That officer must be a man of temperate habits, and one who will enforce discipline at all hazards, otherwise resistance will prove useless."[4]

These comments, and particularly their timing, must have angered Von Zinken, who, from the very first report of Selma's capture, had been endeavoring to do all he could to protect Columbus. If, however, there was any real worry that an able man might not be appointed to overall command of the situation developing in the city, those fears were alleviated that morning when Cobb arrived from Macon to take command of whatever forces Georgia and Alabama could muster.

When Cobb and Von Zinken met on the morning of April 15, the situation must have seemed desperate. Military authorities knew that Federal troops were near Tuskegee, only forty miles away, and thought it likely that they would occupy the town that day. By their calculations, then, depending on how much resistance Buford's small cavalry brigade could throw in their way, the Union advance could reach the outskirts of Columbus as early as the next night, and assault the city on the morning of April 17.

The Federals' rapid advance left little time to finish the earthworks being constructed in Girard or to assemble more soldiers to occupy them.[5]

Contemplating both the preparations being conducted in Columbus and contingencies that might save Macon should Columbus fall, Cobb had his staff in Macon send last-minute dispatches to troops all over south Georgia to prepare their units for action and move with all haste to Columbus and Macon. It was probably with some degree of indignation, too, that Cobb learned that Brown had finally recognized the impending danger posed to Georgia by the rapidly approaching Federal army and had ordered the state's militia "to rendezvous at Columbus as fast as possible." All men who were a part of the militia, had ever previously served, or were capable of doing duty, excepting those between fifty and sixty years of age, were ordered to move to Columbus with "all public arms not in public use." Despite his reluctance to call the men of his state away from their crops, Brown declared that all able men who refused to perform their duty would "be dealt with as deserters" or turned over to regular Confederate service as conscripts.[6]

It was too little, too late, however. Cobb realized that there was little hope that the rest of Georgia's reserves, spread across the northern and eastern part of the state, could march or be transported to Columbus in time to be of assistance, if they could be mustered at all. Cobb would have to rely on local forces and on those reserves who were already en route. He would not simply wait for troops to arrive, either. He would have every available man at his disposal. That day he issued an order stating that "all officers and men belonging to the Confederate States Armies now in Columbus or vicinity, whose leaves of absence or furloughs have expired, or are on their way to rejoin their commands, will report to these Headquarters without delay; for the purpose of being organized into companies for the defense of the city."[7]

Added to Cobb's growing list of concerns was the need to transport out of harm's way all of Columbus's valuable military and industrial supplies, the amount of which had been multiplied to some extent by materiel deposited in the city following Montgomery's fall. Realizing there was a good chance that the Federals might not be stopped at Columbus, or that some flanking movement might force the evacuation of the city, Cobb hurriedly set men to work loading Columbus's vast stores on board trains that would carry them east to Macon and safety. He also instructed the operators in Macon to have the trains from Columbus "unloaded at once and returned" and ordered the state's railroad superintendents to "have all the transportation sent here that the capacity of the road will admit of."[8]

Von Zinken was busy, too. On the morning of April 15, in accordance with the city council's recommendation, he ordered "all liquor establishments in this city . . . to be closed immediately." His instructions made it clear to both businesses and civilians alike that "no liquor will be sold, exchanged, given away, or in any manner disposed of to soldiers." Though it was well intentioned, the order appears to have been largely disregarded.[9]

Shortly thereafter, with the aid of his adjutant, Captain S. Isadore Guillett, Von Zinken directed the troops arriving from both the east and the west into camps to be organized. He also received help from the sick and wounded from the city's hospitals. Those suffering with lesser illnesses and those who believed themselves capable of performing at least some duty were urged to register at the command post for assignment in the field. Many responded to the call and volunteered. As for Guillett himself, while he appears to have served energetically, his mind may have been elsewhere. The young captain, who had only been in Columbus a few months, had recently taken up residence with a local family, the Redds, with whose daughter he had developed a keen love interest. It was over the daughter's strong protests and despite her pronounced anxiety that Guillett carried out the orders of his colonel.[10]

Also working closely with Von Zinken in rallying Columbus's citizens to the colors that morning was Wilkins, who, in stark contrast with the newspaper's attempted undermining of Von Zinken's abilities, urged the people "to sustain and uphold the commandant of the post in all his efforts for our protection and defense, for I am well assured he is doing everything he can . . . for our own good." The *Daily Sun* published pleas for "sober men . . . [to] raise companies to be composed of persons not liable to Confederate or State duty, for the defense of the city." "If such men will take hold of the matter, form a nucleus for volunteer companies," one supporter claimed, "every man in Columbus will attach himself to some organization and, when the emergency arises, will fight to the bitter end."[11]

The urgent requests from Wilkins and others stimulated only a partial reaction. Though many local citizens were arming and forming companies, and men from the surrounding countryside continued to trickle in to the city, many able-bodied townspeople had not volunteered. With time short and matters desperate, Wilkins was determined that "Columbus shall never fall without a strenuous effort made in her defense." On April 15, realizing that the situation warranted "measures . . . which in calmer times might appear arbitrary and tyrannical," he increased Von Zinken's authority to raise troops. "I have advised and counseled that an order be issued that no man capable of bearing arms be permitted to leave the city, and I trust (for I am satisfied that it is essential) every man will see the necessity of such an order," the mayor announced. "Let every man come up and do his whole duty, and Columbus is safe and will be relieved from the degradation of a surrender without a struggle."[12]

While Wilkins was coercing Columbus's less motivated citizens to take action, and Von Zinken was busy overseeing the organization of local troops and the completion of the earthworks in Girard, Cobb continued to try to find available soldiers and get them into positions to help defend the state. Desperate to tap every resource for reinforcements, Cobb sent a message to Colonel George C. Gibbs in Andersonville, directing that "unless it is imperatively necessary that the detachments of the 3rd and 5th Georgia Reserves be retained at Andersonville that they be sent forward at once to Columbus, Ga, with orders to report to [the] commandant of post."[13]

Unfortunately for Cobb, however, the news of the conscript order was already proving to be a major impediment. "With nearly 3,500 prisoners to guard, it is impossible to send any troops from here to Columbus," replied Gibbs, who explained that "since the publication (only yesterday) of the synopsis of . . . [the] order affecting the reserves, many desertions have already occurred—five from one regiment last night." The colonel expected desertion to "continue to a painful extent, and . . . the conduct of some of the officers will stimulate it." Gibbs could not spare a man, either to Cobb or to desertion, and would be unable to assist.[14]

From the moment he heard about the proclamation ordering the breakup of the reserves to go to conscript camps, Cobb had known that it would demoralize his soldiers and hurt Georgia's ability to keep troops in the field. He could only hope that the soldiers already in Columbus, who were as yet unaware of the order, could be prevented from learning of it until after the coming engagement was decided. This, however, was a matter largely outside his control.

While Cobb would not get the men from the 3rd and 5th Georgia reserves on detached duty at Andersonville, before noon a train arrived carrying the majority of the 3rd Georgia Reserve Regiment, which had been forwarded to Columbus from Augusta. While this regiment's arrival was certainly welcomed, their tardiness confirmed to Cobb the poor condition of the state's railroad system. That the regiment's movement from Augusta to Columbus took nearly ten days did not bode well for other troops who might be relying on trains to reach the city.[15]

The developments were not all bad, however. Several other groups of reserves began to arrive during the afternoon. Among the strongest of these were the 3rd Alabama Infantry Reserves and the 4th Battalion Alabama Reserves. Composed of several hundred men, these units were rushed to Montgomery from Mobile before the latter's capture. According to some sources, they were hastily consolidated before leaving Montgomery for Columbus into a makeshift regiment designated the 65th Alabama Infantry.[16]

Whatever their designation, their arrival was certainly welcomed, and they along with the men of the 1st and 2nd regiments of the Georgia State Line, the 3rd Georgia Reserves, and the 26th Battalion Georgia Infantry formed a nucleus around which the remainder of Cobb's forces could be consolidated. It was also to Cobb's good fortune that he was able to enlist the aid of Major John Nisbet, commander of the 26th Battalion, who had been on detached service helping to oversee delivery of the first lot of Union prisoners sent to Mississippi and whose return had been delayed by the movements of Wilson's Raiders.[17]

In addition to these, the men of Columbus's local units helped to fill out the ranks. Among their number were the Columbus City Infantry Battalion (made up of factory workers and detailed men), the Columbus Naval Infantry Battalion, the Columbus Ordnance Battalion, the Columbus City Infantry Provost Guards, and Captain John Pemberton's cavalry. Volunteers from Russell, Muscogee, Chattahoochee, and other surrounding counties further enlarged the garrison.

Supporting them was the very large artillery contingent under Waddell, whose command included Emery's battery, Bellamy's battery, and the 10th Missouri Battery. Clanton's Alabama Battery, Sengstak's Alabama Battery, and possibly a gun of Winston's Tennessee Battery, along with cannoneers who had escaped capture at Selma or who had left their guns at Montgomery and who were put into service with the many guns available at Columbus, helped bolster the force. In total, the Confederate artillerymen fielded thirty-three cannons. All combined, the Confederate command had about three thousand soldiers at its disposal (see appendix 3).[18]

Though Cobb was the ranking officer in Columbus, it appears that Von Zinken, who knew the ground and had been preparing for the city's defense for months, was retained as a field commander and aided in making final preparations. On the afternoon of April 15, Von Zinken ordered the disparate troops that had assembled in the camps on the outskirts of Columbus to form ranks in the streets. "Growing from a company, to a battalion, then to a regiment, and finally to a brigade they came unheralded, their numbers increased by volunteers from Columbus, men over age and boys under age," observed a witness. "[With] few tents to encumber their march and no brass bands to cheer them on their way, and no dress parades to attract an . . . audience, . . . this brigade lined up under the command of Colonel Von Zinken and was marched over the . . . [Franklin] Street Bridge to Girard."[19]

Throughout the rest of that day and into the evening, Cobb and Von Zinken continued to put troops in position and to strengthen their lines. To the discomfort of all, especially the newly assembled citizen soldiers who were not used to life in the field, a drenching spring thunderstorm soaked the ground, filled the rifle pits with water, and forced the troops to huddle under the canvas of their recently erected battlefield bivouacs.

To the west, in Alabama, Buford's cavalry fought a largely unsuccessful delaying action throughout the day, hoping to retard the fast-moving Federal advance. Having evacuated Tuskegee during the morning, east of town they set up barricades made of downed trees and fence rails at every advantageous spot to try to fight the Federal skirmishers to a halt. Outnumbered and outgunned by the Spencer-equipped Union troopers, the Confederate cavalry was forced at nearly every encounter to fire a few shots at the approaching skirmishers and then flee to avoid getting captured or pinned down. At creeks and swamps they tore up bridges or set them on fire, but this proved little hindrance for the large and well-equipped Federal force. Indeed, the torrential rains and heavy thunder and lightning of the late-afternoon storm accomplished more than could the Confederate troopers. It was not enough, and by nightfall the Confederate cavalry had been pushed back to Crawford, Alabama, only eleven miles from Columbus.[20]

In the rain, Cobb and Von Zinken inspected their defenses. The *tête-de-pont* was almost complete. The small unfinished portion of the entrenchments could be held by the more experienced soldiers while the civilians manned the fully prepared sections. "It is a very large and well organized raiding party and in my opinion [they] do not expect to hold the country but intend to destroy and devastate," Cobb surmised of the enemy's plans. "I think it more than likely that they intend, if they can, to destroy southwestern Georgia—and if we drive them from Columbus they may attempt to flank us and move upon that section of the state."[21]

Of more immediate concern to Von Zinken were the numbers of additional soldiers that might be brought into the field from Cobb's command or some other. The colonel was particularly eager to know where Forrest was and whether he would assist in defending the city. It was a question Cobb could not positively answer. "We hope that Forrest may be on their rear," he wrote to his wife on that rainy eve, "but of this we are not advised. If it should be the case, I feel confident we will give the rascals a most wholesome whipping."

When they had finished inspecting the ground over which they would fight, Cobb and Von Zinken retired to their headquarters. As the rain continued to pound the city's hard streets, Cobb took his pen and scrawled out a message.

My Dear Wife—
After an exhausting day's work and before eating my dinner, I write to you this hasty line—It seems now certain that the enemy is ad-

vancing rapidly on this place. His force is estimated by . . . Buford at ten thousand—I have three thousand and shall give him fight. . . . If my men do their duty, he shall pay dearly for Columbus before he gets it. The scouts currently report him within forty miles, and still riding, therefore calculate arriving here by tomorrow night. I have just rode around my lines and given all the necessary orders for putting the troops in position tonight. I am determined not to be surprised, and will give them as warm a welcome as is in my power. . . . I do not know when I may have a chance to write you again. . . . Ever your devoted,
Howell Cobb[22]

While Cobb may have hoped he would not be surprised, not long after he finished the letter to his wife, news arrived from Buford stating that the enemy was no longer near Tuskegee, forty miles distant, but had pushed to within a mile of Crawford, only eleven miles away. The proximity of the Union cavalry meant that the Union soldiers could arrive as early as the next morning if they rode all night, and be in position to attack the city at dawn. Immediately, Cobb and Von Zinken spread the warning to the military commanders and the various government facilities in Columbus. Despite the bad weather, the camps were emptied and "the troops were ordered out to the trenches."[23]

Certain that the next day would bring an engagement, Von Zinken quickly drew up a notice to be printed in the following morning's paper and distributed to Columbus's resident population by the city provosts. The proclamation read: "The public is hereby notified of the rapid approach of the Enemy, but assured that the City of Columbus will be defended to the last. Judging from experience it is believed that the city will be shelled, notice is therefore given to all non-combatants to move away immediately. All who wish to remain are compelled to make preparations for their safety. It is again urged upon all able bodied men of this city to report to these Head Quarters with whatever arms they have to assist the commanding officer in making a resolute defense of their homes."[24]

With preparations made and their wet soldiers in the trenches, Cobb and Von Zinken could only wait for further word from Buford about the approach of the enemy and listen for news of the arrival of the Federal cavalry. In Crawford, Buford planned his next move and watched the campfires of the Federals as they flickered through the trees and swamplands to the west of the hamlet. There was little doubt that the next day would bring battle, and likely determine the fate of Columbus.

7
The Battle Begins
Crawford and Uchee Creek

In the early morning hours of Easter Sunday, April 16, 1865, the Confederate forces at Columbus were roused from their anxious, damp sleep to prepare for the coming action. To their relief, the sky was clear and promised a beautiful spring day. Because the enemy had not yet arrived, some of Columbus's defenders were allowed to leave the trenches and go to church. "There was a very large attendance" at Trinity Episcopal's sunrise service, and "many men were present." "It was most solemn and impressive," remembered Reverend Quintard, who administered the communion. "All hearts were filled with forebodings of what was to come. The enemy was close at hand."[1]

Soon after sunrise, the morning papers and Von Zinken's proclamation were distributed, and the provost marshal, Captain Thomas E. Blanchard, "rode a horse through the town to notify the inhabitants" that the raiders might reach the city at any moment. "There was a perfect panic at the cry that 'the Yankees are coming!'" recalled Confederate surgeon Sam Bemiss. "At one place the women and children were running through the streets like people deranged, and men, with mules and wagons, driving in every direction."[2]

Many of the citizens and refugees in Columbus and Girard frantically began to load their belongings and valuables onto wagons, carts, and animals and take to the roads leading east, toward safety. Terrified at the prospect of being trapped between opposing armies, Mrs. Stanford of Girard and her three daughters recklessly loaded the family wagon and made haste to join the evacuation. This hapless band's ride was cut short, however, when "just a few hundred feet from their house, their horse suddenly stopped, sank to the ground, and died on the spot." Even for those more successful in joining the exodus, there was little consolation to be had. An eyewitness described the "scenes along the road as distressing, but at the same time ludicrous."[3]

In marked contrast to the commotion outside, at about 10:30 A.M. Quintard led another Easter service. The mood was ominous, and the pastor "did not preach, feeling that it was a time for prayer and supplication only." He "stood at the altar for a considerable time administering the sacrament to officers and soldiers who came to receive before going to the field." Some of the soldiers "sang in the choir that morning and then . . . crossed the river bridge with others—old men and young boys . . . to man the trenches in defense of their homes." Additionally, Quintard witnessed a sad scene probably played out in many corners of the city that morning. He recalled: "I was deeply touched by seeing an officer who was very devout, kneel at the chancel rail, and then hasten away, equipped for battle, clasping his wife by the hand as he tore himself from her."[4]

Among those refugees caught in the throng outside the church was General Samuel French, who had recently married and was passing through to take his new bride to the safety of a friend's country home twenty-five miles north of the city. While still in the street, the general was spotted amid the crowd by Cobb, who rode over and, after explaining the situation, implored French "to remain and take command of the forces." "This I declined," recalled French later, "but I promised to return Monday morning and aid him." French's offer was little comfort to Cobb, who feared that by Monday it would be too late.[5]

Throughout the morning, the chaos in Columbus was enhanced by the efforts of the locals to either hide or send to safer quarters their valuables and belongings. Possessions were entrusted to servants, children, and others for safekeeping. A substantial amount of property was buried, "put . . . under mattresses, [or] sent . . . to plantations." Civilians were not the only ones trying to secure their belongings. Lieutenant William W. Carnes, commander of the almost completed ironclad CSS *Jackson,* stationed at the Confederate Navy Yard, recalled: "From what I was able to learn about the Federal command and the force of our troops in Columbus, I considered the capture of the city was inevitable. So I made arrangements accordingly." Carnes loaded his belongings into a trunk and sent it to Macon in trust of his servant.[6]

Even Quintard took no chances with either the morning's offering or his personal belongings. "I had in my possession the money collected at the offertory at the Sunday morning service. This I wrapped up in a piece of rubber cloth and [a] friend put it in the top of a tall pine tree for me," he remembered. The reverend also had in his home "a considerable amount of silver ware," which he "rapidly gathered up, put in a sack and lowered into a well."[7]

While the women, children, and old men either hid their belongings or struck out on the roads away from Columbus, the able-bodied men of the city were forbidden to follow suit. Orders were issued forcing all able males to organize and be armed. At Wilkins's request, Von Zinken issued an order that "all men whether citizens or soldiers able to carry arms in defense of their homes, will not be allowed to leave this city without a pass from the Provost Marshal." In an effort to "prevent spies from entering the city," and to make certain that all eligible males were identified, another order was issued whereby all men in Columbus were "required to obtain city passes from the Provost Marshal" in order to move within the city.[8]

The remaining workers and mechanics from the factories, foundries, shops, mills, and government facilities were assembled into companies and issued arms and ammunition in preparation for deployment west of the river. Alongside them were assembled the men of the local fire companies who were pressed into service. Because of the dire nature of the situation facing the city, standards that normally dictated who was eligible to be compelled to fight were relaxed, and the ranks were filled with "boys from eleven to fourteen years old, and men so old that they could scarcely hold guns."[9]

While it appears that the majority of those called to service in the Confederate earthworks went willingly, there were exceptions. Demoralization gripped portions of the army and Columbus's population who realized that the war and the coming battle could never be won, and that any attempt to defend the city would be a waste of energy and perhaps life. Others apparently feared Wilson's Raiders to such an extent that they were willing to risk all hazards to avoid going to battle with them. In fact, at least three men were shot for refusing to take up arms in defense of their homes. Two were killed, and in a strange set of circumstances, the final execution was botched and the citizen was allowed to be taken to a nearby house where his wounds were tended by his family. While the executions may have forced compliance with the orders to man the trenches, they also seem to have bred resentment and demoralization among many of the otherwise willing soldiers.[10]

Further compounding the problems mounting against Cobb and Von Zinken that morning was the dissemination of news that the reserve forces under their command were to soon be broken up and sent to conscript camps. The timing of the intelligence was indeed inopportune. The revelation that the reserves would soon be forced into conscript camps alongside those who had knowingly shunned duty caused tensions to boil over. It appears that the news of the government's apparent slight was the last straw for many in the reserves, who began to refer to themselves by the derogatory name "conscript" and announced that although they would take the field, they would refuse to fight. Cobb and Von Zinken could say little to rectify the situation. Their best bet was to attach the angry reserves to the few regular units present and hope that their resolve would be broken by the sound of Federal bullets.[11]

The incoming reports of the size and strength of the Union forces may also have been a deterrent for some of the militias and citizen volunteers from Columbus's environs. In Fort Mitchell, for example, on Easter morning the Russell County Reserves were assembled by their commander, Colonel Brannon, who informed his men that due to the large size of the approaching Federal force, he "would not compel them to proceed, but stated that if any of the men wished to volunteer, he would not object to their attempting to reach the city and help defend it." To Brannon's disappointment, there was no general display of courage. According to Charles Martin, "my father [Jacob Martin] immediately stepped to the front and eight others, my eldest brother among them, joined him." Though a few others would ultimately decide to fight, overall it was a pitiful display of the people's broken resolve to sacrifice further for the dying Confederacy.[12]

Despite the demoralization that gripped part of the Confederate forces, not everyone was infected. For days, patients at the several large hospitals in Columbus had been pressured to appear for duty in the works. On April 16, prompted by the imminent danger, soldiers too sick to take the field earlier checked out of the hospitals en masse to join their comrades in the field. Hospital records from Columbus show that at least seventy-six soldiers with all types of illnesses and wounds reported for duty that day at the commandant's post.[13]

Additionally, soldiers and civilians from all over the area surrounding Columbus and Girard continued to trickle in individually as word spread that the Federals were getting close. Mrs. Emma Prescott, who was living with her parents outside Girard while her husband was away in the army, remembered that her father "could not resist the desire to repulse the vandals, and took his gun and hastened on before they reached the city—he was 65 years old." According to Mrs. Clara Watson, her father and her uncle volunteered to fight that day. Her uncle, Colonel Wesley Clark Hodges of the 17th Georgia Infantry, "was at home suffering from . . . [his] last wound, a shattered right shoulder." Hodges "volunteered to assist in commanding the raw troops and, with his right arm in a sling, mounted his horse and, though physically disabled, fought in the . . . battle."[14]

While soldiers and citizens willing to fight continued to arrive in Columbus, Von Zinken and Cobb made careful dispositions and placed their troops in the trenches, behind the earthworks, and out on picket west of

Girard to watch for Federal cavalry. Sixteen-year-old Billy Stanford, a sailor stationed in Columbus who had gone out into the countryside days earlier, had the misfortune of being apprehended by the jumpy sentries who mistook his blue uniform for that of the enemy and accused him of being a spy. He only escaped hanging when an acquaintance arrived who could vouch for him.[15]

Though most of Von Zinken's *tête-de-pont* was ready, and soldiers and prisoners were quickly working to complete a small unfinished portion of the line, other areas of the city were not yet secure. Work on some rifle pits had been begun at the east end of the City Bridge and at the railroad bridge, but they were insufficiently complete to provide protection for the artillerymen manning the cannons stationed there. Taking advantage of the resources on hand, Von Zinken ordered redoubts to be erected using bales of cotton, of which tens of thousands were stored around the city. "We were placed at this point Saturday night," remembered one young Confederate artilleryman, "and we spent . . . Sunday morning rolling bales of cotton out of a nearby warehouse, and constructing some breastworks in front of our pieces, a few yards from the bridge."[16]

Their location behind the cotton-bale redoubt gave the three artillery pieces rolled into position east of the City Bridge a clear shot through the interior of the enclosed wooden span. A fifty-foot-wide section of the floor planking inside the bridge near the Georgia end had been pulled up the night before so as to trap any force that might try to rush through into Columbus. Well aware that they had too few men at their command to adequately protect all of the bridges at Columbus, Von Zinken and Cobb ordered that cotton be stuffed in the cracks between the boards and piled up along the sides of the City Bridge's roadway, and then soaked with turpentine and lamp oil. If the Federals attempted to capture the bridge by charging through it, they would be caught inside by the removed flooring, blasted by the artillery, and potentially trapped inside as flames enveloped the turpentine-saturated cotton and timbers.[17]

The remaining two bridges—the Franklin Street Bridge and the railroad bridge—were protected by the *tête-de-pont*. Even so, Von Zinken and Cobb took no chances. Although the Franklin Street Bridge was already protected by a section of howitzers stationed at the east end, they ordered that it be stuffed with cotton and saturated with flammables—a final precaution in case things went terribly wrong.

Once the bridges at Columbus had been seen to, the only crossing left to consider was the two-part Clapp's Factory Bridge, which spanned the river near Clapp's Factory, three miles north of Columbus. To ensure that Union troops would have no chance of slipping across there, a detachment of soldiers was ordered north that morning to burn the bridge.[18]

While Von Zinken saw to the final arrangements in Girard, Cobb was busy doing what he could to get Columbus's resources and people moved out of danger. He knew that the prospect of beating back the Federal cavalry was slim. At best, he might forestall Columbus's fall until its supplies and equipment could be moved out of harm's way. That morning and early afternoon, everything Cobb had the resources to move, he tried to get loaded on trains bound for Macon. How many trains Cobb was able to send away from Columbus is not clear, but he certainly sent some and was prepared to continue the shipments right up until the enemy arrived. Mrs. Eliza Frances Andrews, on her way via rail from Cuthbert to Macon, recalled meeting the trains and their passengers. "Train upon train of cars was there, all the rolling stock of the Muscogee Road having been run out of Columbus to keep it from being captured, and the cars filled with refugees and their goods," she wrote. "It was pitiful to see them, especially the poor little children, driven from their homes by the frozen-hearted Northern Vandals, but they were all brave and cheerful, laughing and good-naturedly instead of grumbling over their hardships. People have gotten so used to these sort of things that they have learned to bear them with philosophy."[19]

Among the cars that left Columbus that morning were a few carrying sick and wounded patients from the hospitals of Columbus to Macon or elsewhere. Hospital records from Columbus show that of 411 sick and wounded moved by rail from Columbus between April 9 and April 16, 103 departed on April 16.[20]

Ironically, patients were not the only persons leaving. In what can only be characterized as particularly bad timing, Surgeon Samuel H. Stout, the ranking medical officer in Columbus, received orders that had been sent to him ten days earlier from General Lee in Virginia. The orders, written before Lee's surrender, instructed Stout to take his best surgeons and "all of the hospital stores, furniture, bedding, and tents for which he could find transportation" and to proceed as rapidly as possible to Charlotte, North Carolina, from which point he would be directed upon what course to take in order to join Lee's command. "We are almost surrounded by the enemy's cavalry and there is a strong probability that I and my entire corps of medical officers and hospital property will be captured," fumed Stout, adding, "it will be a month before I can get one hospital through."

Nevertheless, all medical personnel were immediately "directed to pack as quickly as possible . . . [their] hospital supplies, surgical instruments, and etc." and were instructed that they should be prepared to evacuate at the first sign that the city had been captured. Thirteen boxes of medical supplies and medicines, enough to fill two railroad cars, were hurriedly carted to the depot and loaded aboard the trains. The president and members of the Columbus Battlefield Relief Committee were summoned to the hospital for instructions on how to take over operations. They were ordered to collect those patients unable to bear transportation out of the city and to transfer them to Columbus's Marshal and Mackall hospitals. Additionally, Cairns Hospital, which had a significant portion of its facilities operating outdoors in tents, was ordered to be closed and its convalescents consolidated with those at Marshal and Mackall.[21]

As it became increasingly obvious that the amount of property to be moved far exceeded the resources at hand to carry it, Cobb sent orders that the freight trains from Columbus be unloaded immediately upon arrival at their destinations and sent back quickly. He also ordered more trains fitted up. "Send every available engine and car to this point at the earliest moment," he demanded of one railroad superintendent, adding, "take them from any roads . . . [and] send them forward with all rapidity possible."[22]

South of town at the Navy Yard, an atmosphere of excitement prevailed as naval officers tried to save their work. Two river steamers, the *Young Rover* and *Marianna,* were loaded with supplies from the yard and sent south out of immediate danger. The ironclad ram CSS *Jackson,* which sat moored at the docks almost ready for service, was quickly packed with ammunition and equipment in anticipation of making an escape downriver as well. The *Young Rover* towed the not quite repaired gunboat CSS *Chattahoochee* "down the river, beyond a bend, out of sight of Columbus," where the steamer anchored.[23]

That same morning, while Columbus was waking to the news of the impending attack and beginning its last-minute preparations, eleven miles to the west, at the town of Crawford, Buford's cavalrymen were preparing for another hard day of skirmishing, still in hopes of delaying the Federal advance. Crawford, in April 1865, was a small village constructed around a main crossroads and was the seat of Russell County. Near the main intersection stood a small brick courthouse. Across the street to the southeast was a two-story wooden building with an outside staircase. It was the local Masonic lodge, but it was also used as a school at that time. Across the street from the courthouse directly to the east stood a small log jailhouse. Crawford's key feature was its crossroads, and a contemporary even described the town as "consisting of but two or three houses and a jail." Even so, at Crawford, troopers from Buford's brigade deployed in a thin line after piling rails and timber as a barricade, and awaited the approach of the Federal skirmishers. To their rear, on the main road from Crawford to Columbus, the rest of Buford's cavalrymen were destroying the bridge over Uchee Creek.[24]

In the Federal camp that morning, the men of the 4th Division were roused early by the noise of the bugles sounding "Boots and Saddles." In the early hours of morning, Upton oversaw the assembling of his forces and watched as his division prepared for the day's march in accordance with his instructions of the previous night. According to Adjutant William Scott of the 4th Iowa Cavalry, "The next morning, the 16th, as the column moved out, it was inspected and prepared for conflict with all the care and rigor that had been observed on the morning of Selma, and every soul was filled with the hopes and fears of another hazardous battle." Lieutenant James O. Vanorsdol, also of the 4th Iowa, remembered: "We began our march early, expecting to meet the foe at Columbus and whip or get whipped."[25]

Following Upton's orders, Alexander, who had recovered sufficiently from his near drowning to retake the saddle, directed his 2nd Brigade into the advance of the corps' line of march. After arranging his three regiments so that the 1st Ohio was in the lead, he dispatched six companies to take the advance and act as skirmishers. Following behind them would be the 7th Ohio and the 5th Iowa.[26]

Bringing up the rear of the brigade and following closely was Rodney's Battery I, 4th U.S. Artillery. Normally, while on the march, the artillery supporting the division traveled in the rear of its lead brigade's baggage train, thus putting it far to the rear of the lead brigade's advance. On this day, however, because the baggage trains for both of the 4th Division's brigades were to follow at the rear of the entire division, Rodney's guns could remain closer to the head of the column to support Alexander's troopers should it become necessary.[27]

In line behind Alexander's brigade was Winslow's 1st Brigade. Of Winslow's three regiments, the troopers of the 4th Iowa took the lead. Behind them marched ten companies of the 10th Missouri, the remaining two companies having been detailed to follow in the rear of the division's baggage train as a rear guard until such time as the six companies of the 3rd Iowa, which had been detached for duty as provost guards in Montgomery, should catch up and take over at that position. Bringing up the rear were the six remaining companies of the 3rd Iowa Cavalry.[28]

Though Upton's 4th Division was well closed up on the road just west of Crawford, the rest of the corps was strung out for miles, with the rear guard still encamped west of Tuskegee. In a circumstance that suited Upton's ambitions, the head of Colonel Robert Minty's 2nd Division was far to the west of the 4th Division's rear and dispersed widely on the road. (Minty had assumed command of the 2nd Division after Long was wounded at Selma.) This meant that once Upton arrived in Columbus, should his march not be significantly hindered, it would be a long time before Minty could get his division onto the field in support. This arrangement suited Upton, who did not wish to share any credit he might earn from the capture of Columbus with anyone else.[29]

Wilson, having spent the night at a plantation six miles east of Tuskegee, was still twenty-four miles west of Crawford and well to the rear of Upton's division on the morning of April 16. He rose early and set out along with his staff and escorts, in an effort to overtake Upton before he reached Columbus. "After a comfortable night in a country with plenty of food for man and beast," remembered Wilson, "we resumed the march at early dawn on a beautiful, clear, spring-like morning, by the road through Crawford, to the twin towns of Girard and Columbus, on opposite sides of the river."[30]

At some point the previous evening or during the beginning of the 4th Division's march toward Crawford on the morning of April 16, Upton received information that would greatly alter his earlier plans for his division's movement toward Columbus. First was the discovery that there were two possible routes from Crawford into Girard. The first was Crawford Road. It was the main road that led directly ahead through the town of Crawford to Girard, eleven miles distant, and crossed Uchee Creek about five miles east of Crawford. The second road, known as the Lower Crawford or Sandfort Road, began at Crawford and led south for a distance before turning east again. It crossed Uchee Creek about nine miles out from Crawford and, if followed on to Girard, entered the town on the south side directly opposite the City Bridge. This route was slightly longer, at about fifteen miles.[31]

The second important piece of information Upton acquired that morning was that there was a bridge at Clapp's Factory, three miles north of Columbus, and that it could be reached by taking a road that bore north and then east from Crawford. Both pieces of information were significant discoveries to Upton, and they helped to shape the course of action and line of march his division would take.[32]

Taking into consideration the new information about the possible routes over Uchee Creek and into Girard, upon arriving outside of Crawford, Upton rode out to the skirmish lines of the six companies of the 1st Ohio under Alexander and made changes to his earlier instructions. He ordered that five companies of the 1st Ohio, upon entering the town, should drive back the defenders upon Crawford Road and capture the bridge over Uchee Creek, as originally planned. To the sixth company, Upton gave special instructions. It was to proceed as rapidly as possibly down the Lower Crawford Road and capture the bridge across Uchee Creek and the swamp, thereby opening an alternate route to Girard. Upton placed Lieutenant Joseph Yeoman, acting aide to Alexander, in charge of this latter action.[33]

Fig. 9. Lieutenant Joseph A. O. Yeoman. Collection of the author.

Several reasons for Upton's change of orders seem obvious. First, if the main road to Girard was occupied by a large force of defenders, or if the bridge had been destroyed, a major delay of his division's movements might be caused. Also, if the Confederates expected him to march upon the most direct and shortest route to his objective, they might have overlooked either defending or destroying the bridges over the creek and swamp on the alternate road. Though a longer route, the Lower Crawford Road might have appeared to provide a faster and less costly passage to Girard. It also had a couple of other advantages, in that it led directly to the City Bridge spanning the Chattahoochee into Columbus, and should the Confederates be expecting his arrival via the shorter and more common route, it might offer his forces a measure of surprise.

Having made his dispositions, at between 8 and 9 A.M. Upton watched as the advance detachment of the 1st Ohio rode off up the hill atop which sat the tiny town, and watched in anticipation of the first action of the day. As the detachment entered the village, the Confederate cavalry was "encountered and driven hastily . . . other squads of reinforcing Rebs joining them as they ran." The few scattered shots exchanged in the streets of Crawford opened the Battle for Columbus.[34]

Buford's cavalry had taken up positions on the east side of the destroyed bridge across Uchee Creek along the Crawford Road, and only a few soldiers were stationed in the town. When the Union skirmishers struck this small detachment it split up, some retreating on the Crawford Road toward the remainder of Buford's brigade, the others heading south on the Lower Crawford Road. Both parties were pursued by the Union troopers as directed by Upton. "The pickets were struck at Crawford cross-roads," recalled Yeoman, and "were followed by the squadron, charging on a dead run for nine miles."[35]

After an intense chase, Yeoman and his company "reached a turn in the road about three hundred yards from the bridge." When the head of the column rounded the bend, they discovered that, in addition to the small force they were chasing, about a dozen Confederates were attempting to ignite the span. The Union troopers' headlong rush had dispersed their formation to some extent, but without hesitation Yeoman and two other soldiers who were in the lead charged ahead, scattered the surprised Confederates at the bridge, and extinguished the flames. "Evidently fearing that there was a larger column coming," the Confederates quickly skedaddled. Within moments, Yeoman's company threw out skirmishers and prepared to defend their prize. The crossing secure, Yeoman dispatched a rider to inform Upton of his success.[36]

The message was soon relayed to the general. With a passage over Uchee Creek secured along the Lower Crawford Road, and having witnessed the large numbers of Confederate cavalry retreating along the Crawford Road, Upton resolved to take advantage of Yeoman's achievement. He directed the head of the 4th Division's approaching column to turn to their right upon reaching the intersection and to follow the Lower Crawford Road, which he was confident would be lightly defended and more expedient than moving via the direct road. At the same time, Upton directed Winslow to send "Captain Young . . . with two hundred of the 10th Missouri to Clapp's factory on the Chattahoochee River, three miles north of Columbus, with orders to seize and hold the bridge there."[37]

Two companies of the 10th Missouri were detached and sent northeast from Crawford toward their target. Their detachment, combined with the earlier detachment of two companies to guard the division trains, left the 10th Missouri with only eight companies moving together with Winslow's brigade. Unfortunately for Young, the Clapp's Factory Bridge was "wholly destroyed before he arrived."[38]

Shortly after the head of the 4th Division's main column arrived in Crawford, but probably after Upton and part of his staff had already set out toward Yeoman's position on the Lower Crawford Road, it was discovered that there was a peculiar prisoner held at the town's jail. A woman by the name of Mrs. Keeling "had been confined in jail for 2 years at . . .

Girard for trying to steal negroes . . . [and] had been removed from there in order to save her life, the citizens of that place . . . [having] threatened to hang her." According to one Federal trooper, Keeling was "a lady of about twenty-one or twenty-two years old," and her liberation was "entirely unexpected." Described as "a refined lady—though a nervous wreck—poorly clad and insane with joy at her unexpected release," when Union soldiers came to her aid "she kissed the men that opened her cell, and fainted." Later, "the prisoner herself stood in plain view . . . with a white handkerchief in her hand, wildly gesticulating her arms and cheering the passing troops."

Shortly thereafter, the jail was set ablaze. This was a minor loss to the village, as, according to Captain Hinrichs of the 10th Missouri, "the whole town would have been laid in ashes, had she not begged for it. . . . The ladies of that town had been very kind to her, and had supplied her with food and clothing." Apparently, the woman was treated well by the Union troopers. "The boys rig up a carriage, secure some clothes, and Mrs. Keeling accompanies us in state," remembered Lieutenant Mitchell of Upton's staff. In the care of her rescuers, the woman rode comfortably toward Columbus and at one point even kept the wounded General Long company in his carriage.[39]

Once Upton arrived at the bridge spanning Uchee Creek, along with the head of the division, he met with Yeoman and "complimented the squadron on the notable feat it had performed." With the one major potential obstruction to his division's advance already secure, Upton ordered Yeoman and the other five companies of the advance, which had been recalled from the Crawford Road, to deploy as skirmishers and to move forward on the Lower Crawford Road and clear the way for the rest of the division. Though Colonel Beroth B. Eggleston, commander of the 1st Ohio, was placed in charge of the movement, "the general supervision" of the advance was again assigned to Yeoman. "General Upton's blood was up," and as the troopers of the advance again deployed the general called to them, "Can you give us the bridge across the Chattahoochee?" "We saluted and said we would try," Yeoman recalled.[40]

Not long after the Federal skirmishers were withdrawn from Crawford Road, Buford realized that the Federals were maneuvering around his defenses and marching toward Girard via the Lower Crawford Road. Though too late to save the bridge across Uchee Creek, the Confederate cavalry was hurriedly shifted southward in order to impede the Union march. Meanwhile, Buford sent word east to Columbus to inform Cobb to expect the approach of the Federals from the southwest along the Lower Crawford Road, known in Columbus as the Sandfort Road.[41]

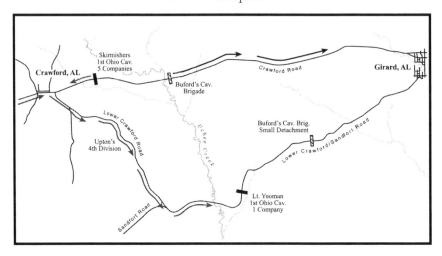

Map 3. Skirmish along the Crawford Road, morning, Sunday, April 16, 1865. Upton led his division southward from Crawford, bypassing Buford's defenses along the Crawford Road.

Unfortunately for Buford, a large portion of his forces would not get into position ahead of the Union column in time to make a unified stand. As the Federal skirmishers exited the swamp and started forward, they were met by a weak but determined Confederate delaying action. The Union "column immediately threw out skirmishers on each side of the road and went driving the enemy at a quick walk and sometimes at a sharp trot along the road to Columbus for nearly five miles." A member of the 7th Alabama Cavalry wrote that "the march of General Wilson was obstructed, as far as the feeble force of Confederate cavalry in his front would permit, at every available point. The bridges and swamps were made skirmish grounds, and every mile of the road to Columbus . . . was marked with blood."[42]

While skirmishing continued along the Lower Crawford or Sandfort Road, at homes along the route the residents watched for signs of the blue-clad soldiers. Though the advance of the 4th Division was occupied with combating the Confederate cavalry, troops further behind took the opportunity to forage and to plunder. At the home of Confederate general James Cantey, who was away at war, Mrs. Martha Cantey, her three small children, and her servants hoped the Union army might overlook them. Unfortunately for them, it did not.

Led to the home by a young black boy envious of his neighbor's pony, Federal soldiers were met by Winter Cantey, the family's free black servant, who "went out and took his stand in the front yard." The bummers soon "swarmed over the house and the grounds," and despite Winter's appeals, ransacked the home. Finding little of value, the soldiers turned on Winter, threatening to kill him if he did not reveal the location of the money and silver. "On his refusal, he felt the cold touch of a pistol against his forehead. Still refusing, as a further trial, they put a rope around his neck and drew him up to the nearest limb. For the second and third time this cruel punishment was repeated without avail. Leaving him then, they approached Mrs. Cantey and demanded the information of her. Then in desperation, they turned to the two slaves at her side, . . . then to Mrs. Cantey again, threatening to kill her, unless she gave them her diamond rings."

At that moment, as if to add insult to injury, the young guide paraded his prize, the Cantey youngster's pony, named Planet, into the front yard. "Look at dat nigger on dem chilluns' pony!" shouted one of the Cantey servants indignantly. When the soldiers ignited a fire in the Cantey's parlor, it looked as if the whole episode might end in tragedy. Much to the relief of the family, however, before the flames had time to spread, a Union officer arrived and ordered the stragglers to extinguish the fire and move on. When the soldiers departed, they did not do so alone. "Winter and Dinah [the family nurse] followed them for two miles, begging for the children's pony, and when these two faithful ones returned . . . Planet [was] with them."[43]

Though they could not protect the inhabitants of the homes along the road to Columbus, the Confederate cavalry did everything they could to slow the Yanks' progress. "The marching was hot and tedious," remembered Captain Francis Morse of Upton's staff. "Every few miles we would meet some portion of the enemy, and a sharp little skirmish would ensue." Even so, by virtue of their being overwhelmingly outnumbered and outgunned, the Confederate efforts proved ineffectual, and they were driven back rapidly for five or six miles, until they gave up and fled to the protection of the defenses at Girard and Columbus.

Their opposition having mostly disappeared, the skirmishers of the 1st Ohio pushed hurriedly forward until, at around 1:30 P.M., they arrived at the crest of a hill southwest of Girard that overlooked the town, the Chattahoochee valley, and their prize—Columbus. "Then as we reached the hill that looked down on Columbus the skirmishers were drawn in, the column was formed by fours, and a mile and a half straight away down the hill, lay the bridge across the Chattahoochee," observed Yeoman, who was still riding in the lead. "It was the prize we sought; could we win it?"[44]

8

The Fight for the City Bridge

In the heat of the afternoon, under the bright Easter sun, at between 1:30 and 2:00 P.M., the Federal advance, led by the 1st Ohio, arrived on the crest of a high ridge just to the southwest of Girard. The skirmishers of the 1st Ohio immediately halted and were drawn in. Quickly, the remainder of the regiments composing the 4th Division's 2nd Brigade began to close up.[1]

The ridge, which towered a little over three hundred vertical feet above the town, afforded the Federal troopers a fantastic view of the Chattahoochee valley. According to Sergeant Conzett of the 5th Iowa, "All at once . . . we saw the Chattahoochee River, Columbus . . . and its suburb Girard, with its strong forts and works at our feet . . . lying in a valley below us. . . We saw their forts and their troops with their bayonets glistening in the sun and their strength and great preparation." The troopers' arrival did not go unnoticed by the Confederates. At the sight of the Federals "the bells were set ringing, whistles from factories shrieked their loudest, and warning salutes were fired to summon the people to arms and defense of their homes against the brutal invaders." To Conzett, "It seemed that all pandemonium had broke loose."[2]

As the wild scene unfolded in the valley, a mile or two to the rear Upton, Alexander, and their staffs rode hard to catch up to the head of the column. Still awaiting the arrival of their commanders, the cavalrymen continued to watch "the marching of the troops into the forts and breastworks—the gunners loading their heavy guns and their officers, generals, and staff riding on full gallop along their lines—giving their orders, and all their other preparations." Conzett of the 5th Iowa remembered afterward: "We could see the people—men, women, and children in Columbus rushing to and fro and even see them pointing their spy glasses towards us. It was a curious and wonderful sight to us, and grand beyond description was the view of [the] river valley and city in its martial array."[3]

At around 2 P.M., Upton and Alexander arrived on the ridge. From atop the high hill, Upton could clearly see that "the lower bridge was defended from the east bank by a rifle-pit, with three pieces of artillery sweeping it," and that "the upper foot and railroad bridges were defended by a *tête-de-pont* consisting of two redoubts connected by a range of rifle pits about three quarters of a mile in length extending across the upper ridge, well strengthened by felled timber in front."[4]

Despite the clear view of the Confederate soldiers who had taken up positions behind the defenses, Upton had come to believe during the morning that Columbus, like Montgomery and Tuskegee, would surrender without a fight. The fact that the Confederate cavalry had suddenly fled from his advance as it neared the outskirts of the town fit perfectly with the pattern of capitulation encountered elsewhere during the campaign. Even so, unlike Montgomery, Columbus could only be reached via the three bridges that spanned the rain-swollen Chattahoochee. Upton could not afford to take chances. Securing one of the bridges upon which the corps could cross into Georgia was critical to his mission. For this reason, despite his confidence that the city would capitulate, Upton immediately set about coordinating a mounted charge to capture the southernmost crossing at the City Bridge.[5]

Upton charged Eggleston of the 1st Ohio with the task of capturing the bridge. As support to the 1st Ohio's movement, the four 12-pounder Napoleons of Rodney's battery were ordered forward. Behind the battery, the troopers of the 7th Ohio and 5th Iowa were held in readiness. Upton, Alexander, and that part of their staffs that were present also prepared to follow the 1st Ohio toward their objective. Finally, any chance of surprise having now been lost, the flags of the division, the brigade, and regiments under Alexander's command were unfurled and a final inspection of the target was made.[6]

The distance from where the 1st Ohio was assembled on the Sandfort Road to the bridge in the valley below was just over a mile. According to a Lieutenant Yeoman of the 1st Ohio, "It was a smooth pike and it looked like a beautiful run down there." The ridge and hillside over which the road gradually descended was bare on its north and east faces. There was "not a bush, tree, or any possible shelter" along the route, and many of the veteran cavalrymen realized that once they were under way, the landscape could provide little protection if the Confederates decided to fight.

Soon the "serious business" of the movement was begun. Yeoman, who had earlier led the charge to capture the bridge over Uchee Creek, was again in the middle of the action. He recalled that "Colonel Eggleston and the staff officers placed themselves at the head of this column [of the

1st Ohio] . . . the order was given to draw sabers, then the bugle rang out the trot, then the gallop, then the wild charge, and away we went, straight down for Columbus."[7]

As the 1st Ohio moved out, Upton, Alexander, and the staff fell in behind and followed the unit down the hill toward Girard. As the troopers raced toward the town, they could see that Confederate soldiers waited behind the earthworks and entrenchments, "but not a gun was fired, and it looked as if the town was at . . . [their] mercy." Upton, Alexander, and the staff followed immediately behind the 1st Ohio until they came to where the ridge they were riding upon formed a low knoll, still slightly southwest of the City Bridge and overlooking Girard. There they halted to watch the action unfold. Ahead of them, the 1st Ohio continued its rapid movement down the ridge toward a bend in the road that would lead them onto Girard's Bridge Street and to the mouth of the covered wooden span.[8]

As the charging column neared the bend, the excitement and anticipation of Upton and those with him grew intense. The guns from the Confederate positions were still silent, and it seemed clear to the commanding general that the city would surrender. Upton dismounted and, taking his field glasses in hand, intensely watched the scene unfold.

While the prospects for success appeared good from Upton's position atop the knoll, nearer the front it was clear that things were not quite as they first appeared. The closer the charging cavalry regiment got to the covered bridge, the more ominous the situation seemed. The troopers could see the waiting Confederate artillerymen on the far side of the bridge silently watching and waiting while the infantry presented their muskets. At the six-gun battery near Fort 1, north of the City Bridge, the gunners trained their pieces and stood with readied lanyards. Suspicions that they might be riding into a trap began to prevail in the Union ranks, and a growing murmur of apprehension began to emanate from the charging column. Finally, convinced that something had to be done, Yeoman, who was riding with Eggleston, called out, "Colonel, I see that the bridge upon the other side has three guns planted at its mouth . . . [so] as to sweep it from end to end. They are certainly loaded with grape and canister, because they have not fired a shot. If we go on the bridge mounted, the first discharge will cut down the head of the column, and fill it up with dead horses, and it will be impossible to get the balance of the command over— the dead horses will choke up the bridge."[9]

While Yeoman pleaded with Eggleston to halt the 1st Ohio's rush toward the span, Upton, back on the knoll, believing that he had accomplished his mission, enthusiastically exclaimed, "Columbus is ours without firing a shot!" The assessment was promptly seconded by several members of the staff, when suddenly, according to Private Ebenezer N. Gilpin, "Almost every Rebel gun in Columbus opened on us—every fort and every musket fired."[10] Waddell's cannoneers targeted the exposed mass of officers on the knoll. "The first round from the forts was shell, and two of our Headquarters' horses were killed," Gilpin reported. "One shell struck our Chief Buglers horse and exploded in him, bursting and tearing him all to pieces. Then came grape and canister more than ever I want to hear again."[11]

Under Cobb's supervision, loosing their destruction on Upton and the staff were the four howitzers of the 10th Missouri Battery that occupied Fort 1 on Red Hill in Girard, near the south end of the *tête-de-pont*. Additionally, six rifled guns from one of the batteries of Waddell's 20th Battalion Alabama Artillery, which was stationed in the street next to the fort, hurled their shells "fast and furious" toward the bare hill. The cannoneers at the east end of the City Bridge, however, held their fire in anticipation of the expected charge through the span. The Confederate infantry occupying the works across the river in Columbus, and also near the south end of the entrenchments in Girard, joined the fight and opened a storm of musketry on the distant blue figures on the knoll as well as at the mounted troopers of the 1st Ohio, who were mostly obscured by the houses and buildings of southern Girard.[12]

To Eggleston, down on Bridge Street, it was obvious that to continue the mounted charge through the bridge would be to invite disaster. "Colonel Eggleston at once assented [to Yeoman's petition], ordered a left oblique on the impulse of the moment, and . . . [the regiment] rode in on the pavement, in shelter of the houses, while orders were at once given to dismount and fight on foot." To cover the movements of the 1st Ohio, Alexander ordered forward Rodney's battery, who had been waiting on the high ridge, to the Union rear.[13]

"With a free roadway, yielded for the purpose," Rodney was quickly able to get his guns rumbling down the hill toward the knoll where the generals and staff were observing the action. "The thrilling effect of 'battery forward, action front,' so impressive when executed in the heat and smoke of battle, was measurably supplied by the skill and promptitude of the maneuver," remembered Major James Latta of Upton's staff, and within moments the four "Napoleons were unlimbered . . . shotted and fired. . . . The discharge by battery brought a prompt response from [the Confederate] long-ranged rifled guns, deadly in its effect to several of the battery men."[14]

Following the battery forward was the remainder of the 2nd Brigade. These troopers rushed ahead to within a short distance of the generals, bat-

Fig. 10. Colonel Beroth
B. Eggleston. Courtesy
Massachusetts Com-
mandery, MOLLUS, and
the U.S. Army Military
History Institute.

tery, and staff and lay down along the ridge near the road. According to one
trooper, the Confederates "trained their guns on us and shot and shell flew
over us pretty lively, and their sharpshooters tried their best to hit some of
us, but they did us no harm as we laid low."[15]

As the savage artillery duel continued, in the streets of Girard part of
the dismounted troopers of the 1st Ohio deployed as sharpshooters, taking cover inside and behind the houses and other structures of the town.
Another group began to reconnoiter the ground to the north of the City
Bridge to see whether there might be a way to get at Fort 1 and silence its
guns as well as those stationed nearby. Noticing that there was a footbridge
spanning the steep Mill Creek, which divided Girard in half, one Union
trooper galloped "over the little creek which separated the earthworks from
the town . . . and rode almost up to the works, and then rode back again."
Despite its being, as Yeoman observed, "a gallant and an inspiring thing to
do," the ride also proved to the Confederates manning the nearby trenches
that the Mill Creek footbridge should be destroyed.[16]

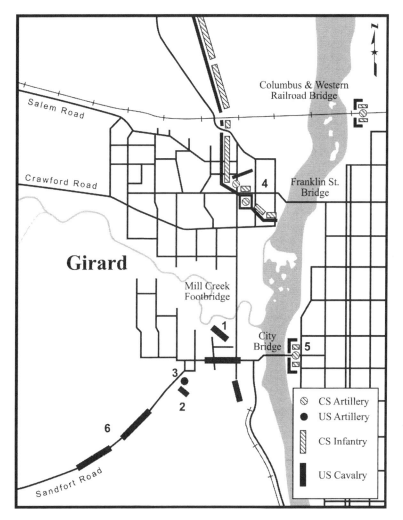

Map 4. Charge for the City Bridge, 2:00 P.M., Sunday, April 16, 1865. (1) The 1st Ohio halts in the street, throws out skirmishers, and forms for a charge to capture the City Bridge. (2) Upton and the staff overlook the battle. (3) Rodney's battery opens counter-battery fire on Fort 1 and Confederates east of the City Bridge. (4) The guns of the 20th Battalion Alabama Artillery open fire on the Federals. (5) Three-gun battery opens fire prematurely. (6) Alexander's brigade lies down along the road to observe the action.

To prevent the Federals from using the footbridge to launch an assault on Fort 1, a small body of Confederate skirmishers were deployed from the south end of the defenses. According to Captain Morse of Upton's staff, "Away to our left we saw a line of skirmishers coming out on the full run; the manner they acted convinced us that no troops but veterans could conduct themselves with so much regularity, under the circumstances." Soon, the Union troopers forming in Girard encountered "fire from a small Confederate force near the creek bridge in Girard, and from the battery on the Red Hill near the upper bridge." The Confederate skirmishers quickly doused the footbridge in combustibles and set it aflame, thus preventing any movement of the enemy across the creek. Their mission complete, they rapidly retired back to the protection of their earthworks.[17]

Eggleston knew he had to act quickly if his men were going to have any chance of capturing the City Bridge. With the fire from the Confederates starting to have some effect, the colonel threw part of his now dismounted regiment into a hastily assembled column and then, himself in the lead, charged into the street toward the City Bridge, prepared to fight through on foot. As the column surged forward, the rest of the regiment spread out, taking shelter amid the houses and other buildings, and began to cover their comrades with rapid fire from their Spencers.[18]

Eggleston's column had not gotten far, however, when it "was received with a heavy fire of artillery and musketry" on its left flank and from the guns stationed across the Chattahoochee. "We plowed wide furrows through their ranks as they approached the bridge," remembered Private Kingman P. Moore of the Griffin Light Artillery, who, along with other men from his section, trained their guns on the mass of blue soldiers across the river.[19]

When the head of the Union column reached the entrance to the span, they found that the bridge "had previously been strewed with cotton [and] saturated with turpentine." "But more than this," observed Captain Rankin of the 7th Ohio Cavalry, "on the further side of the bridge, just beyond the center, the plank had been removed for about fifty feet; so it was intended to trap the column and have it precipitate itself into the Chattahoochee." The "dash at the lower bridge" was halted at the entrance, and many of the troopers began "firing through it when they found their passage stopped by the tearing up of the flooring."[20]

The Confederate command quickly determined that the moment had come to ignite the span. The Federals had discovered their trap, and there was no use risking having them gain possession of the bridge. The order was given for the battery on the Columbus end to cease firing. "The bridge was ordered to be burned," remembered Moore, whose piece of ar-

Fig. 11. The City Bridge as it appeared after reconstruction. The bridge that was fought over during the battle would have been almost identical. Courtesy Historic Columbus Foundation.

tillery fell silent, "and some men under heavy fire from the Yankees entered the covered-in bridge . . . and spoiled our fun of filling it with dead Yankees." In an act of "conspicuous gallantry," Captain Christopher C. McGehee, the commander of one of the Naval Infantry Battalion's companies, "crawled out onto the wooden framework" and attempted to torch the flammables.[21]

On the Alabama side of the river, for a moment there was hesitation within the Union ranks as Eggleston tried to determine how to continue. Before he could devise some means, however, suddenly "one of the men on the bridge shot down one of the [Confederate] gunners; as he fell, he pulled the lanyard, the gun discharged, and immediately the flame from the gun caught the bridge." The other cannoneers, thinking the order had been given, blasted the bridge with their pieces. Fortunately for McGehee, the canister whizzed over his head and ripped along the interior of the structure. His efforts aided by the flash from the cannon's muzzles, "tarred and cottoned for the occasion, flames and smoke burst from every crevice." According to Yeoman, on the Union side, "so quickly did the flames spread that the men standing at this end of the bridge caught the breath of the fire in their very faces."[22]

His goal now unattainable, Eggleston ordered his column to retreat to the safety of the town and take cover. Though the prize was lost, the contest was not over. Still, "the 1st Ohio were fighting bravely through the streets of Girard," and according to Private Gilpin, "the Rebs shelled their horses and poured such a deadly fire into them that they were forced to fall back."[23]

On the knoll just to the southwest, Upton and Alexander watched as their hopes of a quick victory went up in smoke. With both the City Bridge and the footbridge across Mill Creek aflame, the generals soon realized that there was no way to quickly or effectively launch another assault from their position. Within a few minutes, the 1st Ohio "received orders from General Alexander to retire gradually beyond the crest of the hill and rejoin the brigade there."[24]

As the 1st Ohio regrouped and prepared to flee the town, the shells of the Confederate artillery near Fort 1 continued to streak over the rooftops of the houses in Girard toward the cavalrymen in the streets and the staff on the hill. Captain Edward C. Dale, who was observing to the rear of the staff, recalled: "I had a very fine sight of the firing at this place, I laid on top of a ridge and watched the firing from the fort which commanded the bridge across the river leading to the city. The shells would come screaming toward us like some fiery demon." Some of the "demons" found their mark. "A piece of a shell struck . . . [Upton's] Division flag breaking the staff, and three bullets went through the flag." Many of the staff officers' horses were killed or injured, and even Alexander's prized mount, Max, was slain.[25]

Upton took his field glasses in hand and contemplated the deteriorating situation as he scanned the countryside for another possible line of attack. Though he had often been praised for his conspicuous coolness in combat, Upton was apparently so absorbed in his thoughts about his next move that he ignored the danger posed by the "severe artillery fire." Morse, who was with Upton and Alexander, recalled: "We were on a bare hill, in full view of the rebels, and for fifteen minutes we sat on our horses, taking our chances of being torn to pieces, while the general made observations of the works." Upton's seeming obliviousness to the fire to which the staff was being subjected even prompted Gilpin to observe that, "Glass in hand, General Upton stood like 'patience on a monument' . . . in plain view and point blank range watching the Rebs leisurely regardless of the volleys that were fired into us incessantly, and so 'peculiarly near.'"[26]

While Upton and Alexander examined the field, Rodney's battery continued to exchange shots with the Confederates in Girard and across the river in Columbus. The firing of Rodney's battery uncovered "a force planted to hold the [river] crossing, if means were at hand by boat or pontoon to attempt it. There were neither."[27]

Soon the 1st Ohio retreated out of Girard on the Sandfort Road back toward the ridge where the movement started. "An aid was sent back to hurry up the division," and Alexander's brigade was "placed in line of battle on the hill in front of the rebel left." Eventually, the fire from the Confederates' long-range rifle battery made the generals' situation on the knoll "too hot to hold." "The brass guns [of Rodney's battery] couldn't reach effectively," remembered Major Latta, "the cannonading ceased and the effort . . . was abandoned." At about 3 P.M., once Upton "had fully satisfied himself respecting the enemy's position," he ordered his staff to retire farther back up the ridge out of range of the Confederate artillery.[28]

Once the withdrawal orders were relayed, the unnerved staff and members of Rodney's battery wasted no time in beating a hasty retreat. Their movement was anything but orderly. "I did not stand upon the order of my going, but got out of there as fast as 'Charley' could take me," recalled Gilpin. "A bridge that spanned a little ravine had been torn away; there was no time to think, and my horse took the gap at a tremendous leap, but the distance was too great; he caught the opposite bank with his fore feet and held until I flung myself over his head. My brave 'Charley' brought me out safely, but I found that he had been wounded by a piece of shell that cut a tendon, and it was necessary to kill him and thus end his suffering."[29]

After the Union staff and battery withdrew from the knoll, Alexander ordered out part of the 1st and 7th Ohio cavalries to act as skirmishers and videttes. The thin blue line was stationed along the ridge to either side of the Sandfort Road near and overlooking Girard. The remainder of Alexander's brigade took up positions on the high hills farther south, out of reach of the Confederate artillery, which continued to fire for a few minutes longer. Finally, only about an hour after the first major engagement of the battle had begun, as the last of the serious firing died away, Winslow, at the head of his brigade, came riding up along the Sandfort Road ready for action.[30]

Winslow's troopers had ridden hard to keep up with the swift-moving advance, and were anticipating a fight. "The day was a hot one and the column moved on in more than usual silence," recalled Captain Lot Abraham of the 4th Iowa, "until the booming cannon broke the stillness with all its usual enlivening spirit, echoing far over the hills, straightening every trooper in his saddle, and driving away the cares of thought." With Winslow in the lead, the last four miles to Girard passed quickly, "the horses stepping more lively at the sound of well known music." At last, Winslow's troopers topped the hill overlooking the valley and gained a view of the Confederate works and Alexander's brigade "fast forming [in] line on foot, and just out of the Rebel range."[31]

Within the Confederate lines, as the burning City Bridge collapsed into the muddy waters of the Chattahoochee, there pervaded a sense of relief. They had met the enemy, turned him back, and suffered little loss. There was little time for celebration, however. "The fire from our guns had set our breastworks on fire," remembered Private Moore, stationed at the City Bridge, "and as the Yankees had retired from Girard, we spent the remainder of the afternoon trying to extinguish the burning bales of cotton."[32]

Though Cobb and Von Zinken must have been disappointed that their trap had been foiled and that the bridge was destroyed, its loss was not unexpected. Furthermore, with the City Bridge destroyed, many of their forces stationed on the Georgia side were now free to join the other soldiers manning the trenches of the *tête-de-pont*. Though they had won this round, Cobb and Von Zinken realized that the battle was far from over. They also realized, considering how quickly the Federals had arrived and attacked, that it might be prudent to move their headquarters from the Alabama side of the river into Columbus.[33]

9
The Lost Brigade

By the time Winslow arrived on the field near the outskirts of Girard at the head of his brigade, Upton had already formulated his strategy and plan of attack. The remaining bridge across the Chattahoochee (the Franklin Street Bridge), which lay behind the Confederate earthworks north of Mill Creek, would be his objective. Upton's plan was to make a two-pronged assault. The majority of Alexander's brigade would remain "in position along the crest of the lower ridge," out of reach of the Confederate artillery, "while Winslow's brigade, making a wide detour . . . [would march], under cover, across to the upper ridge." When Winslow got in position he would assault what Upton believed was the Confederate far right. Simultaneously, Alexander would move his men off the hills and, after finding some way to cross Mill Creek, attack the Confederate left and left-center. This, they hoped, would divide the defenders and allow Federal troops to break through and capture the Franklin Street Bridge before it could be burned.[1]

Upton's plan had three key elements. First, because it was already approximately 3 P.M., it would be important that Winslow's brigade move into position quickly. Second, the movement needed to be concealed as far as possible from the observations of the enemy so as to achieve maximum effect through surprise. And third, while Winslow positioned his brigade, Upton and his staff needed to reconnoiter the enemy positions and discover some weak spot at which to aim the brunt of the attack.

Shortly after arriving on the hills overlooking Girard, Winslow met with Upton, who instructed him to move his brigade west, then north, behind the hills that would mask his movements, to a new position on what Upton believed was the Confederate right flank. Upton ordered Winslow to conceal his brigade near a road that could not be seen from their position, but which Upton believed ran from the Franklin Street Bridge in Columbus to the town of Opelika to the west. Upton did not know the name of the road, nor did he realize that there were two roads matching his description.[2]

The Salem Road ran slightly northwest from Girard, paralleling the Columbus and Western Railroad, through a valley from the Franklin Street Bridge to Opelika. It was upon this road that Upton wished to assemble Winslow's brigade for their attack. Unknown to Upton at the time, however, was that the Summerville Road lay just north of the Salem Road. The Summerville Road ran directly northwest from Girard and the Franklin Street Bridge, up Ingersoll Hill, through the town of Summerville, and ultimately to Opelika. This situation would prove to complicate the arrangements.

Furthermore, it seems likely that there arose a lack of accurate communication caused by the growing friction between Upton and Winslow. Still smarting from his displacement by the appointment of Upton over him in command, and further agitated by their clash of egos, Winslow believed that his "personality and conduct on the field was lost sight of or at least, in part, overshadowed by that of Upton." According to Winslow, Upton's West Pointer status and "companionship with Wilson gave him . . . greater influence in the corps than . . . any other officer." Hindered by this poor working relationship, and when combined with the insufficient information available about the terrain, Winslow likely emerged from the meeting with only a murky sense of his intended purpose.[3]

Following the meeting, Upton detached the 5th Iowa from Alexander's brigade and attached it to Winslow's command. The 5th Iowa was instructed to march north in advance of Winslow's brigade in order to find the most expedient route, and to drive off any skirmishers or pickets they might encounter. Additionally, Rodney's battery was also assigned to Winslow's brigade, and would bring up the rear of the column. Confident that everything was going as planned, Winslow set out. With the men of the 5th Iowa leading the way, and Rodney's battery rolling along behind, Winslow's brigade marched by "a circuitous and concealed route" in a wide arch around Girard. The troopers encountered no resistance as they crossed Crawford Road, passed around several abandoned forts, and forded Mill Creek. "Marching in a column of fours along a road hidden in the woods and entirely covered by the hills along the route, we crossed the railroad and the Opelika-Salem road and arrived at the exact place named and described by Upton to me in person," remembered Winslow, adding, "I was there to await instructions."[4]

The whole movement took between one and a half and two hours to complete. Though Winslow believed he had arrived at the spot intended by Upton, he had actually moved too far north. Rather than halting south of the Salem Road, as Upton had desired, the entire force was "concentrated and dismounted along the trees in position . . . covering the Summerville road which ran . . . to the bridge and city." Upton had instructed Winslow to conceal his brigade from enemy observation upon arrival and to wait there for further orders. Within moments of their halt, Winslow's troopers vanished into the lush green foliage of the densely wooded valley.[5]

While Winslow was busy moving his brigade, Upton embarked on his part of the plan. Followed by his staff and personal escort (the latter composed of the troopers of the 4th Iowa's Company G), Upton "set out at zealous speed upon a general reconnaissance of the defenses." Within a short time he encountered one of Girard's outlying forts. Wanting to know if it was manned, he called on several of his bodyguards "to lead a 'Forlorn Hope' and charge on . . . [the] huge fort that loomed up in . . . [their] direct front." "Boys, do you see yon fort?" inquired Upton of the selected horsemen. "Ride into it or ride until you draw its fire," he commanded. Fortunately for the troopers, their maneuver was met with nothing but silence as the fort proved to be one not incorporated into the Confederates' defensive plan.[6]

Shifting his focus, Upton "divided his staff into as many observing parties as there were officers, reduced his escort to a squad, to provide orderlies enough, and exhorted all to the utmost diligence." The area Upton and his staff next chose to inspect they thought constituted the right (or northern) flank of the Confederate line. In actuality, the earthworks they encountered made up the central section of the *tête-de-pont*. For well over an hour, Upton and his small band stealthily maneuvered over the rough and often densely wooded terrain west of the defenses in an attempt to learn something of the Confederate positions and strength. "Emulating the fearless example of their chief," remembered Adjutant William Scott of the 4th Iowa, "[some of the] officers rode almost under the guns of the enemy, two of them, Major [William] Woods and Lieutenant Sloan Keck of the Fourth Iowa, actually coming upon the enemy's exterior line at different places, and escaping only by the speed of their horses, each of them losing an orderly, captured."[7]

Unfortunately, Upton learned little from his efforts at reconnaissance. The rugged terrain and his misunderstanding of the extent of the Confederate defenses made much of the endeavor fruitless. The splitting up of his staff and escort cost Upton valuable time and gained him little usable information. It also cost him soldiers whom he hoped would not disclose his plans to their captors.

Behind the walls of the Girard's forts and earthworks, as half the Federal cavalry division in their front was moving north, Cobb, Von Zinken, and Buford were making arrangements to meet the attack they expected might come at any moment. They shifted their troops from positions east of the destroyed City Bridge northward and across the river into the trenches. Buford's brigade, after reassembling in Columbus, "was divided into detachments" and dispatched to guard several posts. One detachment marched across the Franklin Street Bridge to "watch the unfinished line of works and fill the gap in the infantry line on the west bank of the Chattahoochee River," while "the other two detachments were stationed above and below the city upon the east bank to prevent any attempt of the enemy to cross in boats." The 3rd Georgia Reserves were shifted northward from their position at the south end of the *tête-de-pont* to a position "three hundred yards northwest of the railway bridge." Even the 26th Battalion Georgia Infantry was shifted north and positioned "in the center, citizens being on . . . [their] right and left."[8]

As the afternoon passed, Confederate pickets and skirmishers as well as the artillery probed the surrounding hills and valleys trying to keep track of the Union movements. Private Alphonza Jackson of the 2nd Regiment of the Georgia State Line recalled, "We could see the Yankee officers reconnoitering in the evening and were expecting an attack." Confederate batteries stationed along the southern end of the *tête-de-pont* fired out into the countryside to see if they could locate the enemy. They also kept up an intermittent fire upon the men of Alexander's brigade who remained atop the high hills to the southwest of town, but the range was too great. According to one Union officer, "They shell us incessantly from the forts and light batteries without effect, at which we—smile."[9]

The shelling did produce some casualties, however. In the late afternoon, "the premature explosion of a shell as it was leaving the muzzle of a cannon, killed one of the Confederate gunmen and wounded several others." One small group of Confederate militia found this "so depressing" that one of the veterans in the unit "laughed at them and told them that this was nothing [compared] to what they would see in a short time."[10]

Following the failed attempt to capture the City Bridge and the withdrawal of Alexander's brigade to the hilltop southwest of Girard, Alexander deployed skirmishers along the southern ridge to watch for any suspicious Confederate movements. Late in the afternoon, much to the surprise of the Federal videttes posted along the ridge overlooking the town, an unsuspecting train steamed into the abandoned Mobile and Girard Railroad Depot located just south of the burned City Bridge carrying Confederate reserves and civilians ready to man the trenches. Unmolested, "when the engine and coach containing this small band . . . reached the depot without seeing or hearing anything of the enemy" they disembarked and set out to reach the Confederate lines. Intrigued by the sight, a small party of Union soldiers quickly assembled and struck out to investigate.[11]

The Confederate reinforcements were men from the Fort Mitchell area, including the few brave volunteers of the Russell County Reserves. Though "the party only had three guns and a few rounds of cartridges," with one wounded veteran as their guide they "went forward until they reached the top of a long hill in the suburbs of Girard." There they ran into the curious Union skirmishers. "The boys heard them coming, hid behind a fence and waited until they could see the whites of their eyes and then fired on them," recalled Charles Martin, the brother of one of the Confederate soldiers. "This caused a stampede among them and before they could rally and come again, the boys reloaded their guns and gave them another round. . . . The boys then ran behind a house" and secured their escape. After serious effort, the party safely entered the Confederate lines and were sent into Columbus to be armed. "Receiving better guns and ammunition, they returned to the Confederate breastworks in Girard, having fired six rounds of ammunition, killing a Yankee soldier and a horse as they afterwards found out."[12]

Trains from Alabama were not the only ones arriving. From the east, engineers continued to bring into Columbus small numbers of reinforcements and to take on board passengers and supplies to be moved away to more secure locations. Cobb also ordered a train to be kept in waiting, pointed east toward Macon with the steam up, so that it might be used in case of disaster to make an escape. The train's presence seems to have been no secret, and a considerable portion of the Confederate force appears to have been aware of this contingency.[13]

In the countryside to the west of the Confederate lines, Upton, having finished his reconnaissance along the Salem Road, set out to locate Winslow's brigade. He sent word back to Alexander that his brigade should wait in readiness to launch their attack as soon as they heard the start of the action to the north. Unfortunately, however, when Upton and his staff rode to the position where they expected to find Winslow, they found only empty woods.[14]

It was already approximately 5 P.M., and the late-afternoon sun demonstrated that there was little time left to execute an attack. Upton desperately wanted to begin the assault before the arrival of Minty's 2nd Division, who might steal some of his glory, and before darkness closed the day's operations. Up and down the hills west of Girard, along the Salem Road and part of the Summerville Road, Upton searched with no success. Growing ever more irritated by the series of events that seemed to be frustrating his plans, he wandered over the western hills surrounding the Chattahoochee valley for more than two hours.[15]

As Upton searched, back on the high hills southwest of Girard the troopers of the 2nd Brigade waited patiently for some sign of the engagement. Gilpin, whose horse had been mortally wounded in the earlier attack, stayed behind with Alexander. "I took up my position on a very high hill from which I could see every house in Columbus," he recalled. "The hills around the city form a perfect circle—a dim blue line as far as eye can see encircles the plain in which the city nestles—so shady and beautiful; and I could but think if that was *my* home, I'd die, sooner than see an enemy's army enter it." The excellent vantage of Alexander's brigade provided the idle troopers with an entertaining diversion. According to one officer, "Every soldier is a general today, planning the attack and estimating the strength of the foe."[16]

Meanwhile, as Alexander's brigade waited for the start of the attack and Upton rode frantically around the countryside in search of the 1st Brigade, Winslow waited patiently for orders. "The entire force rested quietly in the woods for fully two hours," recalled the general, "during which I received no further word." Indeed, according to Captain Abraham of the 4th Iowa, "We halt, dismount, and many go to sleep!—which I could do very easy, but prevent it by walking about and watching for items."[17]

Though the time Winslow spent waiting for Upton to arrive could have been completely wasted, a stroke of good luck turned the otherwise frustrated battle preparations at least partially in favor of the Federals. Winslow "encountered a man who was well acquainted with the city, its fortifications and with the roads and general situation. He prepared for me a rough sketch of the defenses," remembered Winslow, and "in a quiet manner I personally examined the ground in front of the woods and endeavored to locate certain positions which had been described by this informant." According to Winslow, "From the edge of the woods we occupied the ground was open for some distance in the direction of the city and descended gradually toward the river, but there were two forts on a ridge between us and the bridge."[18]

The outline of the works that was provided to Winslow was indeed "rough" and, while helpful, showed nothing of the Confederate main line of defense, outlining only the forts (Forts 2 and 3) and entrenchments that composed the curtain to the main line. Armed with the sketch, Winslow reconnoitered the position of the two forts that lay on either side of the Summerville Road facing his position. Forts 2 and 3 and the rifle pits that connected them appeared to Winslow to constitute the central portion of the Confederate right flank. Unknown to him, the main line actually lay to the east of the Summerville Road, south of where it passed between the forts. This main line of defenses (extending from Fort 2 to Fort 1) could not be seen from Winslow's position and went completely undetected.[19]

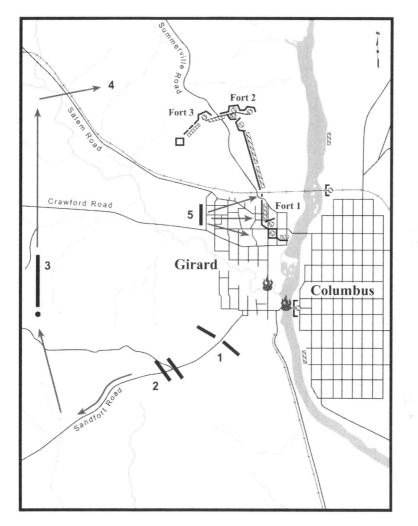

Map 5. Winslow's flank march and Upton's reconnaissance, 3:00–5:00 P.M., Sunday, April 16, 1865. (1) Skirmishers of the 1st and 7th Ohio. (2) Alexander's brigade remains atop high hills. (3) Winslow's brigade and Rodney's battery move north and then disappear into wooded valley (4) north of Salem Road. (5) Upton and his staff reconnoiter Confederate lines along Salem Road.

Feeling confident in what he had learned, Winslow met with his regimental commanders, outlined the situation as he knew it, and acquainted them with what they were likely to face along the Summerville Road. It was probably at about this time, too, that the two companies of the 10th Missouri that had been detached at Crawford to capture the Clapp's Factory Bridge returned with the news that they had found the bridge already burned and that no passage could be made there. It was now clear to Winslow and the other officers of his brigade that there remained no alternate route into Columbus. If they were to be successful in their mission to force their way into Georgia, they would have to capture the Franklin Street Bridge. They could not do that, however, without orders from Upton.[20]

The sun was already sinking toward the horizon when General Wilson arrived on the hills west of Girard. His ride had been long, and his escort was "very tired." By time they halted overlooking the valley, Wilson and his staff had ridden approximately forty miles in order to overtake the 4th Division and make it to Columbus by late afternoon. Though they had made few halts along the way, Wilson and his men had stopped for a quick dinner near Crawford. At a small store near that town, as Wilson and his escort "drew near, one of the old Scotch women . . . tied a white sheet on a quilting frame and ordered one of the fifteen-year-old boys to stand in the road and wave this flag of peace." In response, "General Wilson placed a guard around the store" and ate with the family. Meanwhile, "on the porch of the store, barrels of brandy were brought from the distilling plant . . . and peach and apple brandy was given . . . to the weary soldiers of the Federal Army." Although Wilson almost certainly did not imbibe—for he was opposed to the consumption of alcohol—according to one witness, "General Wilson is said to have referred to that occasion as the greatest 'treat' of the conflict."[21]

Despite the warm reception received near Crawford, Wilson and his escort did not dawdle over dinner and made rapid progress toward the east. When they arrived around sunset "on the bluff overlooking the valley and the city of Columbus beyond," it was obvious that the city's defenses were still manned by Confederate soldiers and that passage over the river had not been secured. From his position on the bluff, Wilson could see Winslow's brigade concealed in a wooded valley nearby, but he did not see Winslow or Upton. Soon, however, according to Wilson, "Upton crossed my front within two hundred yards, riding rapidly to the north. Supposing that he had seen me, but was placing his troops and perfecting his dispositions, I neither hailed nor recalled him till he had entirely disappeared. After waiting patiently ten or fifteen minutes for his return," the general remembered, "I sent a staff officer after him, but it was fully a half hour before he reached my position."[22]

At about the same time Wilson arrived in Columbus, Winslow began to wonder if something was wrong, as he had not "communicated with Upton" in several hours. At first he believed that Upton "was occupied with Alexander's brigade," cognizant of "how energetic and careful Upton was about topographical matters and thought he was making his plans." By near 7 P.M., however, Winslow began to think that perhaps it was he who was in error.[23]

Eventually, Upton was hailed by Wilson's staff officer and returned to Wilson's position. Perturbed at the loss of time spent searching for Winslow's brigade, upon "riding up rapidly and saluting with impatience," Upton announced: "Everything is ready for the assault, but I cannot find Winslow and must delay the attack till he is in position." Surely to the surprise of Upton, Wilson then replied that he had "passed Winslow and his command properly concealed in a wooded valley close by." In disbelief, Upton rode out to observe the spot, followed by Wilson. There they were spotted by Winslow, who recalled: "As the sun had gone down and the twilight in the south is of short duration, I began to fear there was a misunderstanding, when I discovered Upton with others riding to a slight elevation a few hundred yards away and in the open fields in our front. I galloped at once to him as did also General Wilson who joined us."[24]

Within moments, "the three generals were . . . in consultation." According to Winslow, "The serious loss of time had evidently made Upton nervous and he began to upbraid me in no gentle terms for not obeying his verbal instructions." Adjutant Scott, who was observing, recalled that "Winslow, vexed at the possibility of any criticism in respect to the delay, at once said that he was ready to attack at any time, and would do it now." To Wilson, Upton protested, "But it is now too late. It will be dark before I can get him into position and lead the division to the attack." "My command [is] . . . in position just where he . . . ordered me to place it," Winslow rebutted, tempers flaring. Furthermore, Winslow added, he had concealed his brigade and "had been anxiously awaiting . . . further orders," as Upton had instructed.[25]

For the next few moments, the verbal salvos between Upton and Winslow continued. According to Winslow, Upton "said he had been unable to find me or my brigade. As this appeared almost absurd when there were more then sixteen hundred horsemen present for duty," recalled Winslow, "I could say little more." Upton again charged that because of Winslow's failure to follow instructions, he "had lost the opportunity for fighting." "Whereupon I remarked," recounted Winslow, "that if he wished, we could attack immediately and have every chance of success."[26]

Wilson stepped in and took control of the situation. Turning to Upton, he said, "if Winslow wants to fight in the dark let him do it. He has obeyed your instructions." Though there remained much hostility between the generals, according to Winslow, "this remark relieved the situation and soothed our feelings." Wilson then asked Upton to explain his plan and was given the details of the proposed two-pronged attack to be led by Winslow's brigade upon the Confederate right flank. Desiring to demonstrate that he too had been actively involved in accomplishing the mission, Winslow then volunteered the information he gathered about the Confederate defenses along the Summerville Road. He informed Wilson and Upton that the right of the Confederate lines lay not along the Salem Road but across the Summerville Road nearby, and that he had already acquainted the officers of his brigade with the situation. Wilson weighed the options, and remembered later: "As we had already become pretty accustomed to night fighting and its advantages, it occurred to me that an attack after dark would be accompanied by less loss and greater success than one in full daylight. As the position was a formidable one, . . . I felt that no mistake should be made. So far as could be seen the works were well manned, . . . and every indication led to the belief that we should have a sharp and vigorous fight, which might possibly end in our discomfiture."[27]

Even so, there were few options. To postpone would only work to the advantage of the Confederates, who would either use the time to strengthen their defenses and garrison or else abandon their Alabama line during the night and burn the bridges behind them, cutting off any route across the Chattahoochee and forcing a long detour or delay. The decision was made. "Wilson said that the men were not green soldiers," remembered Adjutant Scott, "and that they had showed at Franklin and Selma that they could fight by night." According to Wilson, "After learning Upton's plan, and satisfying myself by careful scrutiny that it was the best that could be devised, I expressed my approval and then said: 'But it is not too late to carry the plan into effect to-night; you will make all your arrangements to attack at 8:30.' With flashing eyes he [Upton] exclaimed: 'Do you mean it? It will be dark as midnight by that hour and that will be a night attack, indeed!' Assuring him that it was just what I wanted and that it should be made . . . I instructed him to get everything ready to carry it into effect."[28]

Upton, who had been "much disappointed" at the prospect of having to delay the attack any further, "seized the proposal with pleasure," even though Wilson informed him that the assault would be directed toward the newly uncovered defenses along the Summerville Road, with which Winslow's officers were already familiar. Excited by the novelty of a night attack, Upton, "with enthusiastic promptitude . . . exclaimed: 'By jingo, I'll do it; and I'll sweep everything before me!'"[29]

10

The Stage Is Set

With the night attack decided upon, Wilson asked Upton "if he wanted any help" and offered to "order up the rest of the corps." Upton, clamorous for a victory to his sole credit and aware that the 2nd Division was several hours' ride from Girard, denied the offer. According to Captain Morse, Upton replied that he "thought the 4th Division was sufficient to gain a victory over all the troops opposed to us." Even so, "It was understood . . . this was not to be mentioned to my men present," remembered Winslow, "i.e. to leave the men to understand that the whole force was near at hand in order to prevent the real fact getting to the enemy in any way."[1]

Shortly after the generals concluded their meeting, they set out to get the 1st Brigade into position to launch their assault at 8:30 P.M. According to Winslow, "Upton then directed me to fight my command and I returned with the two generals to where the brigade was halted and at once made all the dispositions and gave the orders which . . . became the order of battle." As Winslow did so, the last glow of twilight faded and finally disappeared. In a strange set of circumstances, as it got dark at around 7:30 P.M. it became apparent that there was no moon, the light from which might aid the troopers in making their movements. The moon had set that morning at around 10:00 and would not rise again until nearly 12:15 A.M., too late to be of any help to the soldiers preparing for the engagement.[2]

The Union commanders believed that Forts 2 and 3 were part of the main line of defenses that encompassed the Summerville Road. Winslow's earlier reconnaissance had demonstrated that the ground before Fort 3 was flatter than the steep and rugged slope that lay before Fort 2. It would be toward Fort 3 that the first wave of the night assault would be directed. If Fort 3 could be taken, the troops of the brigade could then charge down the road inside the enemy's line and capture the bridge—or so the Union commanders thought.[3]

While Winslow began moving his brigade out of the wooded valley and up the steep hillside to positions along the Summerville Road, Upton wished to substantiate Winslow's intelligence as to the position of the defenses. To verify the exact location of the western fort, and to drive in any pickets who might be stationed in advance and who might cause Winslow's dispositions to be revealed, Upton ordered out the 5th Iowa. According to Colonel Young of the 5th, "Companies A and F, under special direction of . . . Upton, opened the assault upon Columbus, charging upon the enemy's right and drawing their infantry and artillery fire." The remainder of the "regiment took a slight part in this engagement by driving in the enemy's outposts and skirmish line in their front and center."[4]

The "handsomely conducted charge" of Companies A and F of the 5th Iowa against the defenses near Fort 3 was never meant to capture the Confederate positions. Its purpose was simply to expose the enemy's location and draw their attention. After a sharp but brief confrontation, the two companies withdrew to the safety of a small valley where they "lay down, under fire from the enemy's artillery, and awaited further orders" alongside the rest of their regiment. "It was a tedious and tiresome wait for us as [we] were in such a cramped position, but we had to stand it," remembered Sergeant Conzett of the 5th's Company E. "To stand or even sit up, [we] would be sure to be killed or at least wounded."[5]

Eventually, as darkness obscured the landscape, the firing died down and a tense quiet prevailed along the Confederate lines. The Confederate commanders, not realizing that the 5th Iowa's charge was just a demonstration, believed they had stopped a Federal assault. "The enemy made several charges during the evening," reported Cobb afterward, "but was handsomely repulsed."[6]

Though Upton had been unable to discover Winslow's brigade during the afternoon, the Confederate forces occupying the area around Forts 2 and 3 had seen indications of movement on their flank throughout the evening. Cobb and his subordinates began to suspect that the long delay was to allow the entire Union force to get into position, and that when attacked, they might face ten thousand or more of the enemy. When the 5th Iowa made its demonstration, the fact that Federals were massing on the Confederate right was made plain. As the last traces of dusk slipped away, additional defenders were silently shifted north to reinforce the line.[7]

"While preparations were being made, darkness stole over the scene," remembered Winslow. "There was absolute quiet along the lines of the enemy. We might have been miles away so far as indications were manifested." His first priority was the placement of the brigade surgeon, Dr. William Robinson, who was ordered to set up his hospital in a depression not far from where the brigade would form.[8]

Soon afterward, Winslow directed Noble to dismount the six compa-

nies of the 3rd Iowa present (A, B, C, L, I, and K) and to align them facing
Fort 3 with their left flank anchored on the Summerville Road. Though
it was customary for cavalry, when fighting on foot, to leave the horses in
the charge of every fourth man, Winslow wanted every soldier he could
put into line, and his brigade was instructed to leave in the rear only every
eighth soldier. With its left flank abutting the Summerville Road, the 3rd
Iowa's soldiers spread out in a single rank along a ridge that extended per-
pendicular from the road facing Fort 3. The right of the line stopped adjacent to the left of where Companies E, L, and M of the 5th Iowa were deployed as skirmishers, in a little valley in advance of the remainder of their
regiment.[9]

In the meantime, as the part of the 3rd Iowa that was with Noble prepared for action, the balance of the regiment arrived in Girard. They had
been detached at Montgomery and had spent the last couple of days rac-
ing to catch up with their comrades. Their arrival was not known to either Noble or Winslow, however, and thus the detachment assumed their
responsibilities "as train guard for the night."[10]

The next regiment to be formed into line was the 10th Missouri. This
unit, led by Lieutenant Colonel Benteen, "mounted without the bugle sound"
and marched out of the wooded valley, up the hill to the Summerville
Road. Captain Hinrichs, in command of Company L, recalled: "We were
ordered to be quiet, not to speak aloud, and all noisy things such as tin
buckets and pans, were ordered to be thrown away. We halted and waited
for the signal; it got as dark as pitch—not a sound would be heard anywhere."[11] The regiment halted on the Summerville Road "in column of
fours, mounted, the front facing the direction of the bridge and not far from
and in rear of the line formed by the 3rd Iowa." According to Winslow,
"Benteen and his adjutant were at the head of his men. Captain Robert
McGlasson was in front, the senior officer of the two companies there."[12]

The last of the regiments under Winslow's direct command to be positioned was the 4th Iowa. Led by Lieutenant Colonel Peters, they came up
mounted on a road that led through a woods to the rear of the 3rd Iowa's
line. The 4th Iowa marched to where this "blind road" through the woods
intersected the Summerville Road close to the point where the head of
the 10th Missouri was positioned. The regiment then halted and remained
mounted. They were to act as the reserve.[13]

While the cavalry were being placed by Winslow, under the direction of
Upton, the guns of Rodney's battery spread out and took positions on the
surrounding hills. From there they could cover the assault and also confuse
the enemy by firing on them from different points. Rodney was also instructed to open the engagement by firing a salute at the proper time.[14]

Despite the tumultuous circumstances that surrounded it, the meeting

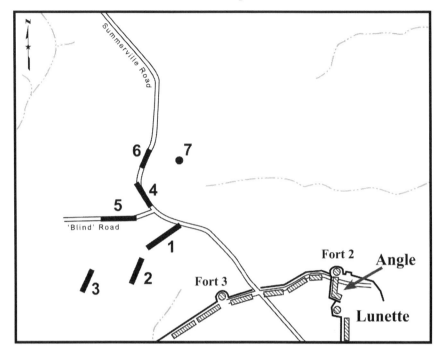

Map 6. Winslow's brigade moves into position, 8:00 P.M., April 16, 1865. (1) The 3rd Iowa dismounted with left anchored on road. (2) Companies E, L, and M of the 5th Iowa. (3) Remainder of the 5th Iowa. (4) The 10th Missouri mounted on road. (5) The 4th Iowa mounted on "Blind" Road. (6) The 4th U.S. waits with General Wilson. (7) Part of Rodney's battery.

between Wilson, Upton, and Winslow earlier in the evening had led to the development of a plan of attack of some novelty in Civil War combat. The plan pitted a Union cavalry division against a fortified enemy superior in numbers, shielded by a mile-and-a-half-long series of well-constructed entrenchments anchored by three heavy forts, protected by a large number of well-manned artillery, in complete darkness. Fortunately, the strategy was fairly simple. The Federal commanders believed that the Confederate entrenchments extended in front of them, across the Summerville Road, to a point west of Fort 3 located on the western side of the road. They believed that beyond Fort 3 the defenses curved back southward to encircle the Summerville Road inside a ring of earthworks. The 3rd Iowa would charge Fort 3, which lay on ground far less rugged than that in front of Fort 2 to the east of the road, would capture it, and would drive off the defenders from that part of the line. This movement would be followed by a mounted charge by the 10th Missouri, who would ride down the road, into the interior of the Confederate defenses, to the mouth of the bridge. The 10th Missouri was to capture the bridge and hold it until the 4th Iowa could be sent in, mounted, to support them. The bridge was the primary objective. According to Adjutant Scott of the 4th Iowa, "Both Upton and Winslow . . . ordered that no prisoners be taken, so that the bridge might be reached with the greatest speed." The men of the brigade were ordered to simply command the Confederates who might surrender to throw away their arms and to stay put. Any prisoners that might be taken were of secondary importance.[15]

In addition to the assault of Winslow's brigade on the Confederate right, Alexander, who was still waiting atop the hills to the southwest of Girard, would join the attack once he heard it commence. His attack would, it was hoped, break through the Confederate lines to the south near the bridge, or at least create sufficient pressure there to divert manpower away from the Confederate right, thereby making it easier for Winslow's troops to break through the lines and make a dash for the bridge. When all the troops were finally in position, and everything grew still in anticipation of the order to attack, the total Union force assembled to participate in the night assault numbered about 2,880 soldiers.[16]

Inside the Confederate lines, final preparations were completed to meet the enemy, which Cobb, Buford, and Von Zinken all expected would attack at any moment. Inside Fort 3, Confederate cannoneers manning three artillery pieces prepared to discharge their guns at the first sign of movement on the part of the 3rd and 5th Iowa cavalries who were formed in their front. Helping to man the fort and the surrounding works were the Columbus Government Mechanics and, possibly, soldiers from the 3rd Regiment and 4th Battalion Alabama Reserves.

Across the Summerville Road to the east, in Fort 2, the men of Clanton's Alabama Battery scanned the darkness for movement and prepared to pour shot and shell from their four cannons.[17] Alongside them, determined Confederate infantrymen, one of whom carried the second national flag of Austin's 14th Battalion Louisiana Sharpshooters, waited anxiously for any sign that the battle was beginning.[18] Just to the right of the fort, a single gun, possibly manned by cannoneers from Winston's Tennessee Battery, was loaded and pointed out the embrasure of a small redoubt into the inky blackness in the direction of the Federals on the Summerville Road.[19]

South of Fort 2, inside the Confederate's actual main line, members of the 1st and 2nd regiments of the Georgia State Line took position inside a series of rifle pits and trenches that formed an abrupt angle near the two-gun lunette (U-shaped redoubt). Inside the lunette, two Confederate artillery pieces, 12-pounder Napoleons, sat in positions that allowed their gunners to cover the rear of Fort 3, to the west of Summerville Road, and to rake the road with enfilading fire.[20]

Farther south, in the trenches just northeast of where the Columbus and Western Railroad ran through the lines, members of the 3rd Georgia Reserves watched patiently as the darkness gathered, while surrounding them and covering the rest of the line both north and south was a motley amalgamation of armed civilians. At the unfinished section of the line, near where the Summerville Road entered the defenses, soldiers of one battalion of the 7th Alabama Cavalry stood alongside members of the Russell County Reserves and the militia from Fort Mitchell. At about sunset, Waddell, who had been directing his batteries at the north end of the defenses, rode south, inspecting the lines as he passed. To the nervous soldiers, Waddell called out: "Men, this position must be held at all hazards." Recognizing a friend, Jacob Martin, among the group, Waddell halted and with assurance announced, "Martin, I know that you will hold it."[21]

Farther south, just to the north of Fort 1, members of Waddell's artillery battalion manned six rifled cannon, mostly Parrotts, which were stationed near Jackson Street. They were protected by a low set of hastily constructed earthworks forming an inner semicircle surrounding the entrance to the Franklin Street Bridge, but through which passed two streets that led to the bridge's mouth. Inside Fort 1, members of Barrett's 10th Missouri Battery manned four 12-pounder howitzers. Also inside the fort were members of one of the Georgia reserve regiments that had earlier proclaimed they would not fight, as well as a few veteran Confederate soldiers. Additionally, a guard of about fifty men was stationed at the entrance to the bridge.[22]

On the east end of the Franklin Street Bridge, Georgia and Alabama artillerymen, including members of Ward's (Cruse's) Alabama Battery who had escaped capture at Selma, manned a section of 12-pounder howitzers (two guns) under the supervision of the Georgia militia's chief of staff, General Robert Toombs. Toombs was famous for the dogged defense he and his brigade of Georgians had made against General Ambrose Burnside at the Battle of Sharpsburg in 1862. Here, as before, Toombs was charged with the defense of a bridge. The two howitzers were loaded with canister and pointed toward the bridge's exit in such a position as to allow the gunners to rake the bridge's roadway and blast any Federals who might attempt to cross the span into Columbus.[23]

Toombs was not the only prominent Georgian, other than Cobb, ready to make a stand on Georgia's western bank. Recently returned from the failed POW transfer negotiations in Florida was Colonel Charles Lamar, who while in transit back to southwest Georgia had learned that both Governor Brown and President Davis had finally approved the plans he had submitted two months earlier to make a series of blockade runs in exchange for Northern goods.[24]

Though some uncertainty remains as to the exact nature of Lamar's activities in Columbus during the days immediately prior to the battle, it is likely that the colonel hoped to coordinate his efforts with the maiden tour of the Confederate ironclad *Jackson,* which was nearing completion in Columbus in April 1865 and which was projected to take up active operations within a couple of weeks, or with the newly constructed torpedo boat *Viper.* Certainly, the unexpected appearance of an ironclad and torpedo boat at Apalachicola would have provided the perfect distraction for Lamar's two blockade runners to slip past the Federal warships and either run up the river or break out into the Gulf. It is also likely, however, that Lamar had simply come to Columbus as part of his responsibilities as an aide to Cobb, or to meet with him about the failed prisoner exchange.

Whatever his intentions, Lamar could not pass up the opportunity to scrap with the Federals. On the evening of April 16 he was given the task of organizing a small infantry unit, probably composed of civilians from the city, that would be held in reserve on the Georgia side of the Franklin Street Bridge. Also in reserve in Columbus were two detachments of the 7th Alabama Cavalry, one north and one south of town, to watch for any attempted amphibious crossing. Additionally, batteries were stationed in the cotton bale defenses at the east end of the railroad bridge and in the smoldering redoubt that covered the destroyed City Bridge.[25]

The rest of the units present, including the militias and civilian companies, Colonel J. C. Cole's Battalion, the City Defense Battalion, the Naval Works Battalion, Captain E. E. Arnold's Company, Colonel Thomas Dorough's command, the battalion from the 3rd Georgia Cavalry, Lieutenant Hunt's Dismounted Cavalry, Captain B. F. White's command, the local fire companies, and other units were put in positions at points all along the Confederate lines in Girard. In total, by the time darkness fell over the battlefield, the Confederate entrenchments were manned by approximately 3,300 defenders.[26]

For about forty-five minutes—from the time Federal forces finished moving into position until nearly 8:30—the hills of Girard were silent and dark. While many Confederate soldiers, inexperienced and unable to make anything of the inky blackness, sat in anxious anticipation of any sign of the enemy, the Union troopers waited with far less trepidation. Accustomed to war, some of the tired Northern veterans even took the opportunity to dismount and sleep. "After all arrangements were completed, the men . . . passed an hour in absolute rest, while Upton waited for the appointed minute with confidence and patience," remembered Wilson. "I allowed him the amplest latitude, but every detail of his plan was submitted for my supervision and approval."[27]

If things appeared to be going as planned within the Union ranks at the north side of Girard, such did not appear to be the case at the south. On the hills southwest of Girard, having received no word from Upton for many hours and without any sign of an engagement, Alexander "thought the attack had been abandoned." According to Lieutenant Yeoman, "Alexander waited till after nightfall for the charge to be made . . . [then] retired about six or seven hundred yards in the rear of his line" for the night.[28]

In Columbus, citizens who had heard and seen the afternoon's engagement climbed atop hills and rooftops to get a view of Girard. Near the navy yard in Columbus, citizens and naval officers watched the sky for flashes from the guns and listened intently for sounds that might reveal in the darkness what was happening across the river. Thus stood the two armies, Union and Confederate, in the pitch-black darkness, at approximately 8:30 P.M., ready to engage in battle over the fate of the city of Columbus.[29]

The Night Attack

Assault on Fort 3

Wrapped in shadows inside the Confederate lines, old men stood beside schoolboys, cavalrymen beside naval officers, and veterans beside hastily assembled militia, all watching in the intense darkness for any sign of the approach of the enemy. Most were there because they wanted to be, some because they were supposed to be, and a number because they were forced to be by a government that they felt had overstepped its bounds in a cause that was obviously lost. Stretched out in a thin line, the hope of Columbus, numbering just over three thousand men, prepared to defend a set of entrenchments stretching more than a mile from the Franklin Street Bridge in the south to Forts 2 and 3 on Ingersoll Hill to the north. Nervous fingers rested on readied triggers as many of the untrained and undisciplined citizen soldiers faced the frightening prospect of fighting an enemy they could not see.

According to Private John F. Benton of Emery's battery, the anxiousness of the untrained Southerners drove some to seek courage in the bottle, despite strict orders to the contrary. "I blush to say there was drinking, and lots of it," he recalled of that tense evening. Never one to drink "crazed or scared," Benton did not partake, preferring instead that "if death had to come . . . to see it with both eyes." Even so, he remembered, "it was in those days, kinder like it is now—many a poor fellow had to pour the spirits down to keep the spirits up."[1]

Within the Union lines, as the appointed time for the beginning of the engagement closed in, members of the six companies of the 3rd Iowa who were lying in front of Fort 3 waited in uneasy anticipation of the order to attack. Peering into the night, they could distinguish very little of the Confederate lines from the surrounding blackness. Quietly, the soldiers stuffed the extra ammunition they had been issued into their pockets. They checked and rechecked their equipment, making sure their magazines were filled and their cartridge boxes were within easy reach. Soon the officers of the regiment began to whisper to their men, informing them of Winslow's most recent order. The general had instructed the whole brigade to yell loudly as soon as the attack commenced in order to scare and confuse the enemy.[2]

Behind and to the right of the 3rd Iowa's line, the 5th Iowa lay in the position they had assumed after their earlier charge. Three companies of the 5th Iowa were deployed in a skirmish line in front of the regiment and immediately to the right of the 3rd Iowa. Disoriented by the darkness and believing that the skirmishers of the 5th Iowa were a part of the 3rd Iowa, two of Upton's staff officers mistakenly ordered them to assist in assailing the walls of Fort 3 as soon as the attack commenced. No order or message was ever relayed to the regiment's colonel, however, to inform him that his skirmishers would soon be advancing on the Confederate positions. Rapidly, the three companies were drawn together in the night and were held in readiness by their officers. "Companies, E, L, and M, being my advance skirmish line, were ordered forward without my knowledge," Colonel Young later reported, "and took part in the general assault."[3]

At approximately 8:30 P.M., just as Rodney's battery was preparing to fire the guns they thought would open the engagement, and to the surprise of the men of the 3rd and 5th Iowa who were lying in front of Fort 3, rockets streaked brilliantly skyward from the Confederate lines. Whether the rockets had been launched for signal purposes or to light the battlefield in order to give the defenders a chance to view the positions of the Federal troopers, a blizzard of artillery fire and musketry was then loosed from the entire curtain of Confederate defenses along the Summerville Road. "We saw several rockets fly up in the air; that was the signal, and the Rebs saw it also and knew it was now or never for them," recalled Sergeant Conzett of the 5th Iowa's Company E. "They at once opened every gun they had on us, and the rattle of their muskets was steady and regular."[4]

Once the rockets were launched the fight was on—there could be no turning back. The defenders opened up with everything they had. The three guns of Fort 3 commenced firing, as did the four guns of Clanton's battery in Fort 2. An additional gun stationed to the right of the eastern fort joined the bombardment, and all along the line Confederate infantry discharged their muskets into the ebony atmosphere toward their unseen foe.[5]

Though their fire was highly inaccurate because of the darkness, the Confederates discharged their weapons with spectacular intensity. "All of a sudden there was a shot, another, and in a second 10,000 more; the whole country seemed to be alive with demons," recalled Hinrichs, who, along with the 10th Missouri, was waiting on the Summerville Road just to the rear of the 3rd Iowa. "The first thing to break the stillness is a deafening volley of musketry and so very close that the flash lights up the woods all around us," recalled Captain Abraham of the 4th Iowa, "but after time enough to draw one long breath, bugles open and then the yell—tis wild!"[6]

When the firing commenced, the men of Winslow's brigade began to shout. According to Sergeant Chauncy Graham of the 4th Iowa, "The balance of the command . . . had orders to holler and make as much noise as possible." Winslow had ordered the brigade's buglers to scatter out so as to confuse the enemy by sounding the charge from different directions. For a few moments the countryside around northern Girard rang with the cries of the Union soldiers, but soon the nearness of the incoming Confederate missiles silenced the force. "Such a yell was never heard, but we did not yell long," admitted Hinrichs. "The next sound brought the balls of the enemy by the thousands over our heads and the shells moved their way in every direction, leaving a fiery streak behind them. This was the first time that I saw shelling during night time. It is a beautiful but awful spectacle."[7]

Many of the Federal cavalrymen believed that by their shouting they were exposing themselves needlessly to injury, though this is unlikely given the shroud of darkness that enveloped them. "The Rebels commenced shelling us from elevated forts on each side of us," explained a particularly concerned Sergeant Graham, "they knowing where to throw their shells by our hollering."[8]

With the engagement having begun prematurely, there was confusion within the lines of the 3rd and 5th Iowa for a few moments. Some men of the 3rd Iowa, "forgetting their orders . . . began firing." The troopers of both regiments pressed themselves against the ground in order to avoid the incoming projectiles. "When the Rebel cannons opened on us with grape, canister, and shell, you ought to have seen us hug mother earth for a few minutes," remembered Corporal George Healey of the 5th Iowa's Company E. At the same instant, Rodney ordered the 4th U.S. Artillery to bombard the Confederate positions. According to Sergeant Conzett, also of Company E, Rodney's artillery "kept up a steady fire until they heard us charge, then they stopped, fearing they would fire into us."[9]

In an attempt to regain control of the situation, the officers of the 3rd Iowa frantically called to their men to hold their fire so as not to give away their position. The effort was in vain. Despite calls from their officers, the Union troopers could no longer be restrained. According to Private John C. Leach of the 3rd Iowa's Company D, it was at about this point when "Captain [Thomas J.] Miller started along the front of the Company and gave the order to cease firing."[10]

Miller had only recently taken command of Company D. He was noted to have remarked upon reenlistment with the regiment as a veteran, shortly before the start of the campaign, that "he should never return alive." The opening shots of the night assault would fulfill Miller's prediction. According to Private Leach, "Just then, this battery to our left opened on us sending a cannon ball right down the line striking Captain Miller, tearing away one side of his body. . . . Then we were ordered forward and only a very few of the company knew that the captain was hit, and no other officer took command of the company."[11]

The men of the three companies of the 5th Iowa, on the 3rd Iowa's right, had no orders to hold their fire and blazed away at the enemy positions. The sight of their firing and the anxiousness of the men in the 3rd Iowa's line was too much. Despite the best efforts of the officers to get them to stop, the 3rd Iowa joined the firefight. Realizing that, like it or not, the battle was on, within a few moments of the Confederates opening fire, Noble ordered his men to charge.[12] "The dismounted cavalrymen, without a moment's hesitation, rushed from their concealment, elbow to elbow, to the attack. The white road through the works was their sole guide and directrix," observed General Wilson. "The starlight was so faint, however, that nothing could be clearly seen except the flash of firearms. The roar of artillery and musketry was continuous and appalling."[13]

The troopers of the 3rd Iowa, followed by the men of the three companies of the 5th Iowa, leaped from their positions and in a single rank surged forward toward Fort 3 in an all-out dash. As they ran they worked the actions of their Spencers and yelled at the top of their lungs. "Up and at 'em boys! Get in them works and don't stop until you are in, and there hold them," shouted the officers of the 5th Iowa as they charged toward the enemy lines. "Up and away on full run we rushed, our carbines in full play, and they were pumped never before faster," recalled Conzett. "Their shell and shot, as well as their musket or infantry balls, flew screaming over our heads. . . . Their rapid fire from . . . their entrenchments lit up the darkness and made the night look bright as day, but it blinded us so that no doubt our aim was bad, but we shot straight ahead and just as fast as we could work our carbines."[14]

Rapidly the Union troopers plunged into the swale before Fort 3 and began to battle their way up the slope. The cannoneers inside the fort continued to load and fire frantically, but "their guns were not depressed low enough" and they "fired so high that they did but little harm to . . . [the] dismounted men." The bottom of the swale was thirty-two vertical feet lower than the ridge atop which the fort sat, only approximately two hundred yards distant. This depression, in conjunction with the darkness, sheltered the advancing Federals to a large degree from the effects of much of the Confederate fire. "Darkness was their best protection, and, being veterans of four years' experience, they continued their advance unshaken and almost unharmed," observed Wilson, who was watching from nearby. "Although the rattle and roar of the conflict made night hideous, it was far more noisy than destructive."[15]

"The air was alive" with the sights and sounds of missiles that screamed across the darkened field as the Union troopers clambered up the hill and pressed forward toward the parapets of the fort. "Such musketry [and] cannonading beat the devil," recalled Healey of the 5th Iowa, adding, "it was dark when the ball commenced, [and] the heavens were in a perfect blaze— a sheet of fire." Hastily, the Confederates shot into the darkness toward the sounds of the Union soldiers scrambling to gain the crest of the hill.[16]

For several minutes there was one unending roar from the fort and surrounding works, but then, as the Federal troopers began to gain the top and approach the breastworks, the Union fusillade was unleashed. Soon a perfect hail of lead from the Federals' Spencers forced the defenders to cower behind their pounded entrenchments. Under the pressure, the Confederates began to break and flee into the darkness. The 3rd and 5th Iowa pushed on, and "before ten minutes had passed they closed in and swarmed over the outlying entrenchments and had them firmly in their possession." Blasting away at an incredible rate with their Spencers, the troopers mounted the ramparts and quickly "cleaned the works," while "the defenders fell back in confusion."[17]

"With deadly Spencer guns [we] drove [the] Rebel breastworks and the day was ours—or should I say, the night!" recalled Healey. As the men of the 3rd and 5th Iowa scattered the defenders of the fort and rifle pits, the firing from both sides died down. Noble and the other Federal commanders all believed they had penetrated the Confederates' main line. In reality, they had only secured the curtain to the actual main line, which was obscured by the shroud of night and the sparsely wooded terrain. The lull in the firing by the Confederates near Fort 2 was to allow those escaping from the first line to fall back into the actual main line of earthworks. The Confederate main line was still silently awaiting the order to open fire and was still unknown to the Union force.[18]

Some of the defenders east of the Summerville Road, when they witnessed the vicious firefight and capture of Fort 3, became demoralized. Though there was no way to see the enemy, they accurately surmised that they were massing again out in the dark. They also realized that there was no way they could hope to stand up to the overwhelming volume of fire produced by the Federals' Spencers. Indeed, because of the constant rattle of the Union repeaters, many of the Confederates quickly became convinced that they were facing an enemy force vastly superior in numbers.[19]

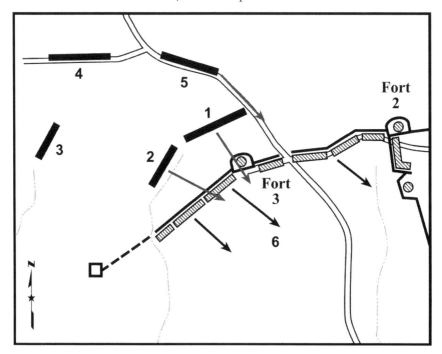

Map 7. Assault on Fort 3, 8:30 P.M., Sunday, April 16, 1865. (1) The 3rd Iowa assaults and captures Fort 3 with help from the three companies (2) of the 5th Iowa. (3) The remainder of the 5th Iowa stays out of action. (4) Men of the 4th Iowa cheer loudly as the firing begins. (5) When the firing dies away, General Wilson orders the 10th Missouri to charge through the works and capture the bridge. (6) Confederates flee south and to their main works.

During the moments following the capture of Fort 3 west of the Summerville Road, confusion reigned on both sides. Fleeing Confederates ran southward along the Summerville Road and eastward to the protection of the main line of entrenchments. Many of the Federal troopers, disorganized and scattered in the assault, tried with mixed success to re-form to the rear of the captured fort. Private Leach of the 3rd Iowa's Company D fell into a deep ravine filled with blackberry briars.[20] After thrashing in the tangle for some time, he extricated himself and climbed out of the ditch, only to find himself alone. Excited, bleeding, and severely disoriented, he turned toward the noise of the shooting continuing from Fort 2 and "started up a gradual rise taking . . . direction by the firing and flash of the guns." Little did he realize that, instead of hurrying toward his comrades, he was headed directly for the Confederate main line. "I . . . soon reached a breastwork and heard men talking, then I was sure I had caught up with the line," remembered Leach. "I heard a man rail out, 'Here, where are you going? Now you get back into that ditch, or I will box your jaws.' . . . "Well, I thought that curious language for any of our officers to use," Leach explained, "but yet I did not suspect it not being our line."

> So I climbed up on the loose dirt and then saw a rifle pit full of men. I stooped down to slip into the ditch among them and that brought my eyes closer . . . and I saw that they had on gray hats and coats. I was on the point of saying, "Well you drove them out, did you boys?" But when I saw where I was, I didn't say it. They didn't say anything to me; they hadn't noticed me, in fact. I saw their heads were turned and they were all looking at the tussle of the officer and the soldier who started to run. After realizing what I had run into, my next thought was Andersonville, the next was to make my get away . . . so I raised up, turned round, stepped down off the breastwork, started slowly and cautiously back till I thought I was out of sight, then I started to run. . . . Where I got clear of the downed brush, you had better bet I tried my speed. I don't think there was a horse in the regiment that could have kept with me.[21]

When they ceased firing, the men of the 3rd and 5th Iowa instantly disappeared into the night. Unable to determine what the Federals who had captured Fort 3 were doing or where they might be, the Confederate command began to fear that they were attempting to slip quietly down the Summerville Road toward the bridge. In an effort to establish whether such was the case, several Confederate units were ordered out of the trenches to meet the enemy. Included in this number were the soldiers of the 3rd Georgia Reserves, including eighteen-year-old Private Charles Henderson of Company F, who at the order to leave the safety of the rifle pits was reported to have retorted in disgust: "They will get me now."

It did not take long for the officers in command of the maneuver to think better of the situation and return the troops to the protection of the defenses. The blackness of the night, the rough ground, and the inexperience of some of the soldiers severely inhibited the coordination of the movement and negated any possible benefit to leaving the protection of the rifle pits. "After a moment we were ordered: 'Fall to the trenches,'" Henderson remembered. He also remembered how, even at that early stage in the battle, the Confederates were beginning to anticipate the worst. "Henry Greene of Chattahoochee County stood at my left, a brave boy," recounted Henderson. "He said to me: 'If I get killed, I want you to take care of me.' I said the same to him."[22]

12

The Night Attack

"A Speedy Journey to Hell"

Under the impression, because of the lull in the firing, that the Confederate defenses had been penetrated and that its defenders were fleeing, Wilson, back out on the Summerville Road, could not help but involve himself in the engagement, and "personally ordered Benteen with the 10th Missouri, in column of fours, to enter the captured works and follow the road . . . to the bridge." With Benteen in the lead, first at a trot, then at a gallop, the column of the 10th Missouri started south along the Summerville Road, watching carefully through the darkness in order to stay on the faintly discernible path.[1]

Winslow was on the Summerville Road near where Noble's men were re-forming behind the captured fort. Upton was riding close by, trying to establish for certain if the Confederate defenses were broken and whether it was safe to order the 10th Missouri forward. Neither Winslow nor Upton, who were directing the actions of the 3rd and 5th Iowa inside the captured defenses, knew that Wilson had already given the order to the 10th Missouri to commence their attack.[2]

As they galloped toward the point where the road entered the works, to the shock and horror of the men of the 10th Missouri as well as Upton, Winslow, and the troopers of the 3rd and 5th Iowa, Cobb ordered the Confederate soldiers manning the main line of entrenchments to open up. Instantly, the flash of musketry illuminated the field and the Confederate bullets zipped over the road and rattled into the woods to the west. The piercing sound of artillery cut the night, and the gunners blasted the Summerville Road area with enfilading fire. The two-gun lunette, placed so as to rake the road, and batteries of artillery farther south all targeted the avenue over which the 10th Missouri would shortly pass. Strangely, however, Captain Clanton drastically overestimated the range of the road and ordered his battery, stationed in Fort 2, "to commence firing at an estimated distance of fifteen hundred yards"—more than three times the actual distance to the enemy.[3]

Already surprised by the realization that there yet remained a well-defended set of fortifications, Upton experienced further consternation when the head of the 10th Missouri emerged unexpectedly out of the darkness, riding fast toward him and directly into the flanking fire of the Confederates. "The order came for us to charge," remembered Hinrichs of the 10th Missouri. "[It is] a sweet thing, I can tell you, to charge the enemy works when it is dark as pitch, and you don't know where and what they are, particularly sweet when every second your eyes are blinded by the blue light of the shells exploding all round you and passing within four or five feet of the ground across the road you have to travel, not speaking of the grapes, canister and small bullets which . . . you can not see but only hear whizzing by, or striking trees or something else."[4]

Within the few seconds between the time he caught sight of the approaching 10th Missouri and when they rode up to where he sat astride his horse, Upton took in the situation and pondered what to do. He knew that if they continued, the mounted column would have to pass for three quarters of a mile or more down the road while the fire from the Confederate lines blasted their flank. He also knew that even if they could penetrate the inner set of works farther south, from there to the bridge they would have to run a gauntlet of resistance. Having had only seconds to reach a determination, Upton called over the roar of the battle to Benteen as he passed to halt his regiment. It was a calamitous decision.[5]

When the head of Benteen's regiment came to an abrupt halt, the following companies smashed into them. Confusion, then panic, soon followed as horses and riders crashed together and reeled in the darkness. The galloping rear companies piled into those ahead of them. Unit cohesion in the center and rear of the regiment was immediately lost. Officers began shouting to one another and to their men to try to rally the regiment, but it was no use. Still under the heavy fire of the Confederate defenders in the trenches, fort, and lunette on their flank, the regiment began to break up within moments, each trooper trying to get off the road and out of danger.[6]

"Well, while we were a-going, all of a sudden the column in front stopped," recalled Hinrichs, who was in the middle of the chaos. "I heard some holler: 'Here is no road.' Others hollered, 'go to the right,' others . . . 'go to the left.' In short, the company . . . in my front got tangled up." With the exception of the two lead companies, the 10th Missouri fell apart. "I turned to where the most went, to the right," remembered Hinrichs, but

Fig. 12. Lieutenant Colonel Frederick Benteen. Courtesy Massachusetts Commandery, MOLLUS, and the U.S. Army Military History Institute.

"the company in my rear charged in on me. . . . To add to this confusion, it happened that a shell fell among us killing three horses and one man. At the same time, a tremendous fire was opened . . . with small arms. . . . The bullets were coming thick and fast. The enemy now commenced . . . to treat us with shell and canister. . . . They came by the basket full. Several officers asked me to take the men away from there and reform. . . . We tried to retrace our steps, but were so mixed up that we took a road leading direct to the fort of the enemy, who . . . sent a half dozen shells whizzing over our heads."[7]

Seeing the confusion that immediately gripped the majority of the 10th Missouri, Upton second-guessed his initial order. While riding ahead to the bridge was dangerous, it was even more dangerous to remain exposed out on the road. A quick survey of the regiment told that the damage was already done. Only the lead two companies retained any composure. Shouting above the noise, Upton commanded Benteen to "detach two companies to carry out the mission which had been entrusted to the whole regiment." The two lead companies (I and K), under the guidance of Captain McGlasson, "charged furiously down the . . . road leading to the bridge over the Chattahoochee."[8]

As McGlasson and Companies I and K rode into the darkness, Benteen immediately set about trying to rally his soldiers. Winslow, hoping to salvage what he could of the battle plan, galloped over and "directed Benteen to dismount the other companies of his regiment" and prepare to make a dismounted charge toward the Confederate position. "Benteen repeated the order 'prepare to fight on foot,' but found that the column had been thrown into some confusion by the constant and terrible fire of the enemy and had edged off or obliqued into the woods on the right of the road." Within moments, despite Benteen's urgent orders, what remained of the regiment broke and fled to the shelter of the forest to the west, and in other directions. The usually quiet Benteen flew into a rage and began to curse violently at his skedaddling troopers.[9]

Benteen was not the only officer of the 10th Missouri incensed by the rapidly deteriorating situation. Confused and disoriented, in a futile attempt to regain command of his company, Hinrichs inadvertently led the remainder of his men not toward safety but toward Fort 2, whose gunners had by this time corrected their range. Exposed and under fire, Hinrichs could not maintain control of his soldiers. "We were hardly formed when a solid shot struck right between us," he remembered. "The men stood. A second afterward, a shell struck and exploded within four feet of my horse, covering myself and company with mud. The most of the men broke . . . I found myself left with a half dozen men. I was never so mad in my life."[10]

If Hinrichs thought for a moment that he might receive some assistance from his commander, Benteen, he was sorely mistaken. Shortly after the breakup of the regiment, as Benteen rode past, Hinrichs reported to him that in his company "several of the men were wounded and horses killed." Benteen, irate at the conduct of his soldiers, shouted angrily at Hinrichs and the surrounding cavalrymen, "I'll give a god damn, if the last god damn one gets killed." Equally frustrated by the situation, those troopers who overheard the colonel jeered back at their commander and "wished him a speedy journey to hell."[11]

The Confederate main line, plainly visible now from the flash of the guns, maintained their fire and continued blasting into the darkness toward the Summerville Road. In particular, the cannons of Clanton's battery inside Fort 2 and the two Napoleons stationed behind the lunette stood out as major obstacles to the continuation of the Union plan. The 10th Missouri in chaos, Winslow again turned his attention toward Noble and the mostly re-formed 3rd Iowa, whom he hoped might be able to silence the guns and secure a foothold in the earthworks. According to Noble, "My detachment was now ordered to 'go for the battery'—upon which I gave the command so as to make a left wheel of the whole line." Swinging to their left, the soldiers turned toward the newly discovered foe. Even though "the ground over which this evolution had to be performed was very much broken," within a few moments the troopers of Noble's 3rd Iowa and parts of the 5th Iowa re-formed parallel with the Summerville Road facing the fort and lunette.[12]

When they reached that position, Noble ordered the charge and the "men went forward with a cheer, passing in the profound darkness over fences, ditches and sloughs, with no other guide than the light and roar of the Rebels' fire." While Noble and Winslow could see the muzzle flashes of the Confederates opposite them, they could tell nothing of the ground between the Summerville Road and the earthworks. From all indications, the enemy fire came from a line of trenches that appeared to be directly ahead on ground that rose slightly from their position, and which was between two and three hundred yards distant. This, however, was not the case.[13]

As soon as Noble's line started forward they began to descend into a deep ravine, which at its deepest point lay almost forty vertical feet below the Confederate trenches. Noble's troopers plunged ahead rapidly, and once they neared the bottom they found themselves safe from the fire of the Confederates, who, unable to see their enemy clearly, aimed blindly in the direction of the Summerville Road and overshot their targets. The ravine had, as Noble remembered, "an almost impassable swamp at the bottom and immediately beyond on the opposite hill was an abatis of pines felled outward from the works . . . with the limbs broken, sharpened, and interlaced."[14]

Led by Noble, the Iowans "scrambled across the ravine and through the marshy brook, and then rose through the slashing on the slope of the works." Winslow, eager to observe the movement, followed Noble "until he entered the slashing" and then turned back to see to the rest of his brigade. Upton also joined the movement and rode forward with the troops, directing the action at the right of the 3rd Iowa's line. Alerted by the cheers of the Union troopers, "the enemy, apparently expecting the new attack, now increased their fire." According to Adjutant Scott, "From the vast noise they made, it seemed as if the Rebels would annihilate the last of their assailants, but all of their fire was still too high."[15]

Upon reaching the slashing of downed trees one hundred yards in depth, the advance of Noble's regiment slowed dramatically as the troopers tried to work their way through the entanglements. The fire from the Confed-

Fig. 13. Colonel John W.
Noble. Courtesy Mark Warren.

erates continued, the bullets clattering amid the timbers. Within moments, what organization the 3rd Iowa had retained during its charge broke up. Men stumbled and fell among the tangle, and those who came out at the far end did so in small, scattered groups and "supposed that their comrades were destroyed." When Noble reached the far side of the slashing, he tried to lead his regiment forward to assail the battlements. To his consternation, however, few men seemed to be emerging from the slashing, and within moments Noble came to the conclusion that his regiment had been decimated by the terrible Confederate fire.[16]

Believing his regiment had been cut to pieces, Noble ordered his men to fall back to the Summerville Road. Back down into the slashing and then through the ravine scrambled the part of the 3rd Iowa that could be readily rallied. The attack had failed, or so Noble thought. What he did not realize at that moment was that much of the unit was still alive but was badly scattered while fighting its way through the slashing. Even as Noble and part of the regiment fell back, fighting that concentrated around a series of rifle pits near the south corner of Fort 2 raged on.[17]

Immediately south of Fort 2, between it and the lunette, lay a short

Fig. 14. Private Andrew W. Tibbets earned the Medal of Honor for his actions at Columbus. Courtesy Bill Elswick Collection, U.S. Army Military History Institute.

stretch of entrenchments that made a sharp angle near its south end. It was there, while most of the 3rd Iowa had been forced to fall back, that under the supervision of Upton, "parts of nearly, if not quite all the companies engaged, gained a lodgment in the works." Under the heavy covering fire of their Spencer repeaters, the disorganized but determined troopers of the 3rd Iowa "crowned the works" and smashed through the Confederate line. Federal soldiers surged into the interior of the entrenchments. One group, led by Captain Samuel McKee, turned immediately on the nearby fort and charged. The movement was short lived, however. The artillerymen of Clanton's Alabama Battery inside the fort continued their destructive work, and their infantry support opened a withering storm of musketry on the Union party forcing them to fall back, but not before Private Andrew W. Tibbets of the 3rd Iowa managed to capture the flag of Austin's 14th Battalion Louisiana Sharpshooters along with the sergeant who bore it.[18]

Unfortunately for Tibbets, however, the capture went far from smoothly.

After forcing the surrender of the standard and bearer, Tibbets was suddenly blinded by the nearby flash of artillery from Fort 2. His vision completely impaired, and caught with his prisoner and trophy between the lines, according to his company commander, "Tibbets had to go through an ordeal which is almost beyond human endurance." Relying on his other senses, and with his prisoner in tow, Tibbets groped and stumbled his way back to the safety of his own lines. Though he would later earn the Medal of Honor for his actions, the episode left him so incapacitated that he had to be led around by his fellow soldiers for nearly a week after the engagement before finally being admitted to a hospital, where his eyesight slowly returned.[19]

While some of the Confederate defenders near the angle in the entrenchments skedaddled at the first sign that the line had been broken, enough of a resistance was established to push back the Federals, and a savage firefight developed as the Confederates tried to retake the works. From positions on opposite sides of the rifle pits, Union and Confederate soldiers exchanged a brief but intense fire, each determined to hold onto the trench line. Exposed and without additional support, many of the Union soldiers abandoned the rifle pits. "Considerable portions of [Companies] 'A' 'B' [and] 'C'" of the 3rd Iowa took the prisoners they had captured in their assault and started back toward the Summerville Road. The remainder doggedly held on, obstinately vying with the Confederates for possession of the angle.[20]

In the meantime, Winslow sent a messenger back to Lieutenant Colonel Peters of the 4th Iowa, who with his regiment had been "awaiting in column of fours, orders to charge the enemy and gain possession of the bridge." Wasting no time, Peters and the 4th Iowa started "forward at a walk," mounted, on the Summerville Road. When the head of the column reached the point where the road passed to the interior of the abandoned first line "directly opposite of the fort," they were met by one of Upton's staff. Following the instructions of the officer, "the 1st Battalion . . . and the 2nd . . . were dismounted and the 3rd Battalion under Maj. Dee [was] ordered to remain mounted and await orders."[21]

"The First Battalion, led by Captain [Lot] Abraham, and the Second, by Captain [Newell] Dana, ran down the road to a point a little lower than that recently occupied by the Third Iowa." There Abraham met Upton and Winslow and was questioned about the whereabouts of Peters. Abraham had thought that Peters was right behind and would lead the detachment. He did not realize that Peters had stayed behind to oversee the deployment of the remainder of the regiment. "Where is he?" demanded Winslow of Abraham, who, after a moment of hesitation, admitted that he did not know. Wasting no time, Upton interjected, "Who is the next in rank?" "I am," responded Abraham. "You'll do!"[22]

"Then followed my instructions," remembered Abraham, "mingled with the wildest oaths man could utter." Winslow commanded Abraham and the two battalions to "pass the slashing and abatis and charge through the line, turn to the right, and push forward inside the works as rapidly as possible to the bridge." His orders received, without hesitation Abraham and his men hastened down the road toward the position from which his attack would begin. According to Winslow, "While these companies were passing, I repeated the orders to the other officers and men constantly as they went and always ended by saying, 'Go for the bridge; do not stop to take prisoners.'" By the general's exhortations it was made clear to the passing troopers that the fight was to be a "knock down, drag out." Even Upton "joined in repeating to the remaining companies as they passed 'Go for the bridge,' and added 'Charge 'em.'"[23]

When Abraham and the head of the column reached the designated spot, the two battalions of the 4th Iowa immediately faced toward the enemy and set off down the slope toward the ravine. As they did, many confused and disoriented soldiers of the 3rd Iowa and the three companies of the 5th Iowa, seeing the advance of a Federal line, which they supposed in the darkness must be their own, "bravely took position to the left of the Fourth, and joined in the charge."[24]

As they had done during the 3rd Iowa's first assault on the Confederate main line, Upton and Winslow followed the troopers of the 4th Iowa down the slope, shouting instructions to them until they reached the ravine and the slashing, then started back toward the Summerville Road. "Boys, go for the bridge—don't stop to take prisoners, they are all ours anyhow—they can't get away, but kill, and cripple, and crush all opposition. Don't stop till you get to the bridge!" Winslow's piercing voice rang out. "They have a few guns up there in that fort yet, but they might fire away till hell freezes over & not hurt anybody." The generals' were not the only voices ringing above the din. "The battle-cry was *Selma!*" recalled Adjutant Scott of the 4th Iowa. "With great cheers the officers and men plunged into the ravine and up the slope, finding ways among the fallen trees as if by instinct, and still under the fire of all the guns and of the rifle-pits in their front not held by the Third Iowa."[25]

The dismounted men of the 4th Iowa, their ranks strengthened along the way by the lost soldiers of other regiments, marched into the ravine, slogged through the creek, and then, while blasting away with their Spencers, worked carefully through the slashing and "crawled up to within a

Fig. 15. Captain Lot Abraham.
Courtesy 4th Iowa Cavalry
Association.

few yards" of the enemy's trenches. To protect themselves from the enemy fire, many of the troopers of the 4th Iowa, upon entering the slashing, crawled upon their stomachs while pumping away with their repeaters in hopes of breaking the Confederates' resolve with their overwhelming firepower. This slower method of approach also allowed them to retain some measure of organization and allowed some time for those who got caught in the entanglements to fight their way out and catch up with the regiment.[26]

Within the Confederate lines there was consternation bordering on panic. A sense of impending doom was manifested ever more intensely as the inexperienced reserves and citizen soldiers prepared to meet another, more determined attack. The repeated cracking of the enemy's carbines and the distinctive thud of the bullets as they slammed into the breastworks, pitching dirt into the air, convinced many of the Confederates that they would at any moment be overwhelmed by a numerically far superior force. "I heard the minie balls Sh-Sh, hiss near my ears," remembered Private Henderson of the 3rd Georgia, "and the clanking of the swords of the

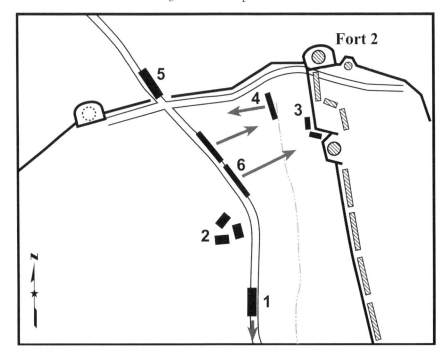

Map 8. Assault on the Confederate main line, night, Sunday, April 16, 1865. (1) Mc-Glasson's two companies charge south, while the remainder of the 10th Missouri (2) flees into the woods west of the road. (3) The 3rd Iowa assaults the works and captures a portion of the defenses, but the remainder of the regiment (4) and Noble fall back to the road. (5) The 4th Iowa is ordered forward. At the entrance to the works, two battalions are dismounted. (6) The 1st and 2nd battalions of the 4th Iowa assail the defenses near the lunette and the angle.

Federal cavalrymen in front of me. The whole battle line of the Confederates popped like firecrackers," he observed, and "the battery cut off the tops of many pines in front of me."[27]

Despite the impassioned pleas of Von Zinken, who was riding along the lines, the prospect of being suddenly rushed upon by an unseen enemy amplified the anxiety of the Confederates. Soon the Federal soldiers themselves began to harass the defenders. "Throw down your gun and surrender," some Union troopers crawling toward the Confederates shouted. "It was too dark to tell friend from foe," remembered one Confederate reserve, and soon it became hard to distinguish the Confederate orders from those being shouted by the enemy. "An officer rode in front of me," remembered Henderson, and ordered, "Fire oblique to the right." "That's a Yankee," announced an observing Confederate, and Henderson recalled, "I have always thought it was so, for it uncovered the fire on the Federals." Primed by confusion, disaster needed only to be catalyzed by the charge of the shadowy figures inching ever closer to the Confederate battlements.[28]

When within easy reach of the Confederate ramparts, Captain Abraham, who was leading the Union advance, heard voices from within the trenches that questioned, "And who are you?" "Who are you?" responded Abraham. "We're 3rd Georgia, we're Confederates," the bewildered Southerners replied. Turning to his own men, Abraham shouted, "Go for 'em."[29] At that the emboldened Federals sprang to their feet. Whether spontaneously or otherwise, when the troopers of the 4th Iowa stood and dashed forward through the last line of sharpened stakes and onto the earthworks and the parapets of the two-gun lunette, they shouted loudly a battle cry of "Selma!" According to one Union trooper, when the order was finally given "we swept down on them like an avalanche covering their works."[30] "The obstinate possession of the Third [Iowa] and this new assault were too much for the enemy. They broke from all the works in the vicinity of the lunette . . . and the new assailants were quickly on the parapets . . . and below, crying 'Surrender! Throw down your arms!' to the dismayed Confederates."[31]

"The main body of the enemy, dismounted and acting as infantry, crawled up to within a few yards of our line," recalled Cobb. "Several bodies . . . then charged our line at several points," and "when our men rose to fire, the infantry of the enemy poured a deadly fire into our line and then charged." The civilians and city companies immediately gave way to the Federal troopers who clambered up the earthen walls and tumbled into the trenches. Despite the violence of the charge, Cobb, who was riding nearby, could see that the "two regiments of State Line [and] one and a half regiments of reserves was in firmly and unshaken." For a moment the Confederate lines near him held, and Cobb erroneously "supposed that the day was won." It would not take long for his supposition to be proved incorrect, however. Soon "it was discovered that the Columbus Mechanics had given way." According to Cobb, "The enemy pressed through the brush, and in an instant all was confusion."[32]

The Federals streamed through the gaps created near the lunette and at the angle in the rifle pits where the savage struggle to retain the works had continued to rage right up until the 4th Iowa made its assault. The rapidity with which the envelopment occurred caught some of the Confederate defenders off guard. When the Union soldiers poured over the embrasure, they met the surprised Confederates at close quarters, and a struggle for several flags ensued. A bitter scrap took place over one of the banners that was ultimately captured by Private John Hays of the 4th Iowa's Company F.

Hays "captured the standard and bearer, who tore it from the staff and tried to escape." The bearer "fired two shots from his revolver, wounding one man of my regiment at my side," Hays recounted. Another flag, belonging to the "Dillard Greys," was captured by Corporal Richard Morgan of the 4th Iowa's Company A.[33]

The successful charge of the 4th Iowa began the collapse of the Confederate battle line. Most of the Confederates manning the northern end of the entrenchments immediately broke and ran for the rear. Men from the convalescent companies, the Columbus Mechanics, the Georgia and Alabama reserves, and the Georgia State Line at once took to their heels. The rout was wild and general. Confederate officers and enlisted alike, realizing that their only route of escape lay across the Franklin Street Bridge or the railroad bridge, struck out at breakneck speed, leaving behind everything that could encumber their movements. "They had broken the lines on our left, and were just coming up . . . undisturbed, but when we began to cross fire, they returned the fire right up to the trenches," remembered Private Alphonza Jackson of the Georgia State Line's Company G. Jackson, who was among the first to abandon his compatriots and take to flight, explained: "We, of course, leaped out of our ditches and made for the bridges and while running down a steep slant, I remember running against Lieutenant Colonel [Beverly] Evans and knocking off his hat. I recognized him by his voice; I never stopped though to pick it up for him, for every fellow was for self now, and while running through a field in the darkness, I ran into a gully over my head. . . . We finally came to a fence, I remember that I climbed to the top of it and being almost out of breath, just fell off."[34]

While the 4th Iowa was attacking the north end of the Confederate defenses, Companies I and K of the 10th Missouri Cavalry, under Captain McGlasson, continued south along the Summerville Road in search of the bridge over the Chattahoochee. Riding hard and without firing, McGlasson's troopers passed down the road virtually undetected by the Confederates, who were focused on repulsing the charges at the north end of their line. It was not long before McGlasson, "much to his surprise . . . found himself in front of an inner line of fortifications" and, according to Wilson, "rode coolly through an opening in their parapet, lined on either side with Confederate soldiers, who evidently mistook his command for a part of their own forces." McGlasson's "apparent temerity deceived the enemy and, mistaken in the darkness for their own troops, they were permitted to pass without resistance" past the battery stationed near Fort 1 and down the hill to the bridge.[35]

Upon reaching the bridge, McGlasson's cavalry surprised and captured the fifty men acting as bridge guards as well as other Confederate soldiers and officers. McGlasson then dispatched Lieutenant Frederick Owen, one of his subordinates, to secure the far end of the bridge, which he did by taking a detachment on a mounted charge through the long, dark interior of the turpentine-saturated span. Upon arrival at the Columbus end of the Franklin Street Bridge, Owen and his men quickly surrounded the artillerymen manning the two howitzers posted there and forced them to surrender without a contest.[36]

If there was a moment of satisfaction for McGlasson after securing his objective, it did not last long. As soon as the bridge guard and the section at the far end of the bridge were captured, the misunderstanding that had shielded his men from attack up to that point disappeared and Confederate forces stationed nearby immediately raised the alarm. Within a few moments, "the enemy discovering what had happened . . . began to close in upon him, firing from all sides." As he was becoming enveloped, McGlasson looked for support from either the remainder of his regiment or from the 4th Iowa, whom he believed would be following close behind. To his disappointment, however, there was no sign of reinforcements.[37]

"Having no shelter, and seeing that he must lose his command or ride back the way he came, [McGlasson] . . . preferred the ride." He hurriedly recalled the detachment of troopers under Owen, and "finding his situation critical released the fifty prisoners he had taken." Fortunately for the men of his two companies, McGlasson recognized the danger of the situation and pulled out before Confederate forces had time to mass and overwhelm his party. Having regrouped, McGlasson "led a tearing gallop back through the lines, all the time under fire," with the loss of but one man mortally wounded and a couple captured. Again outside the battlements, McGlasson and his troopers galloped back up the Summerville Road toward where their ride had begun.[38]

Although McGlasson's efforts had failed to secure the Franklin Street Bridge, they did have a profound effect upon the Confederates stationed at the south of the defenses. The reserves and civilians who were already disoriented by the darkness and frightened by the sights and sounds of the battle now had to deal with what seemed like the very real threat that the Federals had somehow gotten in their rear and were about to surround them. It also made any indistinguishable figure or body of soldiers moving in the darkness behind the Confederate lines a potential enemy.[39]

In addition, the Confederates in the trenches realized that their only route of escape lay to their rear, over either the Franklin Street Bridge or the railroad bridge. The countryside to the west of the area encompassed by the Confederate earthworks was in Union possession, and any attempt at escape in that direction was almost sure to mean capture. If the Federals seized the bridge before they could make their escape, the Confederates in Girard would be trapped.

Further compounding Confederate anxieties, as McGlasson's men were just making their escape from within the dark entrenchments, the 4th Iowa's dismounted troopers successfully assailed the works at the north end of the Confederate lines, sending skedaddling Rebs hurtling southward toward the bridges in order to escape. The onrushing shadowy figures were indistinguishable as either friend or foe to those Confederates who were still resolved to fight, and added much to the confusion of both the officers and men manning the southern defenses.[40]

In addition to McGlasson's ride and the events unfolding to the north, the soldiers of Alexander's brigade were also assisting. At dusk, having surmised that the attack had been postponed, Alexander moved to the rear of the high hill atop which his forces had waited all afternoon for a sign of the engagement's beginning. There the majority of the brigade bedded down for the evening, supposing the assault would take place at dawn. A portion of the brigade, including men from the 7th Ohio, who had been serving as videttes and skirmishers throughout the afternoon, were advanced to the outskirts of Girard to keep a watch out for the enemy. According to Lieutenant Yeoman, it was to the surprise of Alexander and his resting troopers that "suddenly, as if hell itself had broken loose, we heard the rattle and roar . . . and saw the flames from the guns leaping into the night." Roused to excitement, the soldiers of Alexander's brigade were hastily assembled and, taking direction from the "flash of Winslow's guns like fire-flies," set out down the hill toward Girard.[41]

Into the town and through the streets the Federal troopers galloped in hopes of supporting the Union effort. Soon, however, they discovered that the Confederates had destroyed all of the bridges over Mill Creek in Girard and that crossing the stream's treacherous banks would prove a major obstacle. Yeoman recalled: "The order was immediately given for our brigade to advance, but we found it almost impossible to get across the ravine, and drifted down to a lower crossing." It took Alexander's brigade until very late in the action to ford the creek, and by the time the 2nd Brigade got fully assembled they could only "assist in completing victory."[42]

Even so, it appears that Confederate troops at the south of the *tête-de-pont* knew there were Federal troops in their front. They had watched them on the hills southwest of Girard and had skirmished with them throughout the afternoon. Though Alexander's brigade failed to launch a successful major assault during the night, Confederate forces certainly expected an attack. Furthermore, the Federal troopers, who had already crossed the creek and were waiting for the balance of their units to assemble, were seen by

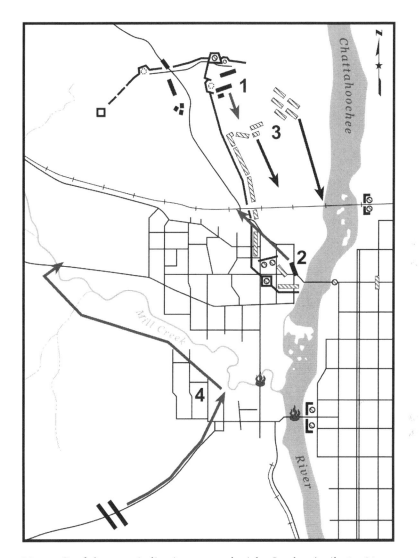

Map 9. Confederate main line is penetrated, night, Sunday, April 16, 1865. (1) 4th Iowa regroups and charges south inside the lines. (2) McGlasson's troopers capture the bridge but are forced to retreat back north. (3) Confederate forces from the breach flee toward the bridges. (4) Alexander's brigade cannot cross Mill Creek in Girard and is forced to ride west in search of a place to cross.

the light of some buildings that the Confederates had purposely set on fire to reveal the movements of the enemy and prevent the structures from being used by sharpshooters. The circumstances and timing of the 4th Iowa's charge, combined with McGlasson's ride and Alexander's movement, severely weakened the defenders' chances of success and hastened the engagement's result.[43]

13
The Night Attack
"Then Commenced the Rough and Tumble Fight"

Back on the Summerville Road near the north end of the *tête-de-pont,* after capturing or driving away the Confederates at the breach in the earth-works, the Federal troopers of the 1st and 2nd battalions of the 4th Iowa quickly drew themselves into semi-coordinated companies. Some of the members of the 3rd and 5th Iowa that had been swept along in the 4th Iowa's charge, once inside the enemy's trenches, simply set out to clear the rifle pits of their defenders. A small group of troopers composed mainly of men from the 3rd Iowa, upon rushing over the parapets, turned to their left and began battling up the rifle pits toward Fort 2. The majority of the 3rd and 5th Iowa, however, remained attached to the 4th Iowa as it prepared to set out inside the Confederate defenses toward the south.[1]

Captain Abraham of the 4th Iowa's 1st Battalion shouted to his soldiers to form up and wheel to their right. As they did, he noticed that at least one company still retained much of its organization. To keep the pressure on the Confederates, he called to Vanorsdol: "Lieutenant Van, take Company K and push ahead." According to Vanorsdol, "Then commenced the rough and tumble fight. Every fellow for himself and the devil for us all. A charge and a forlorn hope made in a night attack can be more easily imag-ined than described. . . . Company K, being an 'Eli' company, got there, you bet. How well the order was obeyed none knows better than Captain Abraham."[2]

Following Company K, both battalions of the 4th Iowa began tracing the line of rifle pits southward in more of a mass than a formation. Ac-cording to Winslow, they found they "were in almost a hollow shell. . . . It demonstrated . . . that, once inside, the game would be ours."[3]

As the last of his battalion readied themselves to press their gains, Abra-ham sent a messenger to the rear to inform Winslow that he was "hastening with several companies to the bridge, leaving the others to follow." The messenger delivered the news to Winslow only moments before Upton, who had been observing the action on another part of the field, rode up to Winslow to inquire of the situation. What followed was the generals' second major altercation of the evening.[4] According to Winslow, "Upton asked me, as soon as he was at my side, how things were going, and I told him we had broken the line and the front companies were now on their way inside the line to the bridge." Winslow's timing could not have been worse. At that very moment, Noble of the 3rd Iowa, thinking his regiment had been decimated in its recent assault, approached Winslow and informed the general that "he had found it impossible to arrive at the works on account of the nature of the obstructions along the creek and on the sides of the ravine." Compounding Winslow's already seemingly poor position, "at this moment the two companies of the 10th Missouri returned, going to the rear." McGlasson reported that "he had entered the line where it crossed the road" but had been sent no support, and had been forced to abandon the bridge after it was already in his possession.[5]

Before Winslow could explain the situation, Upton turned on him and angrily questioned: "I understood you to state that we were inside the lines." His tone brought a sharp response from Winslow, who apparently blamed Upton for disrupting the battle arrangements by halting the 10th Missouri and throwing part of the Union force into chaos. Unwilling at that moment to be distracted from the events at hand, Winslow replied, "*We are there, as will be these men now passing us.*"[6]

Though Winslow could have opted to exchange verbal blows with Upton, he turned on Noble to vent his frustration. Winslow pointed out Noble's failure to take the works but commented that other soldiers had not failed and had gained possession of the battlements. Winslow and Noble were already on less than cordial terms. Just days before the battle, Noble was "reprimanded by Winslow in an unjust and critical manner" for watering his horse while his troops were forming for the day's march. It was apparent to Winslow now that his recent comment did not sit well with the colonel. "I regretted later that I had made this curt statement in the presence of Noble," the general recalled, "whom I gave orders to again push his men forward and make prisoners of all the men he found."[7]

Angry at Winslow and already upset by what he feared was the near annihilation of his regiment, Noble immediately appealed to Upton for orders more sympathetic to the risk of danger to his men. Noble was reluctant to throw the remainder of his unit into another costly charge, particularly against the massive and still active Fort 2. "Finding the left too weak to take the fort," he recounted after the battle, "I so reported to General Upton and was ordered to let the fort go and hold the entrenchments."

With permission from Upton not to attempt another useless assault on the huge, well-manned fort, Noble quickly began organizing his few remaining troopers for another effort to take and hold the trenches and rifle pits near where his regiment had first gained a foothold and where at that moment the 4th Iowa was already clearing the works.[8]

While Upton and Winslow were having words on the road, Wilson, who had been waiting near the rear, "came down to look on" and witness the action. When his regiment halted on the road, one of the troopers from the 4th U.S. Cavalry snatched a small book from his pocket and scrawled in it these few lines, extraordinary for their timing: "Fighting is being briskly carried on at this time and even now I hear the balls whizzing in every direction. The fighting is terrible but it seems we are driving the enemy. This is the first time I have undertaken to write on the field of battle."[9]

The fighting that initially had been somewhat coordinated on the Confederate side now quickly degenerated into pockets of resistance that were either rapidly overwhelmed by the firepower of the advancing troopers or broke before them and fled southward, further frustrating the Confederates at that end. Confederates fleeing from the breach at the north end of the line were thought by their comrades to be the enemy, while in other instances the enemy were thought to be fellow Confederates. Even experienced Rebel officers and soldiers found it difficult to know just what to do, and a sense of dread gripped the entire force.[10]

The discomposure of the civilians was even greater. George Burrus was a young Columbus resident at the time of the battle but was "eager to account for one man" and was stationed in the trenches south of the breakthrough. "His sense of duty overcame his fear," and during the engagement he "picked up a dilapidated old gun" and prepared to do his part. "He was afraid of the oncoming Yankees. . . . Cautiously he aimed at one of the enemy. 'If you don't go off, I will,' he addressed the gun, trembling. . . . The gun snapped and off went young Burrus."[11]

Though there was some scattered fighting, for the most part the Confederate resistance along Ingersoll Hill evaporated before the head of the advancing Federals. Confused and terrified, the Confederates who sprinted southward through the darkness toward the bridges abandoned their weapons, accouterments, and all other encumbrances. According to Private Gilpin, "The Rebels were panic stricken, and where our boys came down among them charging and yelling, they fled in wild rout in all directions—some entered houses and crawled up chimneys, and hid in every corner." Some of the Confederates were so paralyzed with fright that instead of skedaddling they resorted to playing opossum. "When we came up many men [were] lying flat in the trenches playing dead," Gilpin recalled, "and when *rousted out* begged piteously for mercy."[12]

The confused retreat of the Confederate forces, combined with the darkness, helped to shield the soldiers of both sides from inflicting much harm on each other. Neither side could tell friend from foe, and soldiers on both sides were afraid to shoot at the shadowy figures that might be their comrades. Also, many of the Confederates in the trenches continued to fire needlessly into the darkness until they were surprised and overtaken by the men of the 4th Iowa charging down their flank inside the works. Such was the case for Private Ben K. Farrar, who was stationed in the trenches and still firing "into the blackness of night at a point just to the rear of the home of Dr. Ashby Floyd" when suddenly he was informed of his capture by a Federal soldier who surprised him from behind.[13]

Yet even for those Confederates captured, their initial detention was extraordinarily abbreviated. "The Iowans, possessed of one idea, rushed along the rifle-pits, looking eagerly ahead for the bridge, not stopping to take prisoners, only shouting to the rebels to throw down their arms, and leaving them behind in the trenches, in the utmost confusion."[14]

The dismounted men of the 4th Iowa surged rapidly south, sweeping aside all resistance until, upon reaching an area near where the Summerville Road passed to the interior of the defenses, they came under increasing fire from infantry and a battery of six artillery pieces. The guns of Waddell's artillery battalion were stationed across the streets and the lawns north of Fort 1, near the intersection of Jackson and Brodnax streets at the south of the *tête-de-pont,* and were protected by a hastily constructed redoubt. To the north of the battery the Confederates had set several houses and other buildings on fire "for the purpose of showing the assaulting line to their gunners."[15]

As the Union soldiers advanced past the flaming structures, one of the Federal troopers captured during Upton's afternoon reconnaissance escaped. Illuminated as they were by the fires' orange glow, the escapee instantly recognized his comrades among the mass of onrushing Yanks and together with them managed to turn the tables on his captors. For his bravery and cunning in apprehending the colonel (James C. Cole) and adjutant of the unit that had moments before held him prisoner, Private Robert C. Wood was recommended for the Medal of Honor by General Upton (see appendix 5).[16]

Part of the battery stationed near Jackson Street in Girard opened fire on the approaching Federals as their ranks were exposed by the radiance of the flames. Uncertain of what to do but unwilling to blast the many

Confederates who were still in their front, the rest of the battery held their fire. Within moments the cannoneers realized that all was lost and began to abandon their pieces. Some even started cutting loose the horses from the limbers and caissons in order to expedite their withdrawal.[17]

At about the same time, "both Upton and Winslow . . . hurried down the road to the point where it enters the works, and there kept shouting . . . 'Selma! Selma! Go for the bridge! Take no prisoners! Go for the bridge!'" The generals had been "moving along the road parallel with the men led by Abraham and Dana." When they reached the entrance to the works at about the moment when Abraham's battalion was preparing to charge the battery in the street, Upton hollered at the troopers to "clear the road as the guns will sweep it." "The men yelled back, 'Get off the road yourselves,'" then charged.[18]

Without hesitation, Abraham's 1st Battalion, with Vanorsdol's company in the lead, assailed the Confederate positions. "Company K covered themselves all over with glory in this charge as they went rolling, tumbling, stumbling over the enemy's breastworks into the ditches, up the parapets into the very mouths of the cannon," recalled Vanorsdol. In support of the action, Upton roared out "in a high and penetrating voice, plainly heard above the rattle of carbines . . . 'Charge 'em! Charge 'em!'" At the battery, Abraham led his battalion in an intense hand-to-hand melee with a few determined artillerymen, but within moments the remaining Confederate cannoneers broke and fled eastward down the hill toward the bridge.[19]

The 4th Iowa's 2nd Battalion, led by Dana, was following in the rear of Abraham's battalion. "Captain Dana, by luck or a different understanding of orders, left the line of rifle-pits where the [Summerville] road crossed it," remembered Adjutant Scott, "and led his companies, C, F, I, and L, by the road directly toward the bridge." Turning to the east, Dana's battalion ignored the battery being stormed by Abraham's 1st Battalion, and guided by "the rumble of moving wheels . . . passing upon the bridge . . . they ran towards it almost as one man."[20]

As Upton and Winslow rode near the entrance of the road into the works, they were overtaken by the mounted troopers of the 4th Iowa's 3rd Battalion, led by Major Edward Dee. This unit had ridden forward on the road following the action southward. Upton and Winslow fell in at the head of the mounted column and then galloped through the opening in the parapets. "Upton and I called out frequently to the men running along near the works," remembered Winslow. "The men of course were not silent. They yelled and repeated the commands."[21]

Having captured the battery on Jackson Street, Abraham's battalion almost immediately came under fire from Fort 1, just to the south. A piece-

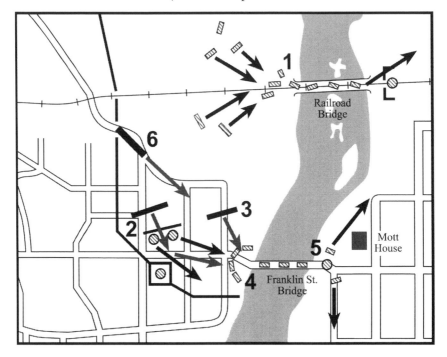

Map 10. Confederate main line collapses, night, Sunday, April 16, 1865. (1) Fleeing Confederates cross the railroad bridge. (2) Abraham's battalion charges and captures the Confederate battery, then rushes toward the bridge. Dana's battalion (3) is joined by Abraham's battalion in the hand-to-hand fight for the bridge. (4) Confederates try to defend the bridgehead but are forced to flee (5) across the bridge and into Columbus. (6) Upton and Winslow, at the head of Dee's mounted battalion, hurry toward the bridge.

meal assault was attempted by part of the 1st Battalion to capture the fort, which anchored the left of the Confederate line, but was repulsed. "The fort . . . opened on us and kept firing until we mounted the works," remembered Sergeant Samuel O. Bereman of the 4th Iowa's Company K. "Several men were knocked down by the very nearness & force of the explosion. Luckily, they fired over our heads, but the deafening roar—we were within twenty feet of them the last time—was awful!"[22]

No second attempt was undertaken. The majority of Abraham's men, seeing their objective, the Franklin Street Bridge, at the foot of the hill, turned and charged down Brodnax Street toward the entrance. As the two Union battalions plunged down the hill parallel to one another on opposite sides of the inner entrenchments, in the darkness and owing to the confusion of the fight, "Abraham's men at one moment took alarm . . . and began firing across the works, but Dana's men cried out, 'Selma, Selma,' and the firing stopped."[23]

As the troopers advanced, routed Confederate forces from all parts of the battlefield raced for the entrance to the bridge to escape capture. Despite the press of their panic-stricken compatriots, a small group of defenders tried desperately to maintain some organization and defense at the bridge-head. Among this group were Cobb, Buford, and Von Zinken. Turning to his staff, Cobb instructed Captain M. Pope Barrow to take the bridge guard across the river and, with the artillery already there, prepare to do all he could to cover the retreat of the army.[24]

Reaching the opposite bank, Barrow drew his soldiers into line with the anxious artillerymen manning the two howitzers and prepared for the worst. "Suddenly, silently, Col. [Charles] Lamar rode up by my side," remembered Barrow. "Colonel, what are you doing here?" questioned Barrow, adding, "we . . . [are] to be sacrificed." "I know it," replied Lamar. "I heard you were down here and I have come to stay with you." At that, Lamar turned and rode back toward his small group of reserves forming nearby on Franklin Street.[25]

Back on the Alabama side of the river, in order to try to save the bridge, a few determined Confederates momentarily made a stand, forming a defensive semicircle around the bridge's entrance, and succeeded in temporarily halting Dana's troopers. The resistance was short lived, however, as just then, from up Brodnax Street, came the head of the mass of soldiers under Abraham determined to smash through to the other side.[26]

Within a few moments, the two battalions of Union cavalrymen crashed into the Confederates, and again hand-to-hand fighting ensued. Soldiers clubbed and shot at one another, and officers were unhorsed as the two sides clashed. Von Zinken, desperate to stem the tide of defeat, shouted urgently to the fleeing Confederates to turn and fight, but it was no use. "The gallant colonel yelled out, 'halt,' but our boys couldn't see it," remembered Private Gilpin. "He raised himself in the saddle and cried, 'Rally round your chief! Rally!' and just then, whack, one of our boys hit him over the head with his carbine, and off the old fellow tumbled among his staff."[27]

During these few chaotic moments the Confederates tried to fire the bridge, which had been saturated with turpentine and lamp oil and stuffed with cotton, much as the lower bridge had been. All efforts proved in vain, however. "One rebel did strike a match," remembered Adjutant Scott, "but he was crushed in the act by a clubbed carbine in the hand of a man of Company K."[28]

Adding to the confusion was not only the darkness but the press of hundreds of routed Confederates, who, having to fight their way through the

Federals and their own soldiers, continued to surge toward the mouth of the bridge in a terrific stampede. At one point, two Yanks interrupted the flight of a Reb toward the bridge and demanded of him, "Lay that gun down." Unwilling to yield just yet, the man "raised it with both hands above his head, . . . brought it down across that Yank's foot," and made his getaway.[29]

As the grappling continued, Captain Guillett, one of Von Zinken's aides, who had been trying to help rally the troops, attempted to save his commander. His efforts cost him dearly, however. Guillett "was shot as he attempted to raise . . . [Von Zinken] on his horse," and toppled to the ground, mortally wounded. Members of Von Zinken's staff did manage to finally raise their dazed commander back onto his animal, and the colonel soon turned and plunged into the dark interior of the bridge in order to escape. Unable to maintain itself under the pressure of the Federal attack and the press of its own retreating men, the resistance at the bridgehead collapsed. Mixed together, shoulder to shoulder, Union and Confederate soldiers bolted through the inky blackness of the thousand-foot-long bridge, bumping and stumbling over one another as they hurtled toward Columbus.[30] "There was a promiscuous rush for the bridges. Friend and foe, horsemen and footmen, artillery wagons and ambulances, were crowded and jammed together in the narrow avenue, which was 'dark as Egypt.' . . . How it was that many were not crushed to death in this tumultuous transit of the Chattahoochee," marveled one contemporary, "seems incomprehensible."[31]

"In going through the bridge at Columbus that night, the scenes were indescribable . . . horses, mules, wagons, everything mingled with the groans of agony," remembered Private Benton of Emery's battery. "One poor fellow had a fit and fainted," but "Dr. Walton and myself dragged him up to one side of the bridge and left him under and behind the braces, inside the bridge, out of the way of horses, wagons and the like."[32]

Bolting through the bridge along with men from both forces were Cobb and Buford. One member of the 7th Alabama Cavalry recalled that "General Buford and his staff dashed through the enemy at the mouth of the bridge and crossed in heavy but uncertain fire." According to Major Latta, "both Cobb and Buford were pursued so closely on the bridge as to be within the reach of sabre-stroke."[33] "The whole space was now filled with the flying rebels and the advancing Iowans," recalled Adjutant Scott of the 4th Iowa. "Indeed, it was so dark that the Iowans passed many of the rebels in the passage without knowing it, and reached the other side before them. The air was full of the odor of turpentine. The angles of the woodwork had been stuffed with cotton saturated with that fluid, so that the whole could be burned instantaneously in case of defeat in the works; but the per-

Fig. 16. Captain M. Pope
Barrow. Courtesy Library
of Congress.

sons charged with the duty of setting the fire could not determine the moment of action, perhaps because enemies appeared before their friends were
all through."[34]

At the east end of the bridge, Barrow's company attempted to maintain their formation despite having their ranks broken by the stamped-
ing throng of soldiers, horses, and wagons. With them, the artillerymen of
Ward's battery, under Toombs's command, stood ready to "rake the roadway" with canister from their two howitzers at the appearance of the Federals. To their dismay, however, from the darkness of the bridge's black interior came a steady stream of Confederates pouring into the streets of
Columbus. Then, suddenly, as it became apparent that the Confederate
resistance on the west bank had been overrun, a wave of intermingled
Union and Confederate soldiers spilled from the bridge and surged toward
the cannons. Heading the column, mingled with Union cavalrymen, were
Von Zinken, Buford, and Cobb. Faced with the choice of losing the bridge

or blasting their own fleeing comrades and commanders, the gunners nervously held their fire, waiting for a clear shot. The shot never came.[35]

According to Toombs, it was "the damnedest mess you ever saw." Uncertain what to do, "the brave cannoneers stood to their guns, waiting for orders and making the best personal defense they could." The determined Federal troopers, upon emerging from the span, "had the benefit of the starlight and came suddenly upon [the] two guns which were placed in readiness to sweep the bridge." One of the first troopers to emerge from the span was Private Nathan Beezly of the 4th Iowa, who "just as he got through the bridge [was] shot through the head." Despite this, the Yanks realized it was time to "push hammer and pound." Without a moment's hesitation, they rushed the section and joined the artillerymen in a vicious brawl.[36]

"For possession of the battery at the east end of the bridge there was a sharp contest," recalled Scott. With dogged determination, the intermingled men of the 1st and 2nd battalions of the 4th Iowa waded into the fray. Von Zinken, still unsteady from being struck by the butt of a carbine and from his earlier fall from his mount, was again unhorsed by a Federal trooper. Sergeant Joseph Jones of the 4th Iowa was shot through the shoulder and killed. Private Richard Cosgriff of the 4th Iowa had a scrap with a Rebel flag-bearer "who fought hard to save his colors, but," according to Cosgriff, "I succeeded in downing him and seized the flag." The cannoneers, unsupported by their fleeing comrades, "tried manfully to save their guns" but were quickly overpowered. According to Wilson, "many were shot at their post, and such as were not killed or wounded were compelled to surrender to the onrushing victors."[37]

Back on the Alabama side, even as Union and Confederate forces continued to cram inside the bridge, the mounted 3rd Battalion of the 4th Iowa arrived at the entrance with Upton and Winslow in the lead. "The second battalion had rushed on foot to the bridge and were on the bridge or had gone through it before we arrived with the mounted battalion at the entrance," remembered Winslow. "Upton started to go over with the mounted companies," and "I remarked 'If you cross over, I will remain in command here and prevent any more rebels from crossing.'"[38]

With Upton in the lead, the mounted column plunged into the span and rode toward the tumult on Franklin Street at the far end. Ahead of their thundering hooves, the column pushed along the remainder of their dismounted counterparts and the routed Confederates in a confused and chaotic stampede. Hurtling toward Columbus's dark streets, the wall of Union and Confederate soldiers that tumbled forth from the dark mouth of the bridge on the Georgia side in advance of the mounted column further confused the fight. Then, suddenly, out burst the mounted troopers.

Together the mounted and dismounted cavalrymen of the 4th Iowa fell upon the Confederates. Captain John S. Pemberton, a Columbus druggist and the future inventor of Coca-Cola, was shot and slashed across the abdomen, but his life was saved when the blow was partially deflected by the money belt he was wearing. Federal troopers attacked Cobb's staff and attempted to capture several officers, one of whom, according to Cobb, "preferred risking his life . . . and had a chase for some fifty yards, more exciting than pleasant. He was shot at twice, but his [mount] being fresh and swift he succeeded in making his escape." Barrow, in command of the bridge guards, was not so fortunate, and was quickly overwhelmed and forced to surrender.[39]

Then, just when it appeared to the Confederates that all was lost, there shone one last glimmer of hope. Moments after the mounted troopers of the 4th Iowa joined the fight on the Georgia side, and before many had exited the bridge into the crowded street, Lamar, at the head of a unit of Confederate infantry, came charging, mounted, up Franklin Street. Brandishing a sword and shouting to his men, he galloped headlong into the fracas, past the Mott House, and toward his fate. According to Charles Martin, "In the dark friend and foe became mixed. My father [Jacob Martin] became separated from his men, fell in crossing a ditch and lost his gun. Just as he crossed the bridge into the city a Yankee soldier arrested him. The soldier was on a horse, my father on foot. At this junction Col. Charles [A.] L. Lamar, a Confederate officer, came galloping down the street, sword in hand, calling to the troops to rally and hold the bridge. . . . The soldier to whom my father had surrendered, when he saw the officer, . . . spurred his horse, knocked my father down, and drawing his gun, shot [at] Col. Lamar."[40]

The bullet sailed wide and missed. At nearly the same instant, the trooper's horse was shot out from under him and collapsed in the street. Unhorsed but still determined, the trooper leaped to his feet, chambered a round in his carbine, and lunged at Lamar as the colonel rode into the tumult. The trooper "stepped in front of Black Cloud, the horse Colonel Lamar was riding, seizing the bit with his left hand, and threw up his carbine with his right, and called on Lamar to surrender. Quick as lightning, . . . [Lamar] plunged his spurs into his horse's sides and tried to ride over his opponent," witnessed Barrow who was nearby. "At that instant, as the horse reared and plunged above the soldier, he fired, and at the crack of the carbine, Lamar fell lifeless to the ground."[41]

Fig. 17. Colonel Charles
A. L. Lamar. Collection of
the author.

"I stood there with two cannon pointed right into the bridge expecting to kill . . . [them] all and before I knew it . . . [they] had possession of the guns and had killed Colonel Lamar right near me," a stunned Toombs recalled. Their commander dead, and with more Union soldiers filling the street and joining the fight, Lamar's reserves broke and ran. With the death of Lamar, so died any hope of saving Columbus, and all organized Confederate resistance on the Georgia side of the Chattahoochee evaporated. Toombs abandoned his position and galloped into the dark streets of the city alongside his skedaddling cannoneers. Von Zinken, still dazed and now on foot, took to his heels to evade capture. "Our men and the enemy crossed the bridge in a confused mass," remembered Cobb. "Failing to rally our forces this side of the bridge . . . [myself] and General Buford concluded that it was time to take care of *Number One*! We rode out of town on the Talbotton road. Fortunately, headquarters had been moved across the river after the fight in the afternoon, otherwise the whole party would have been captured."[42]

Back on the Alabama side of the river, when Upton and the mounted battalion began their movement across the bridge, Winslow stayed behind to ensure the capture of the routed Confederates. Also on that side of the river remained dismounted troopers from several of the 4th Iowa's companies who had not managed to squeeze into the bridge before the arrival of the mounted battalion. When it was clear that the 3rd Battalion would ride through the bridge, Abraham called to Vanorsdol: "Lieutenant Van, form your men here at the side of the embankment and let the mounted men pass." Quickly, the cavalrymen from Vanorsdol's company, as well as men from other companies, formed ranks in the dark.[43]

His attention drawn by the continued shelling from Fort 1 atop Red Hill, Winslow shouted: "Captain Abraham send a storming party to the fort." Immediately the message was relayed, and away charged Vanorsdol and his troopers back up the hill. "At once I gave the order, 'fours left, double quick, march,'" remembered Vanorsdol."[44]

Despite a small show of resistance, the ramparts were quickly scaled, the Union soldiers poured in through the embrasures, and the garrison was forced to surrender. In the assault two flags were captured. Private John Kinney of the 4th Iowa's Company L "had a tussle with the fellow to get the flag" of the 10th Missouri Battery C.S.A. This unit manned the four howitzers that had shelled the Federals during the afternoon and night phases of the action. The other flag was taken by Private Edward Bebb of Company D, who later reported that he picked it up "about 100 yards from the bridge and in the line of works, . . . the rebels near it running away before our men, leaving the flag."[45]

Upon entering the fort, to the surprise of many, the troopers discovered the reason for the light resistance they had encountered. Inside were men of Georgia's Reserve Force who were disgruntled over the government's order to send them to conscript camp and who had even taken to calling themselves by the derogatory name "conscript." Also inside the fort were civilians who had been forced during the morning to take up arms against their will. "The Rebels were almost in mutiny and war among themselves," explained Vanorsdol. "There were some old Confederate soldiers in the fort and probably as many conscripts. The conscripts were twitting the old soldiers for forcing them into the Confederate service, and would say to the old soldiers: 'We told you if you conscripted us we would shoot the other way, as we would not fight at all against the Yankees.'"[46]

Meanwhile, at the north end of the *tête-de-pont* Noble led the remnants of his regiment in another assault on the now mostly abandoned defenses east of the Summerville Road. This time they encountered very little resistance to their advance through the ravine and slashing, and when Noble

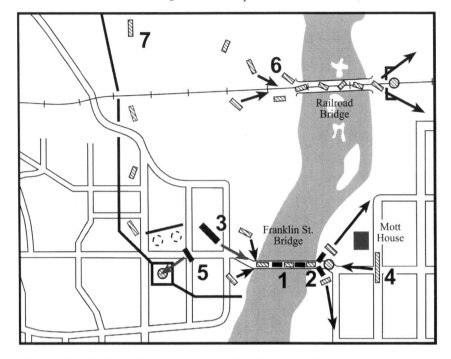

Map 11. Franklin Street Bridge captured, night, Sunday, April 16, 1865. (1) Intermingled Union and Confederate soldiers race across the bridge toward Columbus. (2) A vicious melee ensues at the cannons at the east end of the bridge. (3) Upton and the mounted battalion charge through the bridge and are met by (4) Lamar's Confederates. (5) Vanorsdol's company captures Fort 1. Some Confederates (6) continue to flee over the railroad bridge, while others simply throw away their arms (7) and stay put.

reached the angle in the works south of Fort 2 he found some of his own troopers, who had been swept along in the 4th Iowa's charge, still inside the Confederate lines firing on the fort from its rear.[47]

With the exception of Fort 2, the Confederate defenses were inactive, and all who remained in them were surrendering or trying to escape. Inside Fort 2 the cannoneers of Clanton's battery continued to fire, though now with little effect. Cut off and completely unsupported, it was not long before Captain Clanton called a hurried conference of his officers. "Spike guns and disband," he decided. The fight was over, their duty done. The fort's enormous garrison flag was hurriedly hauled down. "We received the sad and what proved to be the last order 'to take care of ourselves,'" remembered Corporal William W. Grant, and "we left the Girard hills in squads of six to twelve."[48]

"The fire of the battery ceased eventually," remembered Noble, "and

Fig. 18. Captain Nathaniel Clanton. Courtesy State of Alabama Department of Archives and History.

I collected my companies to mount them." The artillery having suddenly fallen silent, a platoon of Federal soldiers dashed ahead, climbed the walls, and "found the guns in the fort loaded, but the enemy fled." Discovering the fort mostly abandoned and the Confederates streaming away into the night, Noble's men immediately pushed forward and pursued the routed enemy. Sergeant Horatio Birdsall of the 3rd Iowa's Company B ran down the soldier trying to escape with the fort's flag and captured both, closing the fight on the Alabama side of the river.[49]

14
The Night Attack

The Battle Concludes

Following the capture of Fort 2, and after establishing details to help round up prisoners, Noble began mounting the portion of his regiment that could be rallied and prepared to move south to enter the city. At the same time, Benteen, who had finally regained control of the 10th Missouri, re-formed his regiment on the Summerville Road. Unlike the 10th Missouri, however, which experienced only slight losses, more than half of the troopers with which Noble had begun the fight were missing.[1] Noble was devastated. He believed that his regiment had taken a severe mauling by the Confederate fire during their first attack on the main line and that his brave soldiers had been slaughtered. Shrouded as the battlefield was in the pitch-black of night, the colonel had no way of assessing his loss and believed that the slashing was filled with the mangled and broken bodies of his soldiers. Seeing the dozens of empty saddles in the faint starlight, Noble became overwrought. As the 10th Missouri and the remainder of the 3rd Iowa slowly reassembled in preparation to move out, Noble wept.[2]

Down at the captured bridge, as soon as Lamar was killed, all organized resistance ceased. Dismounted troopers who had overrun the two pieces of artillery at the east end of the bridge split up and hurried into the streets of Columbus—particularly Bay, Front, and Broad streets—in pursuit of the fleeing Confederates. Shouting above the confusion, Upton instructed his mounted soldiers to give chase. According to Adjutant Scott of the 4th Iowa, "The mounted men rode through the bridge among the last of the dismounted battalions, passed the captured guns, and charged into the streets, meeting the enemy at the first street from the bridge, passing and capturing numbers of them, with desultory firing on both sides, and turning defeat into a hopeless rout."[3]

Confusion reigned as both the mounted and dismounted troopers of the 4th Iowa plunged into the mass of frightened and fleeing Confederates. Disoriented and exhausted from their flight, hundreds of demoralized Confederates began simply to give up and surrender. Many, however, did not, and the scene that played out in the streets of the Columbus was both strange and violent. Shots were exchanged between Union troopers attempting to run down prisoners and Confederates who fired back from within buildings and around corners. In the chaos, several soldiers were killed and wounded, and "in the street three blocks from the bridge" Sergeant Norman Bates of the 4th Iowa's Company E overtook the color-bearer of the 7th Alabama and took the banner as a prize.[4]

According to Wilson, "The bridge was saved and the city penetrated, but the end was not yet, nor could the victory be regarded as complete until the railroad bridge nearby was seized and the rebels retreating over it were captured." Upton immediately dispatched a detail of mounted troopers from the 4th Iowa to secure it. Even as they approached the railroad bridge, the troopers could see the silhouettes of hundreds of Confederate soldiers bolting across the span and then disappearing into the woods north of the city.[5]

Private Jackson of the 2nd Georgia State Line was among those who "crossed the river on the railroad bridge." He remembered of his arrival at the far end: "Once across, I felt safe. Some soldiers had piled up bales of cotton there for a breastworks and begged us to rally, but we were so demoralized and scattered that we didn't." Jackson was among the fortunates able to make an escape. Many Confederates were not so lucky. Their capture by the Union detachment added substantially to the growing tally of prisoners.[6]

Back on Franklin Street, Upton continued to dispatch soldiers to ride down the fleeing enemy and capture strategic points. "One company hastened to seize the battery at the lower bridge," observed Scott, "two others galloped through the streets to capture retreating bodies, and the fourth sought the railway to intercept any train that might be leaving." The darkness greatly hampered this mopping-up operation, however, and one member of the 7th Alabama remembered that "friend and foe alike galloped past each other unrecognized."[7]

Some of the Confederates took advantage of the confusion, including Toombs, who misled a group of Union soldiers into believing that he was a Union officer. As Toombs later admitted to Captain Abraham, "Two soldiers were approaching him. He asked, 'What regiment?' They said, '4th Iowa.' Then trying to make them believe he was a Federal officer, he said, 'Come on boys, let us capture that overloaded train of cars. See 'tis stalled there,' and rode away from them."[8]

Also inhibiting to the operation was the continued skirmishing in the streets of the city, which, were it not so hazardous, might have seemed almost comical. "Everybody blundered around in the dark, fighting pretty much at random," an escaped Confederate later confided to a friend. "If a man met some one he did not know, he asked whether he was a Yank or a Reb, and if the answer did not suit his views he fired. At last everybody became afraid to tell who or what they were."[9]

"There was a general stampede," explained Confederate cannoneer Private Moore of his attempt to avoid injury from the Federal troopers who swept down Broad Street. "We ran in the direction of the main street coming down through the business section of the city, but just as we reached this street, we met the Yankee cavalry advance [and] they ordered us to halt and surrender. I do not know how many of our men obeyed their order, but my legs had stood me well on other occasions," remembered Moore, "and I retreated back toward the river at break-neck speed, and from the Yankee bullets I dodged into the first alleyway I came to and beat it southward."[10]

The haphazard fighting in the streets produced several victims. "Judge Waddell, of Russell County," the brother of Major James Waddell, "was shot and mortally wounded on the upper part of Broad Street." He had been aiding his brother in the coordination of the Confederate artillery and was one of at least six Confederate soldiers killed in the city. William Young, president of Eagle Mills, was wounded when, because of his deafness, he refused to yield to a party of Federals who ordered him to halt his horse. "I with the rest of the old men of the city was upon police duty and being hard of hearing was fired upon by the Union forces," remembered Young, "and received six serious wounds upon my body." Despite his injuries, Young declined to become a prisoner and, though badly bleeding, evaded his pursuers and brought himself successfully to his home.[11]

The Union detachment ordered to seize the battery at the burned lower bridge quickly rode south, picking up prisoners and exchanging scattered shots with those still unwilling to yield on Front, Bay, and Short streets. The battery, now mostly abandoned, was quickly secured, and the party continued its ride southward toward the Confederate Navy Yard.[12]

At the Navy Yard, the troopers discovered the massive, nearly completed ironclad CSS *Jackson* still moored at the docks. She had been loaded with supplies in preparation to sail, but the early arrival of Union forces during the afternoon had prompted the ship's crew to abandon her. The troopers also just missed capturing the torpedo boat *Viper* and a handful of officers and sailors who had stayed behind to observe the engagement. One of these, Lieutenant William Carnes, recalled: "When we heard . . . [the Federals] approaching the location of our navy operations, Mr. Oliver and I went up on the steam launch, which he had ready with steam up, and we quietly dropped down the rapid current of the river. . . . Then under our steam power, we continued until we reached and boarded the wooden gunboat, which had been sent below."[13]

As the troopers approached the *Jackson,* which was still tied up at the river's edge, they drew fire from Confederates hiding in the shadows near the yard. Soon, however, the defenders were driven away or forced to surrender and the troopers got their first close look at the vessel.[14]

Unfamiliar with the layout of the city, the group of Union soldiers bound for the railway depot got lost and misdirected in the darkness and confusion. In the meantime, many Confederates reached the station and boarded the train that had been kept in readiness should the city fall. Steaming out just ahead of the Federals, "a considerable train . . . got away toward Macon, filled with officers, soldiers, and citizens of position." Ironically, Cobb was not aboard, having been separated from his staff during the chaos on Franklin Street. Though most of his staff officers evaded the Federals and reached the depot, Cobb and a handful of others, including Buford, galloped out of Columbus on horseback.[15]

Just outside the city, Cobb encountered a small party of soldiers from the 26th Battalion Georgia Infantry who had been "detailed to stay in camp, guard the wagons, and cook for . . . [their] company." "We were still there listening to the firing . . . when we heard horsemen coming at a gallop," recalled one of the fellows. The horsemen stopped, and one among the group called out, "What are you doing there?" "I'm guarding the wagons," replied the soldier. "I'm General Cobb," the shadowy figure announced, "Wilson's taken the town, you'd better get away!" As the party disappeared down the road, the surprised soldier turned to his pard and suggested, "The jig's up, let's make for home."[16]

Shortly thereafter, Cobb and Buford parted ways. Buford turned off the road into the woods headed north toward West Point, Georgia, to rejoin the remainder of his command. Cobb continued eastward accompanied by the small party of soldiers who had fled Columbus with him. His trek would continue through the night. It would take Cobb a day and a half to secure safe transportation by rail to his headquarters in Macon.[17]

Confederates who were unable to secure a ride out of Columbus via rail sought other avenues of escape. Many of them ran through the streets of Columbus and either started east on one of the roads leading out of the city or melted into the woods to hide. One of the former was Captain Roswell Ellis of the Columbus Guards, who was home recuperating from a shoulder wound. "He got a horse and started at night to go into the country for safety, but in the darkness he and the horse fell into a deep ditch . . . and there he lay unable to extricate himself from his awkward position." It was after midnight before Ellis managed to crawl out of the gully and resume his flight.[18]

Among the latter were soldiers of the 7th Alabama Cavalry. The remaining members of that regiment were obliged to ride a dangerous route around Columbus before striking out toward West Point, "the order of General Buford being that his cavalry, in case of the loss of Columbus, should concentrate [there]." Several times, the 7th stumbled upon Federal troopers and shots were exchanged. "The rear of the regiment was fired into as it crossed the railroad, and narrowly escaped another encounter upon the Macon Road. Just as its rear crossed the latter road, and was hidden in the forest, a Federal regiment galloped past in pursuit."[19]

Some of the routed Confederates never made it out of the city, preferring instead to hide out in town. After beating a hasty retreat across the bridge, civilian volunteer Porter Ingram pitched his musket and ammunition into the bushes of a neighbor's yard and ran home. When convalescent combatant Private James W. Howard, who was stationed at the Franklin Street Bridge, chose the better part of valor, he headed straight for the home of Abbey Stringfield, his sweetheart. "I ran all the way, and just did escape," recalled Howard. He remained at the Stringfields' "all night, and could hear the Federal cavalry charging through the streets." Another soldier managed to secure refuge at the home of a friend but was compelled to jump out of a window and hide in the garden when Union soldiers came to the house looking for escapees.[20]

With the firing dying down near Franklin Street, Upton quickly realized the necessity of placing guards on either end of the bridge to prevent accidental ignition of the turpentine-soaked cotton piled inside. He commanded the officer of the guard "to permit not even a match to be lighted or pipe to be smoked in crossing." While the skirmishing and rounding up of prisoners continued on the battlefield and within the city, Winslow, who had a slight flair for the dramatic, crossed the bridge and, upon reaching the Georgia side, dismounted and climbed onto one of the captured howitzers. Perched atop his new headquarters, he began working with his staff and with Upton to regain control of his scattered brigade. Nearby, the Union soldier who had shot Lamar rooted through the pockets of the fallen colonel. Among other items, he discovered an ornate gold pocket watch, which he took as a souvenir and eventually turned over to Winslow.[21]

As soon as the major fighting had ended, at just before 10 P.M., Wilson assembled his escort and started down the Summerville Road toward the bridge. Mindful of the light skirmishing still taking place, he rode into Girard "with four platoons of cavalry forming a hollow square, the general and two of his staff officers riding in the center." Passing the men of the 3rd Iowa and the 10th Missouri along the way, upon arriving at the bridge, Wilson and the 4th U.S. Cavalry carefully started through to the opposite end. The general's ride was cut short while inside the bridge, however, when a bullet from the skirmishing still taking place in downtown Columbus pierced the bridge's wooden sides and passed through the neck of his prized gray gelding, Sheridan.[22] According to Wilson, Sheridan "was wounded . . . through the neck by a stray bullet in the dark inside the Chattahoochee bridge, at Columbus, and died a week later at Macon." Surprisingly, neither Wilson nor any of his subordinates records how the general entered Columbus. Whether Wilson continued to ride his wounded animal or led it the remainder of the way on foot is a mystery.[23]

Upon arriving at the east end of the bridge, Wilson found Upton and Winslow with their staffs "occupied in sending the officers and men who had already crossed to take and hold . . . all of the enemy." He also found the generals and their soldiers in a state of jubilation over their victory. "A wild exultation seized hold of the soldiers, and I believe our brigade could have whipped *anything* that night," recalled Private Gilpin. "Columbus was ours! It was grand to see and hear."[24]

Near the east end of the bridge, "General Wilson came up and congratulated General Upton, complimenting the 4th Division very highly." Upton, filled with excitement over the victory his soldiers had achieved, forgot how often during the day he had watched his plans crumble when just on the point of development, forcing him to improvise another. With characteristic self-confidence, Upton boasted to Wilson that he could "traverse the Confederacy from end to end, and from side to side, with his single division, carrying any kind of fortifications by assault with which he might come in contact, and defying capture by any kind or amount of force which might be sent against him." Latta shared Upton's confidence in his abilities, proclaiming that "the affair . . . has proven Gen. Upton to be the most thoroughly brave, efficient, energetic, judicious, and indefatigable commanding officer whom we ever met."[25]

After meeting briefly with Upton, Wilson turned his attention to Winslow, who was still seated atop the howitzer in the street. "As a compliment to him upon his brilliant success," Wilson placed Winslow "in command of the city." To him would fall the responsibility of overseeing the occupation and destruction of Columbus.[26]

Exhausted from the day's long ride and the evening's intense fighting, upon arriving in Columbus, Wilson turned his attention to finding a suitable place for his headquarters. He did not have to look far. Only a few yards from the east end of the bridge stood a three-story brick home, atop which sat a large glass-enclosed cupola that would afford the general a magnificent view of the battlefield, captured bridge, and doomed city. Furthermore, the home, known as the Mott House, was owned by a wealthy Virginia-born Southerner and slave owner, yet staunch Unionist, by the name of Colonel Randolph L. Mott.[27]

Mott, a personal friend of Vice President Andrew Johnson (who was already president following Lincoln's assassination on April 15, though this was not known in Columbus at the time), was associated with several businesses in Columbus, including the Palace Mills, and also owned a cotton warehouse in the city. Though he was a Union sympathizer, his commercial interests provided services to the Confederate military, and it appears that he was well treated by his pro-secession neighbors either because of his social standing or because his son, John R. Mott, was in the Confederate service, serving on the staff of the Mott's next-door neighbor, General Henry L. Benning. "It is not known how he [Mott] justified this support to the rebel armies in light of his unionist sympathies," observed one biographer, "but the answer probably lies in evidence that Mott was a capitalist first, and a patriot second."[28]

It is unclear whether Mott personally offered his home to Wilson for use as a headquarters or whether an inquiry by one of Wilson's staff prompted an invitation. In either case, upon meeting with Mott, Wilson was soon convinced that the place "was the property of a Union man . . . [who] claimed with the fervor of a patriot that his house and grounds had never been out of the Union." According to Wilson, Mott further assured his guest of his loyalty by pointing out that "within the dome . . . [of the house] the American flag had been kept flying from the outbreak of the war to that unfortunate day." Within a short time, the property was surrounded by soldiers and staff. For the next two days, the once peaceful riverside home would be the seat of the Union occupation.[29]

Not long after Winslow was given command of the city and Wilson moved off in the direction of the Mott House, Winslow observed the head of a Union column approaching. Noble rode in the lead, followed by a long line of troopers who held the reins to nearly 150 riderless horses. To Winslow's surprise, as Noble approached it became obvious that the colonel was "in a troubled state of mind. . . . In fact, he was shedding tears and said his regiment had lost half its number in passing the abatis and while attacking the enemy's entrenchments connected with a very active battery."[30]

Winslow knew he had to act carefully. He and Noble had already been on shaky terms for several days, a situation that was further exacerbated by Winslow's curt comment during the battle about the failure of Noble and his soldiers to take the Confederate entrenchments. Furthermore, Winslow also knew that if he was not prudent, he might irrevocably alienate one of his best regimental commanders. To Winslow's advantage, however, was that during the fight his position had given him a unique perspective that allowed him to better assess both the effectiveness of the Confederate fire and the dispersion of the Union forces. Armed with that information, Winslow tried to comfort Noble and win back some measure of respect.

"As the avalanche of shells and rifle balls had passed over our heads, I felt confident the aim had been as bad before his men as elsewhere," explained Winslow, "and said in substance, 'Colonel, when your roll is called to-morrow morning you will find nearly all the officers and men present." When Noble eyed the general in disbelief, Winslow replied, "Do not be discouraged. A lot of your men are now in the city having come over dismounted."[31]

The news that a large portion of his regiment was already in Columbus, and that Winslow believed the 3rd Iowa had suffered relatively few casualties, greatly solaced Noble. Additionally, Winslow ordered Noble to "take charge of the city immediately as provost-marshal." Noble eagerly accepted the position, seeing it as a "mark of distinction" that his regiment be so honored "for their services." The colonel was instructed to "establish the outposts and pickets" and to inform Winslow if he should "want anything." As a final gesture of encouragement, at parting, Winslow commented to Noble, "I believe your regiment has not lost twenty-five men." According to Winslow, "This cheered him and as usual he took hold of his allotted task with energy and signal ability."[32]

It did not take long for Noble to confirm Winslow's estimate. As the column started into the streets of Columbus, the colonel began to spy dismounted members of his regiment occupied in rounding up prisoners. He quickly learned that many troopers from the 3rd Iowa had been swept up into the ranks of the 4th Iowa and had joined them in the capture of the bridge and the city. Shortly thereafter, Noble sought out one of the most prominent buildings in Columbus, the massive Perry House Hotel, as his headquarters. He then began to collect the remainder of his regiment and "restore order . . . [his] six companies acting as provost guard."[33]

Following the 3rd Iowa across the bridge into Columbus was the portion of the 10th Missouri that had not been detailed to help collect prisoners on the Alabama side of the river. Benteen, probably still angry over his regiment's performance, appears to have said very little to Winslow or to the other officers as he rode by, but he was instructed to take his regiment through town and halt them for the night on the eastern outskirts. Once on the Georgia side, Benteen dispatched additional details to help round up and guard prisoners and to perform picket duty. The remainder of the regiment, despite "a few shots [which] were fired from the houses," spread out and sought shelter in the abandoned homes and yards of eastern Columbus.[34]

On the battlefield in Girard and in the streets of Columbus, the Confederate soldiers who were compelled to surrender were marched to various locations for holding. On the Alabama side of the river, many of the prisoners were held in the forts they had only a short time before helped to defend. In particular, a large body of prisoners was marched to Fort 1 to be kept under guard until morning. In Columbus, many of those who surrendered were forced to march to the small city stockade, where they would sit out the remainder of the occupation. Additionally, because of the large numbers of prisoners taken, many other locations were used as makeshift penitentiaries, including the lot adjacent to the Mott House. In all, approximately fifteen hundred soldiers—nearly half of the Confederate force— were captured and placed under armed watch.[35]

According to Winslow, after the capture of Columbus "the more humble citizens and colored people were greatly excited and at first somewhat out of hand." Most of the civilians who remained in the city, however, passed the hours just after the battle in concern over what might follow. At the home of Judge Thomas, "Mrs. Thomas was sitting by a parlor window, and seeing some men in the yard, she asked, 'Who are you there?'" "Yanks," came the reply; "you did not expect us so soon, did you?"[36] Over the protests of the family, the soldiers were soon inside. "They went through everything in the house, Judge Thomas with them," remembered a family friend, "and by his engaging manners he got them by the baggage room, and saved things there." Despite his best efforts, the judge was too slow to prevent the discovery of a chest in the basement, which the Union soldiers dragged outside, "thinking they had a prize." To their disappointment, however, the raiders found the chest filled with crockery, which they began to smash until Mrs. Thomas's entreaties halted their wreckage.[37]

Though there were some minor injuries at several homes around Columbus during the evening, by about 11 P.M., with the help of Noble's provost guards, "there was no more noise, except the occasional cheers of the victors." Private Gilpin even noted in his diary: "Now that the battle is over and we are in the city all is changed, strict discipline is enforced, and all is going on quietly." A few officers even took the opportunity to enjoy what was left of the holiday. "Had a big supper prepared for us at a fine house . . . [and] plenty of eggs for Easter," remembered Captain Abraham, "but 'twas almost too late to eat them on Easter, the night being far spent."[38]

Of the soldiers composing the 4th Division who arrived at Columbus prior to the start of the night attack, after the battle only the 4th Iowa, the 10th Missouri, the 4th U.S. Cavalry, and the six companies of the 3rd Iowa that had participated in the assault crossed the bridge into Columbus to stay. During the night, after things had settled in the city, the members of the three companies of the 5th Iowa who had taken part in the engagement made their way back over the bridge to where the rest of their regiment had encamped, close to the same ground where they had lain under the fire from Fort 3. Joining them near where the battle had taken place were the artillerymen of Rodney's battery, who likewise bedded down for the evening. The men from Alexander's brigade, who had arrived too late to help in anything but the mopping-up phase, returned to their camp southwest of Girard for the night, satisfied that their division's mission had been accomplished.[39]

Unsure exactly what the results of the battle were, however, were the troops who brought up the rear of the 4th Division. Both the 1st Wisconsin, which had been attached to the 4th Division after leaving Montgomery, and the six companies of the 3rd Iowa, which had been detailed as baggage guards, arrived late and witnessed the night attack from the hills surrounding the Chattahoochee valley. According to Major Shipman of the 1st Wisconsin, "The result we could not learn until about one o'clock at night when general call sound, and it was announced to the great delight of our men that Columbus was in our possession." Ironically, the men of the 3rd Iowa's six detached companies never received any word of the battle's outcome and would not learn of their comrades' extraordinary victory until the next morning.[40]

In Columbus, as it got late, soldiers who were not on duty began to bed down for the evening. Members of the 3rd Iowa who had not been selected for the provost guard were instructed to "scatter out and find supper and lodging among the citizens and see that no harm came to civilians or their property." The extent to which they obeyed this order varied greatly. At occupied homes, the troopers pitched camp in the yards and persuaded the residents to prepare something for them to eat. At homes where the owners were absent, the soldiers simply helped themselves. Left with little alternative and hoping their homes would be spared the torch, some of Columbus's residents were apparently quite cordial to the invaders. The situation was not uniformly benign, however. Mrs. Emma Prescott, who was living with her parents and sisters, and whose father had participated in the fight in Columbus, remembered of the soldiers' arrival at the house: "Mother met them at the door. An officer pointed a pistol at her, cursed and demanded her watch. 'I never owned one,' was her reply. They rushed in and demanded money, but found none, so they broke into trunks, wardrobes, and dressers taking whatever they saw fit, mostly men's clothes. Then they went into the kitchen and demanded of the servants something to eat and made them cook it."[41]

Late in the evening, after meeting with Wilson at the Mott House, Upton rode back into Girard to examine the battlefield, accompanied only by Morse, his aide. Meanwhile, the rest of Upton's staff as well as his bodyguard, composed of Company G of the 4th Iowa, searched in Columbus for a suitable place to establish the general's headquarters. The place they chose was known as the Battle House.[42]

Though a headquarters for the 4th Division had been selected in Columbus, Upton did not sleep there that night. After riding over the quiet battlefield in Girard, the general, who was extremely fatigued after the day's long march and hard fight, opted to sleep upon the site of his great victory. According to Captain Morse, "The general and I were alone. . . . Near the rifle pits was a large house up to which we rode. I dismounted and gained admittance by kicking open the door. The place was deserted and I built a fire out of an old chair. The general remembered that he had seen a man in charge of the rebel General Buford's dinner, and I went for and captured the man and the dinner—both poor stuff. After dining we went to sleep."[43]

Despite the relative quiet that descended again on the Chattahoochee valley by around midnight, activity continued. One of the last persons to meet with Winslow while the general was still seated astride the cannon on Franklin Street in Columbus was Dr. Robinson, the 1st Brigade's senior surgeon. At Winslow's instruction, Robinson had set up his field hospital just prior to the start of the engagement near the Summerville Road, but he quickly discovered that it had been placed "at point blank range, where the shells not only flew over his tables, but many dropped in the hollow where they were waiting for patients." Robinson "kindly added that he then had the intention of shooting someone (preferably me) and that he had changed his base without hesitation," remembered Winslow.[44]

Suspended following the start of the night assault, Union medical operations were not resumed until Robinson and the other surgeons entered the city. It was not until late in the evening of April 16 and early in the morning of April 17 that the Federal surgeons located and assumed control of Columbus's hospitals. Before the surgeons arrived, however, many of the Confederate convalescents who had claimed to be unfit to take up arms or help to defend the city somehow found the strength to make their escape into the dark streets of Columbus in hopes of evading capture.[45]

With the hospitals finally in operation, by the light of the moon which rose at about 12:15 A.M., ambulances from the division were dispatched to bring in the Union wounded. The Confederate wounded were a low priority, and while those whom the ambulances encountered were transported to the hospitals, many would have to wait until help came for them in the morning. The rough terrain, slashings, and entanglements of the battlefield inhibited the process of finding and recovering the wounded, and despite the best efforts of the dedicated men of the ambulance corps, "all night long the slow rumbling to the hospitals" continued.[46]

The Union soldiers, armed with their rapid-fire Spencer repeaters, "had done considerable execution" near the south end of the Confederate defenses. Shortly after the battle, Captain Hinrichs noted that "many a dead rebel covered the ground [and] on the bridge they laid thick." Fortunately for those who survived the battle but lay wounded on the field, both the victors and the vanquished attempted to administer aid and comfort until the ambulances arrived. Vanorsdol of the 4th Iowa recalled years after the war: "On the field of battle lay a wounded Rebel. . . . I know not how bad the wound nor who he was. He asked for a drink. I ordered someone to give him a drink, and as he took the canteen from his lips he exclaimed: 'Oh, what will become of my poor, widowed mother?' Thirty years have passed and gone, but I still wonder who he was, and whether he recovered to meet that mother."[47]

Late in the evening, as Columbus's citizens maintained a sleepless watch over their homes and loved ones, all around them exhausted Federal soldiers "lay themselves down to dream of victories yet to come." Huddled together and "moving like a restless sea," the Confederate prisoners had a long, cool night ahead in which to contemplate their fate. The excitement of the fight having begun to subside, Captain Barrow's thoughts turned to his friend Colonel Lamar, who lay lifeless in the street. "I asked permission to go out and recover his body," recalled Barrow. "It was granted, and under guard, four of us prisoners went out and found him right where he fell. We carried him into the place where we were confined, composed his limbs, as he lay on the ground, then laid ourselves down by his side. He slept that night with his friends."[48]

Despite the calm that prevailed in the captured city, sleep eluded some of the Union soldiers. For those few, the night was spent in reflection over the day's events or in wandering. "The burning buildings in Girard, which the Rebels had fired to light their operations, continued to cast a lurid glow upon the scene of conflict," and macabre were the recollections of those whose roaming led them back to the ravaged landscape.[49] "Still sleepless I ride back over the river to look upon the battlefield by moonlight," recalled Lieutenant Mitchell of Upton's staff. "Starting at the railroad bridge, I follow up the line of works that was so short time ago occupied by

Rebels. The ground is strewn with blankets, guns, haversacks, and camp debris while at intervals stand silent abandoned cannon. There are but few dead and wounded left on the field, but here and there is a marble face, or a wounded man who has raised himself up to hail the chance passer, or beg for water. It is all impressive, even weird, and rendered more so by the added light of some nearby burning building. As I turn back the ambulance corps with lights and stretchers comes out to pick up the unfortunates."[50]

Though the Union pickets and videttes would watch vigilantly for signs of danger, the night would hold little more excitement. The same held true for most of the prisoners, with the exception of a few who, under the watch of eyes heavy with sleep, were able to slip away into the shadows. The Battle for Columbus was ended. The occupation had begun.

From its opening shots in Crawford to its conclusion in the streets of Columbus, the Battle for Columbus lasted for more than fourteen hours. The major action, from the initial attack on the City Bridge until the capture of the Franklin Street Bridge, took eight hours and involved a combined total of more than six thousand soldiers. The night attack, which resulted in the defeat of Columbus's defenders and the capture of the city, took just over an hour to complete. Despite the intense fighting, particularly during the night phase of the battle, casualties on both sides were relatively light. The combined loss for both sides numbered only about 140 soldiers killed or wounded. Additionally, however, the Confederates lost nearly half their force—fifteen hundred men—to capture.[51]

More important than the casualties or the prisoners, both to the armies and to the residents of Columbus, was control of the city. For Wilson's Union forces, bent on smashing their way into Georgia and crushing the Confederate army's means of survival, the battle had been an unparalleled success. They had captured the Confederacy's second-leading producer of war material and had secured easy passage over the Chattahoochee, opening the door for further advancement of the campaign. For Cobb's Confederates, the battle had been a disaster. Georgia's and Alabama's reserves had been soundly beaten, scattered, and sent reeling back toward Macon, where they had little hope of assembling a force large enough to confront another thrust by the enemy. For Columbus, the consequences of the battle were even more tangible. Resting around the city were sleeping soldiers of an army dedicated to raining total war on all who opposed them. Dawn would begin Columbus's punishment—the price of revolution and resistance.

15
The Conflagration Begins

As the sun rose over Columbus on Monday, April 17, its rays fell on a city about to undergo the most tumultuous and destructive two days in its history. As a general rule, cities that surrendered to Wilson's Raiders or put up no resistance fared much better than those that chose the confrontational option. In either case, however, the Federal army would have to feed and provision itself by foraging from the locals, and would ensure the destruction of captured Confederate military supplies and infrastructure. In cities where no fight had occasioned the Union occupation, such as Montgomery and Tuskegee, Wilson had attempted to restrain his soldiers and confine their demolition to strictly military and government targets. Yet this policy would provide Columbus little protection. Columbus's role as the Confederacy's second-leading overall producer of war material and its largest remaining manufacturing center, combined with the vigorous yet futile defense it had made, meant that the city was sure to face the full brunt of total war.

Although the city stood on the brink of calamity and inferno, the early hours of Monday morning were calm and relatively peaceful. "Though our eyes are heavy for sleep, we resolve to keep them open," remembered Lieutenant Mitchell, who, like others, was eager to discover the full extent of the previous night's intense struggle. With spirits high after their victory, and with all indications that it would be "a delightful morning," many of the Federal troopers awoke with the expectation of spending the day resting from the incessant hard marching of the campaign and securing needed items.[1]

Less enthusiastic about the prospects of the day were those citizens who had opted to remain in their homes. "From tops of houses and the hillsides around the city, groups of frightened women and children watched the battle" during the night, and they knew that the fight had been a horrendous defeat. Concerned guardians, male and female, had spent the night sleeplessly watching over their families and property, and the morning found them still alert to any possible danger. Uncertainty weighed heavily on many hearts, too, while hours passed without word about the fates of loved ones who had gone to man the trenches. Adding to their uneasiness was the host of young Federal soldiers who now began to emerge from their rest and move through the streets.[2]

At the edge of town, where the Union pickets were keeping watch over their wakening comrades, there was still some excitement to be had. At the 10th Missouri's camp on the city's eastern edge, "several Rebs came in and gave up about daybreak." Shortly after that, "the videttes fired" and Hinrichs and three other Union troopers rode out to investigate. According to the captain, "About a dozen of the enemy had shown themselves and were fired upon. They had fled, I started in pursuit, and after a run of several miles, captured three of them and one mule, with saddle and bridle."[3]

Less comfortable that morning than their Federal captors were the many Confederate soldiers who had been taken prisoner during the battle and who sat huddled together inside the forts or in the small stockade in the city. For them, the night had been an unpleasant one in which many had contemplated their future fortunes and whether they would be sent north to occupy prison camps. For many of the civilians who had taken up arms and had been captured, there was a composed but nervous anticipation of the worst. Times were hard enough already. The prospects of an extended detention created intense uncertainty among those whose absence would leave wives and families without provision.[4]

For at least one of the prisoners, however, the morning brought an unexpected reunion that proved favorable to his situation. According to Major John Nisbet of the 26th Battalion Georgia Infantry, "The next morning I awoke in the camp of the Yankee provost guard. A tall cavalryman called out to me: 'Hello, Major Nisbet!' I went over to the guard and asked: 'Do you know me?' He answered: 'Don't you remember taking a batch of prisoners in 1864, from Sherman's army to Andersonville? I was one of those fellers. We all agreed that you treated us well for prisoners, and now I am going to do what I can for you.' He went away, [and] soon returned with a good breakfast."[5]

Though breakfast with a Federal soldier suited Nisbet just fine, for others that morning the experience was less pleasant. Such was the case for a young boy named George F. Peabody. The previous night he had "listened to the artillery firing on the Alabama side and was vastly excited by it—he thought it was grand. The next morning just as the Peabody family was about to sit down to breakfast, in marched a squad of Federal troops who coolly sat down at the table and ate that breakfast, apparently with great

relish." It was a defining moment for young Peabody, who later would an-
nounce: "I thought I knew something about war, but really did not know
what war was until I saw that man eating my breakfast." Unfortunately for
many of Columbus's residents, the lessons of war would not be learned so
innocuously.[6]

As soon as it was light, despite the potential hazards, the curiosity of
many citizens overcame their fear and large numbers began to venture
out into the streets. Almost en masse, hundreds of women, especially mill
workers, began to make their way downtown on foot, hoping to locate
relatives captured in the fighting, establish the safety of their friends and
neighbors, and secure food and other supplies, which most assumed would
soon be destroyed or made otherwise unavailable.[7]

So, too, many of the older men and those workers who had been ex-
empted from doing service under arms began to emerge from their residences. In Columbus lay their livelihoods. The shops and stores that lined
Broad Street and that were scattered around the rest of the city represented
their life's work and their means of survival. For many who were factory,
foundry, or mill workers, concern over their places of employment came
foremost to their minds, while running a close second was inquisitiveness
over the blue-clad strangers who were already busily preparing for the day's
activity.

The Union soldiers, too, were interested in all that was going on in the
city and in the masses that gathered to see them. "Hundreds of workmen
group about the streets as dazed and stupid as bees when robbed of their
honey," observed Lieutenant Mitchell, "but none receive so much attention
and sympathy as the factory girls, of whom there are nearly a thousand."[8]

Lastly, throngs of black servants and slaves, realizing that the Federal occupation severed their ties to their masters, began to swarm into the streets
to get a look at their liberators and to celebrate the Jubilee. Rumors of the
approaching raid had fueled the anticipation of Columbus's blacks, many
of whom saw Wilson's Raiders as their deliverers. From a nearby plantation, slave Rhodus Walton had listened to the battle the night before and
"followed the progress with keen interest." He remembered that when the
report of the cannons was heard that the other slaves "cried joyfully: 'It
ain't gonna be long now.'" A few, like W. B. Allen of Russell County, had
even become openly defiant in the days prior to the city's capture. "I told
my white folks straight from the shoulder, that . . . while I loved them and
would do any reasonable praying for them, I could not pray against my con-
science," Allen recalled, and "that I not only wanted to be free, but that I
wanted to see all the Negroes freed!"[9]

On the morning of April 17, as the first of the slaves slipped quietly from their quarters and made their way into the streets of Columbus to meet the Federal army, they began to encounter other escapees. Soon the excitement of the growing crowd of contrabands could no longer be contained, and a spirit of rejoicing prevailed. Dancing, singing, and questioning the Union troopers occupied their morning in anticipation of the spoils that freedom would shortly bring. "Oh, how . . . [they] did sing, shout, and pray on their knees in the dusty road," remembered Sergeant Conzett of the 5th Iowa. "The day ob Jubilee am come. Lawd bless the Yankee soldier and the Linkum men," the blacks called out in celebration to their emancipators. "They followed us in great crowds. . . . It was really affecting, and in many cases, pathetic, but it meant freedom . . . to them."[10]

Across the Chattahoochee, "boots & saddles was sounded by the bugles" and the remainder of the 4th Division began to assemble in preparation for moving across the bridge into Columbus. As the troopers made ready, reports of the battle began to circulate. According to Lieutenant William Wycoff of the 3rd Iowa, who was with the baggage train, "It was amazing what wonderful results had been attained." Wilson issued orders instructing the regiments to enter the city with "banners waving and swords drawn," much as they had done at Montgomery and Tuskegee. Surprisingly, the troopers' enthusiasm appears not to have been dampened by having to pass over the ground where the bodies of the fallen and the wreckage of war still lay. "We marched over in column of fours, our brass bands heading the regiments," remembered Conzett. "We put on all the airs we could, and about the whole population turned out to see us, for this was the first time they . . . had ever seen the boys in blue. . . . We were new and a curiosity, especially so to the common or poor people and the negroes."[11]

If some of Columbus's citizens felt somewhat relieved by the peaceful atmosphere of the early morning, it was because they did not know what unpleasant arrangements the Union command was conceiving for them. While the spectacle in the streets near the Franklin Street Bridge provided diversion enough for many of the soldiers and civilians, downtown at the Perry House Hotel, Wilson and the generals of the 4th Division met over breakfast to prepare the day's agenda. According to Wilson, "As Columbus was the last great manufacturing place and storehouse of the Confederacy, and we were still without official information as to what had taken place in Virginia, I resolved to destroy everything within reach that could be made useful for the further continuance of the rebellion."[12]

Winslow, having been placed in command of the city, was given the responsibility of directing the destruction. The entire 4th Division would be at his disposal and would be needed to complete the work. Likewise, Upton and Alexander were to assist in making the demolition proceed as smoothly as possible. Additionally, it was well established by this time in the campaign that the thousands of Federal troopers and contrabands that would soon pass through the city would further accelerate the wreckage.[13]

The principal tool at Winslow's disposal, and the one that would ensure the most rapid and complete consummation of the allotted task, was the torch. Wilson's Raiders were well seasoned in its use, having marched a route through Alabama easily identified by billowy gray clouds. "The smoke of burning houses, cotton, factories, foundries and collieries are to be seen in all directions, telling in thunderous tones to the quaking Rebels along our route that the Yankees are coming," Private Alva C. Griest had bragged a few days earlier. "The progress of our command can be traced plainly by the smoke." With the city's defenders fled or captured, and with thousands of Federals still en route to the city, Columbus now stood quietly on the brink of a similar fate.[14]

Following breakfast, Winslow and Alexander assembled their regimental commanders and instructed them to dispatch troopers to destroy all of the government and military stores in the city, as well as any other property of potential value to the Confederacy. Details were marched to the railroad depots, freight houses, arsenals, foundries, factories, laboratories, and mills, where, while some of the material was cataloged prior to destruction, much was simply torched. "The tasks were varied in character and executed under orders which allowed little rest and no discretion," remembered Winslow. The whole of the city's ability to aid the Confederacy had to be incinerated—and quickly.[15]

By 8 A.M. the occupying force "had broken the crust and was destroying the bread." As soon as the business of war resumed, the mood within the city was dramatically altered. The curiosity that the inhabitants had exhibited shifted to fear as parties of troopers moved through the streets bent on firing everything of importance to the Confederacy. With the exception of the city's poorest citizens and blacks, "the majority of the townspeople closeted themselves in their homes and left the city to the mercy of the invaders." "Soon recurred horrible scenes of destruction," recalled Captain Morse of Upton's staff. "Blocks and blocks burning and falling, shells bursting, and powder exploding made day and night hideous. Whole streets were burned. The fire at Selma was small compared to this."[16]

Within a short time, columns of smoke began to rise from all around the city. At the train depots, soldiers discovered thirteen locomotives and approximately two hundred cars loaded with military supplies that Confederate authorities had been unable to move out of the city in advance of the Union army. Additional cars were loaded with weapons and machinery that had been transported to Columbus from Selma and Montgomery prior to their capture. Hurriedly, the cars and their contents were set ablaze and the engines blown up or smashed. The nearby "machine shops, round-houses, and railway supplies" were also put to the torch, as were "three large warehouses containing 20,000 sacks of corn, an immense amount of quartermaster's property, commissary stores, and valuable machinery, all in readiness for shipment."[17]

Down by the river, the huge multi-level mills, including the Eagle, Howard, Grant, and Carter mills, were ignited. Even Clapp's Factory, which lay three miles north of the city, was burned. The Eagle, Howard, and Grant textile mills alone constituted a collective 80,000 square feet of workspace and contained besides all their other equipment, raw materials, and finished product, 342 looms with 8,400 spindles capable of pumping out a combined 10,700 square yards of woolens, cottons, and oilcloths daily. The fires from these and the other mills lining the Chattahoochee sent flames high into the air and particles of smoldering material drifting over the city. It was "a sight that made a very deep and lasting impression upon me," admitted Tom Ragland, one of the mill's slave workers.[18]

Marked especially for destruction at the hands of the Federals was also a supply of cotton constituting about 125,000 bales. In Montgomery and other places through which Wilson's Raiders had marched during their campaign, the Confederates had adopted the policy of destroying cotton stores in the path of the Union army to keep it from falling into enemy hands. At Columbus, the rapid defeat of the Confederate forces had left them no time to execute such an order. According to Wilson, however, "so long as they took that absurd view of it, I willingly helped them."[19]

That morning, the owners and investors associated with the seven largest cotton warehouses in the city came to Wilson seeking a reprieve. "Before the torch was applied," he recalled, "the warehouse-men came with their books, showing the number of bales on storage, and asked me to take for my own use what I thought proper on the sole condition that I should spare the remainder." Though sometimes prone to pardon when appealed to on the grounds of Christian charity, Wilson was little impressed by the offers. For him, the attempted bribery "made the destruction all the more certain." The warehouse men were quickly turned away, and their cotton, estimated in Columbus to be worth more than forty-three million dollars, and on the Northern or world markets in excess of sixty-two million dollars, was ignited.[20]

"Only one warehouse in the city was spared" from destruction by Wilson's Raiders. According to Wilson, "That was the property of a Union man [Mott], at whose house I made my headquarters. . . . Of course, I ordered his property safeguarded." Additionally, while all of the other mills in the city were put to the torch, in order to alleviate the suffering of the city's hungry poor, Wilson spared Mott's Palace Mill and one other, the gristmill of George Woodruff.[21]

Along the river and near the south side of town, Federal soldiers ransacked Columbus's heavy industry. The Muscogee Iron Works, "consisting of a foundry, machine-shop, and small-arms manufactory, blacksmith shop (30 forges), a large saddler's shop, with tools and . . . one engine," were all destroyed. Nearby, the Columbus Iron Works, which produced "sabers, bayonets, and trace-chains," was demolished after the thousand stand of arms found there were seized. The Naval Iron Works, with its rolling mills, iron foundries, copper and brass foundries, boiler shops, numerous engines, lathes, presses, forges, planers, and all other equipment, was broken up and set ablaze, as was the boathouse and "several offices and drawing rooms, with their contents" which were connected with the operation. Additionally, "5,000 rounds of large ammunition" intended for the CSS *Chattahoochee* and the CSS *Jackson* were exploded or dumped in the river.[22]

Just below the Naval Iron Works lay the Columbus Navy Yard, where moored peacefully at the dock rested the 220-foot-long, 54-foot-wide, 2,000-ton ironclad-ram CSS *Jackson*. Left behind by her engineers, the ship quickly became the center of much attention during the early hours of Monday morning as many troopers not otherwise engaged rode over to have a look. Winslow himself was apparently so impressed with the vessel that he personally examined its interior and workings and submitted a report on his findings to his superiors the following day.

The ship, "which would have been ready for active service in two weeks," and which was only lacking the installation of some of its armor, was found loaded with supplies and ammunition that had been hastily packed aboard before the arrival of enemy forces, in anticipation of a possible cruise downriver. While aboard the vessel, Winslow inspected the six 7-inch Brooke rifles that composed the ship's armament and took as trophies the *Jackson*'s flag as well as twenty-two of its signal colors. Concluding his tour, Winslow watched as the ship was doused with turpentine, set aflame, cut loose from its moorings, and "floated away to complete destruction." Little could Winslow or the other observing Federal soldiers have known as they watched the vessel slip around the bend, but the death of the *Jackson* would be protracted. Floating on the swollen waters of the Chattahoochee, the massive ship would smolder for nearly two weeks as it bumped along downstream until finally sinking thirty miles south of Columbus.[23]

Near the north end of town, two blocks east of Wilson's headquarters, the massive Haiman Brothers Factory complex met a similar fate as the rest

Fig. 19. The ironclad ram CSS *Jackson* on the Chattahoochee at Columbus. A work barge can be seen behind the *Jackson*. Courtesy Historical Collection, Special Collections, Tulane University Library.

of Columbus's industry. Though the factory had begun the war producing tinware, by 1865 the establishment was furnishing the army with weapons and equipment of all sorts. The remarkable success of the business had quickly elevated one of the two brothers—Louis—to prominence. He became a member of the city council, and prior to the battle even helped to coordinate with Mayor Wilkins for the city's defense. Louis's brother, Elias, was absent from Columbus for much of the war, and at this time he was in Europe attempting to buy steel and other supplies for the factory and arrange for its shipment via blockade runner. His was a futile effort, however, for by the end of the day the complex, which employed nearly five hundred workers and included a foundry, sword and bayonet manufactory, tin shop, harness shop, gunsmiths facilities, revolver factory, and other shops for producing tarred canvas belts, boxes, and accoutrements, would be completely incinerated.[24]

In the absence of Mayor Wilkins, who had been detained while serving the night before as leader of the city provosts, on the morning of April 17, Louis Haiman briefly assumed the role of Columbus's mayor. He was quickly relieved from this responsibility, however, when after meeting with Wilson, Wilkins was allowed to resume his position, under the condition that he issue a proclamation ordering the city's residents to provide thirty thousand rations to the hungry Union troopers by noon. For Wilson, the proclamation was a formality. He realized that Wilkins lacked the ability to enforce any measure of control over Columbus's alarmed citizenry, and understood that the deadline for assembling the rations could never be met. Even so, it provided him with justification for the measures that would necessarily be employed in order to provide forage enough for his army, and for the liberties his soldiers would take in securing it.[25]

Aiding greatly the destructiveness of the operations being conducted around Columbus was the discovery and distribution of enormous amounts of ammunition and explosives. By early morning, Union troopers had uncovered 13,000 pounds of gunpowder stored in the city's two magazines, nearly 100,000 rounds of artillery ammunition of all calibers, "large quantities of rockets," and innumerable stores of small-arms ammunition, not counting all that was left in the forts, on the battlefield, at the train depot, and in the wagons abandoned in the streets when Confederate forces fled the city. Additional explosive material was discovered at the navy yard and at the laboratories and other associated works. "By fire and explosives the . . . buildings were scattered in all parts of the city," remembered Adjutant Scott. "There was all that day, on all sides, a roaring of fires and an unceasing crash and rattle of explosions. The scene baffles description. . . . The labor and excitement of it were very fatiguing."[26]

Besides being useful for ensuring the demolition of all sorts of objects and property, the ignition of such quantities of explosives added greatly to the entertainment of many of the Union soldiers, and compounded in many cases the fright of Columbus's residents. Gilpin spent the morning "sitting out on the balcony smoking, talking, and listening to the exploding shell." He noted that while the scene was amusing to watch, "it is far more pleasant hearing them in this way, than out among them."[27]

The balcony upon which Gilpin sat to listen to the explosions was that of Upton's new headquarters. Earlier in the morning, Upton's staff moved the general's headquarters from the Battle House to a new location on Randolph Street (present-day 12th Street). The new site was the unoccupied home of the Rothschild family, which one Union trooper described as "the finest mansion in town." The Rothschilds operated a lucrative tailoring business in Columbus that manufactured uniforms for the Confederate army. Their company constructed at least "5,000 uniforms in the first year of the hostilities," and it "remained a prime producer for the Confederate Quartermaster Department throughout the war." Their home was a "magnificent, circa 1857, Corinthian-columned mansion" with magenta-colored walkways, a trellis garden, slave quarters, and even a two-story dormitory for guests. More importantly, Upton's staff found the place well furnished with a "cellar full of wines and brandies . . . and all manner of 'elegant accoutrements.'" The mansion would be his headquarters for the duration of the army's stay.[28]

The fires ravaging Columbus and the noise of the city's demolition could be seen and heard for miles around. The smoke on the horizon warned inhabitants of the surrounding countryside who had not yet heard of the battle's outcome that something had gone terribly wrong and that danger lurked nearby. For some of the Union soldiers still marching toward Columbus, however, the sights and sounds of the morning caused confusion. Sergeant Benjamin F. McGee was riding with the 72nd Indiana Mounted Infantry toward Columbus that morning when suddenly the men began to hear "heavy and continued firing" coming from the east. According to McGee,

> The 1st and 4th divisions had been ahead of us . . . and we, supposing they were having a hard fight at Columbus, hurried forward. In the course of an hour we got word that our forces had captured the place last night . . . and we felt relieved. The heavy artillery firing still continued, and we supposed there must be some mistake, and hurried on again. Pretty soon we could see vast columns of smoke, black and sulphurous, rising a thousand feet into the air, and we were sure there was a terrible battle raging. By 10 o'clock we were close enough to the city to see that the smoke was not the smoke of battle, but was from burning forts, arsenals, machine shops, steamboats, locomotives, cars, cotton, commissary stores, &c.[29]

Fire and explosives were by no means the only destructive forces at work in Columbus. Shortly after the burning of government property commenced, the remainder of the 4th Division was turned loose upon the city. Within a short time, the soldiers had broken open the stores and shops lining the business district, including "every store on Broad Street." Windows were smashed and doors kicked in at shops all around the city, and merchandise of all kinds was tossed out into the streets in piles to be sifted through by the growing mob of soldiers, poor whites, and contrabands. As news of the looting spread, more soldiers rushed downtown to secure trophies and booty.[30]

The pillaging was widespread and, according to many Union soldiers, a generally accepted part of war. Even Winslow seems to have accepted the fact that the army "to a great extent . . . would leave on its route nothing behind save the people, the buildings, and the land." Some modern historians have emphasized that many of the businesses in Columbus had converted either wholly or in part to supplying goods for the army. This is not surprising given the atmosphere of entrepreneurism fostered by the needs of the war effort. Even businesses that were not directly contracted to produce for the government were more or less involved in the economy that sustained the city's production of materials vitally important to maintaining the army's ability to wage war. Nevertheless, though participation in the Confederate economy may have contributed to the business district's ransacking, it seems obvious that most of the troopers required no justification. Sergeant Conzett probably summed up the troopers' view of the matter best: "Considering the deserted stores and the goods left in them our legitimate property, we soon had them opened up and appropriated whatever we found that we could use."[31]

George Peabody, the young boy who had learned a lesson about war at breakfast, would be taught another before the day was out. That morning young Peabody ventured downtown, probably along with his father, to check on the family business—a general store on Broad Street. Upon arrival, he discovered that soldiers had broken into the store and that looters were rummaging through a large stock of shoes. According to Peabody, "When a man found a pair of shoes that fit him, he stopped his search and rushed out with this find." This "shortsightedness" bothered Peabody a great deal, as he realized that if the culprits "had just taken a little more time . . . [they] might have found several pairs that fit him."[32]

With no compunction about taking whatever was to be had, Conzett joined the other soldiers in looting a bank and a jewelry store. "The jewelry man had managed to get away with most of his stock, but what he left we got," he remembered. "A few cheap watches, finger rings, broaches, and necklaces was about all there was. The banker had taken his books and gold & silver coin, . . . but had locked his vault or large safe. We soon had that open (for powder was plenty), and found it full . . . of Confederate money. Thousands and thousands of dollars, we stuffed our pockets full of it."[33]

The soldiers were not alone in their quest for spoils. As soon as the looting began, some of those onlookers who had earlier watched the blue-clad strangers with curiosity now joined them in the streets. According to Winslow, "There are thousands of almost pauper citizens and negroes, whose rapacity under the circumstances of our occupation, and in consequence of such extensive destruction of property, was seemingly insatiable. The citizens and negroes formed one vast mob, which seized upon and carried off almost everything movable, whether useful or not."[34]

The war had taken its toll on the poorer citizens of Columbus, especially the mill and factory workers. Prices were inflated and goods scarce. With no way to know how much of the city might be spared, the workers, many of whom were young women, charged into the streets in order to save what they could for their own use. Joining them were thousands of newly liberated blacks, who, encouraged by the actions of their emancipators, appear to have quickly been stirred into a thieving frenzy.[35] "It is a strange scene and we watch the free play of human nature," commented Lieutenant Mitchell of the 7th Ohio. "The stores and shops are open, and the contents without cost are at the mercy of fancy or desire. . . . Soldiers are going for the substantials, women for apparel, and niggers for anything red. There is evident demoralization among the females. They frantically jam and jostle in the chaos and seem crazy for plunder."[36]

16

Laid in Ruins

By mid-morning, just when it appeared that the turmoil within the city could not be magnified, the rest of Wilson's Cavalry Corps began to arrive. That part of the 1st Division that was not detached with Croxton in Alabama or with LaGrange in West Point arrived first in Columbus, along with their commander, General McCook. As they moved down off the hills of Alabama toward the bridge leading from Girard into Columbus, the newly arrived soldiers were amazed at the destruction. In Girard alone, the Rock Island Paper Mill, the Girard Nail Factory, two locomotives and fifteen cars, "an extensive round-house and railroad machine-shop," a rope factory, several government blacksmith shops, and a match factory near the Alabama end of the Franklin Street Bridge were all in flames.[1]

Following closely on their heels came the lead regiments of the massive 2nd Division under the command of Colonel Minty (who had taken over command of the division after General Long's wounding at Selma). These soldiers, as they entered Columbus, nearly tripled the Union occupation force, swelling the total within the city to more than nine thousand troops.[2]

In keeping with what had been established as the rule, the victorious soldiers of the 2nd Division entered Columbus in columns of four, buttoned up, and with sabers drawn. The volunteer bands of several units were even assembled at the head of the regiments and played patriotic airs as the columns crossed the bridge and filed through the smoky streets. The 72nd Indiana "moved through the city to the tune of 'Hail Columbia,'" which the unit's surgeon found "appropriate, but somewhat ironical," as it had been Wilson's Raiders who had "given Columbus hail."[3]

While some of the newly arrived cavalrymen were impressed by the pageantry, others were more impressed by the blazing landscape. Sergeant McGee remembered: "The rebels had used a great deal of wood in the construction of the forts west of the river, and these had been set on fire.

There were arsenals and powder houses connected with the forts, and by the time we got to the bridge . . . the shells were bursting and throwing fire and dirt a hundred feet high, making the place a thousand times more noisy than pleasant or safe . . . the explosions were constant and almost deafening."[4]

Throughout the late morning and early afternoon, the men of the 1st and 2nd divisions marched through Columbus to its eastern outskirts where camps and guards were established. This accomplished, the cavalrymen were allowed to make their way back into the city or out into the surrounding countryside to secure forage for themselves, fodder for their animals, and other items as they desired. The troopers were also charged with destroying any property they encountered that could be of value to the Rebel cause. The effect was that within a short time the riotous atmosphere that had gripped the business district was spread to the city's neighborhoods and suburbs. The pursuit of forage and other prizes quickly brought the blue-clad soldiers onto the porches and into the parlors of many Columbusites.[5]

Though apologists for both sides have tended to either exaggerate or diminish the extent to which the Federal raiders' need for provisions was accompanied by a lust for plunder, it appears than in the majority of cases, the two went hand in hand. For example, at the home of aged War of 1812 veteran General Anderson Abercrombie, near Columbus, though a portion of the foraging party quietly entered the property and began to search it for food and livestock, the remainder headed straight for the house. There the unsuspecting general "was sitting in a chair on the front gallery by the door, and the first intimation he had that the thieves were at work was a hand from behind him passing, snakelike, over his shoulder and down to his vest pocket to get his watch." Roused to distress, Abercrombie soon discovered a party of nine soldiers had entered the home and was searching for treasure, going "through every wardrobe, bureau, closet, etc." In addition to a great many other useful things, this gang made off with all of the family's silverware and jewelry.[6]

At a home just north of Columbus, "the raiders caught the mules, . . . took everything out of the smokehouse, and dug up the floor in an effort to find some hidden money." A family member recalled that "the soldiers went through everything in the house, turning up mattresses and rugs, and scattering the contents of trunks and boxes." Even the boardinghouses in Columbus were not overlooked, and an unlucky traveler by the name of Joel Bush observed that "Wilson's Raiders came down on the place and looted every house in town . . . of everything valuable." They even stole Bush's particularly fine violin, which was not recovered until thirty-five years later when Bush's brother happened to spot it while passing through Meridian, Mississippi.[7]

Union soldiers sought out horses, mules, and other livestock for confiscation and carried them off in large numbers. To save their animals from seizure, some of Columbus's residents hid their horses in their homes, cellars, and basements. One of those unable to protect his animal in such a way, however, was young Oscar Straus, son of a Columbus merchant. "Looting began by the town rabble, led by several drunken Federal soldiers; cotton warehouses were burned, the contents of which represented the savings of many, including most of my father's," remembered Oscar. "All horses were seized, and among them our little pony, which I never saw again, though I still retain a vivid picture of him in my mind's eye." Ironically, Straus would go on to become a U.S. ambassador and the secretary of commerce under President Roosevelt and would later comment: "Frequently since, when I have met that . . . old veteran, General Wilson . . . I have jestingly reproached him for taking from me the most treasured possession I ever had."[8]

Not all the foraging and looting took place in Columbus. Soon after their arrival, some of the bummers marched back across the Chattahoochee to scour Girard and the Alabama countryside. "They all had black hair—ugly hair," observed Aunt Fannie Bellamy, a Russell County slave girl, of her unwelcome guests, "an' they jest rambled through the house a-cussin' an' a-carryin' on, an' breakin' up all the dishes. The ole master, he run away." Farther outside town, "the day was filled with dread and terror" as the country folks anticipated the arrival of the enemy at their doorsteps. W. F. Ellison was a young man who was visiting his aunt's plantation for the spring. "We stood out in the yard, both whites and blacks, and watched the smoke coming from the burning gins and piles of cotton kept on the surrounding plantations," he remembered of that suspenseful Monday. "Suddenly, two hundred cavalry dashed up to the front gate and in an instant they were everywhere—ransacking the pantry, the whole house, the dairy, smokehouses—in fact, everything. What havoc they wrought!"[9]

Unfortunately for the people of Columbus and its environs, the influx of persons bent on disorder did not end with the arrival of the last of Minty's division. Following in the extreme rear of Wilson's command came the pontoniers, the baggage train, and the men composing the corps' three newly formed colored regiments. These latter regiments, composed of male contrabands collected at Selma and other points along the march, had been outfitted with surplus horses and mules captured by Wilson's command, and upon arrival in Columbus they filed through the streets in ranks greater than three thousand individuals deep.[10]

Though it is likely that many of the men composing the colored regiments volunteered for duty, there is also evidence that male blacks were forced to join either to get them out of the ranks of the white regiments, where their presence in large numbers was seen by some as an encumbrance, or to provide Wilson with a labor force that could be employed to fix roads, rebuild bridges, and conduct foraging missions. As had been done at other points along the campaign, some of Columbus's newly liberated blacks were either persuaded or coerced into joining the regiments. Rias Body was a slave from just north of Columbus. "In 1865, Yankee soldiers captured him (much against his will), took him, . . . and drilled him for two or three months." Columbus slave George Brooks endured a similar ordeal. After going to meet his liberators, he was captured, corralled with other "recruits," and forced to join the ranks.

In Columbus, the colored brigade was outfitted with captured clothing, equipment, tents, and other items from the city's bountiful stores, and were even armed. According to one Union eyewitness, the black soldiers "were marched along by fours and supplied as they passed by . . . [with] a gun and filled cartridge box a piece; also [to] shoes, socks, caps and underclothes." In addition to the arms found in the stores at Columbus, at least seven hundred of the more than twelve hundred Confederate arms picked up off the battlefield were issued to the black soldiers.[11]

Finally, following in the wake of the colored brigade came a legion of black camp followers who had for some time been trailing the army, scouring the countryside alongside the cavalrymen for subsistence and spoil. "The camp of negroes, which all the time moves in the rear of the trains . . . 'banged' anything in the way of a camp we ever saw or expected to see," remembered Sergeant McGee. "There were negro men, women, and children, on horse-back, ass-back, mule-back, cow-back; in carts, wagons, wheelbarrows, and every other way you could think." Estimates recorded for the number of black refugees who trailed the Federal cavalry to Columbus range from three thousand to as many as seven or eight thousand. When added to the mob of newly liberated blacks already doing damage in the city, it is possible that by Monday afternoon close to ten thousand contrabands ranged the streets.[12]

As the newly arrived blacks crossed the bridge into Columbus, they immediately joined "the poor citizens [who] also were helping themselves freely to everything of the stores what suited their taste and want, and indeed everything seemed to suit them. Of course," explained Hinrichs of the 10th Missouri, "our boys were not very backward neither," and together soldiers, poor whites, and runaway slaves worked in unison to desolate the town's businesses and storehouses. At one point, "an army of negroes . . . which numbered by the thousands, were helping themselves from piles of Confederate clothing to full suits of grey" in the center of downtown.[13]

Winslow, in a report made out the following day, enumerated some of the property in Columbus that was "found in store and issued to the troops and negroes or destroyed." Included in the items dispersed to the soldiers and pilferers were "4,500 suits of Confederate uniform, 5,890 yards of army jeans, 1,000 yards osnaburgs, 8,820 pairs of shoes, 4,750 pairs of cotton drawers, 1,700 gray jackets, 4,700 pairs of pants, 2,000 pairs of socks . . . 400 shirts . . . [and] 650 gray caps." In addition to the uniforms issued to the black regiments or simply carried off by the mob, Union soldiers whose uniforms had been worn out from the vigorous campaigning substituted Rebel garb for their own. "Large numbers of gray uniforms were issued," recalled Private William Barker of the 3rd Iowa, "and scores . . . [of Union men] were dressed in gray from head to foot." Wilson put the total number of uniforms destroyed city-wide around "16,000 suits."[14]

For many of the newly liberated slaves it appeared that the long-awaited "Year of Jubilee" had come. Certainly, the scene surrounding the fall of the city appeared to be the much anticipated day of reckoning, when all slaves would be freed, white wealth would be broken up and redistributed, and the Caucasian grip on the reins of power and authority would forever be loosed. Of course, such was not the case, but for those blacks caught up in the frenzied excitement, for a moment at least, it seemed possible.

Great crowds of contrabands roamed the streets and the countryside eager to exercise their newfound liberty. Prayers and rejoicing greeted many of the Federal soldiers, and the singing of the throngs penetrated the atmosphere. "Us is gonna be free! Jes as sho's anything. God has heard our prayers!" the slaves had exclaimed just prior to the battle. Now, in the wake of emancipation, nine-year-old Ella Hawkins questioned her folks as they rejoiced, "What does free mean?" It was a question that would be a while in the answering.[15]

Despite emancipation and the sense of excitement that prevailed among Columbus's blacks, not all the runaways' new experiences as freedmen were pleasant that day. The "Year of Jubilee," for some, became a rather confusing time. Naturally, the blacks who chose to escape looked upon their liberators for guidance, but in many cases they were led astray or poorly treated. Such was the case for Henry, the slave youth of Trinity Episcopal's Reverend Quintard. "Henry, who was sent to town early in the morning with a letter . . . did not return, but went off with his new friends," remembered the Reverend. "Later in the day he rode up to the house of Captain

Cothran with a soldier and while there, a Federal officer came up and ordered them both out of the yard and gave Henry a sound beating with his sword and cursed him. Such was his first taste of freedom."[16]

The realities of the Federal occupation were experienced in varied ways, too, by those slaves who did not immediately abandon their masters but instead waited to see for themselves whether the troopers could be trusted. For some, the meeting with their liberators was far from positive. When several Federals burst into the kitchen of one Columbus home and demanded dinner, Aunt Minty, the family cook, "was scared out of her wits, and raised her hands, pleading for mercy." "Get some ham and eggs for us quick. Quick, you old dunce!" shouted the troopers, who then ordered her to "bring on the pies." Despite the soldiers' objections that they had never seen "a house as big as that . . . [which] did not have pies in it," Aunt Minty "called on all the saints to witness that she had no pies" and informed her mistress when the soldiers departed: "Them is the meanest people I ever did see."[17]

Numerous similar incidents have been recorded by Columbus historians. At the Shepherd home, the family servant was cautioned not to tell anyone where the family had hidden the silverware and valuables. "But," she protested, "if they threaten to shoot me, I'll haft to tell!" "The Yankees soon came, and when they asked the frightened Negress about the silver," she responded quickly and honestly: "We done sent it to White Sulphur Springs." "The Yankees didn't believe her," and after making "an unsuccessful search" they departed.[18]

Not all the Union soldiers who visited slaves at homes or plantations were as obnoxious, however. In many cases the first impressions they made were quite agreeable. "When the Yankees came through, one of them, I remember, picked up my little brother and kissed him," remembered slave girl Harriet Benton. Interestingly, despite the Federals' apparent affection, Benton remembered that the soldiers "then . . . burned and stole everything of value on the . . . place that they could find."[19] At the nearby Holt plantation, when slave Mary Gladdy complained to the newly arrived Yanks that her brother had been unjustly whipped by a black foreman named Warren a few days previous, her new friends quickly proved their worth. According to Gladdy, when the soldiers turned to the foreman and announced, "'Well, we will see Warren about that . . . ,' he flew from home and didn't come back for a week!"[20]

Gladdy's case was not unique. According to some sources, it was customary for Wilson's Raiders to attempt to find out before visiting a plantation "whether the master was mean or kind and always treated him as he had treated his slaves." In several instances this turned out badly for the owner. In the case of Sam Walton, who lived near Columbus, the Federals had heard so much of Walton's cruelty before arriving that upon reaching his plantation he was taken outside and "given the works," much to the enjoyment of his former chattel.[21]

Despite Union commanders' orders mandating the protection of Columbus's citizens, as each additional regiment or mass of black refugees arrived, the riotous atmosphere in the city and its environs escalated. Federal authorities did try, however, to prevent the burning of private homes and the intentional physical injury of residents. Noble, who had been appointed the city's provost marshal, stationed detachments of men from the 3rd Iowa around the city in order to prevent violence and instructed them to arrest unruly soldiers and civilians. Some of the provosts did good work.[22]

At the home of Mrs. Walker of Columbus, a Union soldier "under the influence of home-made blackberry wine, which he had found concealed in a haystack, became very rowdy and demanded a silver knife and fork with which to eat." When the lady of the house told him that all the silver had been sent away, he "became infuriated and shaking his fist in his informant's face, . . . promised to return . . . to burn the house." Fortunately for Mrs. Walker, one of the provosts was taking a nap in her hallway when "the outraged ruffian returned with torches." The provost was quickly awakened, "a fierce encounter followed, and it was only after force of arms had been used that the incensed 'Yank' was marched off."[23]

Yet despite their admirable intents and deeds, within a short time most of Noble's provosts were completely overwhelmed. Indeed, the colonel's headquarters were swamped by a "great rush . . . for passes and guards," and when Noble attempted to wade through the teeming masses in the streets to inspect his details, he found his work inhibited by a mob of women and blacks. "There are a great many poor people here and the destruction of property was great, though we guarded a great deal," observed the 3rd Iowa's Private Simeon Veatch, who was among those assigned to patrol the streets.[24]

Though the provosts made some arrests, at least a few of them openly participated in ravaging the city. "[I] was put on provost duty," remembered Private William Gray of the 3rd Iowa, and "at this place we took all the flour and bacon that was in the city and give it to the poor, and helped ourselves to anything we wanted." In assessment of their performance, Veatch admitted: "All government property was burnt, . . . the citizens pillaged the town, and we enjoyed the cigars, tobacco, and plenty of good wine and brandy."[25]

The stories recorded by the people of Columbus about the day share many common elements. Numerous are the accounts of stolen food, jewelry, clothes, and other belongings as well as tales of simple vandalism. The discovery of large quantities of liquor stashed in homes and businesses contributed enormously to the intensity of the disturbances. "They poured in every minute of the day," remembered one Columbus woman, keeping the public constantly on alert. At some of the homes, armed soldiers "took the dresses of the young ladies . . . and tied them together to feed horses in. . . . Some of the prettiest ones they gave to the servants, and they gave the horses and carriages . . . to the negroes, too." At other places they took the silverware and "searched every room." A particularly appalled individual reported: "One old fellow went all through my draws." Realizing the futility of resistance, most Columbusites submitted without protest, but in some places families tried at least to appear defiant. One young woman remembered that she "talked pretty brave until the drunken ones came and then . . . had nothing else to say."[26]

At the home of sixty-seven-year-old John Banks, "the soldiers had great privilege, roamed around where they pleased, pillaging where they chose." Lucy Banks, who was staying with her father, recalled: "About twenty came down our lane, half Negroes . . . and commenced forcing open the smoke house . . . they took every ham, all the flour and meal, sugar, coffee . . . and off they went. . . . One old [soldier] grabbed Father's hat, but he held on. Our guard finally came to the rescue and made him give it up."[27]

Despite their losses, the Banks were more fortunate than many other Columbus residents in that the detachment of soldiers camping in their yard provided them with a safeguard. Shortly after the destruction began, residents discovered that the Federal soldiers who quartered in and around their homes were very territorial about their accommodations. Often these soldiers left one or more troopers at the home at all times to protect the residents as well as their own property, and, ironically, civilians of Columbus credit these safeguards with preventing a great deal of personal injury that otherwise might have been perpetrated upon them by the baser elements of the army and the plunder-crazed throngs that roamed the streets.[28]

The problem for the people of Columbus lay in the fact that there were too few safeguards to go around. Many residents had to do without, flee to the protection of their neighbors' safeguards, or try to secure one on their own. While many citizens barricaded themselves in their houses and hoped the mob would pass them by, "the beautiful widow, Julia Hurt Colquitt," was unsatisfied with this option and "took her dead husband's West Point class ring and went to see Gen. Wilson." Her appeal did not go unnoticed. "The general, himself a West Pointer, gave Julia and her family his assurance that they nor any of their property would be harmed," and she received her safeguard.[29]

Other persons were also able to secure safeguards from the Federal commander, but not without some effort. When Reverend Quintard learned that an "infamous scoundrel . . . [had] outraged one of the negro women in the presence of the ladies" at the house adjacent, and had threatened to kill a man who attempted to intercede on her behalf, he decided to obtain sentries for himself and his neighbors. Accompanied by a concerned Union soldier, Quintard was directed to multiple headquarters and given a considerable run-around. Frustrated, he took his grievance straight to the top.[30]

At Wilson's headquarters, Quintard wrote out his complaints on a calling card and waited in the yard for an opportunity to lay the matter before the commanding general. Eventually, the interview was granted, and after relating how "the wretches twice put their pistols to . . . [his friend's] head threatening to shoot him," Wilson is said to have replied "with a good degree of indignation, 'Doctor, I would hang such a man in a moment, if I could but put my hands on him.'" The matter was immediately turned over to Noble, and safeguards were dispatched for Quintard and his neighbors.[31]

For those residents without a safeguard, there was no guarantee of security. In several instances, frustrated, belligerent troopers visited violence and torture on area inhabitants. When Mrs. Annie Nunnally, who was minding the farm in her husband's absence, heard of the Federals' approach, she had all the family's valuables buried in the yard. When the soldiers arrived, however, the spot was soon discovered, the slaves were ordered to dig up the loot, and the soldiers "whipped this Southern white woman on her naked body, inflicting sores that she carried to her dying day." "We were glad when those Yankees left . . . and we had to nurse Miss Annie for some time before she could stir around again," remembered Mary Carpenter, one of the slaves, adding: "If the soldiers hadn't been armed, us niggers would have protected her."[32]

Probably the most horrific act perpetrated on an innocent occurred just outside town at the Thornton House. There, as the elderly Mrs. Thornton lay sick in bed, several Federal soldiers barged into the dwelling and demanded money. "They tried every way they could to make . . . [Mr. Thornton] tell where it was, and took him forcibly out of the house, saying they would hang him, if he did not tell. He refused to tell them anything, so they tied him and hung him up by his thumbs, in full view of his sick wife and left him hanging until they thought he was about to die, and cut him down and left him on the ground." Fortunately, "Some negroes came to his relief, . . . cut the cords, . . . and helped to get him in the house."[33]

Besides demonstrating the depth of the depravity exhibited by a small portion of the Northern army, Mr. Thornton's experience shows that while a significant segment of Columbus's slave population abandoned their owners and joined the chaos in the streets, many others proved both loyal and helpful to their masters and other whites. That afternoon there were numerous occasions when trusted servants helped to protect their families from intruders, watched over children while parents were occupied with saving property, or came to the rescue of a neighbor in distress.[34]

Often, families entrusted their most treasured possessions to the protection of a loyal driver or housekeeper. Such was the case with Jeff, a coachman for a prominent Columbus family. Jeff was sent away to hide the family's silver and jewelry at a distant plantation just prior to the arrival of Federals. On his return, while passing an area "where the land was very poor," he ran into several soldiers.[35] "'Hi' they called out to him, 'Is the land further down any worse than it is here?' 'Yassuh, boss, it sho is. De fu'ther you go, de wuss it gits,' he answered and grinned as he knew he wasn't telling the truth, but was saving his master's possessions."[36]

While there were malignant forces within the Union ranks whose actions stirred up hostility among the population, most of the soldiers harbored no malice toward the people of Columbus. Though the overall devastation visited on the city was widespread, at numerous homes the damage done was light and the terror to the inhabitants minimal. "One of the Yankee soldiers who was camped in our grove came to the back door Monday . . . and asked for something to eat," remembered Miss Redd, who was but a young girl at the time. At the instruction of her mother, Miss Redd took the soldier some fried bread, but "was trembling from head to foot." She recalled: "The man laughed at me when he saw that I was frightened, and said with a grin on his face, 'Is yer skeered, Sis?' I told him, 'No,' but when I looked, all the wafers had slid off the plate."[37]

Aware of the reputation that preceded them, some of the troopers went out of their way to assure civilians that although they intended to take what they needed, they were not without compassion and kindness. At one plantation, as the troopers began to search the premises, they encountered a young slave who was so startled by their sudden appearance that he ran into the house and hid under a bed. The boy, Dave Ramsey, remembered: "That Yankee followed me into the house, dragged me out, lifted me up on his shoulder, and toted me round, just to show me he meant no harm." Of course, young Ramsey did not understand what was happening at the time. "I hollered and yelled awfully, for I was terribly scared!" he recalled.[38]

Captain Hinrichs of the 10th Missouri met "a lot of poor women and children who . . . looked pitiful, indeed." When questioned about their condition, they explained that they were going to seek refuge in the countryside because, with the factories destroyed, "they did not know how to provide food for their starving children." This sad situation so worried Hinrichs that he resolved to help alleviate their suffering. "Just then," he remembered, "I noticed ten or twelve negroes running from town each one with a bag of Confederate meal on their shoulders. I made every one of them turn back and carry their loads to the house of these poor women."[39]

Though officially their duties were to destroy Columbus's ability to make war and to secure adequate supplies to meet the army's needs, it seems clear that most of the blue-clad troopers only wanted to carry out their orders and secure a few comforts that would come in handy when their rapid march resumed. Indeed, many of the soldiers only wanted a break from the grueling pace of the campaign and to find a few hours of entertainment or relaxation. In pursuit of these less sinister goals there occurred "many laughable and ridiculous incidents."[40]

"I was up in a fine old church . . . and found a darkey . . . [and] made him pump for me, while I played the organ," recalled Private Gilpin. "It sounded magnificently, . . . and as there was no one there but the darkey to comment, I ran my fingers up and down the keyboard in lively style, then pulled out the stops and let it have it, rolling out billows of sound that made the old church tremble." The private's enthusiasm must have been great, as "it brought the darkey up with eyes rolling." "Deed, suh, dat's suttinly diffunt fum any playin' I *evah* heard!" the man commented. "That's a cavalry fugue with artillery accompaniment," replied Gilpin, "and the only one of the kind."[41]

Alcohol was a contributing factor in much of the sport undertaken by the cavalrymen. In the afternoon, as a mess from the 72nd Indiana was sitting down to "a good supper of slapjacks and molasses, ham and eggs," no doubt courtesy of the citizens of Columbus, there came rushing toward them one of their fellow messmates who had been out foraging. "He had . . . a wooden bucket of pinetop whiskey in his hand, and some whiskey that wasn't in the bucket. He came for us on the jump," remembered Private John C. Bible of Company E, who was seated beside the fire. "His mule sailed clear over the head of one of the boys and set both hind feet into his tin plate of cakes and molasses. The fellow looked up and said . . . 'I wish you would keep your mule out of my dish,' and went ahead with his supper as though nothing had happened."[42]

Though there was plenty of entertainment to keep the majority of the city's occupiers happy throughout the morning and afternoon, for some there was still unpleasant work to do. By afternoon, the Federal ambulance corps had finished driving the Union wounded across the Chattahoochee to the hospitals in the city, but Federal burial details were still completing the disagreeable work of interring the Northern dead either at the city cemetery or, in some cases, on the battlefield where they perished. Though the burial details made rapid work of disposing of their killed, most of the Confederate casualties were afforded no such courtesy. On both sides of the Chattahoochee, it was left to the townsfolk to dispose of their fallen.[43]

On the Georgia side of the river, where the battle's more prominent personalities fell, the Rebel dead were quickly gathered by concerned citizens and taken to Linwood Cemetery, where they joined the hundreds of other Confederate soldiers already engaged in their final rest. On the battlefield across the river in Alabama, however, the burial of the Confederate dead was left to the discretion of the civilians of that section. In one instance, a Southern cavalryman who was killed on Moses Hill near the southwest corner of Girard during the afternoon fight was buried on the spot where he met his fate. In another case, when a Girard family discovered that a mortally wounded combatant had dragged himself onto their porch before expiring, they arranged to have his remains laid in their family plot. These were the exceptions, however. For many of those slain in the trenches in Girard there was no immediate action taken on their behalf, and it is uncertain how long they lay where they were killed. All indications suggest it may have been until the next day or even later.[44]

Though for the Confederate dead all suffering had ended, such was not the case for the wounded. Even as late as the afternoon of April 17, some Rebel soldiers injured in the previous night's action still awaited medical treatment. Small parties of civilians scoured the battlefield, navigating the wreckage for signs of life. "Our dead had been already gathered, but the Rebs were yet laying about in the works, and they were at work gathering the wounded," observed Hinrichs of the recovery operations.[45]

By afternoon, only the most seriously wounded remained on the field. Those with lesser wounds had either been rounded up along with the other prisoners the night before or had escaped to be treated elsewhere, thus making an accurate estimate of Confederate casualties hard to assess. Nevertheless, when discovered, the casualties that yet remained untended were dealt with in varying ways. Some were taken to the hospitals in Columbus where the Federal surgeons were overseeing operations. From what records remain it appears that at least forty wounded individuals were admitted for care and attended by the Northern doctors. Others were paroled and allowed to be treated by family and friends at homes in the city.

Joining the wounded from the battlefield at the hospitals were those less seriously injured Confederate soldiers who had been captured during the fight and forced to remain with the other prisoners during the night. Additionally, surprisingly large numbers of Confederate prisoners who claimed to have diseases or infirmities like rheumatism, chronic diarrhea, and severe fatigue were given passes allowing them to be transported to the hospitals for care. It would appear, however, that many of the sick and wounded who were transferred to the infirmaries were not unhealthy enough to remain there, and made a break for it at their first opportunity. Records taken at the time show that, of the more than 150 individuals who deserted from Columbus's Marshal and Walker hospitals in the days following the battle, at least 60 were admitted and deserted on the same day—April 17. Private James Howard was among this group. "When the doctor called for the wounded to go to the hospital," he remembered, "I put my arm in a sling so as to get out." Claiming he was suffering from rheumatism, Howard was admitted to Marshal Hospital, then promptly escaped. The remainder of the deserters did not linger much longer, and all were counted as missing by the time of the next enumeration of patients on April 20.[46]

Not all of the Confederate prisoners who were obviously ill or who had some other ailment or injury were taken to the hospitals, however. Many of the officers and elderly citizen prisoners, who were thought trustworthy, were paroled and allowed either to go home or to seek shelter in the city. Included in this number were not only selected individuals from the more than fifteen hundred prisoners that were taken during the battle but also a few of the hundreds of Confederate prisoners who trudged into Columbus in tow of the 1st and 2nd divisions of Wilson's Cavalry Corps.[47]

"I had been very sick just before going into Columbus," recounted Lieutenant Colonel Frank Montgomery of the 1st Mississippi Cavalry, who had been captured at Selma. Along with several other officers, Montgomery appealed for and received a parole from Wilson directly and was allowed to leave. Shortly thereafter, while riding through downtown, he was stopped by a provost guard. "Supposing he wished to see if I were paroled," remembered Montgomery, "I stopped . . . and took my parole from my pocket." "He was now in reach of me and stooping over he lifted my hat from my head saying, 'I don't want to see your parole, I was looking for a better hat than mine, yours is not as good,' and he stuck it back on my head and moved on." "Nothing in my life," remembered Montgomery, "made me so angry, and if I had but a weapon, I believe in spite of the consequences I would have killed him."[48]

Precisely what conditions warranted a parole and to whom paroles were issued appears to have varied a great deal and most likely was at the discretion of those Union commanders able to issue them. Colonel Wesley Hodges of the 17th Georgia was one of the convalescents who had volunteered to fight and was captured in the battle. His son-in-law gave Hodges's guards "money and silver to ensure their kindness to their prisoner." Later in the afternoon, "through the entreaties of his sister . . . [Hodges] was permitted to go home under parole with three Yankee officers detailed to guard him."[49]

Wilson himself appears to have issued several paroles throughout the afternoon, including those to the officers of the 1st Mississippi. He did not, however, just hand them out to anyone who inquired. As one young woman, whose mother was sick and whose father was a prisoner, remembered: "I was sent down to interview General Wilson and ask him to let Father see Mother. General Wilson was sitting in a red plush chair and twirling a riding whip. I went to him and stuttered what I wanted. He stared at me and growled out, 'No! The innocent must suffer for the guilty.' "[50]

For most of those prisoners who were themselves unable to secure a parole, and whose families had been denied, there was nothing they could do but sit and wait. Also, while some of the prisoners were clever enough to fool the guards into believing they were sick so they could go to the hospital and then escape, most were not that cunning. Despite this, all hope of release was not lost. Fourteen-year-old George Fontaine, who had gone to do his duty in the battle, secured his "parole" in another fashion. During the afternoon, George's aunt "went to the stockade to take food and provisions" to the men who were inside. "Following her was a little darkey of about the same size as George and he carried on his head an old-fashioned dinner tray, which was full of delicacies for the soldiers, and covered with a huge white cloth." When George's aunt came around to where he was standing, "he slipped under the tray and the negro slid out. George took the tray all 'round among the prisoners and when his aunt finished distributing the food, he followed her out the gate and made his escape."[51]

At least one other escape, made by a prominent and important person, attests to the Union troopers' preoccupation with their duties and with the scene of destruction that gripped the city. "Among Confederates uncaptured was Col. Leon Von Zinken," whom Private John F. Benton of Emery's battery observed "in civilian clothes and leaving Columbus in a two-horse buggy between 10 and 12 o'clock April 17."[52]

While most Confederates were looking to exit the city by any means possible, at least one was attempting the opposite. When word reached General French, who was north of Columbus, that the city had fallen, he dispatched his orderly, named Hedrick, to ride to Columbus to assess the situation. Fortunately for the orderly, shortly after beginning his journey he met some Confederate soldiers who had managed to escape from West Point. They explained to Hedrick that the fort there had been captured, and gave him the name of the Federal commander.

Shortly thereafter, Hedrick happened upon a Union regiment near Hamilton and, without hesitation, rode up to the colonel and announced that "he was a messenger from the Federal commanding officer at West Point, sent to meet Gen. Wilson." The story was believed, and Hedrick was passed to the rear. Farther on, Hedrick encountered a pair of Federal videttes who were Irishmen, one of whom, when told that Hedrick was carrying a message to General Wilson, replied skeptically, "If you please, none of your blarney to us, for . . . you are a Johnnie Rebel, and are after deceivin' us, you are." But Hedrick protested that "he could not ride through the country with his United States uniform on, and that his clothing was taken from a prisoner." "Of course, he could not wear his own coat," agreed the other vidette, and Hedrick was shown the way into Columbus and even told where he might find Wilson's headquarters. Upon entering town, however, Hedrick vanished from sight and observed the occupation from the safety of a friend's home.[53]

Among those unable to escape from Columbus that afternoon was Colonel Benjamin Franklin Dill, manager and spokesman for the *Memphis Appeal*. The *Appeal,* famous on both sides of the conflict for the intemperate rhetoric it published, had begun printing in Memphis at the outset of the war, but when Federal forces occupied that city the operation was forced to flee to escape capture. Five times before March 1865 the proprietors of the paper had to pack up and run, only to reestablish business in some other city, "adding the name of each place in turn to the title." When Wilson's cavalry approached Montgomery in April 1865, the staff of the *Memphis-Grenada-Jackson-Atlanta-Montgomery Appeal* was constrained once again to load their Hoe Press, boiler, engine, machinery, type, and other materials and supplies into wagons and strike out toward Columbus.[54]

Shortly after arrival in Columbus, with Union forces bearing down on the city, the proprietor of the paper, John R. McClanahan, took part of the press, the boiler and engine, and rode the rails to Macon to escape immediate danger. Behind in Columbus, he left the rest of the *Appeal*'s necessary equipment, machinery, tools, and supplies in the care of the paper's quarter partner, Ben Dill, who apparently was a very socially skilled individual, but whose responsibilities at the paper were largely overseen by his wife, a headstrong and worldly lady by the name of America Carolina Dill. The *Appeal*'s equipment was hurriedly concealed in the basement of the Perry House Hotel, and while the mechanics and other associated hands made their lodgings in the basement alongside the press, Colonel Dill and his wife appropriated one of the more expensive rooms upstairs.

Unfortunately for the Dills, when Columbus was captured and Noble was made provost marshal, Noble chose the Perry House as his headquarters. On the afternoon of April 17, troopers discovered the paper's equipment in the basement. Following a tussle with the fiery Mrs. Dill over some of the *Appeal's* equipment, Colonel Dill, whom Noble believed to be the proprietor of the paper and who was "found [to be] as meek and peaceful . . . as a lamb," was arrested and conducted to Wilson's headquarters. Upon arrival at the Mott House, Noble found Wilson "seated on the floor with his engineer officer, a large military map spread out before them." When Dill was introduced to Wilson, who was well aware of the paper's infamous reputation, the general "jumped to his feet, electric with excitement," and exclaimed, "Have we caught that old fox at last? Well, I'll be damned!"[55]

Though the capture of the *Appeal* was "of minor importance in itself," Wilson remembered it as "one of the most gratifying incidents" of his time in Columbus. "General Wilson gave Colonel Dill the choice of posting a bond of $100,000 not to publish the *Appeal* any more for the duration of the war, or being held prisoner. Dill promptly gave the bond." According to Wilson: "Recalling the eloquent terms in which Colonel Noble had bound the owner of the *Tuskegee Press*, . . . I detailed him again to draw the bond for our captive . . . requiring him henceforth and forever to publish nothing inimical . . . to the sovereignty of the Union." Despite the bond, however, Noble's troopers "seized the plant, and destroyed it with conspicuous care in the principal street."[56]

Later that evening, Noble, obviously impressed by Dill's character, met with the colonel at the Perry House and "gave him some brandy," which Dill "declared better than any he had tasted in two years." After the destruction of the paper's equipment, the hands and pressmen also took refuge in the bottle. One of the black workers "stole a whole barrel of whiskey from the hospital stores and stole a mule and a dray to cart it away." Drunk, the workmen, accompanied by a Union deserter, "filled all the bottles and jugs . . . [they] could carry" and set off to walk home. According to one of the men, not long after departing, a fellow announced, "Look-a-here, boys, we ain't taking anything along to eat." The reply was enthusiastic and to the point: "Eat, hell, look at all the whiskey we got!"[57]

Though it was probably small consolation to the Dills, two of the other local papers suffered a similar fate. Both the *Columbus Times* and the *Columbus Daily Sun* were smashed and put to the torch, leaving only the *Columbus Enquirer* intact. That the *Enquirer* was spared cast some suspicion upon the paper; it was even rumored that "a spy was employed there and thus the plant was saved." It is more likely that the owners were able to demonstrate that they had openly opposed secession in their columns during the conflict's prelude, and were offered similar terms to other newspapers bonded along Wilson's route.[58]

While Columbus was being reduced to a smoldering skeleton of its former self, news of the battle was spreading throughout the countryside. Stories of surprise and rout, destruction and conflagration, were disseminated by Confederates scattered in the fighting and by civilians who had fled from the city. Private Henderson of the 3rd Georgia recalled that his parents were very surprised when into the house near Talbotton he strode on the morning of April 17, after walking all night, and announced: "I have just come from a battle in Columbus."[59]

Eliza F. Andrews was on her way via train from Eufaula, Alabama, to Macon, Georgia, along with "300 volunteers from the exempts going to help fight at Columbus," when she heard the news of the city's fall. "Excitement was intense all along the route," she remembered. At the station near Fort Valley, "fears about the fate of Columbus were confirmed by a soldier on the platform, who shouted . . . 'Columbus gone up the spout!'" When the train finally stopped, she discovered that "soldiers who had made their escape after the fight . . . were camped about everywhere, looking tired and hungry, and more disheartened than the women and children."[60]

At Macon, the trains that carried in Cobb's staff and many soldiers from Columbus helped to spread the alarm in that city, as did the refugees on horseback or in wagons who continually poured in from the west. One noncombatant who rode into the city is said to have felt "like the man chased by a snake, who after running till . . . exhausted . . . found he had been running from a piece of rope hung to the tail of his coat." The news of Columbus's fall was extremely discouraging to the people of Macon. "We are whipped," admitted one individual, "everybody feels it, and there is no use for the men to try to fight any longer."[61]

The news that Columbus had been occupied and that Union forces would likely march on Macon sparked waves of desertions from the Confederate forces gathered in the city. Confederate nurse Kate Cumming noted that, following the announcement, "nearly all the men have taken to the woods." The civilians followed suit. The trains leaving Macon were overloaded with frightened passengers, and "people who could not get inside were hanging on wherever they could find a sticking place . . . clinging on like bees swarming round the doors of a hive."[62]

Adding to the demoralization were growing rumors that General Lee's army was defeated and had surrendered somewhere in Virginia. Furthermore, Cobb's whereabouts were unknown, and it was unclear if he had escaped from Columbus. In a futile effort to keep order, the authorities had all liquor in the city seized and turned out in the streets. Such was the state of affairs, however, that when the kegs were smashed, "men, boys, and negroes [got] down on their knees lapping it up from the gutter like dogs." According to Miss Andrews, "I think there can be no more dreary spectacle in the world than a city on the eve of evacuation, unless it is one that has already fallen into the hands of the enemy."[63]

Back in Columbus, plans were under way for the continuation of the Union offensive into south Georgia. On the morning of April 17, Wilson sent a message to Canby in Mobile informing him of the capture of Columbus by "a most gallant attack" and asking the general to forward the information to Generals Thomas and Grant. At the Mott House, Wilson met with his subordinates to coordinate the corps' efforts to seize their next major objective—Macon. Wilson saw Columbus and Macon as critical to the Confederate war effort, cities without which the Southern armies would "disintegrate for lack of munitions." The rout of Cobb's troops at Columbus greatly encouraged Wilson's belief that should he move quickly, he would encounter "no great difficulty" in defeating the remainder of Georgia's forces and capturing Macon. Furthermore, cut off from all outside communication, Wilson appears to have theorized that should Macon fall quickly, he might be able to move his corps from thence via Augusta into the Carolinas to aid Sherman or Grant in the "final windup of the great drama."[64]

Between Columbus and Macon lay only one major obstacle that might prove an impediment to the progress of Wilson's Raiders: the Flint River. Wilson knew that, because of the heavy rains of the last few weeks, the Flint, which crossed the Union line of march, was likely too deep and swift to be crossed without a bridge. Realizing that there were only a couple of points where bridges crossed the river near the route his corps would need to take to Macon, and also understanding that it would be the intention of the Confederates to try to delay his advance, Wilson felt it urgent to save a crossing before it was too late.[65]

Though they had already marched hard to reach Columbus that morning, after only a few hours of rest Wilson ordered the 3rd Ohio and 4th Michigan cavalries, under the command of Lieutenant Colonel Benjamin Pritchard of the 4th Michigan, to set out on an all-night forced march to save the Double Bridges, which spanned the Flint River near Pleasant Hill, Georgia, almost fifty miles away. At 5:30 P.M. these two regiments struck out toward the east, followed closely by the remainder of Minty's 2nd Division, which also took up its eastward march during the evening and night of April 17.[66]

Joining Minty's division was that part of McCook's division that had moved to Columbus rather than toward West Point. During the morning of April 17, Wilson received word of the successful assault of LaGrange's brigade upon the works at Fort Tyler, overlooking West Point, at around two o'clock the day previous. The fort had been subdued by the Union forces and the bridge and city captured, thereby opening another avenue into the state. McCook would lead his troopers east from Columbus and link up west of Macon with LaGrange, who was ordered to march via a convergent route, thus placing McCook in position to "assault Macon first." Wilson remembered: "Having by these divergent operations secured independent crossings of the Chattahoochee at Columbus and West Point within forty miles of each other, convergent roads were now open to Macon and central Georgia, and every man was confident that nothing could delay or imperil our further progress."[67]

Though the troopers of the 1st and 2nd divisions of the Cavalry Corps were beginning to leave Columbus by the evening of April 17, Wilson, Upton, and the men of the 4th Division remained behind. Upton issued orders that his division was to prepare to move the next morning at 8:30. This meant that the destruction of the remaining war materials had to be speeded up in order to finish in time.[68] To prevent the sort of indiscriminate burning of homes that had taken place in Selma following its capture, Winslow had earlier in the day ordered that there should be "no buildings fired except by order and with proper authority." With the exception of a few structures that, despite the best efforts of the provosts, were burned by malicious soldiers, the order had been obeyed. Now, however, with time fast running out, the burning of war materials was renewed, sometimes with the understanding that homes and tenements might be consumed by the unavoidable spreading of the intentionally set blazes.[69]

By late afternoon, many lesser facilities around the city had yet to be destroyed. Down by the river stood "several blocks of large buildings filled with rolls of cut cloth for soldiers uniforms." Connected with these or standing nearby were factory and mill workers' tenements. The troopers dispatched to ignite the storehouses knew that the lodgments "were very liable to burn" with the factories and delayed carrying out the order for as long as possible. "We wanted to give them time to save what they could," remembered Conzett, "but we had to carry out our orders."[70] The fires were set, and, as predicted, it was not long before the workers' homes were engulfed. "It was a trying job for us, for the people took it very hard of course," recalled the sergeant, "and the lamentations and weeping of the poor women was very affecting to see and hear." In addition to the tenements, at least five houses were accidentally or otherwise set ablaze downtown. At the north side of Columbus, the new fires quickly burned out of control and "all houses on Bridge Street" were reduced to ashes.[71]

The troopers' renewed energies appear to have further agitated the mobs that continued to linger in the streets. The crowd was getting larger and more worrisome, and it began to appear that they might turn violent. "The streets were crowded with soldiers and citizens," recalled Winslow. "In front of the handsome house where my headquarters were located . . . we sat upon the balcony looking at the animated scene. The air was soft and the 'madding crowd' presented a varying and interesting picture."[72] At sunset, Noble and his provost guards were ordered out "to put down [the] disturbance." "Just before dark, the citizens and negroes crowded the streets," remembered Union provost William Gray, "and our company was ordered out to disperse the crowd." The companies of troopers deployed in the city quickly broke up and scattered the large bands and forced them to return to their homes or to move to the outskirts of town or across the bridge into Girard for the night. For the civilians who remained behind and the Union soldiers who continued loitering in the streets, "no disturbances were made or permitted," at least in downtown.[73]

In the evening, with the work of the day completed, many of the officers and soldiers of the 4th Division sought entertainment. Confederate money was to be had in quantity, and the soldiers used it to purchase diversions such as tobacco, alcohol, and female companionship. On the streets, troopers gathered to talk of all that had occurred throughout the day and to watch as the last of the 2nd Division took up its eastward march toward Macon.[74]

"All of the city near the river was in conflagration. What a glare! The arsenal and laboratories catch and the earth trembles with the explosion." It was "a night of fire," remembered Lieutenant Mitchell. "We see flitting forms of frightened citizens as they hurry along the streets to escape from the scene and the dangers." One of those forms was Confederate surgeon W. T. McAllister, who, though he had stayed behind to care for the wounded, believed the time was right to slip quietly out of town. "I rode out of the city by the light of the burning buildings," recalled the doctor, "and my road was lighted for twelve or fifteen miles by the burning city."[75]

At Winslow's headquarters, "the Fourth Iowa regimental band opposite the house was playing the patriotic airs of its somewhat limited repertoire" when immense piles of munitions located at the eastern edge of the city were ignited. To the sounds of the brass band, "bursting bomb and rattling cartridges waged a harmless contest, sonorous and piercing as if great armies were contending." As a finale, one of the large powder magazines was blown up, the explosion from which "made the earth tremble for miles" and shattered the windows in several houses. "The arsenal was burned . . . containing several thousand shells, ready filled," observed Sergeant Bereman of the 4th Iowa, "and of all the horrid noises, that was the horridest."[76]

The activity could not be kept up, and "before midnight the streets were deserted, quiet prevailed and the provost guard patrolled every quarter." As the soldiers trudged back to their camps for a needed rest, the citizens of Columbus again stood guard over their families and what property they had left. At some of the homes, both men and women slept in their clothes, ready to flee should an emergency arise. With the exception of the explosions that would continue intermittently, however, nothing would interrupt the tranquillity of the night.[77]

The eye of the storm was passing over the city. The worst was over. There was still more to come, but for now all was quiet. The troopers were satisfied with their work but were tired and "glad to have it end that night." From the balcony of his headquarters, Winslow watched until well past midnight as "the fires which had been kindled in the principal streets in order to burn the surplus movable army stores were dying out. No unpleasant occurrences happened to disturb the harmony of the situation," Winslow recalled. "The cavalrymen had gone to the camps in the outskirts to sleep until called by the bugles in the morning, for Columbus was to be evacuated."[78]

17

Evacuation of Columbus

"The furious flames, triumphant and victorious subsided, when the hot and grimy ashes and the cessation of the frequent and tremendous explosions, told as daylight broke o'er ruin and destruction that their work was fully done. And further down the town upon the river front, the noiseless but insidious fire clambered ruthlessly about the cotton bales, and all the rich expectant profits in that king of fabrics were generated into useless vaporizing gases." Thus was the dawn observed by Major Latta of Upton's staff on the morning of April 18, 1865, in the wrecked and smoldering shell of the once proud city of Columbus. Before sunup, the Union soldiers were roused from their sleep and coaxed to preparation for the day's march. As the first rays penetrated the billowy columns of smoke that rose from the ashy heaps of the city's incinerated industry, civilians peered out from their windows and porches at the dramatic transformation their city had undergone. The clear, warm morning forecast a beautiful spring day, but the mood was still bleak. The day was to see the end of Columbus's occupation, but not before a few more hours of destructive labor.[1]

At Wilson's headquarters, all was in a bustle as the general received final reports from his subordinates, and his staff and escorts prepared to move eastward. While Wilson appears to have been impressed by Winslow's enumeration of the vast amounts of property destroyed in the city, including the CSS *Jackson,* the "most gratifying" news he received that morning was from Upton's headquarters. In the report, Major Latta estimated the losses for the 4th Division during the Battle for Columbus to be thirty-three killed and wounded. Despite the fact that his report fell slightly shy of the actual total, it was close enough to give Wilson a sense of his corps' loss in relation to the great victory they had won, and the tremendous blow they had struck to the Confederacy.[2]

While Wilson contemplated the comparatively light casualties, over in Girard members of the 3rd Iowa dealt more intimately with the faces of death. According to Colonel Noble, on Monday, Chaplain James Latham of

Fig. 20. Major James W. Latta.
Courtesy 103rd Engineer
Armory NGP Collection,
U.S. Army Military History
Institute.

the 3rd Iowa had "with affectionate regard . . . composed our comrades remains, and with Christian burial secured them decent resting places on the
field where they fell." Yet on the morning of April 18, for reasons that are
not altogether clear, work details were ordered to disinter the remains of
some of the Union dead who had been buried on the battlefield the previous day and move them across the river into Columbus's Linwood Cemetery. Private Leach of the 3rd Iowa's Company D was assigned this unpleasant duty. "[In the] morning we went over to the battle ground and
took up Capt. Miller's body," remembered Leach, "and took him back over
the river to a cemetery in Columbus and reburied him."[3]

At dawn, civilians from Girard and Columbus also resumed the disposal
of their cities' fallen defenders, several of whom still rested lifelessly exposed out on the battlefield, in the rifle pits, and near several homes. Some
of the already decomposing bodies were carted across the Chattahoochee
and laid to rest in the city cemetery. Still others remained until a day or
two later when they were transported north of Columbus to be deposited in the Clapp's Factory Cemetery, alongside Columbus's mill workers
and poor.[4]

As soon as it was light, Winslow surveyed the damage done to the city.
He quickly discovered that there was still enough property that might be
of use to the Confederates to warrant a few more hours of destructive labor. Soldiers were dispatched to fire several structures and to rekindle the

blazes that had gone out prematurely in some of the buildings. As had been the practice the previous day, some of the unexploded ammunition was used to further increase the wreckage. The Federals "set fire to all the buildings containing army stores," remembered Captain R. C. Rankin of the 7th Ohio, "the bursting of shell and the explosion of ammunition, causing the roofs and timbers to ascend heavenward, and the mass of bricks and mortar to fall inward, caused by the vacuum from the explosion."[5]

The previous day, at least sixty-eight pieces of artillery, both field and garrison, had been discovered at various locations around the city. Though most had their trunnions knocked off or their carriages burned, there yet remained innumerable limbers, caissons, wagons, forges, and other related items to destroy. These vehicles the Federals set on fire, and some of the more movable of the artillery tubes they tossed into the river.[6]

Included in the latter was a signal gun known as the *Red Jacket*. This small bronze cannon had accompanied the Columbus Guards to Montgomery in 1861 and had fired the salute after President Jefferson Davis was administered the oath of office by the provisional president of the Confederate Congress, Howell Cobb. Following the last battle in the Confederacy's doomed bid for independence, the *Red Jacket* was irreverently tossed into the muddy waters of the Chattahoochee. It was not until 1869 that the gun was brought up from its resting place when a cotton steamer accidentally snagged it with its anchor.[7]

Of the many items and structures destroyed that morning, probably most significant was the Franklin Street Bridge. This span was the last of the four at Columbus to be ruined. The Confederates had ignited the Clapp's Factory Bridge on April 16 to prevent its capture and use by the Federals. Confederates had torched the City Bridge in Columbus during the afternoon engagement on Easter Sunday after the Union cavalrymen discovered the trap that had been laid for them inside by the tearing up of the bridge's flooring. Of the two bridges that survived the battle, the Columbus and Western Railroad Bridge was fired on April 17, along with the cotton-bale redoubt and the cannons that protected its eastern end. By the morning of April 18, only the Franklin Street Bridge remained.[8]

It was upon possession of this structure that the fate of Columbus and its people had hinged, and upon which so much energy had been focused and expended. Ultimately, it was for the possession of the bridge that the soldiers of both sides spilled their blood. On the morning of April 18, having served its usefulness to the Union army, the Franklin Street Bridge was doused with turpentine and set ablaze. Soon its charred timbers collapsed into the murky waters below and were swept away.[9]

At 8:30 A.M., "the march to the interior of Georgia began." The 4th Division, being "first to enter . . . were the last to leave the city, one in which . . . [they] had passed thirty-five exciting and busy hours." The troopers of Alexander's 2nd Brigade led the march, and the men of the 7th Ohio took the advance until they were detached to ride "along the railroad to burn bridges, depots, etc." "[We are] leaving the doomed city still burning and a reign of confusion and terror behind us," remembered Lieutenant Mitchell of Upton's staff. "We have only destroyed what we must, but the innocent suffer with the guilty."[10]

Soon after Upton's division started east on the Macon Road, they came upon abandoned cannons, limbers, caissons, and wagons full of machinery and supplies that the Confederates had been forced to leave behind in their rout, and items that had been partially destroyed by Minty's and McCook's divisions. Finishing for the Confederates what they had lacked the time to accomplish themselves, the raiders burned the artillery carriages, tore down the camps, and smashed the weapons, leaving behind nothing worth salvaging.[11]

Meanwhile, several miles south of Columbus on the Chattahoochee River, the work of Confederate sailors from the crew of the wooden gunboat CSS *Chattahoochee* reached completion. The ship, which sank due to a boiler explosion in 1863, and which was raised and brought back to Columbus for repairs, had yet to have them completed when it was towed out of Columbus prior to the battle. After the capture and destruction of the Columbus Navy Yard and the Naval Iron Works, the ship's officers realized they could do little but scuttle the craft to prevent its capture by the Federals. On the night of April 17 or during the early morning hours of April 18, "the crew doused the vessel with ten barrels of kerosene and, lighting slow fuses, fled overland." Bobbing on the swollen tide, the smoldering hulk of the *Chattahoochee* drifted down the river until it eventually slipped beneath the water "at Race Pass, twelve miles below Columbus."[12]

Shortly after Alexander's brigade departed, Upton and the head of Winslow's brigade took up their eastward trek, leaving Winslow himself behind to bring up the rear. Wilson also departed Columbus at about this time. Just before leaving the Mott House, however, he was approached by Mott and, in return for his kindness, was offered Frank Bambush, the family manservant, as a gift, if Frank would agree. Wilson "wanted to take Frank with him," but after Mott explained to Frank that he was a free man and able to choose, "he promptly did in favor of staying with his former owner, Col. Mott."[13]

When Wilson "took his leave," he did so in a confiscated "carriage belonging to Mr. James C. Cook." The carriage would be only the first of several conveyances "liberated" for the general's use during the trip to Macon. Though it may have been against Wilson's usual attention to etiquette, it has long been accepted in Columbus that "ensconced in the same vehicle were . . . two of the Cook's family servants, rigged up in high style in clothes belonging to their former owners." This latter part of the story, though possible, seems highly improbable given what one historian noted as Wilson's "businesslike" attitude and attention to "dignity and decorum."[14]

As the long lines of Union horsemen filed through the streets, there recurred scenes from the previous day. The mobs of poor white civilians and blacks again swarmed into town to pick through the remains. "It was a sight to behold," remembered Hinrichs of the 10th Missouri, "the people carrying their plunder from place to place." Reverend Quintard was less impressed: "The stores in town were all pillaged . . . and the scenes were indescribably disgusting. The poor people of this section are the *meanest* of the poor and their outrages show very clearly that we have not as a people reached a very high degree of civilization."[15]

The civilians were not alone in gathering up what remained of value, for "on Tuesday morning," as one local historian wrote, "the raiders began their departure with as much of the portable possessions of the citizens as they could carry off." Many of the saddlebags and haversacks that accompanied the Union troopers out of the city were stuffed with money, jewelry, silverware, and other items. Indeed, one trooper's saddlebag was so packed that when an ornate French pewter canister tumbled out, he did not even bother to stop and pick it up. A local citizen recovered the souvenir and presented it as a gift to one of the city's councilmen.[16]

Not all the comforts heading eastward with Wilson's Raiders were ill-gotten, however. At several homes in and around Columbus, families who had been protected by their Union safeguards during the previous day showed their appreciation by packing food for the soldiers or giving them parting gifts. Despite the total destruction of their large and lucrative factory and other business facilities, the Haiman family, and especially Louis Haiman's daughter and two nieces, had been very accommodating to the officers and enlisted men of the 4th Iowa who had bivouacked in their yard. "There are three young ladies here," noted twenty-three-year-old Sergeant Bereman, and "we are having a gay time of it—singing, playing the piano, and etc." The attention showed to the troopers served the Haimans' interests well. On the morning of April 18, Bereman was "accosted by a negro who asked . . . [if he] didn't want to gobble some money." Though tempted by the offer, when Bereman discovered that the money referred to was buried in the Haimans' yard he dismissed the fellow, "telling him that the folks had treated . . . [him] so well that . . . [he] would not touch a thing of theirs without their consent."[17]

To the delight of Bereman and the other soldiers, the Haimans were generous in showing their appreciation when it came time for the troopers' departure. "Our friends, the Jewesses, gave us some beautiful bouquets of flowers when we started," noted Bereman, "besides something more substantial in the shape of roast fowl, cakes, and pies." Though the lovestruck Bereman seems to have been content to linger at the home, others in his unit were ready to move out. "When lined up and ready to leave, I was presented two bottles of wine and a bouquet by the ladies of the house," remembered Lieutenant Vanorsdol, Bereman's company commander. "Three cheers for the ladies, or the wine, I do not know which," observed the lieutenant, "and we were off."[18]

By about noon on April 18, the rear elements of Wilson's Cavalry Corps were leaving the city. Noble's 3rd Iowa was the last regiment of Winslow's brigade to depart. Winslow, who rode along with his men, later recalled that his troopers "rode forward cheerfully and hopefully." His assessment was in large measure correct. Unlike the grueling campaigns of earlier in the war, from all indications the majority of Wilson's troopers were actually enjoying their traipse across Alabama and Georgia. Their remarkable victories had kindled in them a pronounced *esprit de corps* never before known in the western cavalry. This was the war the troopers had wanted to fight all along.[19]

"On that lovely spring morning we left war in our rear," remembered Winslow. "The column stretched out over the open ground east of Columbus and we went between the fields and through the woods moving steadily onward three miles each hour. . . . As the horses' feet struck the ground, the sabers rattled and the men conversed of the (relatively) bloodless successes in which they had assisted." To the entertainment of many of the Union troopers, as the columns passed slowly over the hills east of the city, the last and largest of the city's powder magazines was touched off. "As we were passing out of Columbus, they were preparing to blow up the magazine," recalled Bereman, adding: "We had gone miles when it was exploded, shaking the earth beneath our feet at that distance." Indeed, this was no minor explosion. According to Reverend Quintard, "when the magazine was fired . . . it shattered the glass in houses two miles away." Eighteen miles from the city, the conductor of a train headed from Macon toward Columbus heard over the noise of the engine what he believed was "heavy cannonading" coming from Columbus; he surmised that "General Forrest was there" and that a great battle was raging. Closer to the action, Sergeant Giles of the 4th U.S. Cavalry witnessed the detonation and observed simply, "It was a grand sight."[20]

Following Winslow and his brigade out of town were the corps' baggage trains, the colored regiments, and Lieutenant Henry S. Boutell of the 4th Michigan and the men of the guard detail. "Paroled all the prisoners we had left and took charge of a new lot," remembered Boutell on taking command of the nearly fifteen hundred soldiers captured at the Battle for Columbus. The prisoners were fortunate to have Boutell as the commander of their guard. He was recognized by men on both sides for his fairness and humane treatment of captives. In fact, in gratitude to Boutell, Colonel Robert Pinson of the 1st Mississippi, who was paroled at Columbus, inscribed a note in the back of Boutell's diary that read: "I earnestly commend Lt. Boutell of the 4th Michigan to the kindness of all Confederate soldiers, in consideration of his uniform kindness to myself and men while in his charge as prisoners of war."[21]

Both on foot and on horseback, the Rebel captives were compelled to trudge along the sandy road toward Macon. Those too old or fatigued to keep up were left along the sides of the road, as were a few whose families had bribed the guards for their release. Most of the rest, however, were forced to march as best they could along the hot, dusty way.[22]

For one weary Confederate, relief came when his former slave, who had been confiscated by the Federals, discovered him among the prisoners. "Dat wont do. Nawsir!" the former slave was recorded to have protested to one of the Union guards. "Cain't yo'all give him my hoss and let me walk?" At first the fellow's inquiries went unheeded, but his persistence eventually paid off and the officer relented, saying, "All right . . . if I can find a nigger as faithful as that, I'll let you." Maybe for the first time, the prisoner took orders from his slave, who demanded, "Yo' come 'ere and get on dis hoss." The two shared the animal the rest of the way to Macon, each taking turns riding five miles while the other walked.[23]

Though small parties of black refugees followed the army all along its route, the largest and most vocal group trailed the corps as it left Columbus. Hordes of contrabands already attached to the army had entered the city the previous day and run rampant in the streets, adding much to the chaos. Now joined by thousands more runaways from Columbus and the surrounding countryside, the masses that crept along behind the army numbered over ten thousand. It was "a picture that will not soon be turned to the wall," remembered Mitchell.[24]

The boisterous celebration and singing of the newly liberated was at first "sweet and fine" to the soldiers, but it soon became an annoyance. When Wilson's Raiders halt for the evening, they discover the stamina of the blacks. "The boys can't sleep," recalled Mitchell of the constant singing, "it grows stronger and goes on." "It is a strange, weird scene," recalled Mitchell, "the dim fires, the darkness, the dusky swaying forms, some singing, some praying, some shouting, but all in ecstatic harmony." Soon the cavalrymen can take no more. According to Mitchell, "We have to quiet them by sending a company of soldiers who frighten them back to sanity."[25]

The contrabands and prisoners were not the only people trailing Wilson's Raiders along the road to Macon. Confederate soldiers who had been hiding in the woods and citizens eager to exact retribution for the destruction wrought on their homes pursued the army, waiting for an opportunity to strike. Throughout the afternoon, Union stragglers, small detached parties of foragers, and runaway slaves were bushwhacked by vengeful Confederate soldiers and civilians.[26]

Cooper Lindsay of Columbus led one of these small bands of irregulars. He and his men "overtook a Yankee captain from Ohio, two white and two negro soldiers robbing the house of Congressman Singleton" near Waverly Hall. After a brief chase, the Union captain had his neck broken by a blow from Lindsay's saber. The other four individuals were arrested and marched back toward Columbus. Their tenure as prisoners was terminated early, however, when "on reaching a swamp about eight miles east of the city, the two whites died very suddenly from an overdose of lead." The remaining two lasted only slightly longer. "In the swamp of what is now . . . Wildwood Park, the niggers collapsed and died from an internal dose of blue whistlers. They had several fine watches, for which all save one, the boys found the owners."[27]

Another ambush had as its object the retrieval of a hat wrongfully divorced from its owner. The young man's hat was of "rather peculiar make— something different from the ordinary hat," which he highly prized and sorely missed. The young man's brother soon joined one of the bands of Confederates waylaying unsuspecting Federals on the Macon Road, and in a few days he returned with the unique piece of headgear. "Where did you get it?" asked the young man. His brother replied, "I got it from a Yankee." Naturally, the next question was, "How did you get it?" "I got him before he got me" was the brother's answer.[28]

Probably the strangest encounter between stragglers from Wilson's command and Confederate guerrillas occurred at a plantation several miles from Columbus, when two belligerent Union soldiers were intercepted and killed by a gang of locals patrolling the area. "In seeking a way to dispose of the bodies, the men noticed the bale packer in the cotton gin on the plantation and decided to put the dead Yankees in with the cotton." The bales were pressed and set aside, marked conspicuously, "not to be sold," but several years thereafter they were accidentally included in a shipment of cotton abroad. "One day a news story appeared in papers in America . . . telling about the discovery of two bodies, dressed in army uniforms . . . in bales of cotton imported from the United States."[29]

Though the activities of the Confederate irregulars proved unfortunate for several Northern cavalrymen who fell behind, the bushwhacking of a few Union stragglers did little more than annoy the Union command. Wilson's Raiders were in "magnificent condition," and both enlisted and officer alike believed that "there was no army, there could be none which would be able to arrest their vigorous and destructive movements." They had swept across Alabama, recalled Winslow, "and now had Georgia under their feet, as they relieved their horses at times, from the weight of their persons." As Adjutant Scott noted, "The victory [at Columbus] was perfect, and the battle one of the most splendid in which . . . [they] had ever fought."[30]

Wilson's Raiders had confidence that their efforts were substantially helping to crush the rebellion and that their "achievements . . . must stand high among the heroic deeds of the war." "They believed in the future," recalled Winslow. "They marched over roads where no Union troops had ever been seen and they thought perhaps the ocean would be reached and offer a limitless expanse to their view. Men of the West were marching toward the eastern horizon." Though the raiders had little idea at that moment, "the Civil War was at an end," and though they did not realize it, Winslow later reflected that "we were en route to peace and our homes."[31]

Back in Columbus, following the departure of Wilson's Raiders, looting continued until late on April 18. Joining the women, children, and blacks who continued to pick through the rubble were some of the city's former defenders. "Went into town and collected a lot of things that had been thrown about," remembered Private Howard, who had escaped from captivity on Monday. Even so, most of the returning Rebels were more concerned with reestablishing order within the city.[32]

Colonel Von Zinken was one of the first to emerge from hiding and resume his responsibilities in Columbus. Joining him were the remnants of his forces who had escaped capture or had been paroled. Steaming up in time to witness the last of the enemy's "rear column just going over Wynn's Hill, east of the city," were men from the Navy Yard. Riding in almost on the heels of the Federals came Confederate cavalry and irregulars who had been harassing Wilson's Raiders during their march through Alabama.[33]

Upon the return of Confederate troops to Columbus, the single remaining cotton warehouse, owned by Mott, was burned in retaliation for the colonel's hospitality to the Federal commander. Shortly thereafter, Von

Zinken dispatched details to put down the rioting and patrol the streets. Recruited to help with this task were the men of Harvey's Scouts, a band of Confederate partisans who had harried Wilson's rear from Selma to Columbus under the command of their audacious young captain, Addison Harvey. These troops were armed with captured Spencers and revolvers, with which they undertook to disperse the crowds. The mob was loath to leave or to desist in their pillaging, however, and when one bold citizen attempted to steal Captain Harvey's horse, a fisticuff ensued and Harvey knocked the man down with his pistol. "Not long afterwards, finding Capt. Harvey alone," remembered Sergeant Wiley Nash, the man "slipped up behind him and shot Harvey through the head."[34]

Despite Harvey's murder, by the late afternoon of April 18 the crowds began to thin and an uncertain calm again settled on the banks of the Chattahoochee. Somehow, Von Zinken got a message to Cobb in Macon: "Please grant me forty-eight hours leave of absence to visit your headquarters." Whether Cobb replied is unclear, but shortly after sending the message Von Zinken turned control of the city over to a subordinate and set out at top speed in order to beat Wilson's Raiders to Macon.[35]

With the death of Columbus's last Confederate casualty and the departure of the city's commandant, the final chapter in Columbus's Civil War experience ended. For four years the people of the Chattahoochee valley had labored to expand Columbus's industrial capacity to aid in war production and had sent their men off to fight for independence—an independence they ultimately could not win. Far removed from the darkness of war for much of the conflict, Columbus experienced its greatest trial only after the dawn of peace had already begun to illuminate the reality that the bonds of national union had been preserved.

The blow struck by Wilson's Raiders in the closing days of the war was crippling. The two days of Union occupation that followed the battle transformed Columbus into what one witness described as a "burning, smoking ruins of wasted rebellion." The Confederacy was dead, and for all its patriotic effort and courage in the face of overwhelming odds, Columbus received only disaster. Indeed, the situation was probably best summed up by one of Wilson's Raiders, who likened the destruction of Columbus to God's promise in the book of Isaiah to wipe the kingdom of Babylon from the earth: "Our whole army . . . like a besom of destruction, had swept through one of the fairest cities of the South," observed the soldier, "and left but little of it, and nothing in it."[36]

18
Aftermath

After leaving Columbus on the morning of April 18, Wilson's Cavalry Corps moved rapidly east toward Macon. In the afternoon, Wilson received word from the men of the 3rd Ohio and 4th Michigan that their all-night forced march had proved successful and that they had managed to surprise the small band of Confederates guarding the Double Bridges over the Flint River ten miles west of Thomaston. In their haste to get away, the skedaddling Rebs fired only a few scattered shots in the bridge's defense, and lost a significant number of their men to capture. For Wilson's Raiders, the way was open to Macon.[1]

In Macon on April 18, wildly exaggerated reports of the Battle for Columbus carried in by soldiers and civilians who had managed to escape the city were disseminated in the streets and in the newspaper. Meanwhile, in Cobb's absence, General William Mackall attempted to rally what was left of Georgia's defenders and get them into position behind the fortifications being hastily thrown up by gangs of black workers on the Columbus Road. Even after Cobb arrived in the city during the afternoon, his appeals to the citizens to take up arms went largely unheeded as many demoralized individuals sought escape from the city and certain defeat.[2]

On April 19 the continued rush for outbound trains led to chaos on the platforms, and a woman noted that she "saw one man knock a woman down and run right over her" to secure a space in the car. Cotton bales were rolled into the streets to form barricades in the vain hope that should the outer defenses be penetrated, sharpshooters might succeed in stopping the Federal cavalry short of the city. Despite the preparations and the determination of the "few ragged foot soldiers" who were seen passing through the streets, rumors of the surrender of General Lee in Virginia and of a cease-fire in the Carolinas circulated freely and were generally believed. "I heard fresh rumors of Lee's surrender," recalled one Macon refugee. "No one seems to doubt it, and everybody feels ready to give up hope."[3]

Strangely, as late as the morning of April 20, despite overwhelming evidence that the war's end had finally come, the Macon newspapers printed reports that the Army of Northern Virginia had won two great battles in which "General Lee was gloriously victorious, inflicting tremendous loss on the enemy." If the reports were believed by anyone, they were not believed for long. That morning, Cobb received confirmation that, indeed, Lee had surrendered in Virginia, and instructions from General Pierre Beauregard in North Carolina to cease hostilities.[4]

That afternoon, cavalrymen of Wilson's advance met a force of about four hundred Confederates entrenched behind the Tobesofkee Creek at Mimm's Mill near Spring Hill, fifteen miles from Macon. Without hesitation, the Union cavalrymen charged, and within moments the Confederates were routed. Shortly thereafter, "Colonel White, with his Seventeenth Indiana . . . was suddenly confronted by another party carrying a white flag." Led by General Felix Robertson, the party carried a copy of a telegram sent to Cobb from Beauregard in North Carolina. The message ordered Cobb to "inform [the] General commanding enemy's forces . . . that a truce for the purpose of a final settlement was agreed upon." The message also stated that "contending forces [were] to occupy their present position, forty-eight hours notice being given in the event of resumption of hostilities."[5]

Fearing that the truce was a ruse and that the Confederates were trying to buy time to dig in at Macon, the advance of the Union column charged ahead, scattering the truce party and other Confederate units along the road. At Rocky Creek, just outside town, the bridge was captured and the fires that had been set to destroy it were extinguished. Though some scattered firing from Confederates along the road persisted, when the Union column charged through Macon's defenses, the Confederates inside surrendered without hesitation.[6]

At around 8 P.M., Wilson arrived in the city to find that his troopers had already stripped the garrison of its arms, locked them in the city stockade, and begun patrolling the streets. During a brief but heated meeting with Cobb and his subordinate officers at the city hall, Wilson learned that Grant had beaten Lee in Virginia eleven days earlier. A telegram from Sherman arrived the next day confirming the truth. The war was over.[7]

News of the war's end was met with varying reactions by different elements of Wilson's command. In Macon the revelation was met mainly with celebration. Upon reaching Upton's headquarters in the city, Captain Morse recalled seeing the "staff acting in the wildest kind of a way. [Major] Latta, especially, was performing the most athletic kind of tumbling," remembered the captain, adding: "If General Grant has all the health we drank for him that night, there will not be a vacant lieutenant generalship by death for upwards of two hundred years."[8]

Others were not so enthusiastic. Sergeant Giles of the 4th U.S. Cavalry realized that with the campaign at an end, Wilson's corps would be required to occupy the country. This was not an appealing prospect to Giles, since they were well behind the lines and would have no supplies on which to draw; nor could they continue to live off the country. "Surely, the war can't be over and we here so far from our own lines," Giles complained. "What will we do? How will we live? God grant that such a thing not be."[9]

Most of Wilson's Raiders, however, reacted to the news with complete surprise and then almost paralyzing shock. They had known that the end was near, but none of them had suspected it would come so soon or so suddenly. Near Forsyth on the night of April 20, men of the 4th Iowa Cavalry were engaged in tearing up the railroad, burning the ties, and bending rails when the news of the surrender halted all activity. "On returning to the railway, it was surprising to see that none of the men were working," remembered Adjutant Scott, who had strayed away to get something to eat. "They stood about in groups, thrown into relief by the line of fires in which ties were burning, and were talking, though very quietly and not much. . . . [T]hey had heard the news . . . and indeed nobody could believe it."[10]

The next day, as the regiment rode toward Macon to reunite with their command, Scott observed the mood: "The men were disturbed and nervous . . . there was no strictness in the order of march. . . . Nobody could believe the report. . . . It was much easier to think of the probability of a battle at Macon, and as mile after mile went by all ears were more and more alert to hear the guns in action. Even when at last the works were seen, with no sign of defenders about them, the impression was only that . . . [it] was unreal and that something real would happen at any moment. So it was like a dream to ride at a walk by frowning bastions mounting silent guns, and down through a city at peace."[11]

Just over one hundred miles to the southwest, in Columbus, too, there was shock and disbelief, not at any news, but at what two days of Union occupation had left behind. "For a few seconds my pulse must have ceased to throb," remembered one young woman upon witnessing the devastated landscape. "The scene was so unreal that . . . I was thinking of biting my fingers to make sure I was really awake."[12]

After the departure of Wilson's Raiders, Columbus was merely a shell of its former self. All of the great factories were gone, reduced to piles of smoldering rubble. The partially crumbled walls of the fire-hollowed mills stood stark and silent along the river's banks. "All quiet," recorded one observer of the scene of desolation downtown, adding, "the city looks very lonesome and dull." The bridges spanning the Chattahoochee were gone, the vacant pillars rising to nothing. Only foundations remained of the city's once overflowing warehouses and depots. Both on the outskirts of Columbus and across the river in Girard, the twisted rails and piles of blackened ties told as surely as did the smashed and broken engines and rows of wheels without cars that the city was now isolated from any traffic except that which could reach it from downstream. "All along the river the enemy left a scene of desolation and ruin," observed Reverend Quintard, adding, "the destruction is said to have involved . . . millions of dollars."[13]

In addition to the wrecking of its industry, infrastructure, and private business, Columbus had also lost its communications. With the railroads leading to the city ripped up, the telegraph cables cut, the postal service collapsed, and little or no river traffic to be had, only information immediately verifiable by proximity could be known. Though the news of the war's end and the surrender of Generals Lee and Johnston reached Macon by April 20, in Columbus, only one hundred miles away, it would take more than a week for that information to be received. In the meantime, however, there was work to do.[14]

Between the departure of Wilson's Raiders on April 18 and the end of May, the city government demonstrated remarkable foresight and swiftness of action in trying to put the city back on a footing from which it might begin to function once more. On April 19 the city authorities met to discuss what should be done to ensure order in the city and to decide how best to secure a few basic services. The council recognized Colonel James C. Cole, whom Wilson had paroled, as the new commandant of Columbus and charged him with securing whatever provisions and government property might be found about the city. They also assembled a commission to oversee the procurement of transportation across the Chattahoochee either by boats or by pontoon bridge. As the latter was outside the means at hand, the former option was employed and a makeshift ferry was put into operation using flatboats and canoes. Confederate soldiers and citizens were enlisted to help patrol the streets and prevent any further looting. Parties were even charged with gathering up some of the supplies needed by the city authorities that had been taken by the mob.[15]

Despite all their efforts, however, the one major area in which the authorities could offer little assistance to the local population was in the distribution of food. It was, however, in just this area that help was most needed. With but a few exceptions, Wilson's Raiders, with the help of the mob, had stripped the homes and stores of Columbus of provisions. The hungry men and horses of the Union army had consumed much of the residents' surplus eatables, and what they did not devour they mostly destroyed. Hit hardest and most immediately by the loss of their employment and the lack of food were mill workers and their children, especially those who had lost their homes in the tenements to the flames. Added to these were large numbers of refugees who had come to Columbus in the days after Atlanta's fall and who had poured into the city from Alabama in advance of Wilson's troopers. All told, nearly one third of Columbus's population was left destitute, of whom "more than 5,000 . . . [were] thrown upon the community for other support."[16]

Compounding the problems relating to the poor and hungry in the city was that even when possessed, Confederate money retained almost no value, and was of little help to its owners or the city authorities in procuring the few provisions that became available for barter. A barrel of flour that cost nine dollars at the beginning of the war and fifty dollars in 1863 now cost more than four hundred dollars, placing it well outside the reach of most of Columbus's neediest inhabitants. The limited numbers of horses and mules left in the city made riding into the countryside in search of provisions impractical, particularly as the Union bummers had in large measure combed over the area surrounding the city for some distance.[17]

Additionally, fear of being captured by the Federals—who, so far as the people knew, could still be patrolling nearby—kept them from dispersing and setting out for other locations, as did the fear of Confederate deserters and gangs of marauders, whose reputation for violence had grown more worrisome in recent months, but especially in the light of the near collapse of civil authority. In Columbus, "during the days immediately following the raid, hungry men and women were seen snatching burned ears of corn from the warehouses" and trying to find nutrition in the provender left behind in the Federal camps.[18]

Nor was the food shortage restricted to the former mill workers and refugees. For the large numbers of newly emancipated slaves, prospects for subsistence were even more bleak than for the whites. "At the first blush of freedom," remembered Priscilla Albright, a Columbus-area slave, "the Negroes . . . joys knew no bounds; they went wild. Some had hysterics, some shouted, some prayed and . . . sang, and many took to the highways and by-ways, just to exercise their independence, and walked and roamed aimlessly for days!" The wanderings of many of the slaves who had been employed on the farms and plantations surrounding the city brought them into Columbus, only to discover that the Federals had left and that they were on their own. The revelry and excitement of emancipation quickly gave way to desperation and uncertainty. Supplies of food taken during the fall of the city were either quickly used up or confiscated by the city authorities and placed under guard. Left with little alternative, many of the blacks turned to thievery as a means of subsistence, an activity that, while it met the immediate need, stirred up a great deal of hostility among Columbus's white population.[19]

Despite the widespread food shortage, a few Columbus families had managed to save some of their eatables. At the home of Mrs. Walker of Columbus, though "the larder was swept perfectly bare, . . . rations that had been hid behind the huge chimneys on top of the house, by way of a secret stair-case, remained to tide over the lean days." At the Lion House, too, "hams and side-meat were hung in the upstairs rooms" and saved from confiscation, though the smell and the grease that dripped on the walls and floors proved "difficult to conceal later." On the whole, however, the threat of starvation was the city's most serious crisis. And yet for Columbus, crises were in abundance.[20]

On April 25 the prisoners taken at the Battle for Columbus were paroled in Macon and released. As a portion of these soldiers made their way back to Columbus, they brought with them the news that indeed the war had ended. On their heels followed a ragged procession of war-weary veterans from Virginia and the Carolinas. These soldiers at first trickled into the city as they passed through to the south and west, but during the later days of April and into the first weeks of May the stream grew larger and more difficult to provide for.[21]

In Macon, Wilson's soldiers, with the assistance of Cobb and the Confederate commissary officers, provided the penniless, hungry former Confederates with food secured from parts of the state left untouched by the war. This was not an option in Columbus, however, so Colonel Cole attempted to conserve the meager government stores he had managed to collect so that he might issue three days' rations to the soldiers passing through, and provide meals for the sick and wounded being cared for at the hospitals.[22]

To the consternation of Columbus's leaders, following the returning Confederate soldiers along their route were bandits and lowlifes who took the opportunity to rob and outrage the already suffering community. Across the river in Alabama, a party of Union cavalry under General Benjamin H. Grierson was yet scouring the country around Girard for provisions, destroying what remained of the rail lines and communications, and threatening to cross the Chattahoochee and further disturb the already precarious situation in the city. In fact, as late as April 25, Grierson was himself planning to raid Columbus. And added to these extraordinary troubles, in early

May, incensed that food was being issued to soldiers and withheld from themselves, the city's poor whites and blacks began to threaten again to riot and pillage.[23]

With all direct communication cut off between Columbus and Wilson's command in Macon, Cole sent a desperate plea downriver to Eufaula, Alabama, to Grierson in hopes that the latter might have telegraphic contact with Wilson or that he might come to the city's rescue himself. "General Wilson promised, that if my forces were not sufficient to suppress marauding parties in my vicinity during the present armistice, to furnish me a force," Cole's urgent message read. "Can you do the same immediately, until I can get a courier to him? A strong force is necessary at this post to suppress riot and preserve public stores as well as private."[24]

Though his message reached Grierson and was forwarded to Wilson in Macon, Cole would receive no immediate assistance. Grierson had received word of the armistice and orders that his forces were to be confined to the area west of the Chattahoochee. In Macon, though Wilson received Cole's petition, he also could spare no troopers to garrison Columbus just yet. His men were combing the state in search of America's most wanted fugitive, Jefferson Davis, whom they ultimately captured at Irwinville on May 10.[25]

Realizing the volatility of the situation he faced, on May 12 Cole requested permission from Wilson to start feeding Columbus's needy. "If I do not, I am fearful my guard will be forced and all stores seized by the mob," he explained, but "I can quiet them by giving them a small quantity until your officers arrive here to take charge." Wilson granted the request and also instructed Cole to supply food to the orphan asylum, which had run completely out. Two days later, a detachment of troopers from the 17th Indiana Mounted Infantry under the command of Captain John C. Lamson was dispatched to Columbus to take over command of the city.[26]

Lamson's troops quickly set about "restrain[ing] the rush for commissary stores" and began patrolling the streets to prevent unruly behavior. His soldiers also began to distribute provisions to the poor on a regular schedule and made arrangements for the parole of Confederate soldiers, more than thirty-seven hundred of whom would take the oath in the city. Yet, food shortages remained a problem in Columbus, as elsewhere in the state, and in response to urgent requests for assistance that inundated his headquarters during May 1865, Wilson explained, "I can scarcely supply my own command with corn, much less a large indigent population. Unless General Canby displays great activity in depositing grain at Apalachicola, we shall experience much trouble."[27]

Fortunately for Captain Lamson and the people of the Columbus area,

on June 6 the first of the relief shipments arrived at Columbus from Apalachicola aboard the steamer *Young*. Afterward, according to Columbus historian Louis DuBose, "supplies were issued by the military forces every
two weeks and it was a thankful father who could take home a piece of
side meat and a portion of meal to his desperate family." From that point
forward, while there would still be hunger, there would be no real threat
of starvation. The rations issued to the needy calmed the tense situation in
the city, and both the breadline and the patrolling of the Union soldiers
became a welcome sight.[28]

Along with the arrival of the small yet effective Federal garrison and the
shipments of food came the security and stability necessary to begin the
cleanup. In late May, former mill workers and others were hired to clean
and stack the piles of bricks left over from the city's conflagration. "I got
work cleaning brick at forty cents a thousand," remembered former Confederate James Howard, who had been living off government handouts
since the city's fall. "I had to clean and stack them, and I wore the ends of
my fingers off," he recalled, but was happy for the opportunity. The bricks
were piled and counted in preparation either for reuse in the reconstruction of mills and warehouses or for sale to those who might use them for
building homes.[29]

In the hopes of overcoming the paralysis inflicted upon the city by Wilson's Raiders, and in an effort to unite Columbus's citizens behind the goal
of putting aside the bitter feelings associated with the fall of the Confederacy, a public city meeting was held at Columbus's Temperance Hall
on May 27. At this meeting a committee of some of Columbus's leading
Unionists and businesspeople, chaired by former congressman and Columbus lawyer James Johnson, resolved, in order to better secure the prosperity
of the city, to fully cooperate with the Reconstruction government.[30] In
denouncing the actions of the mob during the days after the battle and in
affirming their commitment to upholding the civil government, Johnson
announced: "We saw on the 17th of April last what our own people did
when all government was for the time destroyed and the passions and cu-
pidity of men had free scope. Every store was robbed and the labor of years
[was] swept away. . . . Society can't exist a moment without government.
That the United States can secure to us life, property and order, no one
doubts."[31]

Additional resolutions agreed upon included the establishment of a panel
of persons, including Colonel Mott, who would petition General Wilson
to allow the detachment of soldiers from the 17th Indiana to remain as the
city's garrison. The thanks of the city were bestowed on Captain Lamson
and his men, and the resolution served as a testimony to their good con-

duct. Finally, Johnson exhorted that "every person . . . resort forthwith to their usual avocations, such being necessary for the support and subsistence of the country."[32]

Not long after this meeting, President Andrew Johnson selected James Johnson to take over as Georgia's provisional governor. On June 17, Johnson took control of the state and was authorized to appoint civil administrators who would be loyal to the United States and would work quickly to restore order. Shortly thereafter he issued a call for delegates to be selected for a state convention, whose purpose would be "to repudiate the debt, to acknowledge the abolishment of slavery, and to cancel the act of secession" so that the state could be speedily readmitted to the Union.[33]

Although some of Columbus's leading men exhorted the people of the city to get back to work, the consequences of the Battle for Columbus, in combination with the death of the Confederate government, made resuming industry of any sort difficult and slow. Had Columbus surrendered to Wilson's Raiders and not put up such a stern defense, it is likely that much of the fiery calamity would have been avoided and the loss to the public would have been far less substantial. Though Columbus would have faced postwar occupation and Reconstruction whether or not it had fought, surrender might have led to the preservation of the majority of its facilities.

Furthermore, if word had reached Columbus of the war's end prior to April 16, there would have been no need to fight. According to Winslow, "If our officers had but known that our fighting days (and nights) were finally ended, and that we were to enter upon the paths of brotherly peace, how gladly we would have joined hands with the thousands who, in . . . Columbus, were deprived of property and the means of living or procuring the supplies necessary for their families." As it happened, however, no such word was received, and the battle and ensuing desolation served to retard Columbus's postwar recovery by months, if not years.[34]

Particularly injurious to the city's ability to resume commerce was the destruction of its railroads and bridges. Without these avenues of trade, the city lay isolated, unable to get the supplies and machinery it needed to resume its commercial enterprises. Realizing this, the city borrowed twenty thousand dollars from one of its elite businessmen, and with these and other funds it contracted in June for the reconstruction of the City Bridge. Though the council had hoped the project would be completed within two months, it would not be until February 1866 that the span was finally finished. As for the Columbus and Western Railroad Bridge and the Franklin Street Bridge, they would not be fully rebuilt until 1868.[35]

Even more important than the bridges to the resumption of normal trade or traffic was the rebuilding of the railroads. Columbus had the unfortunate distinction of having been completely cut off by rail from any of its major neighbors by the labors of Wilson's Raiders. From the west, the Mobile and Girard and the Montgomery and West Point railroads were destroyed, as was the track connecting Columbus and Opelika. To the east at least six bridges—the biggest one spanning the Flint River—along the lines running from Columbus to Macon had been burned, and although their renovation began almost immediately, it was more than three months before they began to be reopened. In the meantime, traffic reaching Columbus from the east had to be brought a long and uncomfortable distance by hack or else moved to Eufaula and brought upriver by steamer. In spite of this latter option, however, the city's business during the summer of 1865 was so inactive that one visitor remarked, "there is but little for boats to do."[36]

Most inhibiting to the resumption of normal trade and commerce in Columbus, however, was the widespread poverty and loss of capital brought about by the city's destruction after the Battle for Columbus and the other effects of the fall of the Confederacy, including the devaluation of Confederate currency and abolition of slavery. With a few exceptions, the looting that had taken place in downtown Columbus after the battle left many of the city's smaller businessmen struggling to secure means with which to renew their vocations. Druggist John Pemberton lost nearly the entire contents of his store, and months after the battle he was still appealing to local people to return his "drug furniture, . . . jars, tincture bottles, scales, mortars, graduate measures, pill tiles and spatulas." In hopes of securing the return of the store's books, the doctor explained: "They are of no service to any one except ourselves, and it is impossible to carry on our business without them."[37]

The Straus family lost not only their business but the bulk of their savings to the "depredations of the soldiers, the fires . . . and the general confusion which reigned [after the battle]." According to son Isidor, "So disheartened and discouraged [was] my father, that he made up his mind that he did not care to waste away the time which he feared would be consumed before normal conditions could be established. And it was on this account that he took his family north."[38]

Even the plantation owners of the Columbus area were not spared from hardship. Though they retained their land and would be able to feed themselves, any hope of profit for 1865 was largely gone. "Wilson's troops camped two days on my place," related Columbus-area planter Martin Crawford to a friend, "and destroyed all my provisions of every sort, got all our clothes, some of our silverware, and when leaving fired my gin house, cotton, two presses, and burnt them up—indeed, they did their best to ruin me." A Co-

lumbus woman noted that her "grandmother suffered greatly from the rav-
ages of war. . . . Not a mule or horse was left to plow a field, the slaves were
set free, and she was reduced from affluence to poverty."[39]

The vanishing of the Confederacy also brought about the evaporation
of all assets tied to the Confederate state. Confederate money, while admittedly worth little by the war's end, became completely valueless. One
Columbus widow who had her savings tied up in forty thousand dollars'
worth of Confederate money found herself penniless and was forced to
leave town to live with relatives. Even those in and around Columbus who
had been savvy enough to make more substantive investments lost heavily.
The tens of thousands of bales of cotton burned in Columbus and at the
plantations outside the city represented the bulk of many families' worth
and cost them their only means of securing capital with which to begin
again.[40]

Additionally, the sudden abolition of slavery, though it would have occurred without a visit by Wilson's men, proved immediately detrimental.
With the coming of Wilson's Raiders, hundreds of thousands of dollars' in
personal investments literally walked away, never to return. "I owned about
two hundred negroes, in which my property mostly consisted," lamented
John Banks of Columbus, adding, "This leaves me poor."[41]

Those who suffered most, however, were Columbus's former slaves who
sought refuge in town, as well as the city's war widows, orphans, and elderly. This was especially the case when, during the summer, the Federal garrison suspended providing rations. In writing from Columbus in
the summer of 1865, a Northern correspondent pondered: "There are vast
numbers of poor widows and helpless people who must exist somehow,
though my wits are taxed to know how. . . . The poverty of the people is
exemplified in a hundred ways—in their language, their appearance, their
habits, and," observed the reporter, "direct appeals for money are of common occurrence."[42]

Given these circumstances, Columbus's immediate postwar prospects
seemed dim. "Hundreds of workmen walked the streets," notes historian
Louis DuBose, "their number augmented by freed negroes who had nothing to do, and made their living by looting and stealing from the whites."
Business, when any could be had, was slow, and even the landscape looked
oppressive. Upon visiting Columbus shortly after the battle, Mrs. Parthenia
Hague remarked: "I beheld the ruins of grim-visaged war, whichever way
I cast my eyes."[43] Yet despite the setbacks and the disillusionment of some
of Columbus's inhabitants, the war itself had provided a lesson in resolve,
resourcefulness, and perseverance in the face of overwhelming odds. What

Columbus's people lacked in capital and infrastructure, they soon resolved to make up for with energy and a firm commitment to set right their prospects for a bright future.

Notwithstanding its losses, Columbus retained many redeeming qualities that boded well for its future progress. The city's location at the head of navigation on the Chattahoochee, the feature that led to its founding, remained an important attribute. The river's falling waters, used to power the highly productive wartime mills, were still flowing, and it was estimated that, put to full use, they could provide enough power "to drive one and a quarter million spindles." Once cotton production was reestablished, shipment of thousands of bales would be facilitated by the river's steamboats, which had already resumed plying the river's winding waters. Furthermore, the Chattahoochee valley was noted for fostering "excellent health and remarkable freedom from epidemics." And there was a white population eager for work of any sort.[44]

Getting Columbus back on track would take remarkable fortitude and quite a bit of entrepreneurship. With little money circulating, people obtained the necessities of life and business by barter. "Our people are in want of many articles . . . but have no currency to purchase, even if the market were supplied as it was in old times," remarked a writer for the *Columbus Enquirer,* who advised: "Our country friends ought to bring in their vegetables, chickens, eggs, butter, etc. They may dispose of them to good advantage by bartering if not for money." Indeed, the economic hardships thrust upon the city and its environs "reintroduced frontier conditions" that the valley had not seen in years and from which not even the upper crust could escape. "The best families are day after day living on corn bread, bacon, and buttermilk, with, perhaps, an occasional chicken," remarked a visitor to the city. Yet this too worked to Columbus's advantage in that through their shared hardships was fostered a spirit of common reliance and interest that would help see the community through the darker and more turbulent days of Reconstruction that lay ahead.[45]

With summer well under way, small signs of renewed commercial life began to appear amid the rubble. To the delight of the investors of the Porter, McIlhenny, and Company Foundry, they discovered that though their losses had been substantial, they possessed or could obtain all the equipment and facilities they needed to get back in business in short order. The foundry was quickly rebuilt, a pattern maker was hired, and, with the brass and iron salvageable in the city, the workers began turning out "a large assortment of hollow-ware, such as pots, ovens, skillets, spiders, and lids." They also advertised the ability to manufacture gin gearing and machinery for sawmills and gristmills. Of course, without a circulating currency, they offered instead to "exchange any thing in . . . [their] line for any kind of country produce, at old prices."[46]

In downtown Columbus, several smaller establishments again set up shop and tried to make a new start. At Dr. Noble's dentist office, the physician had managed to save some of his equipment and resumed offering cavity repair and artificial teeth "on short notice." The general store offered salt in exchange for bacon, lard, flour, or produce, and the *Columbus Enquirer* offered printing "in the neatest style of art." Some enterprises even took advantage of the ruination caused by Wilson's Raiders to do business that otherwise would probably not have fared so well. Included in these were coach services, which, in the absence of more efficient means of travel, offered transportation to points unconnected by water.[47]

Though Columbus still was years away from claiming even a fraction of its former commercial standing, that there were even the smallest signs of renewal by midsummer of 1865 portended well the city's ultimate revival. On visiting the city in June 1867, one traveler observed: "Tis true that evidence of the devastating hand of war are viable on every side, but never-the-less your city, phoenix like, is rising from its ashes again."[48]

After turning command of the post at Columbus over to Colonel French Woodall of the 151st Illinois Infantry on July 28, 1865, Captain Lamson and the men of the 17th Indiana set out toward their homes and a return to civilian life. Preceding them in this transition was the majority of Wilson's Cavalry Corps, which had been officially disbanded on July 2.[49] In writing to Sherman shortly before their dissolution, Wilson called upon the general to remember his disappointment with the branch less than a year earlier and pronounced of the change since then, "our cavalry is cavalry at last." In touting the great successes they achieved and the minimal losses they sustained, Wilson endorsed the corps "as a model for modern cavalry in organization, armament, and discipline," and added, "I . . . hazard nothing in saying that it embodies more of the virtues of the three arms . . . than any similar number of men in the world." Wilson's enthusiasm for his corps and their splendid campaign was not lost on the soldiers themselves. When the troopers departed for their homes that summer they were "animated by a perfect esprit de corps . . . and confident now that they could do anything that men may dare," recalled Adjutant Scott.[50]

Those who participated in the Battle for Columbus took pride not only in having been part of the last real battle of America's greatest and most terrible conflict, but also in having been instrumental players in what their commander called "one of the most remarkable exploits in the history of modern cavalry." "Though the great events of the preceding fortnight in

Virginia and North Carolina had made the engagement unnecessary," explained a member of Upton's division, "it should be remembered that it was fought by men who were ignorant of those events, and who were inspired only by a determination to succeed and by the belief that they were fighting a great battle for the cause."[51]

Wilson saw the Battle for Columbus as a "magnificent achievement." Upton believed that the battle was "unparalleled in cavalry service, and with but few parallels in infantry," and the troopers of his division took tremendous pride not only in having won the war's last battle but in having won it big, by routing a well-fortified enemy, seizing over twenty-seven guns in action, taking eight battle flags, and capturing half the opposing force, with only minimal losses. In praise of actions like these, Wilson announced to his hard-riding and tenacious fighters: "You have learned to believe yourselves invincible, and contemplating your favorable deeds, may justly cherish that belief." For Wilson's Raiders, the Battle for Columbus was the triumphant, dramatic conclusion to a great and noble endeavor.[52]

The Battle for Columbus was seen differently, however, by many Confederate veterans of the engagement and by the residents of Columbus and Girard. Some saw the battle as a feeble attempt undertaken against forces they had no hope of besting. For many, however, though defeat was seen as ultimately inevitable, there was great pride felt in simply having tried to defend Columbus and in having made a courageous stand in the face of overwhelming odds. Despite the disaster that the relatively inexperienced and disillusioned Confederate soldiers met with on the night of April 16, Columbus had been "relieved the degradation of surrender without a struggle."[53]

Following the rout, veterans and citizens cast blame in all directions. For some, fault lay with Georgia's governor and the Confederate government for not calling up the militia sooner, and for heavy-handedness with regard to the conscript ordinance. Cobb and some of his officers blamed the poor resolve demonstrated by some of their troops. Still others placed responsibility for the defeat squarely on the shoulders of Cobb and the Confederate command. After the battle, Private Henderson of the 3rd Georgia confidently announced: "If our men had been stationed on the east side of the Chattahoochee with the aid of the citizens of Columbus with shotguns and pistols, the Federals would never have gotten into Columbus." Furthermore, he proclaimed, "it is bad tactics for any army to have a river in its rear."[54]

Though many factors contributed to the Confederates' trouncing, probably the most important two had to do with the forces themselves. The troops assembled to defend the city, an amalgamation of a few veteran soldiers mixed with reserves, homeguards, convalescents, and civilians, were not sufficiently prepared to be effective in combat, and demonstrate the degraded state of the armies and the South by 1865. By contrast, Wilson's Raiders were some of the best-trained, finest-equipped, and most magnificently armed veteran cavalrymen in the Union army. The outcome of the battle was inevitable, and was best summed up by a Confederate prisoner who admitted to his guard after the fight, "There was no men in the army that would stand before such shooting and yelling as . . . [you] done." "I think it is about so," replied the guard.[55]

To some modern historians, because it was fought after the war had essentially ended, and because it had no significant effect on its outcome, the Battle for Columbus is seen as a tragic final episode in our nation's most costly conflict. Had word of the war's end traveled faster to south Georgia, or had Columbus surrendered to the Union forces, there would have been no battle—no effort, injury, or loss of life. The suffering of those soldiers who were killed, wounded, or captured during the fighting might have been spared.[56]

Others see the Battle for Columbus as somewhat fortunate. As in all wars, there must always be a last battle and a last sacrifice of life. In all conflicts, men die even after the outcome is certain. The men who gave their lives or were injured during the Battle for Columbus unknowingly drew that lot of fate that would require of them the full measure of their resolve in the war's last battle, though too late to influence either side's cause. Fortunate, however, were soldiers on both sides whom circumstances shielded from harm. The burning of the City Bridge, the long delay in the afternoon, the cover of darkness during the night assault, the terrain, and even the confusion of the battle's conclusion helped to protect many of the combatants from peril. That a day-long engagement between six thousand soldiers yielded only approximately 140 casualties is not only extraordinary but also fortunate for the men who participated in the fight.

Despite its significance to Wilson's Raiders and the people of the Chattahoochee valley, the Battle for Columbus never received any major attention in the national press. In fact, most contemporary news outlets and postwar historians made little or no mention of Wilson's Raid. This is due to several important factors and to the timing of the battle.

Wilson and Upton, who had hoped to gain recognition, advancement, and possibly even fame for the accomplishments of their daring cavalrymen at Columbus, soon found that nothing could be further from the truth. Wilson credits the oversight in part to the lack of an attached war correspondent who could chronicle the corps' achievements. "It was a great misfortune to the fame of the Cavalry Corps," explained Wilson after the war, "that all communication was cut off with the North and that neither photographers nor reporters thought it safe to go along with us."

Though Wilson may have regretted after the campaign not having an attached correspondent, that situation was likely of his own doing. Just prior to the campaign's launch, he made known his displeasure concerning the news coverage his recent exploits in the East had received and confided to a friend, Colonel Adam Badeau, that the incident "shows how very politic one ought to be when brought in contact with the representatives of a free press." Nevertheless, with no one dedicated to heralding the actions of Wilson's Raiders to the rest of the nation, the only records of the campaign's successes were to be found in the official reports of Wilson and his subordinates and in the letters and diaries of the soldiers who had participated.[57]

Yet probably the factor most detrimental to the cause of promoting awareness about the Battle for Columbus was the timing of the engagement itself. From the time Wilson's Raiders captured Macon and hostilities were brought to a close in the latter part of April 1865 until June of that year, newspapers North and South were overwhelmed by the other important developments surrounding the close of the war. In April, the news of the fall and destruction of Richmond, the pursuit and surrender of the Army of Northern Virginia, the disarmament of Lee's army, the capture of Mobile, the cessation of hostilities in the Carolinas, the assassination of President Lincoln and succession of President Johnson, the signing of the Johnston-Sherman Armistice, the disapproval of the armistice, the surrender of the Army of Tennessee, and the pursuit of John Wilkes Booth all combined to ensure that nothing of any significance would be published about the Battle for Columbus or the city's capture. Furthermore, throughout May the headlines of every newspaper were dominated by stories concerning the chase and capture of President Davis, the lifting of the blockade, the occupation of Southern cities, the Grand Review of the U.S. armies in Washington, the surrender of all Confederate troops west of the Mississippi, concerns over emancipation, and the growing fears that soon the United States would go to war with the French in Mexico to overthrow the Maximilian government.[58]

Not even in the city where the battle was fought would there be any serious published mention. When Wilson's Raiders burned Columbus and Girard they destroyed all but one of the city's newspapers—the *Columbus Enquirer*—which they placed under bond not to print anything against the government or its armies. When it finally began publishing again around April 24, the *Enquirer* was conspicuously lacking in details concerning what one might imagine would have been the biggest story in the city's history—

the Battle for Columbus and its destructive aftermath. Yet, within the pages of the April 27 issue of the *Enquirer* was to be found "the first and only local account written near the time of the battle," consisting of nothing more than a brief summary of the engagement based largely, it appears, on speculation and rumor.[59]

Almost from the moment it was concluded, the Battle for Columbus and the conflagration of the city fell into complete national obscurity, where it has remained for over 140 years. During the Reconstruction era, there apparently was some aversion to recalling to memory the specifics of the battle and its aftermath, and later there seems to have been but a passing interest on the part of Columbusites to commemorate the event. Even in 1898, when General Wilson made a visit to the troops stationed near Columbus who were gearing up for the Spanish-American War, it was noted that his reception was rather cool and that he was "not extensively entertained." When asked about the battle by a young reporter, Wilson passed over the subject lightly, and it was assumed that "he thought it would not be in such good taste, during this visit in times of peace and goodwill, to dwell too extensively on bayonet, musket, and torch activities."[60]

Despite his reluctance to engage in recollection of the battle during his visit, Wilson did give significant mention to the Battle for Columbus and its consequences in his memoirs, which were published in 1912. Shortly thereafter, Columbus historian Charles J. Swift took up the cause of recognizing the Battle for Columbus as the war's last real battle and corresponded with Wilson, Winslow, and others concerning their participation. On and off from that time forward through the mid-1960s, several efforts were made to commemorate the struggle that took place on the banks of the Chattahoochee. The most successful of these efforts was Georgia representative Bryant T. Castellow's introduction of a bill in 1935 recommending that Congress make available ten thousand dollars for the construction of a monument commemorating the fight. Enthusiasm for the project waned, however, when in 1936 the bill was amended to reduce the amount of the award to one thousand dollars after the Department of the Interior declined to be drawn into the uncomfortable position of having to decide which among several contesting sites should be officially considered that of the war's last battle. Since then, efforts to memorialize the struggle or raise popular interest have been largely hindered by there never having been any attempt to comprehensively investigate or document the engagement.[61]

Likewise, since the Civil War there has been no serious, concerted effort to preserve any portion of the battlefield. In 1865 and 1866, blacks found loitering in Columbus were rounded up by the Federal soldiers and put to work leveling the fortifications. With but a few exceptions, their efforts obliterated all traces of the rifle pits and gun emplacements. In only two small areas, both privately owned, can any trace of the massive forts of Von Zinken's *tête-de-pont* be distinguished.[62]

Furthermore, residential and commercial development has obscured much of the battlefield's face. Today, thousands of people live and work on the very spots where the Battle for Columbus was fought, oblivious to the area's significance to our national or regional history. With the exception of a few historical markers, most of which have been recently installed, and one inconspicuous little monument at the intersection of Broadway and Franklin Street (14th Street) near where the battle reached its climax, there is nothing to remind the people of Columbus or Girard (today called Phenix City) of the great struggle and sacrifice made on that Easter Sunday.

Writing in 1915, William Grant, a Confederate veteran of the Battle for Columbus, observed of the Easter engagement: "Big battles and events are told and retold in story and song, while the little ones, though often significant and important in the construction of a complete narrative, are either not mentioned or are treated so lightly as to discredit the truth of history." To some extent, General Upton had realized this much earlier, and with the understanding that the heroic efforts made on the hills of Girard and in the streets of Columbus were already passing into obscurity, he announced to his soldiers: "Though many of you have not received the reward to which your gallantry has entitled you, you have never-the-less received the commendation of your superior officers and won the admiration and gratitude of your countrymen." With that the veterans would have to be satisfied, for up until now, the Battle for Columbus has remained nothing more than a mostly forgotten footnote in history.[63]

Appendix 1
The Last Real *Battle*
of the Civil War

In addition to its importance to the advancement of Wilson's Raid and as an event significant in the history of the Chattahoochee valley, and despite the fact that it has been almost forgotten, the Battle for Columbus continues to have an even greater national significance than has ever been fully appreciated. This significance springs from the battle's status as probably the most legitimate contender among a field of no less than a dozen localities that lay claim to the site of the Civil War's last real battle.

The endeavor to classify the war's thousands of combats and to ascribe to each its proper measure of significance within the conflict's overall narrative is an activity as old as the war itself. Almost as soon as the guns fell silent in 1865, in an effort to make sense of the tremendous expense both in material and lives expended during the contest, titles began to be associated with distinguishing events. Examples include the "opening shot" at Fort Sumter, the "bloodiest day" at Antietam, the "high tide of the Confederacy" at Gettysburg, and literally hundreds of others.

In the decades following the war, soldiers on both sides, and indeed the people of the areas where the events took place, began to take a keen interest in preserving for themselves or their localities a special position within the grand scheme of America's greatest conflict. Out of these exercises there naturally arose differences of opinion, many of which persist to this day. Historians familiar with the Battle for Columbus, though admittedly few in number, remain embroiled in just such a controversy—whether or not the Battle for Columbus is truly the last real battle of the Civil War.

No fewer than a dozen places claim to be the site of the final land battle between the North and South. (There were later naval engagements.) They range in location from Virginia to Texas, and in chronology, generally, from April 6 to May 13, 1865. Some are well known to Civil War historians and enthusiasts, while others are almost unheard of. How then is one to determine which is actually the last?

One of the surprising aspects of the debate is that chronology is one of the least-contested components. It is relatively easy to compile a list of combats that took place during the winding-up phase of the war and to arrange them in chronological order. What is not so easy is to determine which ones were battles and which were skirmishes. This is because, although the U.S. War Department's historical classification terminology is useful as a general guide, it is somewhat ambiguous and overlapping in application. Furthermore, according to former director of the U.S. Department of the Interior Arno B. Cammerer, the government employs "no positive standard to determine just how large or how small an engagement of troops must be to justify its classification as a battle." In fact, it was for this very reason, and because the Department of the Interior did not wish to expose itself to controversy, that in the 1930s requests that the Battle for Columbus be recognized as the Civil War's last battle were rejected. Yet, in spite of the government's disinterest in settling the question, the contention among historians has continued.[1]

How then might one determine which of the most likely combats is actually the last battle? The key to answering this question lies in accurately defining what constitutes a battle as opposed to a skirmish. The challenge to this approach, as alluded to above, lies in that there is no single, uniformly recognized, positive standard from which to derive the definitions. Simple definitions of *battle* and *skirmish* can be found in any dictionary, and probably could be formulated nearly as accurately by anyone with minimal exposure to military history and terminology. More comprehensive definitions may be found in any number of military dictionaries and treatises, where descriptive analysis of the components of a battle or skirmish vary in length from a few paragraphs to many pages.

A careful examination of the field of possible definitions yields a diverse and often confusing array of standards. Among the variables that help to determine what should be considered a battle as opposed to a skirmish are factors such as scale (large versus small), intensity (high versus low), duration (long versus short), casualties (numerous versus few), and objectives (part of a larger campaign versus no predetermined objective). But in addition to these are less concrete factors, such as control (which suggests a difference between a highly ordered and directed combat versus more independent and desultory fighting) and dignity (which suggests a scale of honor ranging from the decisive or "pitched" combat down to the mere ambush, massacre, or brawl).

In addition, it also appears necessary to weigh the combat against the additional standard of similarity—how similar the combat is to other recognized battles or skirmishes within the same conflict. Obviously, the degree to which the various standards combine to compose a battle during the Civil War will be different from those constituting battles during the Revolutionary War, or World War II, and so forth. This element also relates to how each combat was viewed at the time by participants in the fighting and their contemporaries. And finally, further complicating the analysis, under the blanket definition of a battle there exist subtypes that have their own sets of specific determiners that distinguish, for example, an action from an engagement.[2]

For the sake of brevity, it is possible to distill the most pertinent components from many sources, excluding those that do not seem universal or that are obviously limited by the contemporary considerations of their writers, and to assemble definitions that are both reasonably comprehensive and that also yield predictable determinations when gauged against known battles and skirmishes. Using these composite definitions, a *battle* is *a general engagement, of high intensity, between soldiers of opposing allegiances, that takes place as a part of a larger campaign.* The essential part of this definition is the word *general,* which conveys two separate ideas. One is a sense of scale. For something to be *general,* it must be large, comprehensive, or broad. The other idea is a sense of commonality. For something to be *general,* it must be common, usual, or typical. Therefore, it may be said that for a combat to be considered a battle it must take place (1) between opposing forces, (2) involving large numbers of soldiers as participants, (3) in which the fighting is intense, (4) occurring as a part of a larger military strategy, and (5) which is similar to other recognized battles of the same conflict.

In contrast, a *skirmish* may be defined as *a limited combat between soldiers of opposing allegiances, generally, though not necessarily of short duration, sometimes occurring as a part of a larger battle, which is similar to other skirmishes of the same conflict.* An important term in the definition of a skirmish is *limited.* For a combat to be limited it must be of relatively small scale, and the fighting must be of light to moderate intensity. Therefore, the functional definition of a skirmish is a combat (1) between opposing forces, (2) involving a small number of soldiers, (3) in which the fighting is of light to moderate intensity, (4) usually, though not necessarily, lasting a short time, (5) which may, or may not, be a part of a larger battle, and (6) is similar to other recognized skirmishes of the same conflict.

By weighing the facts relating to a combat against these standards, one may gauge whether or not a combat is a battle or a skirmish. Again, for the sake of brevity, all of the combats that lay some claim to the title of the Civil War's last battle need not be analyzed individually in this appendix.

Instead, the author has narrowed the field to the five most legitimate candidate combats:

1. Fort Blakely, Alabama—April 9, 1865
2. West Point, Georgia—April 16, 1865
3. Columbus, Georgia—April 16, 1865
4. Munford's Station, Alabama—April 23, 1865
5. Palmetto Ranch, Texas—May 12–13, 1865

Fort Blakely

The Battle of Fort Blakely, Alabama, took place on the evening of April 9, 1865, and was the culmination of Union general Edward Canby's campaign to capture Mobile. The Confederate forces, approximately four thousand strong, held a well-fortified, two-and-a-half-mile stretch of earthworks and redoubts known as Fort Blakely, which had already withstood an eight-day siege. These works were strengthened by palisades, abatis, slashings, wire entanglements, and land mines designed to discomfit any attacker. Yet despite the obstacles and obstructions, by the evening of April 9, the Union forces, numbering sixteen thousand soldiers, had finished a series of entrenchments close to the Confederate lines and were prepared for an assault. In a combined attack, the Federals charged the Confederate lines, smashed through the defenses, and pursued the retreating enemy until nearly the entire Rebel force became trapped with their backs to the river and surrendered. Union forces suffered approximately 800 casualties, while the Confederates lost (especially to capture) about 3,700 soldiers. The combined number of killed in the action numbered about 250.[3]

When weighed against the classification criteria, it quickly becomes obvious that the fighting that took place at Fort Blakely was a battle. The fight was between opposing forces and involved a large number of soldiers (about twenty thousand in total), far too many to generally be considered a skirmish within the context of the Civil War. Also in conformity with the definition of a battle, the combat was well calculated beforehand and took place as part of Canby's campaign to capture Mobile, and against Confederate designs to the contrary. The charges made by Canby's soldiers against the well-fortified and significantly defended entrenchments as well as the number of casualties sustained on both sides undeniably evinces a high level of intensity to the fight. And finally, the struggle was universally seen by contemporaries as a battle, and may still be seen as such when compared to other recognized battles of the Civil War. Today, Fort Blakely is a state historic park, and the battle is classified by the Department of the Interior as a Class A battle, or one that had a "decisive impact on a campaign and a direct impact on the course of the war."[4]

Although it seems beyond doubt that the combat at Fort Blakely was a real battle, significant debate continues over whether it was the last of the Civil War. Proponents have long claimed that the Battle of Fort Blakely was the "last major battle of the Civil War" because it was the largest combat to occur after the surrender at Appomattox Courthouse. (It occurred several hours after the surrender.) Others have challenged this claim on the grounds that recognition as the *largest* battle to occur after the surrender is not necessarily synonymous with standing as the war's *final* battle.

Some historians have even claimed that the last battle of the Civil War occurred before the Battle of Fort Blakely. The main support for this theory arises from the rather subjective interpretation that the last battle of any conflict is that battle after which there is no hope of victory for one side or the other. Advocates of this position see the Battle of Sailor's Creek in Virginia, on April 6, 1865, as the event from which no recovery by the Confederacy was possible. The standard, however, is fairly open to interpretation, and depending on one's view of the war's course might also be applied to several other possible "turning point" battles, such as Gettysburg, Vicksburg, Franklin, Atlanta, and so forth.[5]

West Point (Fort Tyler)

Next on the list of likely candidates is the combat at West Point fought on the afternoon of April 16, 1865. Engaged were the Union forces of Oscar LaGrange's brigade of Wilson's Cavalry Corps and a Confederate force composed of a brigade of Confederate cavalrymen and the garrison of Fort Tyler, a small, square bastion situated on a prominent hill overlooking the town of West Point and the Chattahoochee River, which served to protect the bridge over the river from capture. The engagement was part of Wilson's campaign to destroy the South's remaining industrial centers at Selma, Columbus, and Macon. LaGrange's mission was to secure an alternate passage over the Chattahoochee so that, if Wilson's Raiders failed to take the bridges at Columbus by assault, the corps could cross the river at West Point and move on Columbus from the north.[6]

After a running fight with the Confederate cavalry, upon reaching West Point the Union troopers managed to put the Rebel horsemen to flight and capture the bridge. Though they were outnumbered almost five to one, the Confederate garrison of the fort, under the leadership of General Robert Tyler, made a defiant stand. From their position overlooking the bridge, with their three artillery pieces, including a massive 32-pounder, the Confederates began shelling the Union cavalry and the span. In response, the Union cannoneers bombarded the fort and eventually managed to dismount the 32-pounder and disable the other guns. Union soldiers then encircled the fort.

Attacking simultaneously from three sides, the Federals charged up the hill toward the ramparts where they met the Confederate defenders who poured on a heavy musketry fire and hurled lighted shells over the walls like hand grenades. Leading the assault was a body of Union soldiers who carried bridges made from sections of picket fence taken from the yards of surrounding homes. These makeshift bridges were laid across the water-filled ditches so that the onrushing Federals could race over onto the parapets.

After a brief but costly fight in which General Tyler was killed, the Union soldiers forced the surrender of the fort shortly before sunset. In total about 1,700 soldiers participated in the fight, of whom more than 80 were killed or wounded. Additionally, the remaining 220 men of the garrison were made prisoners.[7]

Whether the fight at West Point may be considered a battle remains open to debate. Several key characteristics of a battle are amply demonstrated by the facts of the fight, particularly that the combat which took place was intense and that it occurred as a part of a larger campaign. That the defenders made such a resolute stand, undergoing both serious bombardment and finally an all-out envelopment facilitated by the Federals' use of the improvised scaling ramps and the covering fire of three assaulting columns, provides evidence of the high intensity of the struggle. It is also well established that both Union and Confederate commanders expected an armed clash at West Point and that they prepared to meet each other to contest possession of the bridge spanning the river in order to accomplish the larger objectives of their commands. The progress of the fight is similar to that of other battles that took place over possession of a prepared installation or stronghold, and the combat appears to have not lasted an inordinately short time (several hours).

But one important characteristic—that of scale—stands out as being more closely related to a skirmish than to a battle. In total, the forces involved in the struggle for possession of the bridge and fort fall well below the numbers generally associated with Civil War battles. Of the approximately 1,700 soldiers who participated in the fight, the Confederate cavalry force that confronted LaGrange's brigade consisted of only a few hundred troopers. The garrison that ultimately succumbed to the overwhelming numbers and firepower of the Federals consisted of only about 265 soldiers.

With this exception, however, the fight seems to rise to the level of a battle. It certainly did in the eyes of those soldiers who participated in it and witnessed it. When the *Official Records* were compiled after the war, the combat at West Point was classified in a peculiar manner. Rather than receiving a classification as either a skirmish, action, engagement, or battle, which appears to have been the ranking sequence, the combat was classified as an "attack," a title that leaves open the question of its actual standing. For purposes of this analysis, however, because with the exception of the number of participants the fight appears to meet the qualifications of a battle, and in an effort to give each of the prospective candidates a fair review, the combat at West Point will be accepted as a battle—a small one, but a battle no less.[8]

If a battle, was the combat at West Point the last battle of the Civil War? This claim has been made repeatedly since the time of the fight, and advocates for its recognition still stand by their contention. Assuming that West Point was actually a battle, it displaces Fort Blakely as the site of the last battle of the Civil War, as it was fought seven days later (Fort Blakely on April 9, West Point on April 16).

Columbus

The next fight that has been hailed as the last battle of the Civil War took place at Columbus, Georgia, and is the subject of this study. The combat was fought on April 16 between General Emory Upton's division of General James H. Wilson's Cavalry Corps and the combined Alabama and Georgia forces of Generals Howell Cobb and Abraham Buford. The Union objective was to capture one of the bridges spanning the Chattahoochee River at Columbus, thereby opening a way for the army across that swollen stream into Georgia where they could destroy the industrial complexes of Columbus and Macon. Confederate forces sought to turn back the Federals and save Georgia's resources in hopes of continuing the war.

At Columbus, over six thousand Union and Confederate soldiers fought for more than eight hours (fourteen, if the fighting between Crawford and Girard is included) for possession of the bridges and a series of forts and earthworks stretching more than a mile and a half. The fight took place in two stages. The first was a mounted charge to capture one of the bridges during the afternoon, which the Confederates thwarted by igniting the span and bombarding the Union horsemen into retreat. During the afternoon, as sporadic firing continued, half of the Union force slipped quietly around the Confederates' northern flank. After dark, the major fighting was renewed in a two-pronged assault. Dismounted Union troopers charged over the outer defensive works and followed up their early success with a mounted charge that failed to capture the remaining footbridge.

Reinforcements were called in, and after meeting stubborn resistance the Union troopers managed to scale the parapets and put half the Rebel force to flight.

Additional Federal units were funneled into the action, collapsing what was left of the Confederate line. At the remaining bridge a stiff hand-to-hand struggle occurred, and again on the far side of the wooden enclosure the soldiers clashed in a decisive melee that turned the Confederate retreat into hopeless rout. Eventually, the fighting died away in the streets of Columbus as the last of the Confederates surrendered or fled the city. In all, over 140 soldiers were killed or wounded in the struggle, and approximately half of the Confederate force (over 1,500 men) was captured. Also taken in the fight were eight battle flags and at least twenty-seven pieces of artillery.

Determining whether the combat at Columbus should be classified as a battle or a skirmish is of utmost importance in answering the question presented by this appendix. That the combat took place between opposing Union and Confederate forces is obvious, yet when it comes to analysis of this particular combat, this element seems to be the only one that has escaped dispute. The others warrant a closer investigation.

Whether the combat at Columbus took place as a part of a larger campaign is the first of several contested standards. Critics have argued that what has been termed "Wilson's Raid" did not constitute a campaign. (By "Wilson's Raid" I mean the series of operations between March 22 and April 30 that pitted General James H. Wilson's 13,000 Union cavalry, artillery, and mounted infantry against the Confederate forces of General Nathan B. Forrest in Alabama and General Howell Cobb in Georgia.) Adherents to this position postulate that it is essential to designation as a campaign that two entire, officially designated "armies" face off in prolonged strategic movements (for example, the entire Army of the Potomac versus the entire Army of Northern Virginia). It is their position that no matter how large the forces, how prolonged the conduct of the operations, how extensive the geographic confines, or how grand, protracted, deadly, or decisive any combats that might occur therein, any operation involving less than the total combined weight of two whole armies cannot be a campaign. Supporters of this view also claim that no combat occurring as a part of any lesser operation may be considered a battle, and have even gone so far as to declare that the Battle of Selma, Alabama (April 2, 1865), should not be regarded as such.[9]

Though espoused by some, the above view is an extreme one. The more measured view of what constitutes a campaign is that it is an important part of a war that involves major operations designed to achieve specific objectives and that consists of at least one—but usually more than one—battle and is confined to a certain geographic area. By this definition (or one of its many variations), it is clear that Wilson's Raid constitutes a campaign. It was conducted as such from its conception by Wilson, who was given independent command of his Cavalry Corps (the largest corps in the army at that time) until the end of the war halted his operations, and by Forrest, who, though unable ultimately to completely ready his forces for it, fought Wilson's command until defeated at the largest battle of the campaign, at Selma. It is also a matter of record that had not the surrenders of Lee and Johnston so suddenly terminated his efforts, Wilson would have driven his corps across Georgia in order to fulfill his mission of linking up with Sherman or Grant in either the Carolinas or Virginia and thereby extended his campaign even further, or begun a new one.[10]

The next oft-disputed major factor regarding the combat at Columbus involves determining the level of intensity to which the fighting rose. Past critics have often proposed that the fighting was nothing more than random or desultory and that it never achieved more than low to moderate intensity. In their defense, these historians have had to make evaluations based on a surprisingly small and fragmentary amount of information, which was easily misinterpreted. Today, however, it is easy to demonstrate that the fight at Columbus occasioned a strenuous and sustained contest of arms and wills. This is evidenced by the testimony of those involved, by the number of casualties, and by the fact that the fight included at least four separate incidents of unit-level hand-to-hand combat, a degree of conflict not generally associated with a skirmish.[11]

Two other factors that have not escaped comment are closely related. They revolve around questions of sufficient scale, and whether the combat conforms generally to the model of a Civil War battle. Again, misinterpretation of what sources have been easily accessible has led to past confusion about the scale of the fight. An example of this can be found in numerous references that take Upton's after-action report and misconstrue his enumeration of Union combatants during one particular phase of the fight (300 soldiers) to be representative of the whole force that was involved. This has also been done, as mentioned above, in relation to the number of casualties sustained, particularly by the Confederates at Columbus. Over-reliance on a particular source (a newspaper account), which itself does not purport to be comprehensive, has been the source of recurring error in underestimating the losses. In reality, though the combat at Columbus was not nearly as grand in scale as some of the war's mega-battles, the number of soldiers engaged (over six thousand) was roughly equivalent to many other recognized battles in the western theater, including the battles of Allatoona Pass, Brown's Mill, Lovejoy Station, Buck Head Creek, Monroe's Crossroads, Honey Hill, and Griswoldville, among others. In comparison to these other recognized battles, the combat at Columbus does conform to the standard of what constitutes a battle within the context of the Civil War.[12]

One final criticism has been actively advanced with regard to Columbus's battle status. This criticism concerns the fight's classification in the *Official Records*' "Summary of Principal Events." Despite the fact that the commanders and participants uniformly described the combat at Columbus as a battle, in the chronological summary the combat was classified as an "action." Much has been made of this wording, which some have attempted to suggest makes the combat at Columbus something less than a battle. This conclusion, however, is an oversimplification.[13]

Just as with the terms *battle* and *skirmish,* there are various interpretations of what constitutes other intermediate levels of combat, and a growing suspicion that ambiguities in the records themselves may have affected how the combat at Columbus was classified. Generally, according to the classification scheme, combats were ranked from lowest to highest—skirmish, action, engagement, battle. Full battle designations were generally reserved for what might be termed "mega-battles"—Gettysburg, Franklin, or Atlanta. Lesser combats, though still considered battles, were generally referred to as either engagements or actions in the *Official Records.* Both of these designations carry with them various component factors that, just as with the definitions of what constitutes a battle or skirmish, are often matters of degree and subject to overlap.

The most obvious distinguishing features of these designations are the components of scale and duration. An engagement is a battle that lasts anywhere from several hours to a few days and in which the forces engaged do not exceed division strength on either side. Also, an engagement may be a stand-alone combat or it may be a part of a larger battle. An action is similar in that it may or may not be a part of a larger battle, but it is distinguished from an engagement in that it is smaller and of shorter duration, lasting anywhere from a few minutes up to, but not longer than, a single day.[14]

It appears that the combat at Columbus was ranked as an action based upon the compilers' impressions of the materials relating to the fight's duration, scale, and location. Apparently, the same after-action reports that have caused confusion among historians attempting to understand the combat also confused the compilers of the *Official Records,* who appear not to have been able to distinguish how the disparate reports fit together to form a single combat. When one considers that the fighting occurred in several stages, in two different cities (Girard and Columbus), and also across state boundaries (Alabama and Georgia), it is easy to see how one unfamiliar with the particulars of the fight could develop a fractured understanding of the situation from reading the reports filed by the participants. That the compilers mistakenly viewed the morning, afternoon, and night phases of the battle as separate combats is evidenced by the arrangement of the list. It is almost certain that instead of seeing the battle as an hours-long contest between the entire 4th Division of Wilson's corps and the slightly more numerous Confederate defenders of the city, the compilers instead saw several smaller actions between lesser elements.[15]

Whatever the reasons for the disparity, the position that the combat may be gauged based solely upon the *Official Records'* summary is tenuous at best. A far better measure of the combat's standing may be found in the reports themselves and in the objective examination of the fighting and all of its circumstances as a whole. When this is done, there can be little doubt that the combat that took place at Columbus reaches the standard of classification as a real battle—regardless of whether it is considered an action or an engagement. The obvious question then is, was it the last of the Civil War?

The Battle for Columbus was fought on April 16, obviously displacing the Battle of Fort Blakely, which was fought on April 9. But what about the Battle of West Point (if it is actually considered a battle)? The Battle of West Point was fought on April 16, the same day as the Battle for Columbus. The Battle at West Point, however, concluded with the surrender of Fort Tyler and the capture of its garrison at or before sunset on that Easter Sunday afternoon. The Battle for Columbus, on the other hand, continued for several more hours. In fact, the night assault at Columbus did not begin until after dark, at about 8:30 P.M., and the last of the fighting in Columbus did not die away until about 11:00 P.M. Therefore, although it was only a matter of several hours, the Battle for Columbus occurred later than the Battle of West Point.

Munford's Station

The fourth combat that has been touted as the Civil War's last battle is the fight at Munford's Station, Alabama. This combat was fought between the forces of Union general John Croxton of Wilson's Cavalry Corps and a brigade of soldiers under the command of Confederate general Benjamin Hill on April 23, 1865. Croxton's brigade had been detached from Wilson's main body early in Wilson's Raid, and having failed to rejoin the main body at the appointed time, was left behind to catch up as best they could. While passing through Talladega, Croxton learned that a few hundred Confederates were guarding a nearby supply depot at Munford's Station near Blue Mountain and moved in that direction.

Hill's Confederates numbered only about five hundred infantry and a section of artillery. When this small force observed the approach of Croxton's fifteen-hundred-man brigade they quickly became demoralized. Croxton sent two companies ahead mounted, followed by two regiments from his brigade. The Confederates who did not immediately flee the field opened a sporadic fire on the approaching Federals, and their artillery managed to get off several rounds. When within a short distance of the Confederate position, the Federal cavalrymen charged. The resistance collapsed before the sight of the galloping horsemen, and the Confederates abandoned their artillery and broke for the woods. Within five minutes the fight was over. Two Union soldiers and one Confederate were killed. Additionally, the Confederate cannon was captured, as were about 150 of Hill's Rebels.[16]

In assessing whether the fight at Munford's Station may be considered a battle, the circumstances show that the fight probably involved fewer than one thousand combatants—significantly fewer than other recognized battles. An objective analysis of the fighting indicates a level of engagement not exceeding low to moderate intensity. This is further demonstrated by the short duration of the fight and the few casualties. It is mainly in extenuation that the combat at Munford's Station may be considered a part of a larger military strategy. Though Croxton's Raid was part of the larger campaign known as Wilson's Raid, its objectives had been realized well before this fight; indeed, by this point Croxton's attention appears to have been focused on locating and reuniting with his command's main body.

However, when compared with the standard conception of what constitutes a skirmish, the fight at Munford's Station seems a good fit. It involved a comparatively small number of combatants, lasted a short time, and was conducted with a light to moderate level of engagement. Furthermore, its circumstances seem much more like other recognized skirmishes of the same campaign and conflict. Even its participants and contemporaries viewed the fight as a skirmish. It is also recognized that Croxton did not wish to risk a general engagement with Hill even had the Confederates resisted more sternly because of a shortage of ammunition. Accordingly, the combat at Munford's Station may be accurately classified as a skirmish.[17]

Palmetto Ranch

The most famous of the combats that claim the title of the last battle of the Civil War took place at Palmetto Ranch, Texas. It occurred in May 1865 when, without plausible explanation other than a desire for glory, and despite knowledge that the war had already ended and that there existed an informal cease-fire, Colonel Theodore H. Barrett, the commander of the Federal garrison at Brazos Island (in the Gulf of Mexico), undertook an expedition into the Confederate-held mainland of Texas. With a force of approximately three hundred soldiers, Barrett began his inland march on May 11. After being spotted by a small detachment of Confederate cavalry on May 12, the Federals continued toward Palmetto Ranch, scattered the Confederate outpost stationed there, and captured three of the enemy who were too ill to flee. Later that day, approximately sixty Confederate cavalrymen showed themselves nearby and Barrett ordered his soldiers to withdraw to White's Ranch. That night, the Union and Confederate forces were reinforced.[18]

On May 13, Union forces again advanced inland toward Palmetto Ranch. The suspicious Confederate cavalry shadowed the Union movements but stayed mostly out of range. After a few hours' rest at Palmetto Ranch, two companies of Union skirmishers exchanged fire with a small force of Confederate cavalry who quickly broke off contact and retreated to safety. Barrett, apparently frustrated at his inability to force a fight, turned over command of the expedition to a subordinate, who botched an ambush on a group of observing Confederates. Shortly thereafter, the Federals advanced toward a nearby ridge occupied by the Rebels, but after exchanging some long-range fire they pulled back to rest. In the meantime, the Confederates were reinforced with additional cavalrymen and a battery of artillery and began to deploy in order to surround the idle Federals. The movement was soon discovered, however, and afraid of being trapped with their backs to the Rio Grande, the Union soldiers began a general retreat.[19]

Harassed by the enemy, the Union withdrawal soon escalated into an all-out rout. Exhausted, many of the rear-guard elements were cut off, surrounded, and captured. Eventually, the remnants of Barrett's command managed to reach the safety of the dunes at their landing point on the coast, and the Confederates gave up their pursuit. In all, 920 Union and Confederate soldiers participated in the fight. The total loss for both the Union and Confederate forces during the entire three day episode was three killed and ten wounded. Additionally, the Federals lost about one hundred men to capture.[20]

The issue of chronology is not in doubt when it comes to analysis of the combat at Palmetto Ranch. The fight occurred much later than any of the other combats addressed in this appendix, and it is probably largely for that reason that it has been historically so easy to point to the fight there as the last of the war. The question remains, however, not whether there occurred some fighting at Palmetto Ranch or whether it was the last actual fighting, but whether or not the fighting that took place may be considered a battle.

It is obvious that the fighting occurred between opposing forces. It is also fairly easy to establish that the number of soldiers engaged (920) was quite small compared to other recognized Civil War battles. Indeed, with regard to scale, this fight and the skirmish at Munford's Station are the smallest of the field analyzed, and the fight at Palmetto Ranch might possibly rank as even smaller than Munford's Station. Additionally, whereas it can be argued that the combat at Munford's Station was a part of a larger campaign, the same cannot be said of Palmetto Ranch. The expedition onto the mainland of Texas by the small Union force did not constitute an important sub-part or major operation in the context of the war's totality. It was deficient with regard to having a specific objective, and unless the combat at Palmetto Ranch may be so considered, the requirement of at least one battle is not met.

Furthermore, it seems evident that the fighting which took place never rose above the level of moderate intensity, which is evidenced by the fact that despite the opposing forces being in contact for nearly three days and the absence of other intervening circumstances (such as the intense darkness at the Battle for Columbus), there resulted a total combined injury of only three killed and ten wounded.

Lastly, the combat at Palmetto Ranch conforms in a general sense much more closely to the concept of skirmish, and indeed its participants regarded it as such. Even Colonel Barrett made it clear in his reports that what had taken place was a skirmish, going so far as to explain that he had not been willing to join the enemy in a "general engagement"—the definition of a battle. Thus, although it is fair to say that the combat at Palmetto Ranch marks the last armed clash between North and South (on land), it was not a battle. More precisely, it was a skirmish—likely the last of the Civil War.[21]

Conclusion

In review, the five most likely candidates for recognition as the last real battle of the Civil War are as follows:

1. Fort Blakely, Alabama—April 9, 1865 = battle
2. West Point, Georgia—April 16, 1865 = battle/skirmish
3. Columbus, Georgia—April 16, 1865 = battle

4. Munford's Station, Alabama—April 23, 1865 = skirmish
5. Palmetto Ranch, Texas—May 12–13, 1865 = skirmish

All of the combats examined in this appendix, and others that were left out for lack of space, deserve recognition as being a part of the complete story of America's greatest conflict. Recognizing and acknowledging the place and relation of each of these combats to the whole in no way diminishes the honor that properly belongs to those who participated, but instead affords to each the deserved measure of peculiar identity within our larger national narrative. It is hoped that this volume and appendix will renew the memory of those soldiers who participated in all of the Civil War's final combats, including the Battle for Columbus—the last real *battle* of the Civil War.

Appendix 2
Structure of Wilson's Cavalry Corps

Cavalry Corps, Military Division of the Mississippi (Wilson's Raiders):
Maj. Gen. James H. Wilson

Escort: 4th United States Cavalry:
Lt. William O'Connell

1st Division:
Brig. Gen. Edward M. McCook

2nd Division:
Brig. Gen. Eli Long (wounded April 2, 1865)
Col. Robert H. G. Minty (after April 2, 1865)

4th Division:
Maj. Gen. Emory Upton

1st Brigade:
Brig. Gen. John H. Croxton

8th Iowa Cavalry:
Col. Joseph B. Dorr

4th Kentucky Mounted Infantry:
Col. Robert M. Kelly

6th Kentucky Cavalry:
Maj. William H. Fidler

2nd Michigan Cavalry:
Lt. Col. Thomas W. Johnston

1st Brigade:
Col. Abram O. Miller (wounded April 2, 1865)
Col. Jacob G. Vail
Lt. Col. Frank White

98th Illinois Mounted Infantry:
Lt. Col. Edward Kitchell

123rd Illinois Mounted Infantry:
Lt. Col. Jonathan Biggs

17th Indiana Mounted Infantry:
Col. Jacob G. Vail

72nd Indiana Mounted Infantry:
Lt. Col. Chester G. Thomson

1st Brigade:
Brig. Gen. Edward F. Winslow

3rd Iowa Cavalry:
Col. John W. Noble

4th Iowa Cavalry:
Lt. Col. John Peters

10th Missouri Cavalry:
Lt. Col. Frederick W. Benteen

2nd Brigade:
Col. Oscar H. LaGrange

2nd Indiana (Battalion) Cavalry:
Capt. Roswell S. Hill

4th Indiana Cavalry:
Lt. Col. Horace P. Lamson

4th Kentucky Cavalry:
Col. Wickliffe Cooper

7th Kentucky Cavalry:
Lt. Col. William W. Bradley

1st Wisconsin Cavalry:
Lt. Col. Henry Hamden

2nd Brigade:
Brig. Gen. Andrew J. Alexander

5th Iowa Cavalry:
Col. John M. Young

1st Ohio Cavalry:
Col. Beroth B. Eggleston

7th Ohio Cavalry:
Col. Israel Garrard

4th United States Artillery,
Battery I:
Lt. George B. Rodney

2nd Brigade:
Col. Robert H. G. Minty
Lt. Col. Horace N. Howland

4th Michigan Cavalry:
Lt. Col. Benjamin D. Pritchard

3rd Ohio Cavalry:
Lt. Col. Horace N. Howland

4th Ohio Cavalry:
Lt. Col. George W. Dobb

7th Pennsylvania Cavalry:
Col. Charles C. McCormick

18th Battery, Indiana Light Artillery:
Capt. Moses M. Beck

Illinois Light, Chicago Board of Trade Battery:
Capt. George I. Robinson

Colored Brigade (formed at Selma, Ala.): Maj. Martin Archer

1st Division Colored Regiment
(136th United States Colored Troops)

2nd Division Colored Regiment
(137th United States Colored Troops)

4th Division Colored Regiment
(138th United States Colored Troops)

Pontoniers: 12th Missouri Cavalry:
Maj. James M. Hubbard

Appendix 3
Order of Battle, April 16, 1865

Union Forces

Cavalry Corps, Military Division of the Mississippi (CCMDM): Brevet Major General James H. Wilson
4th U.S. Cavalry (Wilson's escort): Lieutenant William O'Connell
4th Division, CCMDM: Brevet Major General Emory Upton
Company G, 4th Iowa Cavalry (Upton's escort): Major William Woods

1st Brigade, 4th Division, CCMDM: Brevet Brigadier General Edward F. Winslow
3rd Iowa Cavalry: Colonel John W. Noble
10th Missouri Cavalry: Lieutenant Colonel Frederick W. Benteen
4th Iowa Cavalry: Lieutenant Colonel John Peters

2nd Brigade, 4th Division, CCMDM: Brevet Brigadier General Andrew J. Alexander
1st Ohio Cavalry: Colonel Beroth B. Eggleston
7th Ohio Cavalry: Colonel Israel Garrard
5th Iowa Cavalry: Colonel John Morris Young
4th U.S. Artillery, Battery I: Lieutenant George B. Rodney

Total: 2,880 (approximate)

Confederate Forces

Georgia forces and overall command: Major General Howell Cobb
Field commander: Colonel Leon Von Zinken
1st Regiment Georgia State Line: Lieutenant Colonel John M. Brown
2nd Regiment Georgia State Line: Colonel James Wilson

26th Battalion Georgia Infantry: Major John W. Nisbet

3rd Georgia Reserves: Colonel John L. Moore

5th Georgia Reserves: Colonel John B. Cumming

3rd Georgia Cavalry: Colonel Robert Thompson

Typo Guards: Commander unknown

Georgia 1st Columbus City Infantry Battalion (Jacques's battalion): Major Samuel R. Jacques

Columbus City Infantry Battalion Provost Guard (City Defense battalion): Major (Mayor) Francis G. Wilkins

Columbus Ordnance Infantry Battalion: Major W. W. Baldwin

Columbus Naval Infantry Battalion (Naval Works/Iron Works Battalion): Major Samuel J. Whiteside

Pemberton's Company, Georgia Cavalry, Local Defense Troops: Captain John S. Pemberton

Columbus and Muscogee County Militias (Citizens): Commander unknown

Columbus's Confederate Convalescents: Commander unknown

Alabama forces: Brigadier General Abraham Buford

7th Alabama Cavalry: Colonel Francis C. Randolph

4th Alabama Cavalry (consolidated with 7th Alabama Cavalry): Colonel Francis C. Randolph

3rd Alabama Infantry Reserves and 4th Battalion Alabama Reserves Consolidated (65th Alabama Infantry): Colonel Edward M. Underhill

Russell County Reserves: Colonel John M. Brannon

20th Battalion Alabama Light Artillery: Major James F. Waddell

20th Battalion Alabama Light Artillery, Company A (Emery's Battery): Captain Winslow D. Emery

20th Battalion Alabama Light Art, Company B (Bellamy's Battery): Captain Richard H. Bellamy

10th Missouri Battery C.S.A. (Barrett's/Rice's Battery): Captain D. A. Rice

2nd Battalion Alabama Light Artillery, Company D (Sengstak's Battery): Captain Henry H. Sengstak.

Clanton's Alabama Battery: Captain Nathaniel H. Clanton

Ward's (Cruse's) Alabama Battery: Commander unknown

Griffin Light Artillery (Scogin's Battery—One Section): Commander unknown

Additional Units

Captain E. E. Arnold's Company

2nd Battalion Georgia Militia Cavalry: Colonel Thomas T. Dorough

Lieutenant Hunt's Dismounted Cavalry Detachment

Captain B. F. White's Command

Colonel James C. Cole's Battalion

Columbus Fire Companies

Columbus Government Mechanics (Youngblood's Battalion Government Mechanics): Major E. H. Youngblood

Dillard Greys

Other units: Many units that are not listed had representatives at the battle.

Total: 3,300 (approximate)

Appendix 4
Casualties at the Battle for Columbus

KIA = killed in action
MW = mortally wounded
WIA = wounded in action
MIA = missing in action
POW = prisoner of war

Union Forces

4th Division of Wilson's Cavalry Corps: Brevet Major General James H. Wilson

4th U.S. Cavalry:	KIA...0	MW...0	WIA...0	MIA...0	POW...0
1st Brigade: Brevet Brigadier General Edward F. Winslow					
3rd Iowa Cavalry:	KIA...3	MW...3	WIA...20	MIA...2	POW...0
4th Iowa Cavalry:	KIA...2	MW...0	WIA...9	MIA...0	POW...0
10th Missouri Cavalry:	KIA...1	MW...1	WIA...3	MIA...0	POW...2
2nd Brigade: Brevet Brigadier General Andrew J. Alexander					
1st Ohio Cavalry:	KIA...0	MW...0	WIA...3	MIA...2	POW...0
7th Ohio Cavalry:	KIA...0	MW...1	WIA...1	MIA...0	POW...0
5th Iowa Cavalry:	KIA...1	MW...0	WIA...1	MIA...0	POW...0
Battery I, 4th U.S. Artillery:	KIA...0	MW...0	WIA...2	MIA...0	POW...0

Subtotal:	KIA...7	MW...5	WIA...39	MIA...4	POW...2
Unknowns:	KIA...5				
Total loss: 62					

Federals killed in the Battle for Columbus were buried in Linwood Cemetery in Columbus until they were removed to Andersonville National Cemetery after the war. Their graves are located in Section B of the cemetery. All but five have been positively identified. Also, the casualty figures given represent my best estimate based on the records available. There may have been others wounded on the Union side who have yet to be identified. This is suggested by some of the reports made out after the close of Wilson's Raid by the individual company commanders of the regiments engaged. Also, the diary of George Hobson of the 4th Iowa Cavalry states his regiment's loss in the battle as four killed and fifteen wounded—two more killed and six more wounded than I have been able to identify. These additional casualties may account for the five unknown dead.[1]

Union Casualties: Killed

1. Captain Thomas J. Miller, Company D, 3rd Iowa Cavalry—KIA. Struck by a shell during first assault of the 3rd Iowa against Fort 3 west of the Summerville Road at the north end of the Confederate defenses. His last words are reported to have been, "like a Christian and a soldier." Miller's body was buried on April 17, 1865, on the battlefield in Girard. The next day his corpse was moved across the river and reburied in Columbus's Linwood Cemetery. Today his body lies in Plot 12,865, Section B, of Andersonville National Cemetery.

2. 1st Sergeant John W. Delay, Company I, 3rd Iowa Cavalry—KIA. Killed during night assault. Buried in Plot 12,866, Section B, Andersonville National Cemetery.

3. Corporal Miles King, Company B, 3rd Iowa Cavalry—MW. Wounded in the breast/abdomen severely. Died April 20, 1865, at Walker Hospital, Columbus, Georgia.

4. Private William Hagler, Company A, 3rd Iowa Cavalry—KIA. Killed during night assault.

5. Private John M. Miller, Company D, 3rd Iowa Cavalry—MW. Wounded in pelvis. Died April 20th, 1865, at Walker Hospital, Columbus, Georgia.

6. Private Samuel Nelson, Company I, 3rd Iowa Cavalry—MW. Wounded during night assault.

7. Sergeant Joseph H. Jones, Company L, 4th Iowa Cavalry—KIA. Wound described as shoulder severe. Killed during hand-to-hand fighting with cannoneers at east end of bridge during the night assault. Buried in Plot 12,879, Section B, Andersonville National Cemetery.

8. Private Nathan Beezley, Company I, 4th Iowa Cavalry—KIA. Shot through the head during hand-to-hand fighting with cannoneers at east end of bridge during the night assault. Buried in Plot 12,864, Section B, Andersonville National Cemetery.

9. Sergeant John Ritchey, Company I, 10th Missouri Cavalry—MW. Possibly wounded during Captain McGlasson's escape from the bridge during the night assault. Listed as wounded in the left "libra" (possibly "libia"). Died April 29, 1865, at Walker Hospital, Columbus, Georgia.

10. Private John Rattles, Company I, 10th Missouri Cavalry—KIA. Possibly killed by exploding shell on Summerville Road during night assault.

11. Private Richard Porter, Company I, 5th Iowa Cavalry—KIA. Killed by the accidental discharge of a gun during night assault.

12. Private Jonathan Kennedy, Company B, 7th Ohio Cavalry—MW. Possibly wounded by friendly fire. Died April 19, 1865, of his injuries.

13–17. Unknown—KIA. Buried in Section B, Andersonville National Cemetery.[2]

Wounded

1. Lieutenant John J. Veatch, Company I, 3rd Iowa Cavalry—WIA. Details unknown.

2. Sergeant William W. Fraser, Company I, 3rd Iowa Cavalry—WIA. Details unknown.

3. Corporal Daniel S. Beers, Company D, 3rd Iowa Cavalry—WIA. Left leg amputated. Corporal Beers died on July 14, 1865. It is not known whether his death was directly related to his wounding at the Battle for Columbus and the amputation of his leg or whether it was due to other causes. Buried in Plot 13,207 at Andersonville National Cemetery.

4. Corporal Alfred Phillips, Company C, 3rd Iowa Cavalry—WIA. Hand slight.

5. Private Jacob Cellan, Company A, 3rd Iowa Cavalry—WIA. Left leg amputated.

6. Private Alonzo Clinkenbeard, Company I, 3rd Iowa Cavalry—WIA. Details unknown.

7. Private Benjamin F. Grant, Company B, 3rd Iowa Cavalry—WIA. Jaw severe.

8. Private George Guthrie, Company D, 3rd Iowa Cavalry—WIA. Head severe.

9. Private William Guthrie, Company D, 3rd Iowa Cavalry—WIA. Slight.

10. Private Samuel L. McDonald, Company I, 3rd Iowa Cavalry—WIA. Details unknown.

11. Private James W. Miller, Company K, 3rd Iowa Cavalry—WIA. Groin dangerous.

12. Private Edward W. Moore, Company A, 3rd Iowa Cavalry—WIA. Union records show as having flesh wound to leg. Columbus hospital records show wounded left shoulder.

13. Private Isaac O'Conner, Company I, 3rd Iowa Cavalry—WIA. Slight.

14. Private Samuel Parsons, Company B, 3rd Iowa Cavalry—WIA. Slight.

15. Private Ernest Pruss, Company I, 3rd Iowa Cavalry—WIA. Slight.

16. Private John W. Randolph, Company A, 3rd Iowa Cavalry—WIA. Left shoulder severe.

17. Private Isaac Stevens, Company I, 3rd Iowa Cavalry—WIA. Foot severe.

18. Private John Stevens, Company D, 3rd Iowa Cavalry—WIA. Left leg severe. Last name possibly "Stephens."

19. Private Andrew W. Tibbets, Company I, 3rd Iowa Cavalry—WIA. Blinded during the night assault, probably by the flash of artillery from Fort 2, after capturing a Confederate flag and its bearer. According to his company commander, "Tibbets had to go through an ordeal which is almost beyond human endurance. . . . The hottest fire & smoke . . . [from] the severest test of this night made him blind, so that he had to be led by his comrades until we reached Macon, Georgia, where he was left in the hospital." Tibbets would remain in the hospital until sometime after the middle of July 1865, before regaining enough vision to be released.

20. Private Abram Wishard, Company A, 3rd Iowa Cavalry—WIA. Neck/side of face severe. First name possibly "Abraham."

21. Sergeant Horton M. Detrick, Company D, 4th Iowa Cavalry—WIA. Shoulder severe.

22. Corporal Joseph C. McCoy, Company D, 4th Iowa Cavalry—WIA. Union reports show wound as face slight, or "powder burned slightly in face."

23. Corporal Elza A. Reeves, Company A, 4th Iowa Cavalry—WIA. Neck slight.

24. Private David M. Anderson, Company K, 4th Iowa Cavalry—WIA. Details unknown.

25. Private William Loomis, Company D, 4th Iowa Cavalry—WIA. One Union report shows wound as face slight, another as "powder burned in eyes severely."

26. Private Elias F. Ogg, Company D, 4th Iowa Cavalry—WIA. Leg slight.

27. Private John S. Shirley, Company A, 4th Iowa Cavalry—WIA. Left side/head and side severe. Last name possibly "Sherley."

28. Private James H. Van Clear, Company I, 4th Iowa Cavalry—WIA. Report of Lieutenant Colonel Peters shows wound as finger slight. Wound described as hand severe by fellow soldier in same company. Last name possibly "Van Cleve."

29. Private Jehoida Worth, Company D, 4th Iowa Cavalry—WIA. Wrist/hand severe.

30. 1st Sergeant Louis Albright, Company L, 10th Missouri Cavalry—WIA. Wounded by canister near Summerville Road.

31. Private Joseph M. Martin, Company A, 10th Missouri Cavalry—WIA. Burned.

32. Private William Penning, Company L/E, 10th Missouri Cavalry—WIA. Wounded by canister near Summerville Road.

33. Sergeant Henry Wheeler, Company D, 1st Ohio Cavalry—WIA. Details unknown.

34. Corporal William Griffith, Company K, 1st Ohio Cavalry—WIA. Details unknown.

35. Private Nathan C. Rolland, Company A, 1st Ohio Cavalry—WIA. Left wrist severe. Last name possibly "Bolin."

36. Private Charles Neville, Company B, 7th Ohio Cavalry—WIA. Wound with laceration.

37. Private Thomas Heirno, Company L, 5th Iowa Cavalry—WIA. Left leg.

38. Private John McGrath, Battery I, 4th U.S. Artillery—WIA. Left leg amputated.

39. Private Lewis Walter, Battery I, 4th U.S. Artillery—WIA. Wound with bruise.

Missing

1. Private William Dunlary, Company M, 3rd Iowa Cavalry—MIA. Admitted to Walker Hospital, Columbus, Georgia, April 20, with severe fatigue.

2. Private John Wilson, Company M, 3rd Iowa Cavalry—MIA. Admitted to Walker Hospital, Columbus, Georgia, April 20, with severe fatigue.

3. Private James Lynch, Company H, 1st Ohio Cavalry—MIA. No further record.

4. Private George W. Mercer, Company H, 1st Ohio Cavalry—MIA. No further record.

Prisoners

1. Private George W./D. Harris, Company K, 10th Missouri Cavalry—POW. Captured April 16, 1865, at Columbus, Georgia.

2. Pvt. William McGill, Company B/K, 10th Missouri Cavalry—POW. Captured April 16, 1865, at Columbus, Georgia.[3]

Confederate Forces

Georgia forces: Major General Howell Cobb
Alabama forces: Brigadier General Abraham Buford
Field command: Colonel Leon Von Zinken
KIA...31 MW...3 WIA...46 MIA...Unknown
Total: 80
POW...1,500 Deserted...850 Total loss: 2,400 [approximate]

This is only a rough approximation. The total for specifically identified Confederate casualties is 60 soldiers killed, mortally wounded, or wounded. This total is increased by 20 Confederate soldiers reported buried in the Clapp's Factory Cemetery. Unfortunately, the cemetery has been almost completely destroyed, including that area containing the Confederate dead, making verification of these graves impossible. Evidence suggests that there were more Confederate combatants killed and wounded than are represented in this appendix, but so far they have eluded specific identification.

Confederate Casualties: Killed

1. Colonel Charles A. L. Lamar—KIA. Shot while attempting to rally the routed Confederates on Franklin Street near the east end of the bridge. His personal effects were looted by soldiers from the 4th Iowa Cavalry, including an ornate gold watch, which was likely kept by Union General Winslow. Years after the war, at the request of Lamar's wife, Winslow returned the watch to the family. Lamar was buried in Columbus after the battle, but his body was later moved to Laurel Grove Cemetery in Savannah. His tombstone reads: "In the morning it flourisheth and groweth up; in the evening it is cut down and witherith."

2. Captain S. Isadore Guillett, 20th Louisiana Infantry and post adjutant and aide to Colonel Von Zinken—MW. Shot from his horse while trying to assist Von Zinken in rallying Confederate forces near the entrance to the bridge on the Alabama side. He is recorded to have been shot from atop the same horse upon which three of his brothers had been killed. He willed the animal to his nephew before his death. He is buried in Linwood Cemetery in Columbus, Georgia.

3. Alexander W. Robison—KIA. Shot at the east end of the bridge, probably while attempting to assist Von Zinken in remounting his horse during the night assault.

4. Judge George Waddell—MW. Shot at the north end of Broad Street after the rout of the Confederate forces, while acting as an aide to his brother, Major James F. Waddell, who was in command of the Confederate artillery.

5. J. J. Jones—KIA. Shot on Broad Street in Columbus.

6. Evan Jones KIA. Shot on Broad Street in Columbus.

7. William Smith—KIA. Shot on Broad Street in Columbus.

8. Unknown—KIA. Killed near brickyard on eastern outskirts of Columbus.

9. Unknown—KIA. Killed near brickyard on eastern outskirts of Columbus.

10. Unknown artilleryman—KIA. Shot while defending the City Bridge during the afternoon engagement on the Georgia side of the river.

11. Unknown artilleryman—KIA. Killed by the premature explosion of a shell at the battery stationed just north of Fort 1 at south end of the Confederate defenses in Girard.

12. Private Washington Kirkland, Company H, 6th Alabama Infantry—KIA.

13. Unknown—MW. Mortally wounded during the night attack, this soldier crawled onto the porch of a house near the battlefield where he was discovered dead by the family the next morning. His remains were buried in the family's plot at Linwood Cemetery. The marker reads "Unknown Confederate Soldier."

14. Unknown cavalryman—KIA. Shot on the battlefield in Girard and buried where he fell. His remains were moved in 1954 to their present location at the Lakeview Memory Gardens. His headstone reads, "In Memory of Unknown Cavalryman Killed by Wilson Raiders on Moses Hill Apr. 16, 1865."

15–34. Unknown—KIA. Buried at Clapp's Factory Cemetery.

Wounded

1. Private John M. Arnett, Company K, 3rd Arkansas Cavalry—WIA. Left leg.

2. Private James Arnold, Company D, 20th Alabama Infantry—WIA. Right knee.

3. Sergeant Francis M. Bailer, Company I, 8th Arkansas Infantry—WIA. Details unknown.

4. Lieutenant John W. Bailey, Company A, 37th Mississippi Infantry—WIA. Left arm.

5. Lieutenant D. E. Banks, 24th Georgia Infantry—WIA. Details unknown.

6. Private Thomas R. Blacksher, Company B, 2nd Georgia State Line—WIA. Wound with bruise.

7. Private Joel M. Bleason, Company D, 3rd Georgia Reserves—WIA. Left leg.

8. Private Joe Bledsoe, 3rd Georgia Reserves—WIA. Leg amputated.

9. Private W. J. Busbee, Company C, 2nd Georgia Cavalry—WIA. Details unknown.

10. Private —— Carden, Russell County Reserves—WIA. Struck with the butt of a rifle.

11. Private Jesse M. Cone, Company I, 3rd Alabama Cavalry—WIA. Left hand.

12. Private W. T. H. Crutcher, Company F, 27th Alabama Infantry—WIA. Details unknown.

13. Corporal Hamilton Dewberry, Company E, 46th Georgia Infantry—WIA. Chest.

14. Lieutenant Robert M. Foster, Jacques' Battalion—WIA. Left thigh.

15. Captain John Gamble, Company H, 33rd Alabama Infantry—WIA. Back.

16. Corporal Samuel A. Garlick, Company A, Waddell's Batt Artillery—WIA. Wound with laceration.

17. Private A. J. Grant, Company E, 36th Alabama Infantry—WIA. Details unknown.

18. Private John Greene, Cole's Batt—WIA. Wound with bruise.

19. Private William H. Hairall, Company K, 4th Alabama Reserves—WIA. Wound with bruise.

20. Private George W. Hamilton, Company B, 28th Tennessee Infantry—WIA. Head.

21. Private Ted Harty, Company D, 3rd Confederate Infantry—WIA. Right leg. First name possibly "Aia."

22. Conscript W. H. Holland—WIA. Wound with laceration.

23. Sergeant William Honeyfin, Company C, Rice's Battery—WIA. Left leg.

24. Private George W. Ivey, Company H, 2nd Georgia State Line—WIA. Left knee.

25. Sergeant Abel J. Kolb, Company E, 3rd Alabama Reserves—WIA. Wound with laceration. Last name possibly "Koll."

26. Lieutenant Edward D. Lee, Company K, 33rd Alabama Infantry—WIA. Left shoulder.

27. Private James W. Logan, Company K, 28th Alabama Infantry—WIA. Right shoulder.

28. Private Charles B. McLendon, Company G, 2nd Arkansas Cavalry—WIA. Left thigh.

29. Private Thomas K. Miller, Company K, 3rd Georgia Cavalry—WIA. Left leg.

30. Private George Washington Morgan, Company C, 9th Georgia Battalion Artillery—WIA. Details unknown.

31. Private John E. Moore, Company A, 47th Tennessee Infantry—WIA. Head.

32. Private Newlil F. Moore, Company K, 22nd Alabama Infantry—WIA. Left hand.

33. Sergeant E. M. Murphy, Company D, 24th Tennessee Infantry—WIA. Details unknown.

34. Sergeant Jerry Newman, Company D, 5th Confederate Infantry—WIA. Right shoulder.

35. Captain John S. Pemberton, Pemberton's Cavalry—WIA. Chest. Pem-

berton was both shot and slashed by a saber near the Franklin Street Bridge during the night assault. "This brush with death left him with an impressive scar across his abdomen and chest; his life was apparently saved by the money belt he wore." Years after the battle, Dr. Pemberton created the recipe for a medicinal tonic known today the world over as Coca-Cola.

36. Private Benton W. Peters, Company I, 15th Alabama Infantry—WIA. Right leg.

37. Private Charles Prichett, Company A, 3rd Alabama Reserves—WIA. Right eye.

38. Private Francis Rumbo, Company A, 5th Alabama Reserves—WIA. Left hip.

39. Private Amos Ryan, Company B, 2nd Alabama Cavalry—WIA. Left knee.

40. Private Edward R. Smith, Company F, 10th Texas Cavalry—WIA. Left side.

41. Private Richard P. Spencer, Company B, 37th Georgia Infantry—WIA. Left leg.

42. Private Dedle Thrash, Company B, 26th Batt Georgia Infantry—WIA. Left foot.

43. Colonel Leon Von Zinken, 20th Louisiana Infantry, Commandant of Post, and Field Commander at Columbus—WIA. Clubbed on the head with a carbine while attempting to rally his troops near the Franklin Street Bridge, he escaped capture and fled the field. At Macon it was reported that "Col. Von Zinken was severely wounded by a horse running against him."

44. Private John J. Wallace, Company E, 23rd Mississippi Infantry—WIA. Left ankle.

45. Sergeant John R. Wilks, Company H, 5th Georgia Reserves—WIA. Right leg.

46. William H. Young—WIA. Shot on Hamilton Avenue in Columbus during the night attack after refusing to heed commands to surrender. He recalled: "I with the rest of the old men of the city was upon police duty & being hard of hearing was fired upon by the Union forces and received six serious wounds upon my body."[4]

Appendix 5
Medal of Honor Recipients

Two months after the Battle for Columbus, in June 1865, seven men of General Edward F. Winslow's 1st Brigade who participated in the night assault at Columbus were awarded the Medal of Honor. Two additional men were recommended for the award but did not receive it.[1]

1. Sergeant Norman F. Bates—Company E, 4th Iowa Cavalry. Citation: "Capture of flag." "Took a Rebel and standard in the street three blocks from the bridge."

2. Private Edward J. Bebb—Company D, 4th Iowa Cavalry. Citation: "Capture of flag." "At Columbus, Ga., April 16, about 100 yards from the bridge and in the line of works, took a flag, the rebels near it running away before our men, leaving the flag."

3. Sergeant Horatio L. Birdsall—Company B, 3rd Iowa Cavalry. Citation: "Capture of flag and bearer." "Captured the bearer and flag while my company was assailing the line of works on left of Summerville road, near Columbus, Ga., April 16, 1865."

4. Private Richard H. Cosgriff—Company L, 4th Iowa Cavalry. Citation: "Capture of flag in personal encounter with its bearer." "Captured a standard and the bearer, having to knock him down with the butt of my gun before I could get possession of the flag."

5. Private John H. Hays—Company F, 4th Iowa Cavalry. Citation: "Capture of flag and bearer, Austin's Battery (C.S.A.) [should be Austin's Battalion]." "Captured the standard and bearer, who tore it from the staff and tried to escape; he fired two shots from his revolver, wounding one man of my regiment at my side."

6. Corporal Richard H. Morgan—Company A, 4th Iowa Cavalry. Citation: "Capture of flag inside the enemy's works, contesting for its possession with its bearer." "I captured the standard and bearer in the first charge my company made, inside the line of works, April 16; the bearer contested with me for its possession."

7. Private Andrew W. Tibbets—Company I, 3rd Iowa Cavalry. Citation: "Capture of flag and bearer, Austin's Battery (C.S.A.) [should be Austin's Battalion]." "At Columbus, Ga., captured the bearer—a sergeant—and flag of Austin's battery, inside the line of works and to the right of the four-gun battery on the right of the enemy's line."

Recommended for Medals of Honor, but never issued

1. Sergeant Robert Skiles—Company G, 4th Iowa Cavalry. Recommended for Medal of Honor by General Upton, who noted: "In an individual encounter with the enemy in the streets of Girard manifested a spirit of bravery and determination which entitles him to the highest commendation and reward."

2. Private Robert C. Wood—Company A, 4th Iowa Cavalry. Recommended for Medal of Honor by General Upton, who noted: "After being captured by the enemy whilst in the line of his duty at Columbus escaped, and, with the aid of a few others, took as prisoners the colonel and adjutant of the regiment that but a short time before held him in custody."

Appendix 6
Discovering the Battle for Columbus

Today's visitor to Columbus, Georgia, will find no battlefield park or other facility dedicated to preserving the story of the Battle for Columbus. Even so, interested individuals can learn more about the battle, view artifacts from the fight, and even take a tour of the battlefield. By utilizing the available resources, both residents and visitors to the city will find discovering Columbus's Civil War past both educational and entertaining.

The National Civil War Naval Museum (located at the intersection of U.S. Highway 280 and Lumpkin Boulevard in south Columbus) is a good place to begin a day's excursion to see the sites connected with the Battle for Columbus. Inside this forty-thousand-square-foot-facility, the remains of both ships destroyed as a result of the battle are on display. The premier exhibit at the museum consists of the hull, guns, and iron plating of the CSS *Jackson,* the iron-clad ram captured by Union forces on April 16, then burned and sent down the river the next day. Also on display is the stern section of the gunboat CSS *Chattahoochee,* which escaped capture at the Battle for Columbus but was later scuttled by its crew. Additionally, the visitor to the museum will enjoy a huge collection of artifacts and displays related to the Civil War navy.

For those who wish to survey the battlefield, forts, and bridges where the Battle for Columbus was fought, the *Battle of Columbus: Audio Driving Tour & Maps* CD is an excellent option. This recording, designed for use with a vehicle's CD player, includes easy-to-follow driving instructions that allow the listener to navigate the battlefield by automobile and view the sites connected with the last battle of the Civil War. The CD, which includes a map and a small brochure, guides tour takers to fifteen stops located around Phenix City (formerly Girard) and Columbus to spots where Union and Confederate soldiers clashed on Easter Sunday, 1865.

The *Battle of Columbus: Audio Driving Tour & Maps* CD may be found at the National Civil War Naval Museum and at other museums, gift shops, and outlets around the city. Besides being a good way to learn more about the battle, the tour is also an excellent way to explore the historic districts of Columbus and Phenix City. At several stops along the route, listeners can get out of their vehicles and explore the battleground. Some of these areas are scenic and are particularly suited for a picnic, stroll, or other activities.

In addition to the above, the Columbus Museum (located on Wynnton Road in Columbus) houses many artifacts relating to Columbus's Civil War history. Visitors to the National Infantry Museum (located at Fort Benning, just outside Columbus) will find a large collection of Civil War uniforms, weapons, and accoutrements, many manufactured by Columbus's wartime industries. Additionally on display at the museum are large collections of artifacts representing all periods of American military history. Finally, the Historic Columbus Foundation, located downtown, offers tours of Columbus's historic homes, including the home of Confederate captain John S. Pemberton, who was wounded at the Battle for Columbus and is most famous for being the inventor of Coca-Cola.

Notes

Abbreviations

ADAH	Alabama Department of Archives and History, Montgomery
CPL	Columbus Public Library, Columbus, Georgia
CSUA	Columbus State University Archives, Columbus, Georgia
GDAH	Georgia Department of Archives and History, Morrow
HRBML	Hargrett Rare Book and Manuscript Library, University of Georgia Libraries, Athens
LC	Library of Congress, Washington, D.C.
NARA	National Archives and Records Administration, Washington, D.C.
OR	*The War of the Rebellion: A Compilation of the Official Records of the Union and Confederate Armies.* 70 vols. in 128 books. Washington, D.C.: Government Printing Office, 1881–1901. Citations are from series 1 unless otherwise noted.
SHC	Southern Historical Collection, Wilson Library, University of North Carolina, Chapel Hill
SHSI-DM	State Historical Society of Iowa, Des Moines
SHSI-IC	State Historical Society of Iowa, Iowa City
USAMHI	United States Army Military History Institute, Carlisle, Pennsylvania

Chapter 1

1. James Harrison Wilson, *Under the Old Flag: Recollections of Military Operations in the War for the Union, the Spanish War, the Boxer Rebellion, etc.* (New York: D. Appleton, 1912), 295; E. N. Gilpin, *The Last Campaign: A Cavalryman's Journal* (Leavenworth, Kans.: Press of Ketcheson Printing Co., 1908; reprinted from *The Journal of the U.S. Cavalry Association,* April 1908), 17 April 1865.

2. Jerry Keenan, *Wilson's Cavalry Corps* (Jefferson, N.C.: McFarland, 1998), 3–9.

3. Edward G. Longacre, *From Union Stars to Top Hat: A Biography of the Extraordinary General James Harrison Wilson* (Harrisburg, Pa.: Stackpole, 1972), 25–106.

4. Ibid., 95–103; J. H. Wilson, *Under the Old Flag,* 292; Spencer Repeating Rifle Company, *The Spencer Repeating Rifle, Carbines, and Sporting Rifle* (Boston: Spencer Repeating Rifle Co., n.d.; reprint, Decatur, Mich.: Johnson Graphics, 1992), 3–32; Francis A. Lord, *Civil War Collector's Encyclopedia,* vol. 1 (Edison, N.J.: Blue and Grey Press, 1995), 237.

5. Longacre, *Union Stars to Top Hat,* 106–57; J. H. Wilson, *Under the Old Flag,* 172.

6. Keenan, *Wilson's Cavalry Corps,* 6–15; Longacre, *Union Stars to Top Hat,* 160–61; James Pickett Jones, *Yankee Blitzkrieg: Wilson's Raid through Alabama and Georgia* (Lexington: University of Kentucky, 1976; reprint 2000), xi–xiv, 9–19; J. H. Wilson, *Under the Old Flag,* 290–91; Robert Underwood Johnson and Clarence Clough Buel, *Battles and Leaders of the Civil War: Being for the Most Part Contributions by Union and Confederate Officers. Based upon "The Century War Series"* (New York: Century, 1887), 4:465.

7. Longacre, *Union Stars to Top Hat,* 159–93; Keenan, *Wilson's Cavalry Corps,* 17–137.

8. J. P. Jones, *Yankee Blitzkrieg,* 9–19; Keenan, *Wilson's Cavalry Corps,* 138–57; J. H. Wilson, *Under the Old Flag,* 160–80, 292; B. F. McGee, *History of the 72nd Indiana Volunteer Infantry of the Mounted Lightning Brigade* (LaFayette, Ind.: S. Vater and Co., "The Journal" Printers, 1882), "Wilder's 'Hatchet' Brigade"; Longacre, *Union Stars to Top Hat,* 195–200; Samuel O. Bereman, Diary, 22 February 1865, courtesy of Garth Hagerman, Fort Bragg, California; *OR,* 49, pt. 1:355. Some debate exists over whether Wilson's Cavalry Corps was outfitted solely with Spencer carbines (short version) or whether some of the units used the longer rifle version. Though carbines would have predominated, a close examination of the troopers' accounts indicates that Wilson's men carried both carbines and rifles. Furthermore, at least five regiments of Wilson's force were composed of mounted infantry, some of whom possessed the Spencer rifle long before this campaign. J. H. Wilson, *Under the Old Flag,* 292; McGee, *History of the 72nd Indiana,* "Wilder's 'Hatchet' Brigade."

9. Keenan, *Wilson's Cavalry Corps,* 141–42; J. P. Jones, *Yankee Blitzkrieg,* 12; *OR,* 34, pt. 1:45.

10. Longacre, *Union Stars to Top Hat,* 198; J. P. Jones, *Yankee Blitzkrieg,* 12–20; Keenan, *Wilson's Cavalry Corps,* 12, 148–49; J. H. Wilson, *Under the Old Flag,* 178–81; Bruce Catton, *Picture History of the Civil War* (New York: American Heritage/ Wings Books, 1988), 561.

11. Keenan, *Wilson's Cavalry Corps,* 138–57; J. P. Jones, *Yankee Blitzkrieg,* 1–29; E. A. Davenport, *History of the Ninth Regiment Illinois Cavalry Volunteers* (Chicago: Donohue and Henneberry, 1888), 174–76.

12. The few Raiders who were not outfitted with Spencers were issued breech-loading carbines that utilized metallic cartridges. J. P. Jones, *Yankee Blitzkrieg,* 1–29; Keenan, *Wilson's Cavalry Corps,* 150–51; *OR,* 49, pt. 1:355–56; Homer Mead, *The Eighth Iowa Cavalry in the Civil War* (Carthage, Ill.: S. C. Davidson, 1927), 45; F. W. Morse, *Personal Experiences in the War of the Great Rebellion* (Albany, N.Y.: Munsell, 1866), 124.

13. *OR,* 34, pt. 1:45; ibid., 49, pt. 1:402–3; William Forse Scott, *The Story of a Cavalry Regiment: The Career of the Fourth Iowa Veteran Volunteers* (New York: Putnam, 1893), 420; James W. Latta, "Pennsylvania in the War: The Campaign of Wilson's Cavalry Corps through Alabama and Georgia in the Spring of 1865: The Capture of Columbus," MS 526, James William Latta Papers 1854–99, LC.

14. W. F. Scott, *Story of a Cavalry Regiment,* 428; J. P. Jones, *Yankee Blitzkrieg,* 19, 34; *OR,* 49, pt. 1:356, 409–10.

15. Keenan, *Wilson's Cavalry Corps,* 84–86; J. H. Wilson, *Under the Old Flag,* 166; Peter S. Michie, *The Life and Letters of Emory Upton* (New York: D. Appleton, 1885), ix–130; W. F. Scott, *Story of a Cavalry Regiment,* 421–22; J. P. Jones, *Yankee Blitzkrieg,* 10–11; Edward F. Winslow, "Columbus, the Final Battle of the War," Winslow Memoirs, Part II, Episode 8, handwritten pages inserted, Edward F. Winslow Papers, Special Collections, SHSI-IC.

16. *OR,* 49, pt. 1:402–3; Keenan, *Wilson's Cavalry Corps,* 27.

17. James H. Wilson, *The Life and Services of Brevet Brigadier-General Andrew Jonathan Alexander* (New York: n.p., 1887), 5–77.

18. *OR,* 49, pt. 1:402–3; W. L. Curry, *Four Years in the Saddle: History of the First Regiment Ohio Volunteer Cavalry* (Jonesboro, Ga.: Freedom Hill Press, reprint 1984), 374–75.

19. *OR,* 49, pt. 1:402–3; R. C. Rankin, *History of the Seventh Ohio Volunteer Cavalry* (Ripley, Ohio: J. C. Newcomb, 1881), 26–27.

20. *OR,* 49, pt. 1:402–3; Josiah Conzett, "My Civil War: Before, During, and After," 49, Memoirs of Josiah Conzett, Josiah Conzett Papers, Special Collections, SHSI-IC.

21. A. A. Stuart, *Iowa Colonels and Regiments* (Des Moines, Iowa: Mills, 1865), 609–20; James H. Wilson, *General Edward Francis Winslow: A Leader of Cavalry in the Great Rebellion* (n.p., 1915), 3–4; W. F. Scott, *Story of a Cavalry Regiment,* 422, 442; "General Edward F. Winslow Biography," 1–2, Edward F. Winslow Papers, Special Collections, SHSI-IC; Winslow, "Columbus, the Final Battle," handwritten pages inserted; J. H. Wilson, *Under the Old Flag,* 167–68. Winslow's memoirs make clear his frustration stemming from Wilson and Upton's close relationship: "General Upton was a distinguished officer of the regular army, the youngest of all the general officers present. . . . He had, however, never commanded cavalry, and was unacquainted with western methods and country. His position and his companionship with Wilson gave him not only greater influence in the corps than that possessed by any other officer but in many ways overshadowed all of them. . . . It was perhaps natural for . . . [Wilson] to place him above all others, not alone in position, but in the reports of his actions during the campaign . . . but as I did not report to or review orders from the corps commander, my personality and conduct on the field was lost sight of or at least, in part, overshadowed by that of Upton . . . [otherwise,] I might have had greater credit for my long experience as a cavalry commander." Winslow, "Columbus, the Final Battle," handwritten pages inserted.

22. *OR,* 49, pt. 1:483; Stuart, *Iowa Colonels and Regiments,* 609.

23. *OR,* 49, pt. 1:483; Stuart, *Iowa Colonels and Regiments,* 597, 605–6.

24. *OR*, 49, pt. 1:483; Charles K. Mills, *Harvest of Barren Regrets: The Army Career of Frederick William Benteen, 1834–1898* (Glendale, Calif.: Arthur H. Clark, 1985), 11–67.

25. J. P. Jones, *Yankee Blitzkrieg*, 28, quoting James Wilson to Adam Badeau, March 20, 1865, Wilson Manuscripts, LC.

Chapter 2

1. J. P. Jones, *Yankee Blitzkrieg*, 20–56; Keenan, *Wilson's Cavalry Corps*, 151–52; W. F. Scott, *Story of a Cavalry Regiment*, 425–28; Longacre, *Union Stars to Top Hat*, 200–202; *OR*, 49, pt. 1:357.

2. Longacre, *Union Stars to Top Hat*, 202–6; W. F. Scott, *Story of a Cavalry Regiment*, 440; Keenan, *Wilson's Cavalry Corps*, 166; J. P. Jones, *Yankee Blitzkrieg*, 67.

3. Keenan, *Wilson's Cavalry Corps*, 166–68; W. F. Scott, *Story of a Cavalry Regiment*, 434–44; Longacre, *Union Stars to Top Hat*, 204–6; J. P. Jones, *Yankee Blitzkrieg*, 84; *OR*, 49, pt. 1:357; Bereman, Diary, 30 March 1865; William H. Barker, "William H. Barker: Private's Autobiography, 1840–1926," 132–33, Unit History 1861–1868, CWTIColl, USAMHI.

4. J. P. Jones, *Yankee Blitzkrieg*, 84–85; W. F. Scott, *Story of a Cavalry Regiment*, 450–53; Keenan, *Wilson's Cavalry Corps*, 168; Longacre, *Union Stars to Top Hat*, 206.

5. Longacre, *Union Stars to Top Hat*, 207–9; Keenan, *Wilson's Cavalry Corps*, 170–71; J. P. Jones, *Yankee Blitzkrieg*, 87–97; Barker, "William H. Barker," 132–33; W. F. Scott, *Story of a Cavalry Regiment*, 453–63; Frank A. Montgomery, *Reminiscences of a Mississippian in Peace and War* (Cincinnati: Robert Clarke, 1901), 239–46.

6. J. P. Jones, *Yankee Blitzkrieg*, 92–97; Keenan, *Wilson's Cavalry Corps*, 172–73.

7. Whitelaw Reid, *After the War: A Southern Tour* (Cincinnati: Moore, Wilstach, and Baldwin, 1866), 384; J. P. Jones, *Yankee Blitzkrieg*, 96; Keenan, *Wilson's Cavalry Corps*, 176;

8. W. F. Scott, *Story of a Cavalry Regiment*, 464–69; *OR*, 49, pt. 1:409–12.

9. W. F. Scott, *Story of a Cavalry Regiment*, 464–69; Longacre, *Union Stars to Top Hat*, 209–10; J. H. Wilson, *Under the Old Flag*, 237–48; *OR*, 49, pt. 1:362.

10. Keenan, *Wilson's Cavalry Corps*, 179–80; J. P. Jones, *Yankee Blitzkrieg*, 100–101; *OR*, 49, pt. 1:409–12; J. H. Wilson, *Alexander*, 87–89; Gilpin, *Last Campaign*, 8 April 1865.

11. *OR*, 49, pt. 1:362; J. H. Wilson, *Under the Old Flag*, 247–48; Orlando E. Carpenter, Diary 1864–1865, 12–13 April 1865, O. E. Carpenter Papers, 1833–1899, MF 305, Bentley Historical Library, University of Michigan, Ann Arbor.

12. J. H. Wilson, *Under the Old Flag*, 247–49; *OR*, 49, pt. 1:818–19; Frederick H. Dyer, *A Compendium of the War of the Rebellion* (Des Moines, Iowa: Dyer, 1908), part 3, p. 1740; Lucy Banks to unknown party, 23 April 1865, Banks Family Papers 1865, MS 1571, box 2, folder 6, HRBML; McGee, *History of the 72nd Indiana*, 574–78; J. P. Jones, *Yankee Blitzkrieg*, 117.

13. Bereman, Diary, 11 April 1865; James H. Wilson, Diary, 11 April 1865, microfilm, Historical Society of Delaware, Wilmington; Elijah Busby, Elijah Busby

Diary, 11 April 1865, SHSI-DM; Charles W. Toothaker, C. W. Toothaker Diary, 4th Iowa Cav., SHSI-DM.

14. W. F. Scott, *Story of a Cavalry Regiment,* 473; Morse, *Personal Experiences,* 137; Malcolm C. McMillan, *The Disintegration of a Confederate State* (Macon, Ga.: Mercer University, 1986), 118–29; J. P. Jones, *Yankee Blitzkrieg,* 110–12; *OR,* 49, pt. 1:504–5; J. H. Wilson, *Under the Old Flag,* 252.

15. Edward C. Dale to his son, 29 May 1865, Dale-Holt-Hensly Family Papers, box A-018, 66, State Historical Society of Missouri, St. Louis; Charles H. Snedeker, Diary, 25 April 1865, Charles H. Snedeker Civil War Diary, RG 844, Special Collections and Archives Department, Auburn University, Auburn, Alabama, available from http://www.lib.auburn.edu/archive/find-aid/844/ff6.pdf; Stephen E. Ambrose, *A Wisconsin Boy in Dixie: The Selected Letters of James K. Newton* (Madison: University of Wisconsin, 1961), 155; J. H. Wilson, *Under the Old Flag,* 252; Gilpin, *Last Campaign,* 12 April 1865.

16. J. H. Wilson, *Under the Old Flag,* 249–54; Barker, "William H. Barker," 138; William Wycoff, "Autobiography," 51, Memoirs of William Wycoff, courtesy Ron Wycoff; Conzett, "My Civil War," 73; Nancy Pape-Findley, *The Invincibles: The Story of the Fourth Ohio Veteran Volunteer Cavalry, 1861–1865* (Tecumseh, Mich.: Blood Road Publishing, 2002), 254; Bereman, Diary, 12 April 1865.

17. W. F. Scott, *Story of a Cavalry Regiment,* 475; J. H. Wilson, *Under the Old Flag,* 254; Charles F. Hinrichs, Diary, 13 April 1865, Charles F. Hinrichs Papers, 1862–1902, Western Historical Manuscripts Collection, University of Missouri, Columbia.

18. *OR,* 49, pt. 1:407; ibid., pt. 2:344–46; J. P. Jones, *Yankee Blitzkrieg,* 115–17; J. H. Wilson, *Under the Old Flag,* 250–54; John W. Noble, Diary, 13 April 1865, John W. Noble Papers, Special Collections, SHSI-IC; William Winkler, Diary, 12 April 1865, Bartholomew County Public Library, Columbus, Indiana; Richard J. Reid, *Fourth Indiana Cavalry Regiment: A History* (Fordsville, Ky.: Sandefur Offset Printing, 1994), 187; Hinrichs, Diary, 13 April 1865.

19. J. H. Wilson, *Under the Old Flag,* 250–58; Michie, *Emory Upton,* xii–xiii, 165; W. F. Scott, *Story of a Cavalry Regiment,* 475–77; *OR,* 49, pt. 2:344–45; Wilson, Diary, 10 April 1865; J. P. Jones, *Yankee Blitzkrieg,* 100–117; *OR,* 49, pt. 1:409–12.

It has been a point of debate whether or not Wilson's Raiders actually needed to fight at Columbus in order to secure a crossing of the Chattahoochee. The crux of this controversy rests on whether or not Wilson's troopers would have been able to cross the river at any desired point without confrontation using their pontoons.

This was impossible for several reasons. Wilson's pontoniers had destroyed eighteen of their thirty canvas pontoons and thirty of their fifty-eight wagons along with their supplies upon crossing the Alabama River at Selma. This would have left far too few pontoons to span the rain-swollen Chattahoochee. Indeed, the thirty original pontoons proved too few to cross the Alabama and had to be augmented by sixteen wooden pontoons and two large barges that were found in Selma.

Furthermore, should Wilson have desired to cross his command at any point on the Chattahoochee near Columbus, it is likely that they would have met resistance from the forces of Generals Cobb and Buford. A further deterrent to laying a pontoon bridge across the Chattahoochee south of Columbus would have been the Confederate naval forces stationed nearby. It would have been easy for the sailors stationed in Columbus to have used their almost completed (and already operational) ram CSS *Jackson,* the torpedo boat *Viper,* and other vessels to disrupt the work.

Finally, even if the bridge could have been laid, doing so probably would have been vetoed in favor of a more rapid and confrontational option. Indeed, Wilson admitted that his soldiers wanted to fight, and at Montgomery they were disappointed in not getting the opportunity. Bypassing the enemy at Columbus would have been not only complicated logistically but also would have been seen as an act of timidity on the part of Wilson and his soldiers.

20. *OR,* 49, pt. 1:432, 492; Stephen Von Shipman, Diary, 14–16 April 1865, Diary of Stephen V. Shipman, Wisconsin State Historical Society, Madison; Busby, Diary, 14 April 1865; Barker, "William H. Barker," 138; Wycoff, "Autobiography," 51–52; *OR,* 49, pt. 2:1245.

21. Hinrichs, Diary, 14 April 1865; McGee, *History of the 72nd Indiana,* 577–78; Bereman, Diary, 14 April 1865; Norman F. Bates, transcript of Civil War Diary, 14 April 1865, courtesy Andrea Crowell, Reno, Nevada.

22. Conzett, "My Civil War," 70.

23. McGee, *History of the 72nd Indiana,* 577. The term "contraband" had been in use for more than three hundred years by the time of the Civil War and was used to describe smuggled goods. Early in the Civil War, Union general Benjamin F. Butler applied the term to the many runaway slaves who were entering the Union lines. The expression was taken up and used by soldiers of all ranks and on both sides of the conflict. Its use became and remains standard in the lexicon of Civil War history. It is worth noting that the term "contraband" generally did not carry with it any negative connotation, but was neutrally descriptive. Darryl Lyman, *Civil War Wordbook: Including Sayings, Phrases, and Expletives* (Conshohocken, Pa.: Combined Books, 1994), 47.

24. J. H. Wilson, *Under the Old Flag,* 255; Thomas Giles, "Union Diary Records Capture of Columbus," *Columbus Ledger-Enquirer Civil War Centennial Edition,* 16 April 1961, 6; Thomas Crofts, *History of the Service of the Third Ohio Veteran Volunteer Cavalry* (Toledo: Stoneman Press, 1910), 198.

25. J. H. Wilson, *Under the Old Flag,* 255; *OR,* 49, pt. 1:504; Virginia P. Brown and Helen M. Akens, *Alabama Heritage* (Huntsville, Ala.: Strode, 1967), 195.

26. Shipman, Diary, 15 April 1865; Alva C. Griest, Diary, 15 April 1865, Alva C. Griest Collection, 1862–1865, SC 0656, Indiana Historical Society, Indianapolis; Carpenter, Diary, 15 April 1865; Henry A. Potter, Diary, 15 April 1865, Henry A. Potter Diary and Letters Transcript, 1865, MF 305, Bentley Historical Library, University of Michigan, Ann Arbor; George Hobson, Diary, 15 April 1865, Hobson Family Papers, Leonard H. Axe Library, Pittsburg State University, Kansas; Toothaker, Diary, 15 April 1865; Bereman, Diary, 15 April 1865.

27. Charles D. Mitchell, Memoirs, 15 April 1865, Charles D. Mitchell Mem-

oirs, MS 636, LC; Lot Abraham, Diary, 15 April 1865, Papers of Lot Abraham, MsC 73, Diary 1865, Special Collections Department, University of Iowa Libraries, Iowa City; Hinrichs, Diary, 15 April 1865; E. N. Gilpin, "Diary of 'The Last Campaign,'" 15 April 1865, E. N. Gilpin Papers, LC.

28. W. F. Scott, *Story of a Cavalry Regiment,* 479–82; *OR,* 49, pt. 2:344–45; Michie, *Emory Upton,* 165; Gilpin, "Diary of 'The Last Campaign,'" 15 April 1865.

29. J. H. Wilson, *Under the Old Flag,* 256–57.

30. "Historic Tuskegee Homes Tour" (brochure, 2003); Conzett, "My Civil War," 70; James O. Vanorsdol, *Four Years for the Union* (n.p., 1888), 72–73, microfiche, SHSI-DM.

31. J. P. Jones, *Yankee Blitzkrieg,* 120–21; J. H. Wilson, *Under the Old Flag,* 257–58.

32. Hinrichs, Diary, 15 April 1865; Gilpin, *Last Campaign,* 15 April 1865; Hobson, Diary, 15 April 1865; W. F. Scott, *Story of a Cavalry Regiment,* 482; Gilpin, "Diary of 'The Last Campaign,'" 15 April 1865; Curry, *Four Years in the Saddle,* 222.

33. W. F. Scott, *Story of a Cavalry Regiment,* 483; Curry, *Four Years in the Saddle,* 222; *OR,* 49, pt. 2:361; Wycoff, "Autobiography," 51–52.

Chapter 3

1. Diffee Standard, *Columbus, Georgia, in the Confederacy: The Social and Industrial Life of the Chattahoochee River Port* (New York: William-Frederick Press, 1954), 11–19, 53–58; Geoffrey C. Ward, *The Civil War: An Illustrated History* (New York: Knopf, 1994), 356–82; Catton, *Picture History,* 563–604; William C. Davis, *The Civil War Wall Chart* (Lincolnwood, Ill.: Publications International, 1990), 1864–65.

2. Ward, *The Civil War,* 356–82; Catton, *Picture History,* 563–604; James Ford Rhodes, *History of the United States from the Compromise of 1850,* vol. 5 (New York: MacMillan, 1904), 162; Jerry Korn, *The Civil War: Pursuit to Appomattox* (Alexandria, Va.: Time-Life Books, 1987), 157, 56–57; *OR,* 17, pt. 3:206.

3. Mears and Co., *The Columbus Directory for 1859–60* (Columbus, Ga.: Sun Book and Job Printing Office, 1859), 1–111; Willoughby, *Flowing through Time: A History of the Lower Chattahoochee River* (Tuscaloosa: University of Alabama Press, 1999), 47–82; Standard, *Columbus, Georgia,* 11–19. I do not mean to suggest that the transportation of cotton to Apalachicola was still continuing in 1865, but rather that cotton's transportation via the Chattahoochee was an important factor in the city's prewar development. For more information see Lynn Willoughby, *Fair to Middlin': The Antebellum Cotton Trade of the Apalachicola/Chattahoochee River Valley* (Tuscaloosa: University of Alabama Press, 1993); or Willoughby, *Flowing through Time.*

4. Nancy Telfair [Louise DuBose], *A History of Columbus, Georgia, 1828–1928* (Columbus, Ga.: Historical Publishing Co., 1929), 79–130; Etta Blanchard Worsley, *Columbus on the Chattahoochee* (Columbus, Ga.: Columbus Office Supply, 1951), 59–291; Joseph B. Mahan, *Columbus: Georgia's Fall Line "Trading Town"* (Northridge, Calif.: Windsor, 1986), 74.

5. I. W. Avery, *History of the State of Georgia from 1850–1881* (New York: Brown

and Derby, 1881) 297; John S. Lupold, "Columbus and Muscogee County in 1860," *Muscogiana* 2, nos. 1–2 (1991): 23–26; Standard, *Columbus, Georgia,* 1–62; Thomas Conn Bryan, *Confederate Georgia* (Athens: University of Georgia, 1964), 102–9; J. P. Jones, *Yankee Blitzkrieg,* 128; *Confederate Papers Relating to Citizens or Business Firms* (Washington, D.C.: National Archives and Records Service, 1961), "Empire Mills" and "George Woodruff," microfilm, accessed at Wallace State College, Hanceville, Alabama; Leslie D. Jensen, "A Survey of Confederate Central Government Quartermaster Issue Jackets" (Rutland, Mass.: The Company of Military Historians, 1989), parts I–III, available at www.military-historians.org/Journal/Confederate/confederate-1.htm.

6. *Confederate Papers Relating to Citizens or Business Firms,* "Empire Mills," "George Woodruff," "Eagle Manufacturing Company," "Columbus Factory," "Clapp Factory," "John Tibbet's Shoe Co. & Gov't Shoe Shops, 15 April 1864," "Columbus Knitting Company," "Greenwood & Gray," "L. Haiman Bro. & Co.," "W. D. Boyd," "Columbus Fire Arms Co.," "Palace Mills," "R. L. Mott," "Goetchius & Hodges," "Bank of Columbus," "Columbus Armory," and "Columbus Gas Co."; Paul Miles, "Columbus Was Center of South's Second-Ranking Industrial Complex," *Columbus Ledger-Enquirer Civil War Centennial Edition,* 16 April 1961, 13–15; Worsley, *Columbus on the Chattahoochee,* 285; Clason F. Kyle, *Images: A Pictorial History of Columbus, Georgia* (Norfolk, Va.: Donning, 1986), 47–48; John M. Land, "Chronology of Clapp's Factory," 1–5, 2002, Clapp Cemetery Preservation Group, courtesy John Land, McKinney, Texas.

7. Claud E. Fuller and Richard D. Steuart, *Firearms of the Confederacy* (Huntington, W.V.: Standard, 1944), 174–79, 282–84; William A. Albaugh III and Edward N. Simmons, *Confederate Arms* (Harrisburg, Pa.: Stackpole, 1957), 17–19, 76, 102–5, 226–27; Larry J. Daniel and Riley W. Gunter, *Confederate Cannon Foundries* (Union City, Tenn.: Pioneer Press, 1977), 34, 68–69; Paul Miles, "Iron Works Here Was Major Contributor to Confederacy's Big Armament," *Columbus Ledger-Enquirer Civil War Centennial Edition,* 16 April 1961, 13–14; Kyle, *Images,* 49; Willoughby, *Flowing through Time,* 89; Robert A. Holcombe, "Columbus Naval Iron Works," in *Encyclopedia of the Confederacy,* ed. Richard N. Current (New York: Simon and Schuster, 1993), 372; Maxine Turner, *Navy Gray: A Story of the Confederate Navy on the Chattahoochee and Apalachicola Rivers* (Tuscaloosa: University of Alabama Press, 1988), 147–61.

8. Telfair, *History of Columbus,* 131–32; Standard, *Columbus, Georgia,* 14–18; Turner, *Navy Gray,* 128–50.

9. W. F. Scott, *Story of a Cavalry Regiment,* 483–86; Russell County Heritage Book Committee, *The Heritage of Russell County Alabama* (Clanton, Ala.: Heritage Publishing Consultants, 2003), 7–8.

10. *Confederate Reminiscences and Letters, 1861–1865,* 21 vols. (Atlanta: Georgia Division of United Daughters of the Confederacy, 1995–99), 9:88–89; J. P. Jones, *Yankee Blitzkrieg,* 131; Telfair, *History of Columbus,* 125–32; W. F. Scott, *Story of a Cavalry Regiment,* 483–89; Russell County Heritage Book Committee, *Heritage of Russell County,* 7–8.

11. Worsley, *Columbus on the Chattahoochee,* 284.

12. W. F. Scott, *Story of a Cavalry Regiment,* 483; Columbus City Council Records, 1865, Clerk of Council's Office, Columbus, Georgia; John S. Lupold and Thomas L. French Jr., *Bridging Deep South Rivers: The Life and Legend of Horace King* (Athens: University of Georgia, 2004), 164–202.

13. The map drawn in the summer of 1865 for inclusion in Wilson's report of the campaign showed an additional bridge south of the City Bridge. At the time of the Battle for Columbus, this bridge (for the Mobile and Girard Railroad) had only its pilings in place. Lupold and French, *Bridging Deep South Rivers,* 198–202; Sketch of Columbus, Georgia, and Its Defenses, by H. S. Heywood, Accompanying the Report of J. H. Wilson, *OR,* 49, 29 June 1865.

14. *OR,* 28, pt. 2:553.

15. Telfair, *History of Columbus,* 131–32.

16. Russell County Heritage Book Committee, *Heritage of Russell County,* 7–8; W. F. Scott, *Story of a Cavalry Regiment,* 483–86; Lawrence Jones, "Review of Fort Gilmer: A Historical Perspective" (a history of Fort Gilmer and wartime Columbus), 1991, courtesy Lawrence Jones, Columbus, Georgia, 1–16; Auburn University Anthropology Deptartment, "Overview of Fort Gilmer Site" (an archeological survey of Fort Gilmer), 1987, Auburn University Department of Sociology, Anthropology, and Social Work, Auburn University, courtesy Lawrence Jones, Columbus, Georgia, 1–10.

17. Horace Montgomery, *Howell Cobb's Confederate Career* (Tuscaloosa: Confederate Publishing Co., 1959), 14–123; John E. Simpson, *Howell Cobb: Politics of Ambition* (Chicago: Adams Press, 1973), 3–173.

18. H. Montgomery, *Cobb's Confederate Career,* 115–17; William Harris Bragg, *Joe Brown's Army* (Macon, Ga.: Mercer University Press, 1987), vii–xi; Simpson, *Howell Cobb,* 169–71; Howell Cobb, Howell Cobb Special Orders, 1864–1865, 86–96, MS 86, HRBML.

19. H. Montgomery, *Cobb's Confederate Career,* 1–123; Simpson, *Howell Cobb,* 169–72; Bragg, *Joe Brown's Army,* vii–xi.

20. Bragg, *Joe Brown's Army,* vii–xi; Simpson, *Howell Cobb,* 169–73.

21. John H. Martin, *Columbus, Geo., from Its Selection as a "Trading Town" in 1827 to Its Partial Destruction by Wilson's Raid in 1865* (Columbus, Ga.: Thos. Gilbert, 1874), 180; "Memorial Day at Savannah, Ga.," *Confederate Veteran Magazine* 3 (1895): 130–31; Tom H. Wells, *The Slave Ship "Wanderer"* (Athens: University of Georgia, 1967), 1–87; Tom H. Wells, "Charles Augustus Lafayette Lamar: Gentleman Slave Trader," *Georgia Historical Quarterly* 47, no. 2 (1963): 158–68; Telfair, *History of Columbus,* 112–15; "The 'Wanderer' Episode," *Savannah Morning News,* week 32, year 2000, available at http://www.savannahnow.com/150years/week32/, 1–3; "Charles Augustus Lafayette Lamar, 1824–1865," available at http://members.aol .com/eleanorcol/LamarBios2.html, 1–2; "Ship Building in Suffolk County," available at http://longislandgeneology.com/shipbuilding.html; *OR,* series 4, 3:158; *Compiled Records Showing Service of Military Units in Confederate Organizations— Georgia* (Washington, D.C.: National Archives and Records Service, 1971), micro-

film, accessed at Wallace State College, Hanceville, Alabama, "C. A. L. Lamar"; Wells, "Charles Augustus Lafayette Lamar," 159–68; Allen D. Candler, *The Confederate Records of the State of Georgia* (Atlanta: Chas. P. Byrd, State Printer, 1909), 878–79; Jacob R. Marcus, *Memoirs of American Jews, 1775–1865* (New York: KTAV Publishing House, 1974), 304–16.

22. Wells, "Charles Augustus Lafayette Lamar," 167; William Jones, comp., "Treatment of Prisoners during the War between the States," *Southern Historical Society Papers* 1 (January–June 1876): 193–96; R. J. Hallett to C. A. L. Lamar, Letter Authorizing Lamar to Oversee Prisoner Exchange, March 1865, Cobb-Erwin-Lamar Collection, MS 86, box 3, folder 12, HRBML; *OR,* series 2, 8:403–4; Thomas R. Hay, "Gazaway Bugg Lamar, Confederate Banker and Business Man," *Georgia Historical Quarterly* 37, no. 2 (1954): 89–128; Gazaway Lamar to William Pettes, 31 January 1865, and Gazaway Lamar to Joseph Burke, Letter Concerning C. A. L. Lamar, 1 February 1865, Gazaway B. Lamar Papers, MS 10, box 1, folder 9, HRBML.

23. "April 10, 1865—Davis Signature," available at http://www.goldbergcoins .net/catalogarchive/20011201/chap015.shtml; Goldberg Coins representative, phone interview by author, 2003; Janet Hewett, ed., *Supplement to the Official Records of the Union and Confederate Armies* (Wilmington, N.C.: Broadfoot, 1994), vol. 3, series 95, pp. 812–14; *OR,* 49, pt. 2:1216.

24. "April 10, 1865—Davis Signature"; Goldberg Coins interview.

25. "April 10, 1865—Davis Signature"; Goldberg Coins interview; Hewett, *Supplement,* vol. 3, series 95, pp. 812–14.

26. Hewett, *Supplement,* vol. 3, series 95, pp. 812–21.

27. Ibid.

28. W. Jones, "Treatment of Prisoners"; Howell Cobb to C. A. L. Lamar, n.d., Cobb-Erwin-Lamar Collection, MS 86, HRBML; C. A. Fraser, "Marion County Prisoner of Rebels Kept Diary in Andersonville Prison," *Centralia, Illinois Evening Sentinel,* available at www.stkusers.com/lindas/jesse.html; *OR,* series 2, 8:403–4.

29. W. Jones, "Treatment of Prisoners"; Cobb, Special Orders, 86–100; R. J. Hallett to C. A. L. Lamar, Letter Authorizing Lamar to Oversee Prisoner Exchange, March 1865, Cobb-Erwin-Lamar Collection, MS 86, box 3, folder 12, HRBML; Hewett, *Supplement,* vol. 3, series 95, pp. 812–21; M. H. Wright to J. W. Mallet, 12 April 1865, RG 109, file M331, roll 274, NARA; "John Newland Maffitt and the Galveston Blockade," available at http://nautarch.tamu.edu/projects/denbigh/ Maffitt.htm.

30. Ella Lonn, *Foreigners in the Confederacy* (Gloucester, Mass.: Peter Smith, 1965), 31; *OR,* 10, pt. 1:502, 507. Some sources refer to Von Zinken as "Leon 'Toll' Von Zinken." "Toll" means essentially "crazy" or "mad," and it is unclear where and how Von Zinken acquired this name. Daniel A. Bellware, "Colonel Leon Von Zinken: Commandant of the Post at Columbus, Georgia," available at http://cvacwrt .tripod.com/zinken.html.

31. *Compiled Service Records of Confederate Soldiers Who Served in Organizations from the State of Louisiana* (Washington, D.C.: National Archives and Records Service, 1961), microfilm, accessed at Wallace State College, Hanceville, Alabama, "Col. Leon Von Zinken" [hereafter cited as "CSR-Louisiana"]; *OR,* 30, pt. 2:201.

32. *OR,* 38, pt. 3:856; CSR-Louisiana, "Leon Von Zinken"; Arthur W. Bergeron Jr., "Colonel Leon Toll Von Zinken, 20th Louisiana Infantry Regiment, Army of Tennessee, C.S.A.," *Confederate Calendar Works,* September 1993; *OR,* 38, pt. 5:1019.

33. CSR-Louisiana, "Leon Von Zinken"; J. H. Martin, *Columbus, Geo.,* 175; Telfair, *History of Columbus,* 126.

34. Telfair, *History of Columbus,* 126–27; J. H. Martin, *Columbus, Geo.,* 175; Worsley, *Columbus on the Chattahoochee,* 293; Cobb, Special Orders, 80.

35. Leon Von Zinken to Howell Cobb, Telegrams, 2 April, 4 April 1865, Howell Cobb Papers, MS 1376, box 70, folder 11, HRBML; William R. Houghton and Mitchell B. Houghton, *Two Boys in the Civil War and After* (Montgomery, Ala.: Paragon Press, 1912), 234–42.

36. *OR,* 49, pt. 1:1011; CSR-Louisiana, "Leon Von Zinken."

37. H. L. Scott, *Military Dictionary: Comprising Technical Definitions; Information on Raising and Keeping Troops; Actual Service, Including Makeshifts and Improved Materiel; and Law, Government, Regulation, and Administration Relating to Land Forces* (New York: D. Van Nostrand and Trubner, 1864), 613; Russell County Heritage Book Committee, *Heritage of Russell County,* 7–8; W. F. Scott, *Story of a Cavalry Regiment,* 483–86; Leon Von Zinken to Lamar Cobb, 5 April 1865, Cobb Papers, MS 1376, box 70, folder 11, HRBML; Michie, *Emory Upton,* 165–66.

38. W. F. Scott, *Story of a Cavalry Regiment,* 483–85; Russell County Heritage Book Committee, *Heritage of Russell County,* 7–8.

39. W. F. Scott, *Story of a Cavalry Regiment,* 483–85; Russell County Heritage Book Committee, *Heritage of Russell County,* 7–8; "The Last Battle," *Columbus Ledger,* 22 February 1895; Standard, *Columbus, Georgia,* 56–59; Von Zinken to Cobb, 5 April 1865, Cobb Papers, MS 1376, box 70, folder 11, HRBML.

40. W. F. Scott, *Story of a Cavalry Regiment,* 483–85; Russell County Heritage Book Committee, *Heritage of Russell County,* 7–8; *OR,* 49, pt. 1:492–95. Fort 1 was located on the spot presently occupied by the Russell County Courthouse. The remains of Fort 2 are located just east of the Summerville Road on 26th Street, near the intersection of 26th Street and 9th Avenue. During the battle, Fort 2 was occupied by Clanton's Alabama Battery and other Confederate troops. Some of the heaviest casualties of the battle occurred around this fort. The remains of part of Fort 3 are found today just west of the Summerville Road on 26th Street. Since 2005, houses have been constructed on the battleground immediately to the north of this fort destroying a substantial portion of the battlefield that had, until then, remained undeveloped. The uncompleted Fort 4 was located on the high hill where Pine Grove Cemetery is now located. Russell County Heritage Book Committee, *Heritage of Russell County,* 7–8.

41. W. F. Scott, *Story of a Cavalry Regiment,* 483–85; *OR,* 49, pt. 1:492–95; "Maptech Terrain Navigator 2002—Alabama," Phenix City Area Elevation data/Line-of-sight/United States Geological Survey Maps (Amesbury, Mass.: Maptech, 2002).

42. Bragg, *Joe Brown's Army,* 98–106, x–xi; H. Montgomery, *Cobb's Confederate Career,* 99–121; Simpson, *Howell Cobb,* 169–73.

Chapter 4

1. Cobb, Special Orders, 81; *OR,* 49, pt. 2:1193; Leon Von Zinken to Braxton Bragg, 20 October 1864, CSR-Lousiana, "Leon Von Zinken"; Leon Von Zinken to Howell Cobb, Telegram Inquiring as to Wofford's Authority, 4 April 1865, and Zinken to Cobb, Telegram, 2 April 1865, Cobb Papers, MS 1376, box 70, folder 10, HRBML; Houghton and Houghton, *Two Boys in the Civil War,* 234–42.

2. *OR,* 49, pt. 2:1193; Cobb, Special Orders, 81.

3. Cobb, Special Orders, 78–79.

4. Bragg, *Joe Brown's Army,* x, 106; Cobb, Special Orders, 86–94; W. Jones, "Treatment of Prisoners"; Howell Cobb to C. A. L. Lamar, n.d., Cobb-Erwin-Lamar Collection, MS 86, HRBML; Fraser, "Marion County Prisoner"; *OR,* series 2, 8:403–4.

5. Cobb, Special Orders, 77, 87, 100; B. H. Newton to Howell Cobb, 4 April 1865, Leon Von Zinken to Howell Cobb, Telegrams from Von Zinken, 4 April 1865, and A. W. Reynolds to Howell Cobb, Telegram Detailing Transfer of Troops and Deserter Troubles, 4 April 1865, Cobb Papers, MS 1376, box 70, folder 11, HRBML.

6. Bragg, *Joe Brown's Army,* x, 106; John Banks, "A Short Biographical Sketch of the Undersigned by Himself," 36, Genealogy and Local History Department, CPL; Cobb, Special Orders, 79–80; Howell Cobb to Birkett Fry, Telegram Granting Furloughs to Troops Bringing in Volunteers, 3 April 1865, and Reynolds to Cobb, 4 April 1865, Cobb Papers, MS 1376, box 70, folder 11, HRBML.

7. *OR,* 49, pt. 2:1208, 1212; Cobb, Special Orders, 83–84.

8. Cobb, Special Orders, 81; *OR,* 49, pt. 2:1193.

9. Leon Von Zinken to Howell Cobb, Telegrams from Von Zinken, 4 April 1865, and Zinken to Cobb, Telegram, 2 April 1865, Cobb Papers, MS 1376, box 70, folder 10, HRBML; Cobb, Special Orders, 80.

10. Leon Von Zinken to Inspector General of Georgia, Telegram, 3 April 1865, and Leon Von Zinken to Howell Cobb, Telegram Calling for State Line to Be Sent, 5 April 1865, Cobb Papers, MS 1376, box 70, folder 11, HRBML; Cobb, Special Orders, 83–84.

11. Russell County Heritage Book Committee, *Heritage of Russell County,* 550; "Alabama Artillery Units: 20th Alabama Artillery Battalion," available at http://www.tarleton.edu/~kjones/alarty.html; Telfair, *History of Columbus,* 143–44; Stewart Sifakis, *Compendium of the Confederate Armies: Alabama* (New York: Facts on File, 1992), 11, 24.

12. "Alabama Artillery Units"; Sifakis, *Compendium,* 8; "10th Missouri Battery CSA," available at http://history-sites.com/cgi-bin/boards/mocwmb/index.cgi?read=819, 1–2.

13. "Alabama Artillery Units"; 1865 Diary of James Latta, 16 April 1865, MS 526, James W. Latta Papers 1854–1899, LC; W. F. Scott, *Story of a Cavalry Regiment,* 485; "10th Missouri Battery CSA," 1–2; Sifakis, *Compendium,* 8–24; Clement A. Evans, *Confederate Military History Extended Edition,* vol. 8, *Alabama* (Wilmington, N.C.: Broadfoot, 1987), 335–36.

14. Leon Von Zinken to Howell Cobb, Telegram on Need to Impress Horses, 4 April 1865, Cobb Papers, MS 1376, box 70, folder 11, HRBML; *Columbus Daily Sun,* April 6, 1865.

15. Von Zinken to Lamar Cobb, 5 April 1865, Cobb Papers, MS 1376, box 70, folder 11, HRBML; *OR,* 49, pt. 1:474, 493–95; W. F. Scott, *Story of a Cavalry Regiment,* 485–97; John C. Leach, Diary, 16 April 1865, James Boyle Papers, 3rd Iowa Cavalry, SHSI-DM.

16. Von Zinken to Lamar Cobb, 5 April 1865, Cobb Papers, MS 1376, box 70, folder 11, HRBML.

17. Cobb, Special Orders, 81.

18. B. G. Ellis, *The Moving Appeal: Mr. McClanahan, Mrs. Dill, and the Civil War's Great Newspaper Run* (Macon, Ga.: Mercer University Press, 2003), 319–49; McMillan, *Disintegration of a Confederate State,* 118–20; William W. Rogers Jr., *Confederate Homefront: Montgomery during the Civil War* (Tuscaloosa: University of Alabama, 1999), 145; Sam Davis Elliott, ed., *Doctor Quintard, Chaplain C.S.A. and Second Bishop of Tennessee: The Memoir and Civil War Diary of Charles Todd Quintard* (Baton Rouge: Louisiana State University Press, 2003), 250–51.

19. David Knapp Jr., *The Confederate Horsemen* (New York: Vantage Press, 1966), 279–80; Ezra J. Warner, *Generals in Gray* (Baton Rouge: Louisiana State University, 1999), 39; Richard N. Current, *Encyclopedia of the Confederacy* (New York: Simon & Schuster, 1993), 239; Marcus B. Buford, "History and Genealogy of the Buford Family in America with Records of a Number of Allied Families," 1924, La Belle, Missouri, Mildred B. Minter, available at www.Afn.org/~rbuford/page11.html; James Dinkins, *1861–1865: By an Old Johnnie, Personal Recollections and Experiences in the Confederate Army* (Dayton, Ohio: Morningside Bookshop, 1975), 255–57; William S. Hoole, ed., *History of the Seventh Alabama Cavalry Regiment* (n.p.: reprint 1984), 4–15; C. C. Andrews, *History of the Campaign of Mobile; Including Gen. Wilsons Cavalry in Alabama* (New York: D. Van Nostrand and Trubner, 1867).

20. Elliott, *Doctor Quintard,* 250–51.

21. *OR,* 49, pt. 2:364; Sifakis, *Compendium,* 55–129; Histories of Alabama Infantry Regiments: 65th Alabama Infantry Regiment, 3rd Infantry Battalion, Alabama Reserves, and 3rd Infantry Regiment, Alabama Reserves, available at http://www.tarleton.edu/~kjones/alinf.html; W. W. Rogers, *Confederate Homefront,* 142–44; Leon Von Zinken to Howell Cobb, Telegram Inquiring as to Sending Troops to Alabama, 3 April 1865, Cobb Papers, MS 1376, box 70, folder 10, HRBML; Elliott, *Doctor Quintard,* 250–51; Daniel Adams to Howell Cobb, Telegram, 4 April 1865, Cobb Papers, MS 1376, box 70, folder 11, HRBML.

22. *OR,* 49, pt. 2:364, 1212; W. W. Rogers, *Confederate Homefront,* 142–45; Gilpin, *Last Campaign,* 12 April 1865.

23. *OR,* 49, pt. 2:1215, 1220.

24. Abraham Buford to Howell Cobb, Telegram on Position of Union Forces, 5 April 1865, and Daniel Adams to Howell Cobb, Telegram Report about Mobile, 5 April 1865, Cobb Papers, MS 1376, box 70, folder 11, HRBML; Abraham Buford to Howell Cobb, Telegram on Troops Moving to Demopolis, 7 April, 1865, Cobb Papers, MS 1376, box 70, folder 12 HRBML; *OR,* 49, pt. 2:1220.

25. Cobb, Special Orders, 87–89.

26. Ibid., 87–88.

27. *OR,* 49, pt. 2:1212.

28. Cobb, Special Orders, 93, 100; W. Jones, "Treatment of Prisoners"; Fraser, "Marion County Prisoner."

29. Cobb, Special Orders, 91–94.

30. Ibid., 91–92.

31. Ibid., 92–94.

32. Bragg, *Joe Brown's Army,* 1–111; Cobb, Special Orders, 94.

33. Cobb, Special Orders, 94–96.

Chapter 5

1. Ellis, *The Moving Appeal,* 319–49; J. P. Jones, *Yankee Blitzkrieg,* 108–11; McMillan, *Disintegration of a Confederate State,* 119–20; Samuel W. Catts, "Wilson's Raid and Other Recital," *Alabama Historical Quarterly* 5 (Winter 1943): 430–34; *OR,* 49, pt. 2:363; W. W. Rogers, *Confederate Homefront,* 143–46; Samuel H. Stout, Proclamation from Medical Department, 10 April 1865, Samuel H. Stout Papers, M695-z, SHC; Hoole, *History of the Seventh Alabama,* 15.

2. W. W. Rogers, *Confederate Homefront,* 145–46.

3. *OR,* 49, pt. 2:364.

4. Bragg, *Joe Brown's Army,* 107.

5. *OR,* 49, pt. 1:504.

6. Ibid., 49, pt. 2:1255.

7. Cobb, Special Orders, 96–100; *Macon Daily Telegraph and Confederate,* 17 April 1865.

8. Cobb, Special Orders, 96; Von Zinken to Inspector General of Georgia, 3 April 1865, and Joseph Brown to Howell Cobb, Telegram to Cobb Outlining Orders to Transfer State Line, 5 April 1865, Cobb Papers, MS 1376, box 70, folder 10, HRBML; Bragg, *Joe Brown's Army,* 107; George Gibbs to Howell Cobb, Letter on the State of Affairs at Andersonville, 15 April 1865, Cobb Papers, MS 1376, box 70, folder 12, HRBML.

9. *OR,* 49, pt. 1:504; Leon Von Zinken to Howell Cobb, Telegram Reporting Call for Alabama Militia, Cobb, Howell, 1815–1868, MS 2345, box 10, folder 10, HRBML.

10. Von Zinken to Cobb, Telegram Reporting Call for Alabama Militia.

11. Charles T. Martin, "A Reminiscence of the War between the States," Easley Progress, 9 September 1926, Info Subject Files—Civil War and Reconstruction, Personal Narratives—Charles T. Martin, Location No. SG 011151, Folder No. 010, ADAH; Russell County Historical Commission, *The History of Russell County, Alabama* (Dallas: National ShareGraphics, 1982), C-45.

12. *Columbus Daily Sun,* April 12, 1865.

13. Ibid.

14. Ibid., April 7–13, 1865.

15. Kingman P. Moore, Memoirs, 19–20, courtesy of the family of Susan Marie Moore Brittain, Thomas M. Brittain, custodian, Tucson, Arizona; Bob Dunnavant, "Athens Man Claimed Unique Honor," available at http://gordonfamilygenealogy .homestead.com/jcjgordon.html; Bob Dunnavant, "The Last Cannon Boomed," available at http://gordonfamilygenealogy.homestead.com/jcjgordon.html; John F. Benton, "John F. Benton's Letter," *Columbus Enquirer-Sun,* 1 May 1925; John F. Benton, "John F. Benton's Letter—Postscript," *Columbus Enquirer-Sun,* 2 May 1925; John F. Benton, "Reminiscences of John F. Benton," *Columbus Enquirer-Sun,* 14–18 May 1925 [hereafter cited as "Benton" with date]; J. H. Martin, *Columbus, Geo.,* 178. The theory, recently advanced, that no Confederate soldiers who escaped capture at the Battle of Selma on 2 April could have made it to Columbus and participated in the fight on 16 April is incorrect. Private Kingman P. Moore of the Griffin Light Artillery (Scogin's battery) was one of at least eleven men from that battery who fought at Selma, escaped capture, trudged into Montgomery among the refugees, and was forwarded to Columbus in time for the fight. Others included men from Ward's battery and soldiers who at Montgomery were assigned to duty with Buford's brigade. Moore, Memoirs, 19–20; Dunnavant, "Athens Man Claimed Unique Honor"; Dunnavant, "The Last Cannon Boomed."

16. *Columbus Daily Sun,* April 12, 1865.

17. Telfair, *History of Columbus,* 133.

18. *OR,* 49, pt. 1:504; Moore, Memoirs, 20; Hoole, *History of the Seventh Alabama,* 15; J. H. Wilson, *Under the Old Flag,* 252; W. W. Rogers, *Confederate Homefront,* 146; Isaac Hermann, *Memoirs of a Veteran Who Served as a Private in the 60's in the War Between the States* (Atlanta: Byrd Printing Company, 1911), chapters 21–27.

19. J. H. Wilson, *Under the Old Flag,* 250–51; Edward C. Dale to his son, 29 May 1865, 66; Pape-Findley, *The Invincibles,* 254; Snedeker, Diary, 25 April 1865; Hoole, *History of the Seventh Alabama,* 15–17; *OR,* 49, pt. 1:387, 504; Winkler, Diary, 12–13 April 1865.

20. Hermann, *Memoirs,* chapters 21–27; Hewett, *Supplement,* part 2, series 86, vol. 74, p. 665.

21. Hermann, *Memoirs,* chapters 27–28.

22. Winkler, Diary, 13 April 1865; R. J. Reid, *Fourth Indiana Cavalry Regiment,* 187; Hermann, *Memoirs,* chapter 28.

23. Hermann, *Memoirs,* chapter 28; *OR,* 49, pt. 1:387; Crofts, *History of the Third Ohio,* 197–98; Hoole, *History of the Seventh Alabama,* 15–17.

24. Banks, "A Short Biographical Sketch," 35–36. Some historians have claimed that John Banks of Columbus was a Unionist, based primarily upon his being listed in John G. Winter's accounting of Union sympathizers residing in that city. However, Winter's writings as they bear upon Bank's loyalty are somewhat questionable, especially in the light of Winter's self-imposed exile to Great Britain during the war beginning in 1861. Furthermore, Winter wrote the letter designating Banks as "an original unionist that gave in seemingly, but now reconciled to the union" in 1864, three years after leaving the Americas. How Winter could have known anything of Banks's intimate feelings after such a prolonged absence is un-

clear. Lastly and most importantly, a diary Banks kept during the Civil War makes it plain that he supported the Confederacy and his sons who fought for it. Though Banks may not have been an ardent secessionist during the crisis of 1860–61, there is no reason to believe he was not supportive of the Southern cause. LeRoy P. Graf and Ralph W. Haskins, "The Letters of a Georgia Unionist: John G. Winter and Secession," *Georgia Historical Quarterly* 45, no. 4 (1962): 385–402; LeRoy P. Graf and Ralph W. Haskins, "Letters of a Georgia Unionist: John G. Winter and the Restoration of the Union," *Georgia Historical Quarterly* 46, no. 1 (1961): 45–58.

25. *Columbus Daily Sun,* 12–16 April 1865.

26. Worsley, *Columbus on the Chattahoochee,* 297; C. T. Martin, "Reminiscence of the War"; Russell County Historical Commission, *History of Russell County,* C-45.

27. Columbus City Council Records, 13 April 1865.

28. Ibid.

29. *Columbus Daily Sun,* 13 April 1865; "The Last Battle," *Columbus Ledger,* 22 February 1895. The unit referred to in period documents as the "Typo Guards" has thus far eluded specific identification. I believe this company was composed of workers from the city's newspapers and their neighbors. This hypothesis is bolstered by the unit's advertisements in the local papers in the days leading up to the battle and by the announcement on 15 April by the *Columbus Daily Sun* editors that it would have to suspend its operations until the emergency passed because its employees had all been pressed into service to defend the city. *Columbus Daily Sun,* 15 April 1865; "The Last Battle," *Columbus Ledger,* 22 February 1895.

30. J. H. Martin, *Columbus, Geo.,* 178; "The Last Battle"; Adolph H. Philips, Alfred J. Millard, and Lee W. Roberts, "What Happened to the Defenders of Columbus?" p. 2, Events Related to CS Soldiers After the Battle, March 1957, Joseph Mahan Files, Genealogy and Local History Department, CPL; Lot Abraham, "More about the Last Days of the Confederacy and Disbanding the Armies," 1, SHSI-DM; *Augusta Tri-Weekly Constitutionalist,* 23 April 1865; "Post Register of Sick and Wounded Soldiers in Hospitals at Columbus, Ga., 1864–1865," Clerk of Council's Office, Columbus Government Center, Columbus, Georgia [hereafter cited as "Post Register"].

31. Elliott, *Doctor Quintard,* 253.

32. Cobb, Special Orders, 101–4.

Chapter 6

1. *Columbus Daily Sun,* 15 April 1865.

2. Ibid.

3. Ibid.

4. Ibid.; Benton, 1 May, 2 May 1925.

5. *OR,* 49, pt. 1:504; Howell Cobb to Mrs. Cobb, 15 April 1865, Cobb Papers, MS 1376, box 70, folder 12, HRBML.

6. Cobb, Special Orders, 103–9; J. P. Jones, *Yankee Blitzkrieg,* 132; *OR,* 52, pt. 2:813.

7. *Columbus Daily Sun,* 15 April 1865.

8. *OR,* 49, pt. 1:485; J. W. Mallet, Telegrams Sent—Superintendent of Labs, April 14–15, 1865, RG 109, Chapter IV, vol. 52, NARA; Cobb, Special Orders, 106.

9. *Columbus Daily Sun,* 15 April 1865; Benton, 1–2 May, 14 May 1925.

10. "Post Register"; Louise J. DuBose, "Women in Columbus, 1828–1928," Louise Jones DuBose Papers, Simon Schwob Memorial Library, CSUA.

11. *Columbus Daily Sun,* 15 April 1865.

12. Ibid.

13. Cobb, Special Orders, 100.

14. George Gibbs to Howell Cobb, Letter to Cobb's Headquarters, 15 April 1865, Cobb Papers, MS 1376, box 70, folder 12, HRBML.

15. Jane Gullatt, "Henderson Tells of Final Conflict Resulting in Capture of Two Cities," *Columbus Ledger-Enquirer Civil War Centennial Edition,* 16 April 1961, 6; *Confederate Reminiscences and Letters,* 9:123; Cobb, Special Orders, 79–80.

16. There is significant debate about the identity of the 65th Alabama Infantry and their connection with the 3rd Alabama Infantry Reserves and 4th Battalion Alabama Reserves. Some experts suggest that these units were not related. Others hold that the 65th Alabama was organized from these units for the purpose of sending the reserves to Mississippi prior to Wilson's Raid. Still others contend that the two units were probably consolidated during Wilson's Raid. All that is certain is that at least the officers of the 65th Alabama participated in the fight, as did the two reserve units, whatever their designations. *OR,* 49, pt. 1:504; Sifakis, *Compendium,* 55–129; Histories of Alabama Infantry Regiments: 65th Alabama Infantry Regiment, 3rd Infantry Battalion, Alabama Reserves, and 3rd Infantry Regiment, Alabama Reserves, available at http://www.tarleton.edu/~kjones/alinf.html.

17. Sifakis, *Compendium,* 55–58, 129; James Cooper Nisbet, *Four Years on the Firing Line* (Wilmington, N.C.: Broadfoot, reprint 1987), 255; W. Jones, "Treatment of Prisoners," 193–95.

18. The breakdown of this number is as follows: Fort 3, 3 guns; Fort 2, 4 guns + 1 gun in redoubt; Lunette, 2 guns; Jackson Street Battery, 6 guns; Fort 1, 4 guns; Franklin Street Bridge section, 2 guns; Railroad Battery, 4 guns; City Bridge Battery, 3 guns; Naval Yard Battery, 4 guns. Sifakis, *Compendium,* 8–24; *OR,* 49, pt. 2:474; Dunnavant, "Athens Man Claimed Unique Honor"; Dunnavant, "The Last Cannon Boomed."

19. J. H. Martin, *Columbus, Geo.,* 180; "The Last Battle," *Columbus Ledger,* 22 February 1895.

20. Hoole, *History of the Seventh Alabama,* 15; Hinrichs, Diary, 15 April 1865; Gilpin, "Diary of 'The Last Campaign,'" 15 April 1865; Curry, *Four Years in the Saddle,* 222.

21. Hoole, *History of the Seventh Alabama,* 15; Howell Cobb to Mrs. Cobb, 15 April 1865, Cobb Papers, MS 1376, box 70, folder 12, HRBML.

22. Howell Cobb to Mrs. Cobb, 15 April 1865, Cobb Papers, MS 1376, box 70, bolder 12, HRBML.

23. Augustus McLaughlin, "McLaughlin Letter Book, 1864–1865," Columbus Naval Yard Log, 15 April 1865, National Civil War Naval Museum at Port Columbus, Columbus, Georgia.

24. Leon Von Zinken, Proclamation to People of Columbus on the Eve of Battle, 15 April 1865, Simon Schwob Memorial Library, CSUA.

Chapter 7

1. Arthur Howard Noll, ed., *Doctor Quintard, Chaplain C.S.A. and Second Bishop of Tennessee; Being His Story of the War (1861–1865)* (Sewaneee, Tenn.: University Press of Sewanee, 1905), 137.

2. Worsley, *Columbus on the Chattahoochee*, 294; Kate Cumming, *A Journal of Hospital Life in the Confederate Army of Tennessee* (Louisville: John P. Morton, 1866), 175.

3. Bob Macomber, "My Daddy Was a Sailor . . . A Confederate Sailor!" available at www.civilwarinteractive.com/ArticleDaddyWasAConfederate.htm; Cumming, *Journal of Hospital Life*, 175.

4. Among the soldiers gathered in the church that Easter morning was General Jesse J. Finley of Florida. Though Finley is documented to have been in Columbus on the morning of the battle, it is not known if he participated in the fight. Noll, *Doctor Quintard*, 137–38; Elliott, *Doctor Quintard*, 120–21; Lynn Willoughby, *A Power for Good: The History of Trinity Parish, Columbus, Georgia* (Columbus, Ga.: Trinity Episcopal Church, 1999), 91; "Political Graveyard: Index to Politicians: Finley," available at http://politicalgraveyard.com/bio.finley.html; "Finley, Jesse Johnson, 1812–1904," available at www.civilwarhistory.com/_122899/jesse_johnson_finley.htm.

5. Samuel G. French, *Two Wars: An Autobiography of Gen. Samuel G. French* (Nashville: Confederate Veteran, 1901), 304–5.

6. Worsley, *Columbus on the Chattahoochee*, 297; William Watts Carnes, Memoirs, p. 204, National Civil War Naval Museum at Port Columbus, Columbus, Georgia.

7. Willoughby, *A Power for Good*, 91–92; Noll, *Doctor Quintard*, 137–39; Elliott, *Doctor Quintard*, 120–21.

8. *Columbus Daily Sun*, 15 April 1865.

9. Telfair, *History of Columbus*, 137.

10. Hinrichs, Diary, 16 April 1865.

11. Vanorsdol, *Four Years for the Union*, 74.

12. C. T. Martin, "Reminiscence of the War"; Russell County Historical Commission, *History of Russell County*, C-45.

13. "Post Register."

14. Emma J. Slade Prescott, Memoirs, 1:80–81, Kenan Research Center, Atlanta History Center, Atlanta; *Confederate Reminiscences and Letters*, 3:137.

15. Macomber, "My Daddy Was a Sailor."

16. J. H. Martin, *Columbus, Geo.*, 178; A. J. Jackson, "Diary of War between the States Kept by A. J. Jackson, Company G, 2nd Georgia State Line Troops From February, 1863 to April, 1865," p. 9, Jackson, Co. G, Ga. State Line, Personal Narratives, drawer 76, box 7–8, GDAH; Moore, Memoirs, 20.

17. W. F. Scott, *Story of a Cavalry Regiment*, 483–86; Moore, Memoirs, 20; J. H. Martin, *Columbus, Geo.*, 178; Curry, *Four Years in the Saddle*, 223–26; Michie, *Emory Upton*, 165–67; Telfair, *History of Columbus*, 134–35.

18. Winslow, "Columbus, the Final Battle," 1; Louise G. Jones, "Some Reminiscences and Incidents of the Last Battle of the Civil War at Columbus, Easter, April 16, 1865," *Columbus Enquirer-Sun*, 16 April 1922.

19. Cobb, Special Orders, 109–11; Eliza Frances Andrews, *The War-Time Journal of a Georgia Girl* (New York: D. Appleton, 1908), 145–47.

20. "Post Register." In "The Civil War Hospitals in Columbus, Georgia," Sandra W. Uzar states: "In April, 1865, with the impending assault of Federal Forces upon Columbus, the patients were moved back to Atlanta" (6). It should be understood, however, that at this time there was no direct rail connection between Columbus and Atlanta. Any passengers moving from Columbus to that point had to travel west toward Opelika before switching back northeast toward Atlanta, or had to head east to Macon before rerouting northward. With this understanding, it is possible that the final destination of Columbus's patients was Atlanta (via Macon); however, this is not specifically what the hospital records indicate. The number of transfers that took place between 5 and 16 April as recorded by the "Post Register" can be broken down thus:

Transferred from Columbus to Macon:	528 patients
Transferred from Columbus to Cuthbert:	65 patients
Transferred from Columbus to Eufaula:	13 patients
Transferred from Columbus to Griffin:	8 patients
Transferred from Columbus to Forsyth:	4 patients
Transferred from Columbus to unknown:	3 patients

Total number of patients transferred from Columbus, 5–16 April 1865: 621

"Post Register"; Sandra W. Uzar, "The Civil War Hospitals in Columbus, Georgia," 1–6, 1989, Clerk of Council's Office, Columbus Government Center, Columbus, Georgia; Sandra W. Uzar, "Confederate Hospitals in Columbus, Georgia," *Muscogiana Magazine* 3, nos. 1–2 (1992–93): 16–21.

21. George B. Douglas to Samuel Stout, 30 April 1865, S. M. Bemiss, Official Order, 15 April 1865, S. M. Bemiss to McPherson, Official Order, 15 April 1865, and S. M. Bemiss to W. H. Brannon, Official Order, 15 April 1865, Stout Papers, SHC; Glenna R. Schroeder-Lein, *Confederate Hospitals on the Move: Samuel H. Stout and the Army of Tennessee* (Columbia: University of South Carolina Press, 1994), 146–47.

22. Cobb, Special Orders, 109–10.

23. There is some dispute over whether the *Chattahoochee* was towed downriver by the *Young Rover*, as is suggested by Lieutenant William W. Carnes, or whether it was taken by the torpedo boat *Viper*. If it was the latter, the *Viper*'s crew wasted little time in their operations, as is evidenced by the boat's reappearance at the Navy Yard in time to take the remainder of Columbus's Confederate naval offi-

cers out of the city at around 9:30 p.m. Turner, *Navy Gray*, 233–34; McLaughlin, "McLaughlin Letter Book, 1864–1865," 16 April 1865; Carnes, Memoirs, 204.

24. Russell County Historical Commission, *History of Russell County*, C-46; Curry, *Four Years in the Saddle*, 222.

25. W. F. Scott, *Story of a Cavalry Regiment*, 482–88; Vanorsdol, *Four Years for the Union*, 73.

26. *OR*, 49, pt. 1:500; Curry, *Four Years in the Saddle*, 222–23.

27. *OR*, 49, pt. 2:361; Latta, "Pennsylvania in the War."

28. Abraham, Diary, 16 April 1865; *OR*, 49, pt. 2:361; ibid., pt. 1:492.

29. Abraham, Diary, 16 April 1865.

30. J. H. Wilson, *Under the Old Flag*, 258.

31. Curry, *Four Years in the Saddle*, 222–23.

32. Michie, *Emory Upton*, 166; W. F. Scott, *Story of a Cavalry Regiment*, 490; Winslow, "Columbus, the Final Battle," 1.

33. Curry, *Four Years in the Saddle*, 222–23.

34. Gilpin, "Diary of 'The Last Campaign,'" 16 April 1865.

35. W. F. Scott, *Story of a Cavalry Regiment*, 488; Curry, *Four Years in the Saddle*, 222.

36. Curry, *Four Years in the Saddle*, 222.

37. Ibid., 222–23; Winslow, "Columbus, the Final Battle," 1.

38. Winslow, "Columbus, the Final Battle," 1.

39. Reports concerning the circumstances of Mrs. Keeling's incarceration are mixed. Some claim she was jailed for attempting to steal slaves, and others claim it was for some act associated with her open displays of Unionism. Neither may be completely accurate. Hinrichs, Diary, 16 April 1865; Abraham, Diary, 16 April 1865; Barker, "William H. Barker," 139; Busby, Diary, 16 April 1865; William A. Gray, Diary, 16 April 1865, available at www.iowa-counties.com/civilwar/3rd_cav/graycw.htm; Mitchell, Memoirs, 16 April 1865.

40. Curry, *Four Years in the Saddle*, 223.

41. Hoole, *History of the Seventh Alabama*, 15; W. F. Scott, *Story of a Cavalry Regiment*, 488; Curry, *Four Years in the Saddle*, 223.

42. Curry, *Four Years in the Saddle*, 223; Hoole, *History of the Seventh Alabama*, 15.

43. Anne Kendrick Walker, *Russell County in Retrospect* (Richmond Dietz Press, 1950), 250–52.

44. Morse, *Personal Experiences*, 138; Curry, *Four Years in the Saddle*, 223.

Chapter 8

1. Curry, *Four Years in the Saddle*, 223.

2. "Maptech Terrain Navigator 2002—Alabama"; Conzett, "My Civil War," 70–71.

3. Conzett, "My Civil War," 70–71.

4. Michie, *Emory Upton*, 166–67.

5. Curry, *Four Years in the Saddle*, 223; Gilpin, "Diary of 'The Last Campaign,'" 16 April 1865; Michie, *Emory Upton*, 167.

6. W. F. Scott, *Story of a Cavalry Regiment*, 487–90; Curry, *Four Years in the Saddle*, 222–24; *OR*, 49, pt. 1:500; Gilpin, "Diary of 'The Last Campaign,'" 16 April 1865; Mitchell, Memoirs, 16 April 1865; Latta, "Pennsylvania in the War"; Conzett, "My Civil War," 71; Edward C. Dale to his son, 29 May 1865, 66–67.

7. Curry, *Four Years in the Saddle*, 223; Conzett, "My Civil War," 71; Michie, *Emory Upton*, 165–67; "Maptech Terrain Navigator 2002—Alabama." It is not clear how much of the 1st Ohio was in position in time to support the action. Some accounts seem to indicate that the whole regiment was on hand, while others state that the assault was performed by only the six companies who had led the advance. What is known for certain is that the 1st Ohio Cavalry (the whole regiment) held the foremost position in the line of march that morning and early afternoon. There is no evidence that the remaining six companies of the regiment, which were not acting as skirmishers, were detached at any point to conduct some other action, and therefore it can be inferred that they were following the six companies that led the brigade. Also, behind the 1st Ohio followed the 7th Ohio, the 5th Iowa, and Battery I of the 4th U.S. Artillery. It is certain that all of those units either came up to support the action or were held in reserve, overlooking the scene, within a few minutes of the start of the movement. Therefore, while it remains a matter of debate how many companies participated in the charge, it seems almost certain that the entire unit was on the scene. Curry, *Four Years in the Saddle*, 223; Conzett, "My Civil War," 71; Michie, *Emory Upton*, 165–67.

8. Gilpin, "Diary of 'The Last Campaign,'" 16 April 1865; Curry, *Four Years in the Saddle*, 223; Latta, "Pennsylvania in the War"; Morse, *Personal Experiences*, 138.

9. Gilpin, "Diary of 'The Last Campaign,'" 16 April 1865; Curry, *Four Years in the Saddle*, 223–24.

10. Curry, *Four Years in the Saddle*, 223–24; Gilpin, "Diary of 'The Last Campaign,'" 16 April 1865.

11. Gilpin, "Diary of 'The Last Campaign,'" 16 April 1865.

12. W. F. Scott, *Story of a Cavalry Regiment*, 487–90; Curry, *Four Years in the Saddle*, 222–24; *OR*, 49, pt. 1:473; Gilpin, "Diary of 'The Last Campaign,'" 16 April 1865; Mitchell, Memoirs, 16 April 1865; Latta, Diary, 16 April 1865.

13. Curry, *Four Years in the Saddle*, 224.

14. Latta, "Pennsylvania in the War."

15. Conzett, "My Civil War," 71; Edward C. Dale to his son, 29 May 1865, 66–67.

16. Curry, *Four Years in the Saddle*, 224–25.

17. There is some degree of discrepancy concerning the exact time at which the Mill (Holland) Creek footbridge was destroyed. Accounts of the action suggest that the bridge was intact when Federal forces first arrived at Girard during the afternoon and that it survived at least until the 1st Ohio made its aborted charge toward the City Bridge. This is evidenced by Sergeant Aden Harper's ride over the bridge in order to get a look at Fort 1. The footbridge did not survive for long after that, however. By the time the 1st Ohio was recalled from Girard following the ignition of the City Bridge, using the Mill Creek footbridge to launch a broader attack on Fort 1 was no longer an option. It is partially for this reason that Upton

ordered Winslow's brigade to march north, around to the Confederate right. It is my impression that the bridge was torched by the Confederate skirmishers who deployed "near the creek bridge in Girard" during the afternoon phase of the engagement. Morse, *Personal Experiences,* 138–39; J. H. Martin, *Columbus, Geo.,* 179; Curry, *Four Years in the Saddle,* 225–26.

18. Curry, *Four Years in the Saddle,* 224.

19. Michie, *Emory Upton,* 167; Moore, Memoirs, 20.

20. Rankin, *History of the Seventh Ohio,* 28; Curry, *Four Years in the Saddle,* 224; J. H. Martin, *Columbus, Geo.,* 179.

21. Moore, Memoirs, 20; Telfair, *History of Columbus,* 135; Worsley, *Columbus on the Chattahoochee,* 295.

22. Given the conflicting accounts, it is hard to state with certainty what took place during those moments. To avoid an extended analysis, I have synthesized all the available information relating to this phase of the battle and presented the most likely scenario. Curry, *Four Years in the Saddle,* 224; Latta, "Pennsylvania in the War"; J. H. Martin, *Columbus, Geo.,* 179; Rankin, *History of the Seventh Ohio,* 28; Moore, Memoirs, 20.

23. Gilpin, "Diary of 'The Last Campaign,'" 16 April 1865.

24. Curry, *Four Years in the Saddle,* 225.

25. Upton's division flag was white and swallow-tailed. It bore in its center a pair of red crossed sabers, above and below which was emblazoned a large blue 4. Other cavalry units during the war had used similar flags, but most featured the silhouettes of sabers sheathed in their scabbards. Upton's flag and, indeed, all the flags of Wilson's Raiders were symbolically unsheathed. Edward C. Dale to his son, 29 May 1865, 66–67; Gilpin, "Diary of 'The Last Campaign,'" 16 April 1865; J. H. Wilson, *Alexander,* 10.

26. Morse, *Personal Experiences,* 138; Gilpin, "Diary of 'The Last Campaign,'" 16 April 1865.

27. Latta, "Pennsylvania in the War."

28. Morse, *Personal Experiences,* 139; Gilpin, "Diary of 'The Last Campaign,'" 16 April 1865; Latta, "Pennsylvania in the War."

29. Gilpin, *Last Campaign,* 6–7.

30. Morse, *Personal Experiences,* 139; J. H. Martin, *Columbus, Geo.,* 179.

31. Abraham, Diary, 16 April 1865.

32. Moore, Memoirs, 20.

33. Howell Cobb to Mrs. Cobb, 19 April 1865, Cobb-Erwin-Lamar Collection, MS 86, box 3, folder 12, HRBML.

Chapter 9

1. Michie, *Emory Upton,* 167; Curry, *Four Years in the Saddle,* 225; Abraham, Diary, 16 April 1865.

2. W. F. Scott, *Story of a Cavalry Regiment,* 490–92; Curry, *Four Years in the Saddle,* 225; Morse, *Personal Experiences,* 139; Michie, *Emory Upton,* 166–67; Winslow, "Columbus, the Final Battle," 4–5.

3. Winslow, "Columbus, the Final Battle," handwritten pages inserted; Stuart, *Iowa Colonels and Regiments,* 620; Michie, *Emory Upton,* xii–xvi.

4. Michie, *Emory Upton,* 167; W. F. Scott, *Story of a Cavalry Regiment,* 490; J. H. Wilson, *Under the Old Flag,* 260; Conzett, "My Civil War," 73; *OR,* 49, pt. 1:497; Abraham, Diary, 16 April 1865; Edward C. Dale to his son, 29 May 1865, 66–67; Winslow, "Columbus, the Final Battle," 4.

5. Winslow, "Columbus, the Final Battle," 5.

6. W. F. Scott, *Story of a Cavalry Regiment,* 490–91; Barker, "William H. Barker," 140.

7. W. F. Scott, *Story of a Cavalry Regiment,* 491; *OR,* 49, pt. 1:499.

8. Hoole, *History of the Seventh Alabama,* 15; Gullatt, "Henderson Tells of Final Conflict," 6; Nisbet, *Four Years on the Firing Line,* 255.

9. J. H. Martin, *Columbus, Geo.,* 179; Jackson, "Diary of War between the States," 9; Mitchell, Memoirs, 16 April 1865.

10. Russell County Historical Commission, *History of Russell County,* C-45–46; C. T. Martin, "Reminiscence of the War."

11. Russell County Historical Commission, *History of Russell County,* C-45–46; C. T. Martin, "Reminiscence of the War."

12. Russell County Historical Commission, *History of Russell County,* C-45–46; C. T. Martin, "Reminiscence of the War."

13. Cobb, Special Orders, 107–11; J. H. Wilson, *Under the Old Flag,* 264–65; Abraham, "More about the Last Days," 1; W. F. Scott, *Story of a Cavalry Regiment,* 499–500.

14. Curry, *Four Years in the Saddle,* 225–26; Morse, *Personal Experiences,* 139; Mitchell, Memoirs, 16 April 1865.

15. W. F. Scott, *Story of a Cavalry Regiment,* 491–92; Winslow, "Columbus, the Final Battle," 4–6; J. H. Wilson, *Under the Old Flag,* 259; *OR,* 49, pt. 1:362.

16. Gilpin, "Diary of 'The Last Campaign,'" 16 April 1865; Mitchell, Memoirs, 16 April 1865.

17. Winslow, "Columbus, the Final Battle," 5; Abraham, Diary, 16 April 1865.

18. It has been suggested in at least one secondary history that the man who offered Winslow information about the Confederate defenses along the Summerville Road was a slave, but I can find no definitive information as to the informant's identity. Winslow, "Columbus, the Final Battle," 5; David Williams, *Rich Man's War: Class, Caste, and Confederate Defeat in the Lower Chattahoochee Valley* (Athens: University of Georgia Press, 1999), 166.

19. W. F. Scott, *Story of a Cavalry Regiment,* 492–93.

20. There is some debate about whether the two hundred men from the 10th Missouri who were dispatched to capture the Clapp's Factory Bridge on the morning of 16 April rejoined their regiment before the night assault or were left out of the action. Considering the chronology of events, and that Young's battalion began their unopposed march to Girard from Crawford at approximately 9 A.M., it would have been easy for this detachment to reach the Clapp's Factory Bridge ahead of the arrival of Alexander's brigade south of the city, but not in time to prevent the structure's destruction. This would have made it possible for Young's detachment to hear and possibly even witness the afternoon attack. The troopers of Winslow's

brigade appear to have known of the destruction of the Clapp's Factory Bridge by as early as their two-hour delay in the wooded valley. It is my impression, then, that Young's detachment rejoined Winslow's command sometime prior to the night assault. It is this idea that I present in the text. It is, however, possible that Young's troopers missed Winslow's brigade during the afternoon. Should that be the case, Young's troopers would not have reunited with Winslow's command and would have had to make the information about the bridge known to either Upton or Wilson, who then relayed it to Winslow. Winslow, "Columbus, the Final Battle," 1, 5; Hinrichs, Diary, 16 April 1865; W. F. Scott, *Story of a Cavalry Regiment,* 490.

21. Giles, "Union Diary Records Capture," 6; J. G. Christy, Diary, 16 April 1865, J. G. Christy, 4th United States Cavalry, SHSI-DM; Wilson, Diary, 16 April 1865; Walker, *Russell County in Retrospect,* 143–44; Longacre, *Union Stars to Top Hat,* 32, 38–39.

22. J. H. Wilson, *Under the Old Flag,* 259.

23. Winslow, "Columbus, the Final Battle," 5.

24. J. H. Wilson, *Under the Old Flag,* 259; Winslow, "Columbus, the Final Battle," 6.

25. W. F. Scott, *Story of a Cavalry Regiment,* 492; *OR,* 49, pt. 1:362; Charles Jewett Swift, *The Last Battle of the Civil War* (Columbus, Ga.: Gilbert Printing Co., 1915), 24–25; Winslow, "Columbus, the Final Battle," handwritten pages inserted, 5–6; J. H. Wilson, *Under the Old Flag,* 259.

26. Winslow, "Columbus, the Final Battle," 5–6. Major discrepancies exist among the various accounts regarding what was said between the three commanders when they met in the fading twilight of 16 April. Because of the heated nature of the exchanges, it may be that none of the accounts is entirely accurate. It also seems that each of the participants and observers, either in an effort to defend his own positions or those of his superiors, was selective in what he recorded about those moments. Additionally, while a resolution was finally made and a course of action agreed upon, the details of the meeting soon became a point of contention among the three generals. This mostly friendly dispute over the actual circumstances and suggestions made at the meeting would continue long after the war, even to the generals' deaths. W. F. Scott, *Story of a Cavalry Regiment,* 492; *OR,* 49, pt. 1:362; Charles Jewett Swift, *The Last Battle of the Civil War* (Columbus, Ga.: Gilbert Printing Co., 1915), 24–25; Winslow, "Columbus, the Final Battle," handwritten pages inserted, 5–6; J. H. Wilson, *Under the Old Flag,* 259.

27. Winslow, "Columbus, the Final Battle," 5–6; J. H. Wilson, *Under the Old Flag,* 259–60.

28. W. F. Scott, *Story of a Cavalry Regiment,* 492; J. H. Wilson, *Under the Old Flag,* 259–60.

29. J. H. Wilson, *Under the Old Flag,* 259–60. Much of the debate that was kept up between the generals after the war was related to who made the suggestion for the night attack at Columbus. All three generals appear to have claimed the honor at various times. In his official report of the campaign, Wilson included the following remarks, which seem to indicate that Upton made the suggestion of a night attack: "Through an accident Winslow did not arrive at his position until after dark,

but Upton proposed to make the assault in the night and coinciding with him in judgment, I ordered the attack."

Despite what he recorded in his official report of the action, after the war, Wilson claimed with vehemence that, indeed, it was he, and not Upton or Winslow, that deserved the credit for developing the plan for the night assault. In a letter written to Charles J. Swift of Columbus, Georgia, in 1913, Wilson defended his claim. He wrote: "I am much obliged to you for your 'last writing on the "last battle."' The only correction I can suggest is that the night attack was suggested by me to Upton as an improvement on his plan for an afternoon attack, which was deranged by his failure to find Winslow at the place and time we had appointed. I may add the change was enthusiastically accepted by Upton and carried out in the masterly manner that characterized all his operations."

In another letter dated 7 January 1915, Wilson again defended his claim for the credit of originating the idea. He wrote: "I notice, since the death of General Winslow, in one or two of his writings, he claims to have made the suggestion of the night attack. While my recollection does not sustain this claim, it is perfectly certain that 'the night attack' could not have been made except by my authority and direction." J. H. Wilson, *Under the Old Flag*, 259–60. *OR*, 49, pt. 1:362; Swift, *Last Battle*, 24–25; Winslow, "Columbus, the Final Battle," 5–6; W. F. Scott, *Story of a Cavalry Regiment*, 492.

Chapter 10

1. Morse, *Personal Experiences*, 139; Winslow, "Columbus, the Final Battle," handwritten pages inserted. After the war, Wilson claimed that the attack at Columbus had been made with "Minty's Division supporting." Whether he wanted to hide the fact that he had approved the night assault without any reserve force in place to assist or whether he was simply mistaken is unclear. In either case, after the war Winslow made it a point in his writings to clarify the situation and demonstrate that Minty's division was not present, a fact confirmed by the following message:

HEADQUARTERS SECOND DIVISION CAVALRY,
Ten Miles from Columbus, April 16, 1865—6.50 p.m.
Major BEAUMONT,
Assistant Adjutant-General, Cavalry Corps:
MAJOR: I have halted here to feed and groom horses. If the general wishes me to move forward to-night please send me word; otherwise I will remain where I am to-night and will march at 4.30 in the morning. They call it forty miles from here to Tuskegee; a pretty long march. If you send an orderly to me let me have the news.
Yours, respectfully,
ROBT. H. G. MINTY, Colonel.

Winslow, "Columbus, the Final Battle," handwritten pages inserted; *OR,* 49, pt. 2:367; ibid., pt. 1:442.

2. Winslow, "Columbus, the Final Battle," 6; U.S. Naval Observatory, Astronomical Applications Department, Sun and Moon Data for One Day, 16 April 1865, 17 April 1865, Columbus, Muscogee County, Georgia (longitude W85.0, latitude N32.5), available at http://aa.usno.navy.mil/cgi-bin/aa_pap.pl.

3. The distance from the Union position on Summerville Road to Fort 2 was approximately 325 yards. Over this distance, however, the ground descended gradually for nearly seventy vertical feet, then rose abruptly before the fort for seventy-nine vertical feet. It would have been obvious to Winslow during his reconnaissance that the terrain alone before Fort 2 might prove a tremendous challenge to any assaulting force. Winslow's brigade would make their charge toward Fort 3 and through the shallower swale before its walls. W. F. Scott, *Story of a Cavalry Regiment,* 492–93.

4. Michie, *Emory Upton,* 167; *OR,* 49, pt. 1:503.

5. Latta, "Pennsylvania in the War"; *OR,* 49, pt. 1:503; Conzett, "My Civil War," 71–72.

6. Conzett, "My Civil War," 72; Howell Cobb to Mrs. Cobb, 19 April 1865, Cobb-Erwin-Lamar Collection, MS 86, box 3, folder 12, HRBML.

7. J. H. Martin, *Columbus, Geo.,* 179; Howell Cobb to Mrs. Cobb, 15 April 1865, Cobb Papers, MS 1376, box 70, folder 12, HRBML

8. Winslow, "Columbus, the Final Battle," 7.

9. Ibid.; W. F. Scott, *Story of a Cavalry Regiment,* 493; J. H. Wilson, *Winslow,* 19.

10. Wycoff, "Autobiography," 52.

11. Hinrichs, Diary, 16 April 1865.

12. Winslow, "Columbus, the Final Battle," 7–8.

13. Ibid., 8; W. F. Scott, *Story of a Cavalry Regiment,* 493; Abraham, Diary, 16 April 1865.

14. J. H. Wilson, *Under the Old Flag,* 260–61.

15. W. F. Scott, *Story of a Cavalry Regiment,* 493–97; Winslow, "Columbus, the Final Battle," 7–20.

16. There is no indication that any of Winslow's troopers, outside of the staff who overheard the generals' meeting, had any idea that the night attack was not their commanders' original intention. Indeed, the majority of diaries, letters, and memoirs I examined indicate that the majority of troopers believed that Upton and Winslow had deliberately delayed the assault so that it could be made under the cover of darkness. Curry, *Four Years in the Saddle,* 224–26; Elbridge Colby, "Wilson's Cavalry Campaign of 1865," *American Military History Foundation Journal* 2, no. 4 (1938): 208.

17. *OR,* 49, pt. 1:493; W. W. Grant, "Recollections of the Last Battle," *Confederate Veteran Magazine* 23 (1915): 163–65.

18. There are several theories regarding the Austin's battalion flag and its appearance at the Battle for Columbus. One theory is that a very small detachment of soldiers from Austin's battalion were in Columbus prior to the battle and, along with

their flag, were pressed into service during the battle. Another is that no members of Austin's battalion participated in the battle but that the flag was transferred to Columbus prior to the engagement and was pressed into service by the hastily assembled local defenders. What seems certain from the evidence available is that the flag was carried by soldiers whose identities remain a mystery but who were stationed near the north end of the entrenchments. It is also well established that the flag was captured during the battle along with the soldier who bore it, whoever that might have been. *OR,* 49, pt. 1:493; *Echoes of Glory: Arms and Equipment of The Confederacy* (Alexandria, Va.: Time-Life Books, 1991), 273; see Arthur W. Bergeron, Bruce Allardice, Greg Biggs, and Ken Legendre, "Austin's 14th LA Sharpshooters," postings on the Louisiana in the Civil War Message Board, available at http://history-sites.com/cgi-bin/boards/lacwmb/index.cgi?read=1024.

19. One gun of Winston's battery was reported to be attached to the 3rd Alabama Reserves at Montgomery, and this gun might have been stationed near Fort 2. However, it is also possible that the piece was manned by a crew from one of several other batteries. *OR,* 49, pt. 2:363.

20. Ibid., pt. 1:493.

21. Gullatt, "Henderson Tells of Final Conflict," 6; Nisbet, *Four Years on the Firing Line,* 255; Hoole, *History of the Seventh Alabama,* 15; C. T. Martin, "Reminiscence of the War"; Russell County Historical Commission, *History of Russell County,* C-46.

22. Michie, *Emory Upton,* 166; W. F. Scott, *Story of a Cavalry Regiment,* 485; Sketch of Columbus, Georgia, and Its Defenses, by H. S. Heywood, Accompanying the Report of J. H. Wilson, *OR,* 49, 29 June 1865; "10th Missouri Battery CSA," available at http://history-sites.com/cgi-bin/boards/mocwmb/index.cgi?read=819, 1–2; *OR,* 49, pt. 1:398; Vanorsdol, *Four Years for the Union,* 74; Winslow, "Columbus, the Final Battle," 8; J. H. Wilson, *Under the Old Flag,* 262–63.

23. Abraham, "More about the Last Days," 1; Dunnavant, "Athens Man Claimed Unique Honor"; Dunnavant, "The Last Cannon Boomed"; Catton, *Picture History,* 239.

24. "April 10, 1865—Davis Signature"; Goldberg Coins interview; *OR,* 49, pt. 2:1216.

25. Lamar might be characterized as the typical Southern hothead. Several times, when criticized in public, he took the (by this period) unpopular approach and challenged the offender to a duel. Once he even shot and seriously wounded a close friend in a dispute at a racetrack. Lamar had no shortage of enemies, and even as late as the month of his death his family was speculating on his most recent escalation in rhetoric with Captain McDuffie and whether it might "end with pistols and coffee for two." Hoole, *History of the Seventh Alabama,* 15; Moore, Memoirs, 20; Cobb Relative to Howell Cobb, Letter from Americus, 6 April 1865, Cobb-Erwin-Lamar Collection, MS 1376, box 70, folder 11, HRBML.

26. Captain E. E. Arnold, mentioned in the text, might be Captain Eugenius C. Arnold, originally of the 11th Georgia Infantry, but at the time commanding a company of cavalry in state service. Howell Cobb to Mrs. Cobb, 15 April 1865,

Cobb Papers, MS 1376, box 70, folder 12, HRBML; Hoole, *History of the Seventh Alabama,* 15.

27. Hinrichs, Diary, 16 April 1865; J. H. Wilson, *Under the Old Flag,* 261; Abraham, Diary, 16 April 1865; Leach, Diary, 16 April 1865.

28. Curry, *Four Years in the Saddle,* 225.

29. Telfair, *History of Columbus,* 136–37; L. G. Jones, "Some Reminiscences."

Chapter 11

1. Benton, 2 May 1925.

2. Winslow, "Columbus, the Final Battle," 9; Abraham, Diary, 16 April 1865.

3. *OR,* 49, pt. 1:396–97, 503.

4. Ibid., 486; Conzett, "My Civil War," 72.

5. Though Wilson and a few other participants in the battle wrote later that the 3rd Iowa's attack had been launched before the Confederates opened fire, the overwhelming majority of the evidence suggests the chronology of events I present in the text. *OR,* 49, pt. 1:493–95; J. H. Wilson, *Under the Old Flag,* 261.

6. Hinrichs, Diary, 16 April 1865; Abraham, Diary, 16 April 1865.

7. Chauncey M. Graham, Civil War Diary, 16 April 1865, Chauncey M. Graham, 4th Iowa Cavalry Reg. Diary, Civil War Miscellaneous Collection, USAMHI; Hinrichs, Diary, 16 April 1865.

8. Graham, Diary, 16 April 1865; Abraham, Diary, 16 April 1865.

9. Leach, Diary, 16 April 1865; George Healey, Civil War Letter Transcripts, p. 57, George Healey Papers, SHSI-DM; Conzett, "My Civil War," 73.

10. Leach, Diary, 16 April 1865.

11. George Curkendall, "Report of Alterations for Co. D, 3rd Regt Iowa Cavalry, from March 31, 1865 to April 1865," SHSI-DM; Historical Data Systems, Inc., "Roster and Record of Iowa Soldiers in the War of Rebellion," Information on Thomas J. Miller, Co D, 3rd Iowa Cavalry, www.civilwardata.com; Stuart, *Iowa Colonels and Regiments,* 605; Leach, Diary, 16 April, 1865.

12. Conzett, "My Civil War," 72–73; *OR,* 49, pt. 1:396–97, 503; Philip St. George Cooke, *Cavalry Tactics or, Regulations for the Instruction, Formation, and Movements of The Cavalry of the Army and Volunteers of the United States* (Philadelphia: Lippincott, 1862).

13. J. H. Wilson, *Under the Old Flag,* 261.

14. Conzett, "My Civil War," 72–73.

15. Ibid., 72; J. H. Wilson, *Under the Old Flag,* 261–62; "Maptech Terrain Navigator 2002—Alabama."

16. Winslow, "Columbus, the Final Battle," 8; Healey, Civil War Letter Transcripts, 56–57.

17. J. H. Wilson, *Under the Old Flag,* 262; John W. Noble, "Report of April 23, 1865," 11, Adjutant General's Collection, SHSI-DM.

18. Healey, Civil War Letter Transcripts, 56; W. F. Scott, *Story of a Cavalry Regiment,* 494–95; Winslow, "Columbus, the Final Battle," 9.

19. Gullatt, "Henderson Tells of Final Conflict," 6; J. H. Martin, *Columbus, Geo.*, 179.

20. Leach, Diary, 16 April 1865.

21. Ibid.

22. Gullatt, "Henderson Tells of Final Conflict," 6.

Chapter 12

1. J. H. Wilson, *Under the Old Flag*, 262.

2. W. F. Scott, *Story of a Cavalry Regiment*, 494; Winslow, "Columbus, the Final Battle," 8–9; *OR*, 49, pt. 1:493–95.

3. *OR*, 49, pt. 1:474; Grant, "Recollections of the Last Battle," 164.

4. Hinrichs, Diary, 16 April 1865.

5. J. H. Wilson, *Under the Old Flag*, 262; W. F. Scott, *Story of a Cavalry Regiment*, 494; Hinrichs, Diary, 16 April 1865.

6. Hinrichs, Diary, 16 April 1865; Winslow, "Columbus, the Final Battle," 9–16.

7. Hinrichs, Diary, 16 April 1865.

8. J. H. Wilson, *Under the Old Flag*, 262; *OR*, 49, pt. 1:492.

9. Winslow, "Columbus, the Final Battle," 9–10; Hinrichs, Diary, 16 April 1865.

10. Hinrichs, Diary, 16 April 1865.

11. Ibid.

12. *OR*, 49, pt. 1:493; W. F. Scott, *Story of a Cavalry Regiment*, 495.

13. *OR*, 49, pt. 1:493.

14. "Maptech Terrain Navigator 2002—Alabama"; *OR*, 49, pt. 1:493; W. F. Scott, *Story of a Cavalry Regiment*, 495–97.

15. W. F. Scott, *Story of a Cavalry Regiment*, 495–96; *OR*, 49, pt. 1:493.

16. W. F. Scott, *Story of a Cavalry Regiment*, 495–96; *OR*, 49, pt. 1:493.

17. *OR*, 49, pt. 1:493; W. F. Scott, *Story of a Cavalry Regiment*, 496; Winslow, "Columbus, the Final Battle," 9–10.

18. *OR*, 49, pt. 1:398, 493; Michie, *Emory Upton*, 168. The flag of Austin's battalion was of the second national pattern, bearing twelve stars on its canton (no center star). Painted below the canton was a pair of red, crossed cannons. At the top of the white field was emblazoned "Austin's Batt," followed beneath by battle honors including Shiloh, Belmont, Chickamauga, Farmington, Perryville, and Murfreesboro. A photograph of the flag is in *Echoes of Glory: Arms and Equipment of The Confederacy*, (Alexandria, Va.: Time-Life Books, 1991), 273.

19. Conzett, "My Civil War," 72–73; Bereman, Diary, 16 April 1865; Gilpin, "Diary of 'The Last Campaign,'" 16 April 1865; William M. Johnson, "Andrew W. Tibbets: Iowa's Medal of Honor Heroes," Iowa Battle Flag Project, SHSI-DM.

20. W. F. Scott, *Story of a Cavalry Regiment*, 496; *OR*, 49, pt. 1:493.

21. *OR*, 49, pt. 1:499; Abraham, Diary, 16 April 1865.

22. W. F. Scott, *Story of a Cavalry Regiment*, 496; Abraham, Diary, 16 April 1865.

23. Winslow, "Columbus, the Final Battle," 10; Vanorsdol, *Four Years for the Union,* 73.

24. W. F. Scott, *Story of a Cavalry Regiment,* 497.

25. Bereman, Diary, 16 April 1865; W. F. Scott, *Story of a Cavalry Regiment,* 497.

26. Howell Cobb to Mrs. Cobb, 19 April 1865, Cobb-Erwin-Lamar Collection, MS 86, box 3, folder 12, HRBML.

27. Gullatt, "Henderson Tells of Final Conflict," 6.

28. Ibid.

29. Abraham, Diary, 16 April 1865.

30. It is not clear if the 4th Iowa's battle cry of "Selma!" was arranged prior to the engagement or occurred spontaneously. The Battle of Selma was the regiment's last major engagement. In it, the regiment made a very similar assault and achieved a spectacular victory. Though I do not believe the cry was prearranged, there is evidence that the word was used by the men of the 4th Iowa during the assault as a sort of code word to help fellow soldiers identify each other in the darkness. W. F. Scott, *Story of a Cavalry Regiment,* 497; Winslow, "Columbus, the Final Battle," 23; Graham, Diary, 16 April 1865.

31. W. F. Scott, *Story of a Cavalry Regiment,* 497.

32. Howell Cobb to Mrs. Cobb, 19 April 1865, Cobb Papers, MS 86, box 3, folder 12, HRBML.

33. W. F. Scott, *Story of a Cavalry Regiment,* 497; *OR,* 49, pt. 1:398; William M. Johnson, "Corp. Richard Morgan: Iowa's Medal of Honor Heroes," Iowa Battle Flag Project, SHSI-DM.

34. W. F. Scott, *Story of a Cavalry Regiment,* 497; Gilpin, "Diary of 'The Last Campaign,'" 16 April 1865; Jackson, "Diary of War between the States," 9.

35. W. F. Scott, *Story of a Cavalry Regiment,* 494–95; Winslow, "Columbus, the Final Battle," 9–10; Michie, *Emory Upton,* 167–68; J. H. Wilson, *Under the Old Flag,* 262; Latta, "Pennsylvania in the War."

36. W. F. Scott, *Story of a Cavalry Regiment,* 494–95; Winslow, "Columbus, the Final Battle," 9; J. H. Wilson, *Under the Old Flag,* 262–63.

37. W. F. Scott, *Story of a Cavalry Regiment,* 495.

38. Ibid.; Winslow, "Columbus, the Final Battle," 9.

39. J. H. Martin, *Columbus, Geo.,* 179–80.

40. Winslow, "Columbus, the Final Battle," 10.

41. Curry, *Four Years in the Saddle,* 225; Mitchell, Memoirs, 16 April 1865.

42. Curry, *Four Years in the Saddle,* 225; Mitchell, Memoirs, 16 April 1865.

43. J. H. Martin, *Columbus, Geo.,* 179; W. F. Scott, *Story of a Cavalry Regiment,* 491–500.

Chapter 13

1. Vanorsdol, *Four Years for the Union,* 73; Winslow, "Columbus, the Final Battle," 14.

2. Vanorsdol, *Four Years for the Union,* 73.

3. Winslow, "Columbus, the Final Battle," 21.

4. Ibid., 10.

5. Ibid.

6. Ibid.

7. Ibid.; Noble, Diary, 12 April 1865.

8. *OR*, 49, pt. 1:493–95; W. F. Scott, *Story of a Cavalry Regiment*, 496.

9. W. F. Scott, *Story of a Cavalry Regiment*, 497; Giles, "Union Diary Records Capture," 6.

10. Hoole, *History of the Seventh Alabama*, 15–16; Gilpin, "Diary of 'The Last Campaign,'" 16 April 1865.

11. Telfair, *History of Columbus*, 139–40.

12. Gullatt, "Henderson Tells of Final Conflict," 6; Mitchell, Memoirs, 16 April 1865; Gilpin, "Diary of 'The Last Campaign,'" 16 April 1865. The quoted account of Confederates playing dead to escape capture is substantiated by the 4th Iowa's Sergeant Bereman, who recorded that on the evening of the battle "we went over ditches, logs, fences—firing, yelling, running—and so the line was taken with nearly 1000 prisoners. They were afraid to run away—so they hid down in the rifle pits." Bereman, Diary, 16 April 1865.

13. "Civil War Veteran Relates Experiences," *Columbus Enquirer*, 30 November 1938.

14. W. F. Scott, *Story of a Cavalry Regiment*, 497.

15. Ibid., 491, 497–98; Abraham, Diary, 16 April 1865; Vanorsdol, *Four Years for the Union*, 73; Sketch of Columbus, Georgia, and Its Defenses, by H. S. Heywood, Accompanying the Report of J. H. Wilson, *OR*, 49, 29 June 1865.

16. W. F. Scott, *Story of a Cavalry Regiment*, 491; *OR*, 49, pt. 1:398.

17. Benton, 15 May 1925.

18. W. F. Scott, *Story of a Cavalry Regiment*, 497; Winslow, "Columbus, the Final Battle," 12.

19. W. F. Scott, *Story of a Cavalry Regiment*, 497–98; Abraham, Diary, 16 April 1865; Vanorsdol, *Four Years for the Union*, 73; J. H. Wilson, *Under the Old Flag*, 263.

20. W. F. Scott, *Story of a Cavalry Regiment*, 498; Winslow, "Columbus, the Final Battle," 10–11.

21. Winslow, "Columbus, the Final Battle," 10–12; W. F. Scott, *Story of a Cavalry Regiment*, 499.

22. W. F. Scott, *Story of a Cavalry Regiment*, 497–98; Vanorsdol, *Four Years for the Union*, 73–75; *OR*, 49, pt. 1:481; Abraham, Diary, 16 April 1865; Bereman, Diary, 16 April 1865.

23. Winslow, "Columbus, the Final Battle," 12. Some discrepancies among the various accounts concerning the assault on Fort 1 have yet to be fully remedied. The main issue is whether the Federals captured the fort before or after they captured the Franklin Street Bridge. Several accounts disagree as to whether there was a failed attempt followed by a later successful capture, or whether the capture was successful the first time. I believe the fort was assailed unsuccessfully once and then later captured after the penetration of the Franklin Street Bridge. Edward C. Dale to his son, 29 May 1865, 67; W. F. Scott, *Story of a Cavalry Regiment*, 498; Bereman, Diary, 16 April 1865; Vanorsdol, *Four Years for the Union*, 73–75; Abraham, Diary, 16 April 1865;

24. Howell Cobb to Mrs. Cobb, 19 April 1865, Cobb Papers, MS 86, box 3,

folder 12, HRBML; Gilpin, "Diary of 'The Last Campaign,'" 16 April 1865; "Memorial Day at Savannah, Ga.," 130.

25. "Memorial Day at Savannah, Ga.," 130–31.

26. *OR,* 49, pt. 1:499.

27. W. F. Scott, *Story of a Cavalry Regiment,* 498–99; Vanorsdol, *Four Years for the Union,* 73; Gilpin, "Diary of 'The Last Campaign,'" 16 April 1865; Hoole, *History of the Seventh Alabama,* 16; Howell Cobb to Mrs. Cobb, 19 April 1865, Cobb Papers, MS 86, box 3, folder 12, HRBML; *OR,* 49, pt. 1:499; Bereman, Diary, 16 April 1865.

28. W. F. Scott, *Story of a Cavalry Regiment,* 499. Accounts differ as to the device used by the Confederate attempting to ignite the bridge. Most identify him as using matches, others a firebrand, and at least one other, a bucket of turpentine and a torch. Vanorsdol, *Four Years for the Union,* 73–74; W. F. Scott, *Story of a Cavalry Regiment,* 499; Bereman, Diary, 16 April 1865; Shipman, Diary, 17 April 1865.

29. Benton, 14 May 1925.

30. Gilpin, "Diary of 'The Last Campaign,'" 16 April 1865; J. H. Martin, *Columbus, Geo.,* 180; J. H. Wilson, *Under the Old Flag,* 264; Latta, "Pennsylvania in the War." According to a local historian, Guillett's three brothers had all been killed earlier in the war, each while riding upon the same horse that Captain S. I. Guillett rode at the Battle for Columbus, and upon which he was seated when he received the wound that would end his life. Before his death, Guillett willed the animal to a nephew. Telfair, *History of Columbus,* 136–37.

31. J. H. Martin, *Columbus, Geo.,* 180.

32. Benton, 15 May 1925.

33. Hoole, *History of the Seventh Alabama,* 16; Latta, "Pennsylvania in the War."

34. W. F. Scott, *Story of a Cavalry Regiment,* 498–99.

35. Abraham, "More about the Last Days," 1; Dunnavant, "The Last Cannon Boomed"; Dunnavant, "Athens Man Claimed Unique Honor"; W. F. Scott, *Story of a Cavalry Regiment,* 494–95, 499; "Memorial Day at Savannah, Ga.," 130–31; J. H. Wilson, *Under the Old Flag,* 264; John A. Nourse, Letters from Soldier with Chicago Board of Trade Battery, 25 April 1865, LeighColl Book 27:27, USAMHI. Some of the Federal soldiers who had captured Confederates on the Alabama side of the river forced them across the span ahead of them. Private Richard Cosgriff remembered: "Then taking half a dozen of the prisoners we marched them across ahead of about fifty of us and told them that if they uttered . . . any alarm we would shoot them down, and furthermore, they were ordered to give the guard at the other end of the bridge the countersign. . . . Our prisoners acted according to our instructions and when they gave the countersign we pushed them aside and rushed for the guns." Walter F. Beyer, *Deeds of Valor: How America's Heroes Won the Medal of Honor* (Detroit: Perrien-Keydel Co., 1907), 537.

36. Abraham, "More about the Last Days," 1; J. H. Wilson, *Under the Old Flag,* 264; Winslow, "Columbus, the Final Battle," 11; Graham, Diary, 16 April 1865; Abraham, Diary, 16 April 1865.

37. W. F. Scott, *Story of a Cavalry Regiment,* 499; John Peters, "Report of Opera-

tions from March 22nd to April 22nd, 1865," p. 17, Adjutant General's Files, SHSI-DM; Beyer, *Deeds of Valor,* 537; *OR,* 49, pt. 1:398–99; J. H. Wilson, *Under the Old Flag,* 264.

38. Winslow, "Columbus, the Final Battle," 11–12.

39. W. F. Scott, *Story of a Cavalry Regiment,* 499; Mark Pendergrast, *For God, Country, and Coca-Cola* (New York: Scribner and Maxwell Macmillan, 1993), 21; Fort Tyler Association, "Battle of West Point: Civil War Trivia," www.forttyler .com/trivia.htm; Howell Cobb to Mrs. Cobb, 19 April 1865, Cobb Papers, MS 86, box 3, folder 12, HRBML; "Memorial Day at Savannah, Ga.," 130–31.

40. J. H. Martin, *Columbus, Geo.,* 180; Telfair, *History of Columbus,* 146; C. T. Martin, "Reminiscence of the War"; Russell County Historical Commission, *History of Russell County,* C-46.

41. "Memorial Day at Savannah, Ga.," 130–31. The participants in the action made various and sometimes contradictory records of Lamar's final moments. In the text I have attempted to synthesize the material and present the best of it in the most plausible scenario. "Memorial Day at Savannah, Ga.," 130–31; J. H. Martin, *Columbus, Geo.,* 180; Telfair, *History of Columbus,* 146; Russell County Historical Commission, *History of Russell County,* C-46; C. T. Martin, "Reminiscence of the War."

42. Abraham, "More about the Last Days," 1; J. H. Martin, *Columbus, Geo.,* 180; W. F. Scott, *Story of a Cavalry Regiment,* 499; Jane Gullatt, "Small, but Well Armed Unit Penetrated Local Defenses on Easter Sunday, 1865," *Columbus Ledger-Enquirer Civil War Centennial Edition,* 16 April 1961, 9; *Macon Daily Telegraph and Confederate,* 18 and 20 April 1865; Howell Cobb to Mrs. Cobb, 19 April 1865, Cobb Papers, MS 86, box 3, folder 12, HRBML.

43. Winslow, "Columbus, the Final Battle," 12; Vanorsdol, *Four Years for the Union,* 73.

44. Vanorsdol, *Four Years for the Union,* 73–75.

45. *OR,* 49, pt. 1:398.

46. Vanorsdol, *Four Years for the Union,* 74; Abraham, Diary, 16 April 1865.

47. *OR,* 49, pt. 1:493–94.

48. Grant, "Recollections of the Last Battle," 164.

49. *OR,* 49, pt. 1:493–94.

Chapter 14

1. Winslow, "Columbus, the Final Battle," 14.

2. W. F. Scott, *Story of a Cavalry Regiment,* 496; Winslow, "Columbus, the Final Battle," 14–15.

3. W. F. Scott, *Story of a Cavalry Regiment,* 499.

4. Ibid., 499–500; Winslow, "Columbus, the Final Battle," 14; *OR,* 49, pt. 1:398, 499; J. H. Martin, *Columbus, Geo.,* 180; Hinrichs, Diary, 16 April 1865; Bates, Diary, 16–17 April 1865.

5. J. H. Wilson, *Under the Old Flag,* 264; Winslow, "Columbus, the Final Battle," 11.

6. Jackson, "Diary of War between the States," 9.

7. W. F. Scott, *Story of a Cavalry Regiment,* 499–500; Hoole, *History of the Seventh Alabama,* 16.

8. Abraham, "More about the Last Days," 1.

9. E. F. Andrews, *War-Time Journal,* 146.

10. Moore, Memoirs, 21.

11. J. H. Martin, *Columbus, Geo.,* 180; Telfair, *History of Columbus,* 137; William H. Young to Andrew Johnson, August 3, 1865, Case Files From Former Confederates for Presidential Pardons ("Amnesty Papers"), 1865–1867, M1003, reel 24, RG 94, quoted in Harold S. Wilson, *Confederate Industry: Manufacturers and Quartermasters in the Civil War* (Jackson: University Press of Mississippi, 2002), 222.

12. Gilpin, "Diary of 'The Last Campaign,'" 16 April 1865.

13. Columbus Naval Yard Log, 16 April 1865; Carnes, Memoirs, 204–5.

14. Gilpin, "Diary of 'The Last Campaign,'" 16 April 1865.

15. W. F. Scott, *Story of a Cavalry Regiment,* 500; J. H. Wilson, *Under the Old Flag,* 264; Cobb, Special Orders, 111–16; Howell Cobb to Mrs. Cobb, 19 April 1865, Cobb Papers, MS 86, box 3, folder 12, HRBML.

16. Philips, Millard, and Roberts, "What Happened to the Defenders of Columbus?" 2.

17. Hoole, *History of the Seventh Alabama,* 16; Cobb, Special Orders, 111–16; Howell Cobb to Mrs. Cobb, 19 April 1865, Cobb Papers, MS 86, box 3, folder 12, HRBML.

18. Jackson, "Diary of War between the States," 9; Gullatt, "Henderson Tells of Final Conflict," 6; Hoole, *History of the Seventh Alabama,* 16; Prescott, Memoirs, 1:82; Moore, Memoirs, 21.

19. Hoole, *History of the Seventh Alabama,* 16; Grant, "Recollections of the Last Battle," 164.

20. Ingram, Letter Outlining Confederate Service of Porter Ingram, Porter Ingram Folder, File II, Names (Record Group 4, Sub-group 2, Series 46), GDAH; James W. Howard, Confederate Diary, 16 April 1865, Simon Schwob Memorial Library, CSUA; C. T. Martin, "Reminiscence of the War."

21. Winslow notes in his memoirs that "Some years after the war a member of his [Lamar's] family wrote me that the watch which was carried by Lamar was lost or taken, and as it was an heirloom its recovery was greatly desired. It was found and at once restored" (13). I believe Winslow had the watch in his possession at the time of the request and that he obtained it either at the close of the battle or later in the month when Wilson's corps was assembled and searched for looted property. Curry, *Four Years in the Saddle,* 226; Winslow, "Columbus, the Final Battle," 13–14; C. T. Martin, "Reminiscence of the War"; Russell County Historical Commission, *History of Russell County,* C-46.

22. Benton, 18 May 1925; Winslow, "Columbus, the Final Battle," 14; J. H. Wilson, *Under the Old Flag,* 230.

23. J. H. Wilson, *Under the Old Flag,* 230.

24. Winslow, "Columbus, the Final Battle," 14; Gilpin, "Diary of 'The Last Campaign,'" 16 April 1865.

25. Gilpin, "Diary of 'The Last Campaign,'" 16 April 1865; Michie, *Emory Upton,* xvi; Abraham, Diary, 16 April 1865; Latta, Diary, 17 April 1865.

26. W. F. Scott, *Story of a Cavalry Regiment,* 501.

27. Swift, *Last Battle,* 27; David Dodd, "Randolph Lawler Mott, 1799–1881: Columbus Businessman, Civic Leader, Unionist," *Muscogiana Magazine,* 8, nos. 1–2 (1997): 56–67.

28. Swift, *Last Battle,* 27; *Confederate Papers Relating to Citizens or Business Firms,* "Randolph L. Mott" and "Palace Mills"; J. H. Wilson, *Under the Old Flag,* 266–67; Worsley, *Columbus on the Chattahoochee,* 298; Ben Walburn, "Mott Remained Loyal to Union throughout War Although Son Wore Uniform of Confederate Army," *Columbus Ledger-Enquirer Civil War Centennial Edition,* 16 April 1961, 7; Dodd, "Randolph Lawler Mott," 58–61.

29. Several local historians have asserted that on the night of the battle, Mott flew a U.S. flag from the cupola of his house, demonstrating his Union sentiments and leading Wilson to establish his headquarters at the home. This seems unlikely, however, for two reasons. First, considering the Confederate forces concentrated around the Mott House, particularly during the afternoon and evening of 16 April, it seems difficult to imagine that such an open show of Unionism would have been tolerated. Second, none of the diaries, letters, or memoirs written by Union and Confederate soldiers or civilians suggests seeing a Union flag atop this prominent home, whose conspicuous location certainly would have made such a symbol hard to miss. Most likely, the flag was displayed inside the home in some prominent spot. Indeed, it is in this manner that the only contemporary account of the flag's display is to be found. This lone first-person account was recorded by Wilson and has been quoted in the text. The key phrase in Wilson's statement, and the one most often overlooked in Columbus's histories of this period, is "within the dome." This statement makes clear that the flag was inside. J. H. Wilson, *Under the Old Flag,* 267.

30. Winslow, "Columbus, the Final Battle," 14.

31. Ibid.

32. Ibid., 14–16; *OR,* 49, pt. 1:494.

33. W. F. Scott, *Story of a Cavalry Regiment,* 496–501; Noble, Diary, 16 April 1865; Winslow, "Columbus, the Final Battle," 14–15.

34. Hinrichs, Diary, 16 April 1865.

35. Morse, *Personal Experiences,* 141; Telfair, *History of Columbus,* 137; *Confederate Reminiscences and Letters,* 3:137; "Memorial Day at Savannah, Ga.," 131; W. F. Scott, *Story of a Cavalry Regiment,* 501; *OR,* 49, pt. 2:383.

36. Winslow, "Columbus, the Final Battle," 16; French, *Two Wars,* 308–9.

37. French, *Two Wars,* 308–9.

38. W. F. Scott, *Story of a Cavalry Regiment,* 500; Gilpin, "Diary of 'The Last Campaign,'" 16 April 1865; Abraham, Diary, 16 April 1865.

39. W. F. Scott, *Story of a Cavalry Regiment,* 500–501; Hinrichs, Diary, 16 April

1865; J. H. Wilson, *Under the Old Flag,* 267; Noble, Diary, 16 April 1865; Christy, Diary, 16 April 1865; Shipman, Diary, 16 April 1865; Wycoff, "Autobiography," 52; Conzett, "My Civil War," 73; Bereman, Diary, 16 April 1865; Abraham, Diary, 16 April 1865.

40. Shipman, Diary, 16 April 1865; Wycoff, "Autobiography," 52.

41. Leach, Diary, 16 April 1865; Prescott, Memoirs, 2:11.

42. Morse, *Personal Experiences,* 140–41; Gilpin, "Diary of 'The Last Campaign,'" 16 April 1865.

43. Morse, *Personal Experiences,* 140–41.

44. Winslow, "Columbus, the Final Battle," 7.

45. Fannie A. Beers, *Memories: A Record of Personal Experience and Adventure during Four Years of War* (Philadelphia: Lippincott, 1891); "Post Register."

46. U.S. Naval Observatory, data for 16–17 April 1865; Gilpin, "Diary of 'The Last Campaign,'" 16 April 1865.

47. Hinrichs, Diary, 16 April 1865; Vanorsdol, *Four Years for the Union,* 74.

48. Mitchell, Memoirs, 16 April 1865; "Memorial Day at Savannah, Ga.," 131.

49. W. F. Scott, *Story of a Cavalry Regiment,* 500.

50. Mitchell, Memoirs, 16 April 1865.

51. *OR,* 49, pt. 2:383.

Chapter 15

1. Mitchell, Memoirs, 17 April 1865.

2. Telfair, *History of Columbus,* 136.

3. Hinrichs, Diary, 17 April 1865.

4. Telfair, *History of Columbus,* 113–30; Standard, *Columbus, Georgia,* 46–62; Worsley, *Columbus on the Chattahoochee,* 283–91; Williams, *Rich Man's War,* 85–115; Tom Sellers, "Cruel Conflict Crushes Valley, But Brings Glory," *Columbus Ledger-Enquirer Civil War Centennial Edition,* 16 April 1961, 2; Ben Walburn, "Council Minutes Tell Graphic Story," *Columbus Ledger-Enquirer Civil War Centennial Edition,* 16 April 1961, 19–24.

5. Nisbet, *Four Years on the Firing Line,* 255–56.

6. W. C. Woodall, "Our Town: After the Battle Was Over," *Columbus Ledger,* 31 January 1966.

7. Conzett, "My Civil War," 73; Mitchell, Memoirs, 17 April 1865.

8. Mitchell, Memoirs, 17 April 1865.

9. *Born in Slavery: Slave Narratives from the Federal Writers' Project, 1936–1938, Georgia Narratives* (Washington, D.C.: Library of Congress), 4, pt. 4:126; ibid., 4, pt. 1:12–13.

10. Conzett, "My Civil War," 73.

11. Wycoff, "Autobiography," 52; Conzett, "My Civil War," 73.

12. J. H. Wilson, *Under the Old Flag,* 266.

13. Ibid., 266–67; W. F. Scott, *Story of a Cavalry Regiment,* 501.

14. Griest, Diary, 11 April 1865.

15. Winslow, "Columbus, the Final Battle," 20. No complete enumeration of

property destroyed by Wilson's Raiders has ever been assembled, and it is probably impossible to estimate exactly. Winslow did, however, attempt to record the major industrial and military assets destroyed in Columbus. Though the report he submitted to Wilson on 18 April is not comprehensive, it provides some insight into the city's loss. W. F. Scott, *Story of a Cavalry Regiment,* 501–3; *OR,* 49, pt. 1:485–87.

16. Winslow, "Columbus, the Final Battle," 21; Standard, *Columbus, Georgia,* 61; Morse, *Personal Experiences,* 141.

17. J. H. Wilson, *Under the Old Flag,* 267; *OR,* 49, pt. 1:485–87.

18. W. F. Scott, *Story of a Cavalry Regiment,* 500–503; *OR,* 49, pt. 1:485–87; Kyle, *Images,* 48–49; Federal Writers Project (Ga.) and George P. Rawick, *The American Slave: A Composite Autobiography* (Westport, Ct.: Greenwood, 1974), 12, pt. 1:243.

19. J. H. Wilson, *Under the Old Flag,* 266–67. Some Southern sources put the total number of bales stored in the city at about half the number given in the text. These figures are disputed by the Union accounts, which consistently state the total as exceeding 100,000 bales. After careful examination of the materials related to the battle, I am inclined to believe that the actual number was closer to the figures given by the Federal authorities. It should be noted that, for some time before its capture, Columbus had its connections to Apalachicola and Savannah cut off by the Union naval blockade and Sherman's March to the Sea. Cotton produced in the Chattahoochee valley and elsewhere in the South piled up with no way to get it out to the markets overseas. Furthermore, Wilson's Raid caused panic in eastern Alabama, and there is reason to believe that cotton might have been moved to Columbus from Montgomery and other points during the period between Selma's fall and the capture of Montgomery to prevent it from falling into Union hands. J. H. Wilson, *Under the Old Flag,* 266–67; Wilson, Diary, 17 April 1865; W. C. Woodall, "More Detailed Credit for General," *Columbus Ledger,* 30 January 1966.

20. J. H. Wilson, *Under the Old Flag,* 266–67; Woodall, "More Detailed Credit for General." The values given in the text are in U.S. currency for 1865. The most conservative estimate of the value of the cotton destroyed in Columbus on 17 April equaled more than the entire real estate valuation of the city in 1928, which was only estimated to be $41,171,911.00. (This figure does not take into account the disparity of currency values between to the two periods. Each figure is given in U.S. dollars for its respective period.) Indeed, according to at least one Columbus historian, the (lowest estimated) value of the cotton destroyed would surpass the real estate valuation of the entire city until as late as 1942.

When one realizes that the savings and investments of many people in the Chattahoochee valley were tied up in cotton, it is easy to see how great a blow the loss of such a substantial portion would have been to the local economy. To help further illustrate the point, if the value of the cotton destroyed in Columbus were adjusted to reflect modern dollars (as of 2004), its value would be an astonishing $726 million (approximately). J. H. Wilson, *Under the Old Flag,* 266–67; Woodall, "More Detailed Credit for General"; "Columbus, Georgia," *Columbus Ledger Centennial Edition,* 1928 (bound copy), Genealogy and Local History Department, CPL; W. C. Woodall, "Columbus, Georgia," *Columbus News,* 12 November 1942,

2–3; Samuel H. Williamson, "What Is the Relative Value?" Economic History Services, April 2004, available at http://www.eh.net/hmit/compare.

21. J. H. Wilson, *Under the Old Flag,* 267; Lupold and French, *Bridging Deep South Rivers,* 178, 190; John S. Lupold, *Industrial Archeology of Columbus, Georgia: A Tour Guide for the 8th Annual Conference of the Society for Industrial Archeology, April 1979* (Columbus, Ga.: J. S. Lupold, 1979), 1–3.

22. *OR,* 49, pt. 1:485–87.

23. Ibid., 485; Bob Holcombe, interview and examination of CSS *Jackson* conducted at the National Civil War Naval Museum at Port Columbus, Georgia, 2005; Cris Calle, "A True and Accurate Account of the Raising of the *CSS Jackson* and the *CSS Chattahoochee,*" *Muscogiana Magazine* 12, no. 1 (2001): 1–8; Turner, *Navy Gray,* 233–34, 247–55; Jerry Franklin, interview and examination of shells conducted at the storage facility of the National Civil War Naval Museum at Port Columbus, 2005; Winslow, "Columbus, the Final Battle," handwritten pages inserted.

24. Louis Bonnigal, Melvin J. Sowards, and R. E. Mildner, "Report on the Role of Private Industry in Columbus, Georgia During the Period 1861–1865," 5–6, 14 March 1957, Joseph Mahan Files, Genealogy and Local History Department, CPL; Jean K. Kent, *Temple Israel of Columbus, Ga., 1854–2000* (Columbus, Ga.: Temple Israel, 1999), 13–14; Kyle, *Images,* 49; W. C. Woodall, "Battle for City Unnecessary," *Columbus Ledger,* 16 April 1969; Marcus, *Memoirs of American Jews,* 305–7; Columbus City Council Records, April 1865; *Confederate Papers Relating to Citizens or Business Firms,* "L. Haiman and Bro. Co."; "Sword Factory Said Largest," *Columbus Ledger-Enquirer Civil War Centennial Edition,* 16 April 1961, 17; Albaugh and Simmons, *Confederate Arms,* 17–19, 76–105; Fuller and Steuart, *Firearms of the Confederacy,* 282–84.

25. Vanorsdol, *Four Years for the Union,* 75; Columbus City Council Records, April 1865; Kimberly B. Cantrell and H. David Williams, "Battle for the Bridges," *America's Civil War,* March 1991, 43; Rita Folse Elliott, *Living in Columbus, Georgia 1828–1869: The Lives of Creeks, Traders, Enslaved African-Americans, Mill Operatives and Others as Told to Archaeologists* (Columbus: City of Columbus, Georgia Department of Community and Economic Development, 2005), 85.

26. *OR,* 49, pt. 1:485–87; J. H. Wilson, *Under the Old Flag,* 267–69; W. F. Scott, *Story of a Cavalry Regiment,* 501–3.

27. Gilpin, "Diary of 'The Last Campaign,'" 17 April 1865.

28. Latta, Diary, 17 April 1865; Gilpin, "Diary of 'The Last Campaign,'" 17 April 1865; Kent, *Temple Israel of Columbus,* 14–15.

29. McGee, *History of the 72nd Indiana,* 580.

30. Woodall, "More Detailed Credit for General"; Kyle, *Images,* 48–49; Paul Miles, "Columbus Was Center of South's Second-Ranking Industrial Complex," *Columbus Ledger-Enquirer Civil War Centennial Edition,* 16 April 1961, 13–15; Conzett, "My Civil War," 73–75; Mitchell, Memoirs, 17 April 1865; Hinrichs, Diary, 17 April 1865.

31. Winslow, "Columbus, the Final Battle," 21; Conzett, "My Civil War," 74.

32. W. C. Woodall, "After the Battle Was Over," *Columbus Ledger,* 30 January 1966; Woodall, "More Detailed Credit for General."

33. Conzett, "My Civil War," 74.

34. *OR,* 49, pt. 1:487; Abraham, Diary, 17 April 1865.

35. Standard, *Columbus, Georgia,* 53–58.

36. Mitchell, Memoirs, 17 April 1865. The potential for this sort of behavior had demonstrated itself on a much smaller scale about two years earlier, when a small mob of hungry women took to the streets of Columbus with weapons, demanding food and supplies from the shops downtown. The disturbance was quickly put down, but it reveals the extent to which the increasing strain of poverty affected the city's poor, especially the mill women. *Columbus Daily Sun,* 11 April 1863.

Chapter 16

1. Crofts, *History of the Third Ohio,* 198–99; Shipman, Diary, 17 April 1865; *OR,* 49, pt. 1:487; Kyle, *Images,* 48–49.

2. *OR,* 49, pt. 1:798; Carpenter, Diary, 17 April 1865.

3. McGee, *History of the 72nd Indiana,* 582; Marilyn C. Davidson, "Patriotic Songs at the White House," www.thenationalanthemproject.org/teachermaterial/naptm_lesson02.html.

4. McGee, *History of the 72nd Indiana,* 581.

5. Carpenter, Diary, 17 April 1865.

6. Mary A. H. Gay, *Life in Dixie during the War* (Atlanta: Charles P. Byrd, 1897), 268–71; Carpenter, Diary, 6 May 1865; Potter, Diary, 3 April 1865; John W. Morton, *The Artillery of Nathan B. Forrest's Cavalry* (Chattanooga: Methodist Episcopal Church, 1909), 311; French, *Two Wars,* 304–8; Carson Johnson, "Anderson Abercrombie Genealogical Information," available at www.carsonjohnson.com/chapter04-Abercrombie.htm. John Winter described Abercrombie as a Unionist in his 1864 letters to Vice President Johnson, but it is unclear to what extent that was true. It does not appear that Abercrombie received any preferential treatment by Wilson's Raiders or that his property was spared by the foragers. Abercrombie owned a large plantation in Russell County, Alabama, and probably another residence on the Georgia side of the Chattahoochee. His son-in-law owned a home in the Columbus suburb of Wynnton, which is where the general died in 1867. The account presented in the text may have occurred at this latter place rather than at the general's own home. Mary F. Abercrombie, the general's daughter, married Confederate General Samuel French in 1865. Graf and Haskins, "Winter and Secession," 399; Graf and Haskins, "Winter and the Restoration of the Union," 51–57.

7. Lillian D. Champion, "Union Troops Raided Harris in Spring of 1865 Entering Homes and Taking Food, Livestock," *Columbus Ledger-Enquirer Civil War Centennial Edition,* 16 April 1961, 3; "A Lost Violin," *Columbus Ledger,* 24 April 1900, 8.

8. Elliott, *Doctor Quintard,* 257; Noll, *Doctor Quintard,* chapter 13; Worsley, *Columbus on the Chattahoochee,* 199; Oscar S. Straus, *Under Four Administrations* (Boston: Houghton Mifflin, 1922), 19; Marcus, *Memoirs of American Jews,* 300.

9. "Aunt Fannie Dies at Well Past 100," *Columbus Ledger,* 8 February 1958; F. A. Ellison, Letter, p. 5, ADAH Public Info Subject Files, Russell County, Hurtsboro, SG 6923, ADAH.

10. *OR,* 49, pt. 2:818–19; J. H. Wilson, *Under the Old Flag,* 295; Carpenter, Diary, 10 and 24 April 1865.

11. J. H. Wilson, *Under the Old Flag,* 295; *OR,* 49, pt. 2:818–19; McGee, *History of the 72nd Indiana,* 577, 579, 582; *American Slave,* 12, pt. 1:74; ibid., 12, pt. 1:133; Carpenter, Diary, 17 April 1865; Hinrichs, Diary, 17 April 1865; Wilson, Diary, 17 April 1865.

12. McGee, *History of the 72nd Indiana,* 579–82; Griest, Diary, 18 April 1865; Lucy Banks to unknown party, 23 April 1865, Banks Family Papers 1865, MS 1571, box 2, folder 6, HRBML; Carpenter, Diary, 24 April 1865.

13. Hinrichs, Diary, 17 April 1865.

14. *OR,* 49, pt. 1:487; Barker, "William H. Barker," 145; Wilson, Diary, 17 April 1865.

15. Conzett, "My Civil War," 73; *American Slave,* 12, pt. 1:1–3, 315.

16. Elliott, *Doctor Quintard,* 257.

17. French, *Two Wars,* 308.

18. Worsley, *Columbus on the Chattahoochee,* 297.

19. *American Slave,* 12, pt. 1:46.

20. *Born in Slavery,* 4, pt. 2:2, 17–18.

21. Ibid., 4, pt. 4:126.

22. *OR,* 49, pt. 1:494; Simeon Veatch, Diary, 17 April 1865, Pomona Public Library, Pomona, California; Noble, Diary, 17 April 1865. Wilson's Raiders, as well as the Confederates and civilians of this period, refer to the destruction of "private property" mainly as it relates to the burning of private homes. This unusual understanding of what constitutes private property was also noted by Columbus historian Stewart C. Edwards in "River City at War: Columbus, Georgia in the Confederacy" (Ph.D. diss., Florida State University, 1998). Though Wilson's Raiders might destroy the smokehouse and other outbuildings, ransack the house, and steal valuables and supplies, unless the actual residential dwelling had been burned, it was generally acknowledged by military and even many civilian authorities, that no "private property" had been destroyed. Edwards, "River City at War," 281–83.

23. *Confederate Reminiscences and Letters,* 15:112–13.

24. Noble, Diary, 17 April 1865; Veatch, Diary, 17 April 1865.

25. Gray, Diary, 17 April 1865; Veatch, Diary, 17 April 1865.

26. Noble, Diary, 17 April 1865; Lucy Banks to unknown party, 23 April 1865; Telfair, *History of Columbus,* 138; *American Slave,* 12, pt. 1:316.

27. Banks, "A Short Biographical Sketch," 36; Lucy Banks to unknown party, 23 April 1865.

28. Banks, "A Short Biographical Sketch," 1–38.

29. Tom Sellers, "Cruel Conflict Crushes Valley, But Brings Glory," *Columbus Ledger-Enquirer Civil War Centennial Edition,* 16 April 1961, 2.

30. Elliott, *Doctor Quintard*, 254–57; Noll, *Doctor Quintard*, 140.

31. Elliott, *Doctor Quintard*, 254–57; Noll, *Doctor Quintard*, 140–44.

32. *American Slave*, 12, pt. 1:143–44.

33. Prescott, Memoirs, 2:1.

34. Ibid.; Telfair, *History of Columbus*, 138–39; Walker, *Russell County in Retrospect*, 250–52; *American Slave*, 12, pt. 1:143–44, 315–16; ibid., 12, pt. 2:669; Worsley, *Columbus on the Chattahoochee*, 296–97; L. G. Jones, "Some Reminiscences."

35. Telfair, *History of Columbus*, 138–39.

36. Ibid., 138.

37. Ibid.; L. G. Jones, "Some Reminiscences."

38. *American Slave*, 12, pt. 2:498.

39. Hinrichs, Diary, 17 April 1865.

40. McGee, *History of the 72nd Indiana*, 582.

41. Gilpin recorded his story about the church organ in his wartime diary and again in his postwar published memoirs. Many discrepancies exist between the two accounts, and it appears that the published version was extensively edited. In the diary the date given is 17 April, at Columbus, but in the edited version it has been moved to 13 April. It is my belief, having reviewed both versions, that the event occurred at Columbus on 17 April. Gilpin, "Diary of 'The Last Campaign,'" 17 April 1865; Gilpin, *Last Campaign*, 13 April 1865.

42. McGee, *History of the 72nd Indiana*, 582–83.

43. *OR*, 49, pt. 1:495; Hinrichs, Diary, 17 April 1865; Leach, Diary, 18 April 1865.

44. Annie —— to G. B. Lamar, 1 May 1865, Letters: April–August 1865, Lamar Papers, MS 10, box 1, folder 11, HRBML; "Memorial Day at Savannah, Ga.," 130–31; Mary J. Galer, *Columbus, Georgia: Lists of People in Town 1828–1852 and Sexton's Reports to 1866* (Athens, Ga.: Iberian Publishing Company, 2000), 253; Jane Gullatt, *Phenix City, Alabama: American Revolution Bi-centennial, 1776–1976* (Phenix City, Ala.: Jane Gullatt Publisher, 1976); cemetery investigation conducted by Charles Misulia; Jane Gullatt, "Several Flourishing Russell Communities Stripped of Manpower," *Columbus Ledger-Enquirer Civil War Centennial Edition*, 16 April 1961, 18; Linda J. Kennedy, interview and site observation conducted at Linwood Cemetery, spring 2004; Hinrichs, Diary, 17 April 1865; George Kryder, Diary, 17 April 1865, MS 163, Center for Archival Collections, Bowling Green State University, Bowling Green, Ohio.

45. Hinrichs, Diary, 17 April 1865.

46. "Post Register"; *Confederate Reminiscences and Letters*, 3:137; Telfair, *History of Columbus*, 140; H. S. Wilson, *Confederate Industry*, 222; Pendergrast, *For God, Country, and Coca-Cola*, 21; Morse, *Personal Experiences*, 140–41; Vanorsdol, *Four Years for the Union*, 75; Bereman, Diary, 16 April 1865; Howard, Diary, 17 April 1865.

47. *Confederate Reminiscences and Letters*, 3:137; Telfair, *History of Columbus*, 140; F. A. Montgomery, *Reminiscences*, 253–54; William H. Hardie Jr., "Brothers in Arms: The Hardie Family in the Civil War," available at www.thornhill.org/bia/index.html; Carpenter, Diary, 14 April 1865.

48. F. A. Montgomery, *Reminiscences*, 253–54.

49. *Confederate Reminiscences and Letters,* 3:137; Telfair, *History of Columbus,* 140.

50. L. G. Jones, "Some Reminiscences."

51. Telfair, *History of Columbus,* 137–38.

52. Gullatt, "Small, but Well Armed," 9; Gullatt, *Phenix City,* 3.

53. French, *Two Wars,* 305–7.

54. Ellis, *The Moving Appeal,* 8–356; J. H. Wilson, *Under the Old Flag,* 268–69; St. John Waddell, *The Commercial Appeal* (Memphis: Memphis Publishing Co., 1965), 1–43.

55. Ellis, *The Moving Appeal,* 342–56; Noble, Diary, 16 April 1865; J. H. Wilson, *Under the Old Flag,* 268–69; W. F. Scott, *Story of a Cavalry Regiment,* 502–3; Waddell, *The Commercial Appeal,* 40. At least one account credits Dill's capture to Colonel Robert Minty, commander of the Cavalry Corps' 2nd Division, and suggests that Minty sought out the paper in revenge for some bad press he had received earlier in the war. This, however, I am disinclined to believe. Not only is every other account of Dill's capture attributed to Colonel Noble, but Noble describes Dill's capture in his personal diary. For this reason I credit Noble with the capture. Ellis, *The Moving Appeal,* 342–56; Noble, Diary, 16 April 1865; J. H. Wilson, *Under the Old Flag,* 268–69; W. F. Scott, *Story of a Cavalry Regiment,* 502–3; Waddell, *The Commercial Appeal,* 40.

56. W. F. Scott, *Story of a Cavalry Regiment,* 502–3; J. H. Wilson, *Under the Old Flag,* 268–69; Waddell, *The Commercial Appeal,* 41.

57. Noble, Diary, 17 April 1865; Waddell, *The Commercial Appeal,* 40–43.

58. W. C. Woodall, "More Detailed Credit for General," *Columbus Ledger,* 30 January 1966; J. P. Jones, *Yankee Blitzkrieg,* 141; Lupold and French, *Bridging Deep South Rivers,* 178; Telfair, *History of Columbus,* 141; Sowell, 9.

59. Gullatt, "Henderson Tells of Final Conflict," 6; Grant, "Recollections of the Last Battle," 164.

60. E. F. Andrews, *War-Time Journal,* 145–47.

61. Cumming, *Journal of Hospital Life,* 175; E. F. Andrews, *War-Time Journal,* 153.

62. Cumming, *Journal of Hospital Life,* 175; E. F. Andrews, *War-Time Journal,* 150.

63. Cobb, Special Orders, 111–15; Spencer B. King Jr., *April in Macon* (Athens: University of Georgia), 150; E. F. Andrews, *War-Time Journal,* 154.

64. *OR,* 49, pt. 2:344, 383; J. H. Wilson, *Under the Old Flag,* 254.

65. J. H. Wilson, *Under the Old Flag,* 270–71; *OR,* 49, pt. 2:379; Crofts, *History of the Third Ohio,* 199; McGee, *History of the 72nd Indiana,* 583.

66. Crofts, *History of the Third Ohio,* 199; Kryder, Diary, 17 April 1865; E. D. Stoltz, ed., *The Civil War Diary of Daniel J. Prickitt, 1861–1865* (Archbold, Ohio: E. D. Stoltz, 1988), 17 April 1865; Isaac Skillman, Diary, 17 April 1865, Diary and Papers, MS 1083, Center for Archival Collections, Bowling Green State University, Bowling Green, Ohio; McGee, *History of the 72nd Indiana,* 583; *OR,* 49, pt. 2:383; Carpenter, Diary, 17 April 1865; Potter, Diary, 17 April 1865.

67. *OR,* 49, pt. 2:367, 379; J. P. Jones, *Yankee Blitzkrieg,* 121–25; Winkler, Diary, 16 April 1865; J. H. Wilson, *Under the Old Flag,* 275.

68. *OR,* 49, pt. 2:379.

69. Ibid., pt. 1:487; Woodall, "More Detailed Credit for General"; Martin J. Crawford to A. H. Stephens, 6 October 1865, Alexander H. Stephens Papers, MS 94, Emory Manuscript, Archives, and Rare Book Library, Emory University, Atlanta; *Confederate Reminiscences and Letters,* 15:112–13.

70. Conzett, "My Civil War," 74.

71. It is possible, though not known for certain, that the tenements described as being destroyed by the ignition of the cloth warehouses in Conzett's memoirs could have been located along Bridge Street. Woodall, "More Detailed Credit for General"; Conzett, "My Civil War," 74.

72. Winslow, "Columbus, the Final Battle," 19–20.

73. Noble, Diary, 17 April 1865; Gray, Diary, 17 April 1865; Winslow, "Columbus, the Final Battle," 20.

74. Hinrichs, Diary, 17 April 1865; Veatch, Diary, 17 April 1865; Hobson, Diary, 17 April 1865; Mitchell, Memoirs, 17 April 1865.

75. Mitchell, Memoirs, 17 April 1865; Beers, *Memories,* 12; George B. Douglas to Samuel Stout, 30 April 1865, Stout Papers, SHC.

76. Winslow, "Columbus, the Final Battle," 20; Latta, "Pennsylvania in the War"; Hinrichs, Diary, 17 April 1865; Elliott, *Doctor Quintard,* 257; Bereman, Diary, 18 April 1865.

77. Winslow, "Columbus, the Final Battle," 20; Lucy Banks to unknown party, 23 April 1865.

78. W. F. Scott, *Story of a Cavalry Regiment,* 503; Winslow, "Columbus, the Final Battle," 20.

Chapter 17

1. Latta, "Pennsylvania in the War."

2. *OR,* 49, pt. 1:475, 485–87; J. H. Wilson, *Under the Old Flag,* 266.

3. *OR,* 49, pt. 1:495; Leach, Diary, 18 April 1865; "Journal of a Trip through Parts of Kentucky, Tennessee, and Georgia Made to Locate the Scattered Graves of Union Soldiers," Record of Burials of Federal Soldiers Prior to Removal to National Cemeteries, RG 92, Entry 685, Record Book (No. 2) 34, 225–28, NARA.

4. Galer, *Columbus, Georgia,* 253; Jim Miles, *Civil War Sites in Georgia* (Nashville: Rutledge Hill Press, 1996), 128–29; Sid Thomas, "Pioneers, Indians, Dixie Soldiers Rest in Forgotten Hilltop Cemetery," *Columbus Ledger-Enquirer,* 4 February 1955; Land, "Chronology of Clapp's Factory," 1–5; Buster W. Wright, "Clapp Cemetery Burials: Abstracted from Newspaper Obituaries, Newspaper Articles, Funeral Records, &c.—Supplemented from Additional Sources," Clapp Cemetery Preservation Group, courtesy John Land, McKinney, Texas, 1–8. Though the sexton's reports of burials after the battle mention only those Confederates killed on the Columbus side of the Chattahoochee as being buried in Linwood Cemetery, I believe that at least a portion of the soldiers buried in Linwood bearing the inscription "Unknown C.S.A." with no unit or death date are casualties from the battle.

The Clapp's Factory Cemetery originally encompassed approximately five acres of land on the banks of the Chattahoochee near the present-day Lake Oliver Dam. Unfortunately, no accurate survey of the site, which fell out of use in the early twentieth century, has survived. Eventually, the site was forgotten and later used as a dump for "old shingles, asphalt, appliances, and other rubbish." It may even have been scraped over with equipment at some point, obliterating any markers or distinguishing features that might have escaped the work of time and neglect. Today, while the nonprofit Clapp Cemetery Preservation Group has begun raising funds and awareness of the cemetery, it is unclear if there is anything left to save. With no physical way to confirm the burial of some twenty Confederate soldiers supposedly killed during the battle and buried at the site, I have had to rely on what fragmentary information has been collected by the members of the preservation group and a few brief mentions in the local newspapers.

Questions also surround why Confederate dead from the battle might have been buried at the Clapp's Factory Cemetery rather than Linwood Cemetery. The answer may lay in the burial options available to the townsfolk, which were (1) to bury the bodies where they fell; (2) to transport the bodies via canoe or flatboat over the Chattahoochee near Columbus, from which point the days-old bodies would need to be carted through the central section of the city to Linwood Cemetery; or (3) to haul the bodies north of town to where the two-part Clapp's Factory Bridge, which connected midstream with an island, was only partly destroyed, and where immediately upon the bridge's eastern terminus lay the Clapp's Factory Cemetery. It is not hard to see how the latter option might have been the more attractive. Galer, *Columbus, Georgia,* 253; Jim Miles, *Civil War Sites in Georgia* (Nashville: Rutledge Hill Press, 1996), 128–29; Sid Thomas, "Pioneers, Indians, Dixie Soldiers Rest in Forgotten Hilltop Cemetery," *Columbus Ledger-Enquirer,* 4 February 1955; Land, "Chronology of Clapp's Factory," 1–5; Buster W. Wright, "Clapp Cemetery Burials: Abstracted from Newspaper Obituaries, Newspaper Articles, Funeral Records, &c.—Supplemented from Additional Sources," Clapp Cemetery Preservation Group, courtesy John Land, McKinney, Texas, 1–8.

5. Rankin, *History of the Seventh Ohio,* 28.

6. *OR,* 49, pt. 1:487; Christy, Diary, 17 April 1865; Veatch, Diary, 18 April 1865.

7. Debate remains over whether Federal soldiers dumped the *Red Jacket* into the river after the capture of Columbus or whether Confederates ran it into the river prior to the city's capture to keep it out of enemy hands. Nothing conclusive, however, has yet been established so far as I am aware. The *Red Jacket* is on display today inside the Columbus Iron Works Convention and Trade Center. Unfortunately, the *Red Jacket* was exploded by pranksters attempting to fire it some years ago and has been pieced back together. A replica of the historic piece may, however, be viewed outside the Cannon Brew-Pub in downtown Columbus. Paul Miles, "Red Jacket Cannon Famed Relic," *Columbus Ledger-Enquirer Civil War Centennial Edition,* 16 April 1961, 46; L. G. Jones, "Some Reminiscences"; J. Miles, *Civil War Sites in Georgia,* 129–30; Jordan Vocational High School, "The Meaning of the Red Jacket," available at www.jordanhs.com/main_history.htm.

8. *OR,* 49, pt. 1:487; Winslow, "Columbus, the Final Battle," 23.

9. *OR,* 49, pt. 1:408.

10. Winslow, "Columbus, the Final Battle," 20; Mitchell, Memoirs, 18 April 1865.

11. Wilson, Diary, 18 April 1865; Hinrichs, Diary, 18 April 1865; *OR,* 49, pt. 1:408; Hobson, Diary, 18 April 1865.

12. Turner, *Navy Gray,* 234, 242–45; Calle, "True and Accurate Account," 1–7; Carnes, Memoirs, 205.

13. *OR,* 49, pt. 2:379; Worsley, *Columbus on the Chattahoochee,* 300; Swift, *Last Battle,* 28.

14. Telfair, *History of Columbus,* 141; French, *Two Wars,* 307; J. P. Jones, *Yankee Blitzkrieg,* 143; David E. Patterson, "'Wilson's Raid' Brought Civil War to Upson," *Thomaston Times,* 15 April 1992.

15. Hinrichs, Diary, 18 April 1865; Elliott, *Doctor Quintard,* 257.

16. Telfair, *History of Columbus,* 141; Clason Kyle, "Under the Old Flag: From Selma to Peking," *Columbus Ledger-Enquirer,* 11 April 1965.

17. Bereman, Diary, 18 April 1865.

18. Ibid.; Vanorsdol, *Four Years for the Union,* 67, 75, 78–79.

19. Gray, Diary, 18 April 1865; Veatch, Diary, 18 April 1865; Winslow, "Columbus, the Final Battle," 22.

20. Winslow, "Columbus, the Final Battle," 22; Bereman, Diary, 18 April 1865; Noll, *Doctor Quintard,* chapter 13; *Macon Telegraph and Confederate,* 19 April 1865; Giles, "Union Diary Records Capture," 6.

21. Henry Boutell, Civil War Diary, 18 April 1865, Emory Manuscript, Archives, and Rare Book Library, Emory University, Atlanta.

22. *Confederate Reminiscences and Letters,* 3:137; J. H. Wilson, *Under the Old Flag,* 247–48.

23. Telfair, *History of Columbus,* 139.

24. McGee, *History of the 72nd Indiana,* 579; Mitchell, Memoirs, 18 April 1865.

25. Mitchell, Memoirs, 18 April 1865.

26. French, *Two Wars,* 306–8; Telfair, *History of Columbus,* 141–42; "Cotton Bale Hides Bodies of 2 Yankees," *Columbus Ledger-Enquirer Civil War Centennial Edition,* 16 April 1961, 26.

27. Telfair, *History of Columbus,* 141–42.

28. Ibid., 142; Benton, 14 April 1925.

29. "Cotton Bale Hides Bodies," 26.

30. *OR,* 49, pt. 2:383; Winslow, "Columbus, the Final Battle," 21–23; W. F. Scott, *Story of a Cavalry Regiment,* 500.

31. Winslow, "Columbus, the Final Battle," 22–23.

32. Howard, Diary, 18 April 1865.

33. Leon Von Zinken to Howell Cobb, Telegram Asking Permission to Leave His Post, 18 April 1865, Cobb Papers, MS 1376, box 70, folder 11, HRBML; John F. H. Claiborne, *A Sketch of Harvey's Scouts* (Starkville, Miss.: Southern Live-Stock Journal Print, 1885), 19–20, 60–62; A. O. Blackmar, 18 April 1865, Blackmar Files, National Civil War Naval Museum at Port Columbus, Columbus, Georgia.

34. Claiborne, *A Sketch of Harvey's Scouts,* 19–20, 60–62. Claiborne says that

Harvey was murdered in Columbus on 19 April, but this conflicts with statements that he was assisting Von Zinken in restoring order in the city during the rioting after the departure of Wilson's Raiders. The rioting, and the fact that Von Zinken telegraphed Cobb and left Columbus on 18 April, arriving in Macon on 20 April, seems to point to 18 April as the date Harvey was killed. The confusion may arise from Harvey's burial, which is likely to have occurred on 19 April. Claiborne, *A Sketch of Harvey's Scouts*, 60–62, 70–71.

35. Von Zinken to Howell Cobb, Telegram Asking Permission to Leave His Post, 18 April 1865, Cobb Papers, MS 1376, box 70, folder 11, HRBML; *Macon Telegraph and Confederate*, 20 April 1865; Abraham, Diary, 18 April 1865.

36. Abraham, Diary, 18 April 1865; McGee, *History of the 72nd Indiana*, 582. "I will also make it a possession for the bittern, and pools of water: and I will sweep it with the besom of destruction, saith the LORD of hosts" (Isaiah 14:23, King James).

Chapter 18

1. Crofts, *History of the Third Ohio*, 199–201; McGee, *History of the 72nd Indiana*, 584–94; Skillman, Diary, 18 April 1865; Kryder, Diary, 18 April 1865; David E. Patterson, "'Wilson's Raid' Brought Civil War to Upson," *Thomaston Times*, 15 April 1992; Carpenter, Diary, 17 April 1865; Potter, Diary, 19 April 1865.

2. E. F. Andrews, *War-Time Journal*, 144–55; *Macon Daily Telegraph and Confederate*, 18–20 April 1865; Cumming, *Journal of Hospital Life*, 175; Jackson, "Diary of War between the States," 9–10; Cobb, Special Orders, 111–18; Lupold and French, *Bridging Deep South Rivers*, 145–47; William G. Whitaker, "A Part of War and Prison Life of Private W. G. Whitaker Company H, Fourth Georgia Regiment," available at www.civilwarsutlery.com/diarytext.html.

3. E. F. Andrews, *War-Time Journal*, 154, 158; *Macon Daily Telegraph and Confederate*, 19 April 1865.

4. *Macon Daily Telegraph and Confederate*, 20 April 1865; *OR*, 49, pt. 1:365–68; J. H. Wilson, *Under the Old Flag*, 280–81.

5. McGee, *History of the 72nd Indiana*, 584–86; W. F. Scott, *Story of a Cavalry Regiment*, 504–11; Howell Cobb, Cobb's Account of His Surrender, Cobb-Erwin-Lamar Collection, MS 86, box 3, folder 12, HRBML; *OR*, 49, pt. 1:365.

6. Crofts, *History of the Third Ohio*, 200–201; McGee, *History of the 72nd Indiana*, 586–88; J. H. Wilson, *Under the Old Flag*, 276–78; *OR*, 49, pt. 1:365; W. F. Scott, *Story of a Cavalry Regiment*, 511–12.

7. J. H. Wilson, *Under the Old Flag*, 278–81; Crofts, *History of the Third Ohio*, 200–201; McGee, *History of the 72nd Indiana*, 586–88; *OR*, 49, pt. 1:366–68.

8. Morse, *Personal Experiences*, 143.

9. Giles, "Union Diary Records Capture," 6.

10. McGee, *History of the 72nd Indiana*, 586–94; W. F. Scott, *Story of a Cavalry Regiment*, 509–13.

11. W. F. Scott, *Story of a Cavalry Regiment*, 513.

12. Parthenia A. Hague, *A Blockaded Family: Life in Southern Alabama during the Civil War* (Boston: Houghton, Mifflin, 1888), 171.

13. Howard, Diary, 19 April 1865; Elliott, *Doctor Quintard*, 257; Noll, *Doctor Quintard*, chapter 13; Mary A. DeCredico, *Patriotism for Profit: Georgia's Urban Entrepreneurs and the Confederate War Effort* (Chapel Hill: University of North Carolina Press, 1990), 135; Dodd, "Randolph Lawler Mott," 58–62; Lupold and French, *Bridging Deep South Rivers*, 178.

14. DeCredico, *Patriotism for Profit*, 135; Howard, Diary, 19 April–1 May 1865; *Columbus Enquirer*, 26 April–6 June 1865; Luke Teasley, "Confederate Troops Moved by Railroads," *Columbus Ledger-Enquirer Civil War Centennial Edition*, 16 April 1961; *Macon Daily Telegraph*, 31 May 1865. One prominent chronicler of Civil War and early Reconstruction history wrote: "Indeed, Columbus's devastation surpassed that of Atlanta: not one factory, machine shop or mill was left standing, and all rail connections to northern Georgia and Alabama were destroyed. Residents and visitors alike were stunned by the universal desolation, and credit reporters, who returned to the city in 1866, could report nothing but 'burnt out' or 'destroyed during Wilson's Raid.'" This assessment is mostly correct, with the exception that in Columbus Wilson spared two gristmills, one of them owned by Colonel Mott. DeCredico, *Patriotism for Profit*, 135.

15. *OR*, 49, pt. 2:585; ibid., pt. 1:499; W. F. Scott, *Story of a Cavalry Regiment*, 491; Columbus City Council Records, 19 April 1865; Lupold and French, *Bridging Deep South Rivers*, 190; Hague, *A Blockaded Family*, 171–72; Laura Comer, Diary, 6 May 1865, Simon Schwob Memorial Library, CSUA; *Columbus Enquirer*, 26 April 1865; Claiborne, *A Sketch of Harvey's Scouts*, 60–62; Howard, Diary, 20 April 1865.

16. Telfair, *History of Columbus*, 142; Netty Sowell, "Local Sentiment after the Battle of Columbus," 1–9, Chappell File, Mahan Civil War Collection, Genealogy and Local History Department, CPL; *OR*, 49, pt. 2:598, 734; Worsley, *Columbus on the Chattahoochee*, 291; *Macon Telegraph and Confederate*, 14 April 1865; Willoughby, *Flowing through Time*, 99; *OR*, 49, pt. 1:485.

17. *Columbus Enquirer*, 9 June 1865; Standard, *Columbus, Georgia*, 47; Straus, *Under Four Administrations*, 19; Prescott, Memoirs, 1:83; Winslow, "Columbus, the Final Battle," 20–22.

18. *OR*, 49, pt. 2:468–69, 597; ibid., pt. 1:301–12, 571; Houghton and Houghton, *Two Boys in the Civil War*, 234–42; Telfair, *History of Columbus*, 142.

19. *American Slave*, 12, pt. 1:2; *Macon Daily Telegraph*, 31 May–June 1865; Worsley, *Columbus on the Chattahoochee*, 303–4; Telfair, *History of Columbus*, 144; *American Slave*, 12, pt. 2:659.

20. Hague, *A Blockaded Family*, 172–73; *Confederate Reminiscences and Letters*, 15:113; Worsley, *Columbus on the Chattahoochee*, 199; *OR*, 49, pt. 2:734, 891; Telfair, *History of Columbus*, 142.

21. *OR*, 49, pt. 2:461, 597, 600, 631.

22. J. H. Wilson, *Under the Old Flag*, 284–85; W. F. Scott, *Story of a Cavalry Regiment*, 532–33; *OR*, 49, pt. 2:600, 631; Howard, Diary, 6 May 1865.

23. *OR,* 49, pt. 1:301–12, 571; ibid., pt. 2:597, 631, 657, 734; *Columbus Enquirer,* 26 April 1865; Houghton and Houghton, *Two Boys in the Civil War,* 234–42.

24. *OR,* 49, pt. 2:597.

25. Ibid., 585, 651, 656–57; ibid., pt. 1:368–81; James P. Jones, "Your Left Arm: James H. Wilson's Letters to Adam Badeau," *Civil War History* 12 (September 1966): 242–45.

26. *OR,* 49, pt. 2:734, 764; Howard, Diary, 18 May 1865.

27. *Macon Daily Telegraph,* 31 May 1865; Telfair, *History of Columbus,* 142; *OR,* 49, pt. 1:415; ibid., pt. 2:891.

28. *OR,* 49, pt. 1:567–68; Telfair, *History of Columbus,* 142; *Macon Daily Telegraph,* 31 May–5 June 1865.

29. Howard, Diary, 23–25 May 1865; Turner, *Navy Gray,* 250.

30. *Macon Daily Telegraph,* 2–5 June 1865; Graf and Haskins, "Winter and the Restoration of the Union," 49–52; Olive H. Shadgett, "James Johnson, Provisional Governor of Georgia," *Georgia Historical Quarterly* 36, no. 1 (1952): 1–3.

31. *Macon Daily Telegraph,* 2–5 June 1865.

32. Ibid.

33. Shadgett, "James Johnson," 1–21; Alan Conway, *The Reconstruction of Georgia* (Minneapolis: University of Minnesota, 1966), 43–51.

34. Winslow, "Columbus, the Final Battle," 21.

35. Lupold and French, *Bridging Deep South Rivers,* 182–201; *Macon Daily Telegraph,* June 1865.

36. J. T. Towbridge, *A Picture of the Desolated States and the Work of Restoration. 1865–1868* (Hartford: L. Stebbins, 1868), 452; *Macon Daily Telegraph,* 12–13, 31 May 1865; *Columbus Enquirer,* 7 July 1865; DeCredico, *Patriotism for Profit,* 135; W. F. Scott, *Story of a Cavalry Regiment,* 534–37; "Georgia: Our Special Correspondent's Journey through the South," *New York World,* 18 July 1865.

37. DeCredico, *Patriotism for Profit,* 135; *Columbus Enquirer,* 5 June 1865; Worsley, *Columbus on the Chattahoochee,* 494–97; Emile D. Murphy, "Coca-Cola's Ghost" (1967), 10, courtesy Ben Salata, Historic Columbus Foundation, Columbus, Georgia.

38. Marcus, *Memoirs of American Jews,* 315–16; Straus, *Under Four Administrations,* 19–21. It has been claimed that the Straus family left Columbus after the war because of a wave of anti-Semitism and not for economic reasons, but the testimony of members of the Straus family does not bear this out. According to the family, the Strauses came to Columbus to escape some anti-Semitism that had taken hold in Talbotton, Georgia, during the war, and found Columbus to be both profitable and hospitable. It was only after the town was destroyed, along with the Straus's shop and much of their savings, that they decided to relocate. Marcus, *Memoirs of American Jews,* 315–16; Straus, *Under Four Administrations,* 19–21; Kent, *Temple Israel of Columbus,* 15–16.

39. Martin J. Crawford to A. H. Stephens, 6 October 1865, Alexander H. Stephens Papers, MS 94, Emory Manuscript, Archives, and Rare Book Library, Emory University, Atlanta; *Confederate Reminiscences and Letters,* 15:113.

40. Crawford to Stephens, 6 October 1865; Worsley, *Columbus on the Chattahoochee*, 298.

41. Banks, "A Short Biographical Sketch," 38.

42. Crawford to Stephens, 6 October 1865; "Georgia: Our Special Correspondent's Journey through the South"; *Macon Daily Telegraph*, 31 May–July 1865; *Columbus Enquirer*, 26 April 1865–17 April 1866; Sidney Andrews, *The South since the War: As Shown by Fourteen Weeks of Travel and Observation in Georgia and the Carolinas* (Boston: Ticknor & Fields, 1866), 377–82.

43. Telfair, *History of Columbus*, 144; *Columbus Enquirer*, 6 July 1865; Hague, *A Blockaded Family*, 170.

44. DeCredico, *Patriotism for Profit*, 135–41; J. H. Martin, *Columbus, Geo.*, 186–89; Lupold and French, *Bridging Deep South Rivers*, 182–88; Willoughby, *Flowing through Time*, 47–61, 100–101.

45. *Columbus Enquirer*, 26 April–August 1865; Turner, *Navy Gray*, 244; "Georgia: Our Special Correspondent's Journey through the South." After order was restored in Columbus during the latter part of May and the early part of June, the city experienced relative calm until about the first of August. A substantial part of the credit is due to the efforts of the men of Captain Lamson's detachment of troopers from the 17th Indiana. I find but a few exceptions to the overall praise of these troops in preserving the peace in the city.

The same cannot be said of the soldiers of the 151st Illinois Infantry, a one-year regiment that took over after the departure of Lamson and his men. Almost from the very arrival of these soldiers, there was trouble. Their service having begun just as the war was coming to a close, instead of the great adventures the enlistees of the 151st Illinois had hoped to embark on, they were assigned the intensely boring duty of patrolling Columbus's streets and neighborhoods. With too little to do and often too much to drink, these soldiers caused major disturbances within the city until their mustering out in January 1866.

Unfortunately for the people of Columbus and the detractors of the Illinois men, the next garrison would nearly cause outright riot. In February 1866 the 103rd United States Colored Troops, composed in large part of runaway slaves from South Carolina, took up patrolling Columbus's streets. Though white Columbusites certainly displayed hostility toward having black soldiers as occupiers, and this may have increased the tension between the parties, it seems also that the black regiment was poorly supervised and prone to provoking the white residents. Tensions exploded when a former Confederate partisan instigated a fight in which one of the black soldiers was wounded, and after which the soldiers retaliated by mortally wounding a civilian passing outside their barracks. After the incident, the black regiment was hurried off and replaced by a white garrison.

Beyond these troubles, Columbus would suffer after July 1865 through 1868 with turmoil between the local black population and other citizens, between the soldiers and blacks, and even between the soldiers and the public. Political and criminal violence, a wave of robberies and other illegal activity, and finally a sensational murder case (the Ashburn case) in 1868 that focused the spotlight of Reconstruction politics on Columbus would further mark the period.

Macon Daily Telegraph, 31 May–July 1865; Whiling H. Boyer, Letter from the Camp of the 151st Illinois Infantry, 12 August 1865, David DeWolf Papers, SC 1852, Abraham Lincoln Presidential Library, Springfield, Illinois; Yvonne Sampelayo, *The Civil War Diary of Clark Black* (n.p., 1974), 31 July–12 December 1865; *Montgomery Daily Advertiser,* 28 November, 16 February 1865; Conway, *The Reconstruction of Georgia,* 154–60; Worsley, *Columbus on the Chattahoochee,* 298–317; Faye L. Jensen, "Power and Progress in the Urban South: Columbus, Georgia, 1850–1885" (Ph.D. diss., Emory University, 1991), 120–45, available at www.military-historians.org/Journal/Confederate/confederate-1.htm; Thomas J. Peddy, comp., "Looking Back through the Files: News of the Sixties," excerpts from Columbus newspapers during the 1860s, 1 September 1865–17 April 1866, Genealogy and Local History Department, CPL; Houghton and Houghton, *Two Boys in the Civil War,* 54–56, 234–42; N. K. Rogers, *History of Chattahoochee County, Georgia* (Columbus, Ga.: Columbus Office Supply, 1933), "Fuller, Hiram 1798–1867," available at http://ftp.rootsweb .com/pub/usgenweb/ga/chattahoochee/bios/gbs586fuller.txt.

46. *Columbus Enquirer,* 2 June 1865.

47. Ibid., 5 June, 5 July 1865; *Macon Daily Telegraph,* 13 May 1865.

48. DeCredico, *Patriotism for Profit,* 135–41; Murphy, "Coca-Cola's Ghost," 10.

49. Dyer, *Compendium,* part 3, pp. 1102, 1125–26; Boyer, 12 August 1865; Sampelayo, *The Civil War Diary of Clark Black,* 26–31 July 1865; W. F. Scott, *Story of a Cavalry Regiment,* 500–548.

50. *OR,* 49, pt. 2:663; W. F. Scott, *Story of a Cavalry Regiment,* 518.

51. Michie, *Emory Upton,* xxv; W. F. Scott, *Story of a Cavalry Regiment,* 500–501.

52. Wilson, Diary, 16 April 1865; Michie, *Emory Upton,* 168; W. F. Scott, *Story of a Cavalry Regiment,* 543.

53. Noll, *Doctor Quintard,* chapters 13–14; Straus, *Under Four Administrations,* 19; *OR,* 49, pt. 2:1253; C. T. Martin, "Reminiscence of the War"; Russell County Historical Commission, *History of Russell County,* C-45–C-46; Telfair, *History of Columbus,* 131–54; Worsley, *Columbus on the Chattahoochee,* 292–99; Grant, "Recollections of the Last Battle," 164; *Columbus Daily Sun,* 15 April 1865.

54. Cobb, Special Orders, 94–96; Bragg, *Joe Brown's Army,* 109; Gullatt, "Henderson Tells of Final Conflict," 6.

55. William N. Parker to Nettie Bowles, 14 May 1865, Jennett Bowles Letters 1865–1868, SHSI-IC.

56. J. P. Jones, *Yankee Blitzkrieg,* 143–44; Standard, *Columbus, Georgia,* 59–62.

57. J. P. Jones "Your Left Arm," 233–41; Winslow, "Columbus, the Final Battle," 22; *Augusta Tri-Weekly Constitutionalist,* 23 April 1865; *Macon Daily Telegraph,* 18–20 April 1865; *New York World,* 25 April–24 July 1865; *New Orleans Picayune,* 23 April 1865; *New York Times,* 26 April 1865; *Atlanta Daily Intelligencer,* 28 April 1865.

58. The only contemporary newspaper account of the battle published outside Columbus that merits any mention was published in Macon on 18 April 1865. The account, no doubt assembled from what could be learned from soldiers who

had fled the fighting, was brief and only partially accurate. *Macon Daily Telegraph,* 18 April 1865.

59. Worsley, *Columbus on the Chattahoochee,* appendix D, 297; *Columbus Enquirer,* 26 April 1865; J. H. Martin, *Columbus, Geo.,* 178–91.

60. W. C. Woodall, "The Battle of Columbus, Georgia," 1, Chappell File, Mahan Civil War Collection, Genealogy and Local History Department, CPL.

61. J. H. Wilson, *Under the Old Flag,* 258–71; Swift, *Last Battle,* 1–32; "Sunset Wednesday: Program of Exercises Arranged for the Ceremonies at Fourteenth Street at 'The Confederate Bridge,'" and "Bronze Tablets Are Unveiled," clippings, 1922, Chappell File, Mahan Civil War Collection, Genealogy and Local History Department, CPL; Theodore F. Allen, "Last Battle of the Civil War," *Journal of the United States Cavalry Association* 13 (April 1908): 785–86; Arno B. Cammerer to Bryant Castellow, 14 May 1934, Alva C. Smith Collection, Simon Schwob Memorial Library, CSUA; "Columbus: Was It the Last Battle of the Civil War?" 1–47, Alva C. Smith Collection; papers related to the Battle for Columbus, Alva C. Smith Collection; U.S. Congress, House, 1935, *Authorizing Erection of Marker at Site of Engagement Fought at Columbus, GA., April 16, 1865,* 74th Cong., 1st sess. H.R. 1890; U.S. Congress, Senate, 1936, *Authorizing Erection of Marker at Site of Engagement Fought at Columbus, GA., April 16, 1865,* 74th Cong. 2nd sess. S.R. 1663.

62. Peddy, "Looking Back through the Files," 14 September 1865, 1 and 3 November 1865, 23 February 1866.

63. Grant, "Recollections of the Last Battle," 164; W. F. Scott, *Story of a Cavalry Regiment,* 542.

Appendix 1

1. Arno B. Cammerer to Bryant Castellow, 14 May 1934, Alva C. Smith Collection; "Columbus: Was It the Last Battle of the Civil War?" Alva C. Smith Collection; U.S. Congress, House, 1935, *Authorizing Erection of Marker at Site of Engagement Fought at Columbus, GA., April 16, 1865,* 74th Cong., 1st sess. H.R. 1890; U.S. Congress, Senate, 1936, *Authorizing Erection of Marker at Site of Engagement Fought at Columbus, GA., April 16, 1865,* 74th Cong. 2nd sess., S.R. 1663.

2. H. L. Scott, *Military Dictionary,* 84–86, 396–401, 562; Carl Von Clausewitz, *On War: The Complete Translation by Colonel J. J. Graham* (London: N. Trubner, 1873); Edward Luttwak and Stuart Koehl, *The Dictionary of Modern War* (New York: Harper Collins, 1991), 81; Jay M. Shafritz, Todd J. A. Shafritz, and David B. Robertson, *The Facts on File Dictionary of Military Science* (New York: Facts on File, 1989), 3, 37–38, 41, 55, 92, 128, 164, 421; Trevor N. Dupuy, Curt Johnson, and Grace P. Hayes, *Dictionary of Military Terms: A Guide to the Language of Warfare and Military Institutions* (New York: H. W. Wilson, 1986), 2, 27, 42, 57–58, 82, 163, 201; John E. Jessup and Louise B. Ketz, *Encyclopedia of the American Military: Studies of the History, Traditions, Policies, Institutions, and Roles of the Armed Forces in War and Peace* (New York: Scribner and Maxwell Macmillan International, 1994), 1201–1219; Samuel Pufendorf, *De Jure Naturae Et Gentium Libri Octo: The Transla-*

tion of the Edition of 1688 by C. H. Oldfather and W. A. Oldfather (Oxford: Clarendon Press and Humphrey Milford, 1934), 1326–28.

3. *OR,* 49, pt. 1:173–259; Heritage Preservation Services, "CWSAC: Battle Summaries, Fort Blakely," available at http://www.cr.nps.gov/hps/abpp/battles/al006.htm; "Fort Blakely," available at http://ehistory.osu.edu/uscw/features/battles/states/alabama/0007.cfm.

4. The class designations used by the Advisory Commission correspond with the degree to which a combat had an impact upon the progress of the war. The sites are ranked A through D, with A listed as "having a decisive influence on a campaign and a direct impact on the course of the war" to D which had "a limited influence on the outcome of their campaign or operation but achieving or affecting important local objectives." Staff of the Civil War Sites Advisory Commission, "Civil War Sites Advisory Commission Report on the Nation's Civil War Battlefields," Profile of Principle Civil War Battlefields, Civil War Battlefields in Each State, Battle Summaries: Fort Blakely, 1993, Civil War Sites Advisory Commission, Washington, D.C., available at www.cr.nps.gov/hps/abpp/cwsac/cws0-1.html.

5. "Columbus: Was It the Last Battle of the Civil War?"

6. Hoole, *History of the Seventh Alabama,* 16–17; Herman, *Memoirs,* chapter 28; W. J. Slatter, "Last Battle of the War," *Confederate Veteran Magazine* 4 (1896): 381–82; Crofts, *History of the Third Ohio,* 198; Alan J. Pitts, "Last Battle of the War, or Last East of the Mississippi?" posting at http://history-sites.com/alcwmb/old-archive/archivefiles/3206.html; Jim Huffman, "10th Regiment, Mississippi Cavalry (aka 12th Battalion, Mississippi Cavalry (excerpt from *A Military History of Mississippi, 1803–1898* by Dunbar Rowland)," 26 March 2000, www.ebicom.net/~moorer/scripts/wwwboard/messages/638.html accessed 25 November 2006; Winkler, Diary, 16 April 1865; R. J. Reid, *Fourth Indiana Cavalry Regiment,* 189–91; W. F. Scott, *Story of a Cavalry Regiment,* 477–82; J. P. Jones, *Yankee Blitzkrieg,* 121–25; Keenan, *Wilson's Cavalry Corps,* 190–94.

7. W. F. Scott, *Story of a Cavalry Regiment,* 479–82; J. P. Jones, *Yankee Blitzkrieg,* 121–24; *OR,* 49, pt. 1:340, 364–65, 384, 386, 408, 428–437; Dyer, *Compendium,* pt. 2, p. 723; Herman, *Memoirs,* chapter 28; Slatter, "Last Battle of the War," 381–82; Keenan, *Wilson's Cavalry Corps,* 190–94; Winkler, Diary, 16 April 1865; R. J. Reid, *Fourth Indiana Cavalry Regiment,* 189–91; Ambrose, *Wisconsin Boy in Dixie,* 155–56; Nathaniel S. Robinson, Diary, 16 April 1865, Surgeon's Diary, March 22–April 22, 1865, Civil War Times Collection, USAMHI.

8. *OR,* 49, pt. 1:340.

9. "Columbus: Was It the Last Battle of the Civil War?"

10. Dupuy, Johnson, and Hayes, *Dictionary of Military Terms,* 42.

11. Lupold and French, *Bridging Deep South Rivers,* 176–81; "Columbus: Was It the Last Battle of the Civil War?"

12. "Columbus: Was It the Last Battle of the Civil War?"

13. Ibid.

14. Dupuy, Johnson, and Hayes, *Dictionary of Military Terms,* 58.

15. Allen, "Last Battle," 785–86; *OR*, 49, pt. 1:340.

16. There is some disagreement as to whether Hill's Confederates had one or two cannons at Munford's Station. Most accounts tend to suggest only one, which was captured. *OR*, 49, pt. 1:340, 368, 387, 418, 423; W. F. Scott, *Story of a Cavalry Regiment*, 516; Marshall P. Thatcher, *A Hundred Battles in the West: St. Louis to Atlanta, 1861–1865—The Second Michigan Cavalry* (Detroit: Marshall Thatcher Publisher, 1884), 242–43; Mead, *Eighth Iowa Cavalry*, 42, 99; J. P. Jones, *Yankee Blitzkrieg*, 158; Keenan, *Wilson's Cavalry Corps*, 209; "Last Battle East of the Mississipi?"; Scott Owens, "The Last Battle," posting at http://history-sites.com/mb/cw/alcwmb/index.cgi?noframes;read=2381518; Clement A. Evans, "Brigadier General Benjamin J. Hill, P.A.C.S.," originally from Clement Evans, *Confederate Military History*, vol. 12 (Atlanta: Confederate Publishing Co., 1899), 146–47, available at http://members.aol.com/jweaver303/tn/hillbj.htm; E. Grace Jemison, *Historic Tales of Talladega* (Montgomery, Ala.: Paragon Press, 1959).

17. W. F. Scott, *Story of a Cavalry Regiment*, 516; *OR*, 49, pt. 1:368, 387; Thatcher, *A Hundred Battles in the West*, 242–43.

18. The combat referred to is known both as the Battle of Palmetto and as the Battle of Palmito Ranch. Jeffrey Wm Hunt, *The Last Battle of the Civil War: Palmetto Ranch* (Austin: University of Texas, 2002), 1–69; Phillip T. Tucker, *The Final Fury: Palmito Ranch, The Last Battle of the Civil War* (Mechanicsburg, Pa.: Stackpole, 2001), 1–90.

19. Hunt, *Last Battle*, 68–72; Tucker, *The Final Fury*, 88–90.

20. Hunt, *Last Battle*, 80–150; Tucker, *The Final Fury*, 110–63.

21. Hunt, *Last Battle*, 173.

Appendix 4

1. Galer, *Columbus, Georgia*, 253; United States, Register of Burials at Andersonville National Cemetery, Andersonville National Historical Site, Andersonville, Georgia; Hewett, *Supplement*, part 1, series 31, vol. 19, pp. 201–317; ibid., part 2, series 41, vol. 29, p. 831; ibid., part 2, series 47, vol. 35, p. 625; Hobson, Diary, 16 April 1865.

2. Leach, Diary, 18 April 1865; *OR*, 49, pt. 1:493; United States, Register of Burials; John W. Noble, "Exhibit of 3rd Iowa Cavalry, Veteran Volunteers, to Accompany Special Report at Macon, Ga., April 28th, 1865," Adjutant General's Files, SHSI-DM; "Post Register"; Peters, "Report of Operations," 16–17; W. F. Scott, *Story of a Cavalry Regiment*, 499; Graham, Diary, 16 April 1865; Winslow, "Columbus, the Final Battle," 9; Len Eagleburger, *The Fighting 10th: The History of the 10th Missouri Cavalry US* (Bloomington, Ind.: 1st Books Library, 2004), 471–77; Hinrichs, Diary, 16 April 1865; J. F. Weaver, "Inventory of Effects and Final Statement of Pvt. Richard Porter, Company I, 5th Iowa Cavalry," 22 June 1865, Adjutant-General's Records, SHSI-DM; "Benton County in the Civil War," Richard Porter Death Record, available at www.rootsweb.com/~iabenton/civil_war/5th_cav.htm; Jim Martin, "Civil War Message Board Portal, Ohio Forum," available at http://

history-sites.net/mb/cw/ohcwmb/index.cgi?read=213 accessed 4 May 2006; Historical Data Systems, Inc., "Official Roster of the Soldiers of the State of Ohio &
Roll of Honor of Ohio Soldiers," 7th Ohio Cavalry Casualty Information, www
.civilwardata.com; Galer, *Columbus, Georgia,* 253; on-site research and interview
conducted by Charles Misulia with Alan Marsh, cultural resources program manager, 3 May 2006, Andersonville National Historic Site.

    3. Leach, Diary, 18 April 1865; *OR,* 49, pt. 1:476, 493; United States, Register
of Burials; site investigation by Charles Misulia; Noble, "Exhibit of 3rd Iowa Cavalry"; "Post Register"; Peters, "Report of Operations," 16–17; W. F. Scott, *Story
of a Cavalry Regiment,* 499, 574; Graham, Diary, 16 April 1865; Winslow, "Columbus, the Final Battle," 9, 13; Eagleburger, *The Fighting 10th,* 321, 393, 438, 463,
471–77; Hinrichs, Diary, 16 April 1865; Weaver, "Inventory of Effects"; "Benton
County in the Civil War"; Jim Martin, "Civil War Message Board Portal, Ohio
Forum"; Historical Data Systems, Inc., "Official Roster of the Soldiers of the State
of Ohio & Roll of Honor of Ohio Soldiers," 7th Ohio Cavalry Casualty Information, www.civilwardata.com; Galer, *Columbus, Georgia,* 253; Marsh interview;
Hewett, *Supplement,* part 1, series 31, vol. 19, p. 249; Franz Arnim, Return of Cap-
tain Franz Arnim, Company I, 3rd Iowa Cavalry, April 1865, Adjutant General's
Files, SHSI-DM; Johnson, "Andrew Tibbets," Iowa Battle Flag Project, SHSI-DM;
John H. Peters, Draft of Report of April 22, 1865, p. 2, Adjutant General's Files,
SHSI-DM; Curry, *Four Years in the Saddle,* Appendix: Roster of 1st Ohio Cavalry,
15, 32; "Union County, Ohio—1883 History—Military Record," Corp. William
Griffith information, available at www.heritagepursuit.com/Union/Unrosta.htm;
Historical Data Systems, Inc., "Official Roster of the Soldiers of the State of
Ohio & The Medical and Surgical History of the Civil War," 1st Ohio Cavalry,
www.civilwardata.com; Jim Martin, "Civil War Message Board Portal, Artillery
Forum," 4th US Light Artillery, Battery I, available at http://history-sites.net/mb/
cw/cwartmb/index.cgi?read=460; Historical Data Systems, Inc., "Index to Com-
piled Service Records & The Medical and Surgical History of the Civil War," 4th
US Light Artillery, Battery I, www.civilwardata.com.

    4. J. H. Martin, *Columbus, Geo.,* 13, 180; C. T. Martin, "Reminiscence of the
War"; "Frankies Confederate Monuments and Memorials of the South," avail-
able at www.geocities.com/Heartland/Pines/3093/pages2.html; Telfair, *History of
Columbus,* 136–37; Louise J. DuBose, "Women in Columbus, 1828–1928," Louise
Jones DuBose Papers, Simon Schwob Memorial Library, CSUA; Galer, *Colum-
bus, Georgia,* 253; Curry, *Four Years in the Saddle,* 224; Marc Willis, "6th Alabama
Company H Roster," information on Washington Kirkland, available at http://
home.att.net/~al_6th_inf/roster/h.htm; Kennedy interview, 2005; Gullatt, *Phenix
City,* 3; Sid Thomas, "Pioneers, Indians, Dixie Soldiers Rest in Forgotten Hill-
top Cemetery," *Columbus Ledger-Enquirer,* 4 February 1955; Land, "Chronology of
Clapp's Factory," 1–5; Wright, "Clapp Cemetery Burials," 1–8; "Post Register";
Doug Carter, "3rd Georgia Reserves/State Troops," posting available at http://
history-sites.com/cgi-bin/boards/gacwmb/index.cgi?read=952; Pendergrast, *For
God, Country, and Coca-Cola,* 20–21; Hewett, *Supplement,* part 2, series 17, vol. 5,

pp. 599, 682; Gilpin, "Diary of 'The Last Campaign,'" 16 April 1865; *Macon Daily Telegraph,* 18 April 1865; H. S. Wilson, *Confederate Industry,* 222.

Appendix 5

1. *The Medal of Honor of the United States Army* (Washington, D.C.: Government Printing Office, 1948), 204; *OR,* 49, pt. 1:477, 504; Bates, Diary, 16–27 April, 4 July 1865; Beyer, *Deeds of Valor,* 537; Johnson, "Richard Morgan," Iowa Battle Flag Project, SHSI-DM; Johnson, "Andrew Tibbets," Iowa Battle Flag Project, SHSI-DM.

Bibliographic Essay

The following is an outline of just a few of the primary and secondary sources, arranged topically, that were essential to the completion of this volume.

Primary Sources

Primary sources made up the greatest part of the research necessary to uncovering the history of the Battle for Columbus. Among the most foundational was the series *The War of the Rebellion: A Compilation of the Official Records of the Union and Confederate Armies* (Washington, D.C.: Government Printing Office, 1880–1901). The reports and other correspondence contained in the *Official Records* provided an excellent starting point for exploring the particulars of Wilson's Raid, the Battle for Columbus, and its aftermath.

Several works illuminated the personalities and actions of the Union command. The longest and most detailed of these was the autobiography of James H. Wilson, titled *Under the Old Flag: Recollections of Military Operations in the War for the Union, the Spanish War, the Boxer Rebellion, etc.* (New York: D. Appleton, 1912). When read together with Wilson's diary, available on microfilm from the Historical Society of Delaware in Wilmington, a good understanding was obtained of the commanding general's objectives, situational awareness, and impressions during the campaign.

The biographies titled *The Life and Services of Brevet Brigadier-General Andrew Jonathan Alexander* (New York: n.p., 1887) and *General Edward Francis Winslow: A Leader of Cavalry in the Great Rebellion* (n.p., 1915), both written by Wilson after the war and drawing in large part upon Wilson's own experiences, were of value, as was also Wilson's introduction to Peter Michie's *The Life and Letters of Emory Upton* (New York: D. Appleton, 1885). Yet probably the most informative work in this group was the chapter in Edward F. Winslow's memoirs entitled "Columbus, the Final Battle of the War," located at the State Historical Society of Iowa in Iowa City. Winslow's work not only outlines in detail the particulars of the fight from the general's perspective, but also illuminates with remarkable honesty and clarity the personal interplay between the prominent officers of the corps and his brigade.

Several Union staff officers produced thorough records of their experiences during the campaign that proved particularly insightful. James W. Latta served as Upton's assistant adjutant-general, and both his diary and a lengthy memoir titled "Pennsylvania in the War: The Campaign of Wilson's Cavalry Corps through Alabama and Georgia in the Spring of 1865" are available from the Library of Congress. Francis W. Morse, who was an aide to Upton, produced *Personal Experiences in the War of the Great Rebellion* (Albany, N.Y.: Munsell Printer, 1866). The diary and published memoirs of Ebenezer N. Gilpin were among the most entertaining encountered on this project. A reader of the latter work should be aware, however, that the memoirs were extensively edited and should make a point of reviewing both ("Diary of 'The Last Campaign," E. N. Gilpin Papers, Library of Congress, Washington; *The Last Campaign* [Leavenworth, Kans.: Press of Ketcheson Printing Co., 1908; reprint from the *Journal of the U.S. Cavalry Association,* April 1908]). Charles D. Mitchell, also of Upton's staff, described in detail the aftermath of the battle and his experiences in Columbus during the occupation. The Mitchell's memoirs are also located at the Library of Congress.

Several Union regimental histories were of particular utility. W. L. Curry's *Four Years in the Saddle* (Columbus, Ohio: Champlin Print. Co., 1898; reprint, Jonesboro, Ga.: Freedom Hill Press, reprint 1984) tells of the participation of the 1st Ohio Cavalry during the morning and afternoon phases of the battle. The chapter on Columbus was written by the hero of that morning's action, J. A. O. Yeoman. William Forse Scott's *The Story of a Cavalry Regiment* (New York: G. P. Putnam's Sons, 1893) tells of the 4th Iowa Cavalry's successful assault on the Confederate defenses during the fight's night phase. And Benjamin F. McGee's *History of the 72nd Indiana Volunteer Infantry of the Mounted Lightning Brigade* (LaFayette, Ind.: S. Vater & Co., "The Journal" Printers, 1882) outlines the experiences of Union soldiers who passed through the city after the battle.

Nearly forty Union diaries, memoirs, and collections of letters helped to develop the full story of the battle and how it was experienced by those who fought in it. Charles F. Hinrichs's diary, available from the Western Historical Manuscripts Collection at the University of Missouri in Columbia, is the single best resource for information about the 10th Missouri. The diary of John C. Leach exposes the confusion and disorientation experienced by the men of the 3rd Iowa during their night assault on Fort 3, and may be reviewed at the State Historical Society of Iowa Library in Des Moines as a part of the James Boyle Papers. William H. Barker's "A Private's Autobiography" is available from the United States Army Military History Institute, now called the U.S. Army Heritage and Education Center, and is distinctive in that Barker served as one of General Upton's bodyguards.

Two resources were helpful in understanding the situation of the 5th Iowa during Wilson's Raid. Josiah Conzett's "My Civil War: Before, During, and After" allows the reader to see the action through the eyes of an average soldier, while the Civil War letter transcripts of George Healey convey their message in an exciting but far more condensed manner. Both collections are available for review at the State Historical Society of Iowa Libraries.

The 4th Iowa had several talented writers whose diaries and memoirs proved revealing. Lot Abraham commanded the dismounted detachment of the regiment during the night assault, and his diary, located at the University of Iowa Library, was an exciting find. James O. Vanorsdol's *Four Years for the Union* (n.p., 1888) tells the story of Company K's heroic efforts and is available for review on microfiche at the State Historical Society of Iowa in Des Moines. Particularly noteworthy for its descriptive detail is the diary of young Samuel O. Bereman, also of Company K, which was graciously provided by Garth Hagerman of Fort Bragg, California. Chauncey Graham's 1865 diary, with its description of the afternoon flank march, was located at the United States Army Military History Institute and rounds out the best of the materials written by members of the 4th Iowa.

Of the many manuscript collections consulted in relation to Union soldiers, by far the most comprehensive and important were the Adjutant General's Files of the State Historical Society of Iowa in Des Moines. This massive collection of papers relating to the service of Iowa troops contained original drafts of reports written by officers of the participating regiments, lists of casualties, inventories of personal effects, and other invaluable documentation.

Information about the Confederate command was drawn principally from collections, including the Howell Cobb Family Papers, the Cobb-Erwin-Lamar Collection, and the Howell Cobb Papers held by the Hargrett Rare Book and Manuscripts Library at the University of Georgia. These collections included revealing letters written by Cobb to his wife as well as telegrams and other correspondence related to military operations in 1865. Howell Cobb's Special Orders Book proved to be the key to understanding the circumstances faced by Cobb and others in the Confederate command who were attempting to assemble Georgia's forces to repel the Union invasion.

Primary documentation produced by Confederate combatants was substantially harder to obtain than that written by their Union adversaries. The best recollection relating to service with Buford's brigade was recorded by Isaac Herman in his autobiography *Memoirs of a Veteran Who Served as a Private in the 60's in the War Between the States* (Atlanta: Byrd Printing Co., 1911). The demoralization of the Confederate reserves during the battle is apparent from "Diary of [the] War Between the States Kept by A. J. Jackson, Company G, 2nd Ga. State Line," available on microfilm at the Georgia Department of Archives and History. The Alabama Department of Archives and History is the repository for Charles Martin's "A Reminiscence of the War Between the States," a short work detailing the service rendered by the Russell County Reserves during the battle. Also, the article published in the *Confederate Veteran Magazine* titled "Memorial Day at Savannah, Ga." vividly relates Pope Barrow's memory of Colonel Lamar's death during the melee at the Franklin Street Bridge.

Three artillerymen produced interesting accounts of the battle. John F. Benton of Emery's Battery offered his version of events in a series of letters published by the *Columbus Enquirer-Sun* in May 1925. William W. Grant served with Clanton's Alabama Battery and described the battery's actions in "Recollections of the Last Battle," an article published in the *Confederate Veteran Magazine* in 1915. Kingman P. Moore started writing a book after the war that featured his daring escape from the Battle of Selma, his retreat to Columbus, and his service with the artillery defending the City Bridge. Though Moore died before completing the work, a typescript copy of the manuscript was provided to the author courtesy of the family of Susan Marie Moore Brittain and Thomas Brittain of Tucson, Arizona.

The experiences of civilians compose a major part of this study. Two compelling accounts of the trials endured by women were found in Eliza F. Andrews's *The War-Time Journal of a Georgia Girl* (New York: D. Appleton, 1908) and Kate Cumming's *A Journal of Hospital Life in the Confederate Army of Tennessee* (Louisville: John P. Morton, 1866). A less formal account was given by Emma J. S. Prescott in her memoirs, which are housed at the Kenan Research Center at the Atlanta History Center. The wonder and apprehension felt by children during the occupation was obvious from the recollections of W. F. Ellison, retained by the Alabama Department of Archives and History in their Public Info Files (Russell County, SG 6923), and Louise G. Jones's "Some Reminiscences and Incidents of the Last Battle of the Civil War at Columbus, Easter, April 16, 1865," which was published in the *Columbus Enquirer-Sun* in 1922.

The autobiography of John A. Banks, available at the Genealogy and Local History Department of the Columbus Public Library, revealed the worry that male civilians felt about their prospects for success in turning back Wilson's Raiders. As to the occupation of Columbus following the battle, no more enlightening description written by a civilian was found than that given by Charles T. Quintard in his autobiographical work, edited by Author Noll, *Doctor Quintard, Chaplain C.S.A. and Second Bishop of Tennessee; Being His Story of the War (1861–1865)* (Sewanee, Tenn.: University of Sewanee Press, 1905). A recent republication of this work (Sam Davis Elliot, ed., *Doctor Quintard, Chaplain C.S.A. and Second Episcopal Bishop of Tennessee: The Memoir and Civil War Diary of Charles Todd Quintard* [Baton Rouge: Louisiana State University Press, 2003]) also includes the bishop's diary. Slave narratives complete the civilian experience and are available in their most concentrated form from the Library of Congress's "Born in Slavery: Slave Narratives from the Federal Writers' Project, 1936–1938" and from George P. Rawick's series *The American Slave: A Composite Autobiography* (Westport, Conn.: Greenwood Press, n.d.) and its supplements.

Government records were used in a variety of ways. The National Archives' "Compiled Service Records" for both Union and Confederate soldiers were used to learn as much as possible about important personalities associated with the battle as well as their units. Iowa's Adjutant General's Files, along with the National Archives' "Journal of a Trip Through Parts of Kentucky, Tennessee, and Georgia Made to Locate the Scattered Graves of Union Soldiers" and the "Register of Burials at Andersonville National Historic Site," were all used to help identify Union casualties. The "Columbus City Council Records, 1865" were helpful in understanding the measures taken by the civil authorities in the days surrounding the battle. The "Post Register of Sick and Wounded Soldiers in Hospitals at Columbus, Ga. 1861–1865" proved to be the single best resource for information on Confederate casualties from the battle, although it should be noted that the register is at least partially incomplete. Both the "Council Records" and "Post Register" may be found in the clerk of council's office in the Columbus Government Center. Additionally, although information on Columbus's contributions to the Confederate war effort were available from several sources, the National Archives' "Confederate Papers Relating to Citizens and Business Firms," available on microfilm, was not matched in usefulness or volume.

Secondary Sources

For their overview of Wilson's Raid and the Battle for Columbus, the following were helpful: James Pickett Jones, *Yankee Blitzkrieg: Wilson's Raid through Alabama and Georgia* (Lexington: University of Kentucky Press, 1976); James Pickett Jones, "Wilson's Raiders Reach Georgia: The Fall of Columbus, 1865," *Georgia Historical Quarterly* 59, no. 3 (1975): 313–29; Jerry Keenan, *Wilson's Cavalry Corps* (Jefferson, N.C.: McFarland, 1998).

Edward F. Longacre's *From Union Stars to Top Hat: A Biography of the Extraordinary General James Harrison Wilson* (Harrisburg, Pa.: Stackpole Books, 1972) provided in-depth background into the life and personality of General Wilson. Similar background information about Howell Cobb came from both Horace Montgomery's *Howell Cobb's Confederate Career* (Tuscaloosa: Confederate Publishing Co., 1959) and John E. Simpson's *Howell Cobb: Politics of Ambition* (Chicago: Adams Press, 1973).

Other biographies that proved useful were Peter S. Michie's *The Life and Services of Emory Upton* (New York: D. Appleton, 1885) and Charles K. Mills's *Harvest of Barren Regrets* (Glendale, Calif.: The Arthur H. Clark Co., 1985), which outlined the turbulent life and controversial career of Frederick Benteen.

Several Columbus histories were of tremendous value. They included Diffee Standard, *Columbus Georgia, in the Confederacy: The Social and Industrial Life of the Chattahoochee River Port* (New York: The William-Frederick Press, 1954); John H. Martin, *Columbus, Geo., from Its Selection as a "Trading Town" in 1827 to its Partial Destruction by Wilson's Raid in 1865* (Columbus, Ga.: Thos. Gilbert, 1874); Nancy Telfair [Louise Dubose], *A History of Columbus, Georgia, 1828–1928* (Columbus, Ga.: The Historical Publishing Co., 1929); and Etta Blanchard Worsley, *Columbus on the Chattahoochee* (Columbus, Ga.: Columbus Office Supply Co., 1951).

Girard (present day Phenix City) and Russell County histories were likewise of importance to this work. They included Russell County Heritage Book Committee, *The Heritage of Russell County, Alabama* (Clanton, Ala.: Heritage Publishing Consultants, 2003); Russell County Historical Commission, *The History of Russell County, Alabama* (Dallas: National Share-Graphics, 1982); and Anne Kendrick Walker, *Russell County in Retrospect* (Richmond: The Dietz Press, 1950).

Columbus's wartime efforts and industrial contributions made it a target for Wilson's Raiders. Information on this activity was gleaned from Diffee Standard's work, mentioned above, and also from Mary A. DeCredico, *Patriotism for Profit: Georgia's Urban Entrepreneurs and the Confederate War Effort* (Chapel Hill: University of North Carolina Press, 1990); Harold S. Wilson, *Confederate Industry: Manufacturers and Quartermasters in the Civil War* (Jackson: University of Mississippi Press, 2002); Stewart C. Edwards, "River City at War: Columbus, Georgia in the Confederacy" (Ph.D. diss., Florida State University, 1998); Faye L. Jensen, "Power and Progress in the Urban South: Columbus, Georgia, 1850–1885" (Ph.D. diss., Emory University, 1991); and *Columbus Ledger-Enquirer Civil War Centennial Edition,* 16 April 1961.

Maxine Turner's *Navy Gray: A Story of the Confederate Navy on the Chattahoochee and Apalachicola Rivers* (Tuscaloosa: University of Alabama Press, 1988) was indispensable for information concerning naval operations in Columbus. William Harris Bragg's popular work *Joe Brown's Army* (Macon, Ga.: Mercer University Press, 1987) was essential for understanding the history of Georgia's State Line Regiments. And both B. G. Ellis's *The Moving Appeal: Mr. McClanahan, Mrs. Dill, and the Civil War's Great Newspaper Run* (Macon, Ga.: Mercer University Press, 2003) and St. John Waddell's *The Commercial Appeal* (Memphis: The Memphis Publishing Co., n.d.) shed light on the curious story of the *Memphis Appeal* newspaper.

Three of the best and easiest to find resources for information concerning Columbus's claim to the site of the Civil War's last battle were The Alva C. Smith Collection, Simon Schwob Memorial Library, Columbus State University Archives; The Mahan Civil War Collection, Genealogy and Local History Department, Columbus Public Library; and Charles Jewett Swift, *The Last Battle of the Civil War* (Columbus, Ga.: Gilbert Printing Co., 1915).

Finally, in learning about the circumstances surrounding the Battle of Palmetto Ranch, the other combat that is widely recognized as the site of the Civil War's last battle, the following were enlightening: Jeffrey Wm. Hunt, *The Last Battle of the Civil War: Palmetto Ranch* (Austin: University of Texas Press, 2002); Phillip Thomas Tucker, *The Final Fury: Palmito Ranch, the Last Battle of the Civil War* (Mechanicsburg, Pa.: Stackpole Books, 2001).

Index